A Guide to the Crime and Disorder Act 1998

Previous titles in the series

A Guide to the Criminal Justice and Public Order Act 1994
A Guide to the Finance Act 1994
A Guide to the Police and Magistrates' Courts Act 1994
A Guide to the Sunday Trading Act 1994
A Guide to the Trade Marks Act 1994
A Guide to the Finance Act 1995
A Guide to the Pensions Act 1995
A Guide to the Criminal Procedure and Investigations Act 1996
A Guide to the Family Law Act 1996
A Guide to the Finance Act 1996
A Guide to the Housing Act 1996
A Guide to the Crime (Sentences) Act 1997
A Guide to the Finance Act 1997
A Guide to the Finance (No 2) Act 1997
A Guide to the Police Act 1997
A Guide to the Finance Act 1998
A Guide to the Data Protection Act 1998

A Guide to the
Crime and Disorder Act 1998

Nicola Padfield, MA (Oxon), Dip Crim (Cantab),
DES (Aix-Marseille), Lecturer, Institute of Criminology,
Fellow of Fitzwilliam College, Cambridge

Butterworths
London, Edinburgh, Dublin
1998

United Kingdom	Butterworths a Division of Reed Elsevier (UK) Ltd, Halsbury House, 35 Chancery Lane, LONDON WC2A 1EL and 4 Hill Street, EDINBURGH EH2 3JZ
Australia	Butterworths, a Division of Reed International Books Australia Pty Ltd, CHATSWOOD, New South Wales
Canada	Butterworths Canada Ltd, MARKHAM, Ontario
Hong Kong	Butterworths Asia (Hong Kong), HONG KONG
India	Butterworths India, NEW DELHI
Ireland	Butterworth (Ireland) Ltd, DUBLIN
Malaysia	Malayan Law Journal Sdn Bhd, KUALA LUMPUR
New Zealand	Butterworths of New Zealand Ltd, WELLINGTON
Singapore	Butterworths Asia, SINGAPORE
South Africa	Butterworths Publishers (Pty) Ltd, DURBAN
USA	Lexis Law Publishing, CHARLOTTESVILLE, Virginia

Any Crown copyright material is reproduced with the permission of the Controller of Her Majesty's Stationery Office.

Nicola Padfield has asserted her right under the Copyright, Designs and Patents Act 1988 to be identified as the author of this work.

A CIP Catalogue record for this book is available from the British Library.

ISBN 0 406 90524 X

Printed and bound in Great Britain by The Cromwell Press, Trowbridge, Wiltshire

Visit us at our website: http//www.butterworths.co.uk

Preface

The Crime and Disorder Act 1998 marks a significant step in the new Labour Government's crusade to be 'tough on crime and tough on the causes of crime'. The Government is fully aware that it was elected by an electorate determined that 'something' should be done about crime and disorder. Whether or not the right things are being done remains to be seen, and much of the Act can be seen as something of an experiment in social engineering, open to criticism on grounds of both principle and practice. Much may turn out to be unworkable. Even those parts which are workable will need considerable resources and energetic determination on the part of local criminal justice partnerships in order to succeed. A number of years will pass before we will be able to judge whether the Crime and Disorder Act 1998 is the important flagship that the Home Secretary believes it to be, or whether it will, in the words of Mr Edward Leigh, 'sail away and be forgotten in a year's time' (HC Report, 23 June 1998, col 950). What does seem certain is that this Act will involve a great deal of work for all those working with offenders, and it will doubtless also result in a huge amount of litigation. However, it is a comfort that there are clear signs of a Government commitment to a codification of sentencing law, an area desperately in need of rationalisation and simplification.

In order to keep this guide to a manageable length some issues may have been glossed over to an extent which readers may find unsatisfactory. However, I have sought to concentrate on those provisions which have already proved to be controversial or may be difficult to apply in practice. I have not discussed the consultation papers which preceded the Bill in any depth, but have quoted liberally from the debates in both the House of Commons and in the House of Lords, in the belief that this will prove to be more valuable to practitioners. It is depressing to record that the quality of debate was frequently higher in the House of Lords than in the House of Commons. In particular, many back bench Labour MPs who spoke enthusiastically in support of the Bill showed little enthusiasm for engaging with the detail. The debates also make curious reading for those of us who have become accustomed over the last 18 years to Labour members in Opposition speaking up in defence of civil liberties. In the debates on this Bill, it was often left to the Liberal Democrats, sometimes with strong Conservative support, to question the implications of some of the measures from the libertarian standpoint.

For those who wish to follow developments in the implementation of the Act, the Home Office has already developed a detailed web site on the Crime and Disorder Act (http://www.homeoffice.gov.uk/cdact). I am particularly grateful to all those at Butterworths who looked after me so well during the production of this guide, supplying me efficiently with the raw materials which I requested. I would also like to express my thanks to Juliet Wheldon, Legal Adviser at the Home Office, who kindly provided me with a copy of the original Notes on Clauses. Needless to say, all the mistakes which may have slipped through are entirely my own responsibility.

Nicola Padfield
September 1998

Contents

Table of Statutes

Table of Cases

1 Introduction

BACKGROUND

The Labour party manifesto

1.1. The Crime and Disorder Act (CDA) 1998 passed swiftly through Parliament, given priority by a new Government determined to show its 'law and order' credentials. The Labour party manifesto published prior to the general election of May 1997 promised to be 'tough on crime and tough on the causes of crime, different from the Labour approach of the past and the Tory policy of today'—

> 'Under the Conservatives, crime has doubled and many more criminals get away with their crimes: the number of people convicted has fallen by a third, with only one crime in 50 leading to a conviction. This is the worst record of any government since the Second World War—and for England and Wales the worst record of any industrialised country. Last year alone violent crime rose 11 per cent.
>
> We propose a new approach to law and order: tough on crime and tough on the causes of crime. We insist on individual responsibility for crime, and we will attack the causes of crime by our measures to relieve social deprivation.
>
> The police have our strong support. They are in the front line of the fight against crime and disorder. The Conservatives have broken their 1992 general election pledge to provide an extra 1,000 police officers. We will relieve the police of unnecessary bureaucratic burdens to get more officers back on the beat.
>
> *Youth crime*
>
> Youth crime and disorder have risen sharply, but very few young offenders end up in court, and when they do half are let off with another warning. Young offenders account for seven million crimes a year.
>
> Far too often young criminals offend again and again while waiting months for a court hearing. We will halve the time it takes to get persistent young offenders from arrest to sentencing; replace wide-spread repeat cautions with a single final warning; bring together Youth Offender Teams in every area; and streamline the system of youth courts to make it far more effective.
>
> New parental responsibility orders will make parents face up to their responsibility for their children's misbehaviour.
>
> *Conviction and sentencing*
>
> The job of the Crown Prosecution Service is to prosecute criminals effectively. There is strong evidence that the CPS is over-centralised, bureaucratic and inefficient, with cases too often dropped, delayed, or downgraded to lesser offences.
>
> Labour will decentralise the CPS, with local crown prosecutors co-operating more effectively with local police forces.

We will implement an effective sentencing system for all the main offences to ensure greater consistency and stricter punishment for serious repeat offenders. The courts will have to spell out what each sentence really means in practice. The Court of Appeal will have a duty to lay down sentencing guidelines for all the main offences. The attorney general's power to appeal unduly lenient sentences will be extended.

The prison service now faces serious financial problems. We will audit the resources available, take proper ministerial responsibility for the service, and seek to ensure that prison regimes are constructive and require inmates to face up to their offending behaviour.

Disorder

The Conservatives have forgotten the 'order' part of 'law and order'. We will tackle the unacceptable level of anti-social behaviour and crime on our streets. Our 'zero tolerance' approach will ensure that petty criminality among young offenders is seriously addressed.

Community safety orders will deal with threatening and disruptive criminal neighbours. Labour has taken the lead in proposing action to tackle the problems of stalking and domestic violence.

Child protection orders will deal with young children suffering neglect by parents because they are left out on their own far too late at night.

Britain is a multiracial and multicultural society. All its members must have the protection of the law. We will create a new offence of racial harassment and a new crime of racially motivated violence to protect ethnic minorities from intimidation.

Drugs

The vicious circle of drugs and crime wrecks lives and threatens communities. Labour will appoint an anti-drugs supremo to co-ordinate our battle against drugs across all government departments. The 'drug czar' will be a symbol of our commitment to tackle the modern menace of drugs in our communities.

We will pilot the use of compulsory drug testing and treatment orders for offenders to ensure that the link between drug addiction and crime is broken. This will be paid for by bringing remand delays down to the national targets.

We will attack the drug problem in prisons. In addition to random drug testing of all prisoners we will aim for a voluntary testing unit in every prison for prisoners ready to prove they are drug-free.

Victims

Victims of crime are too often neglected by the criminal justice system. We will ensure that victims are kept fully informed of the progress of their case, and why charges may have been downgraded or dropped.

Greater protection will be provided for victims in rape and serious sexual offence trials and for those subject to intimidation, including witnesses.

Prevention

We will place a new responsibility on local authorities to develop statutory partnerships to help prevent crime. Local councils will then be required to set targets for the reduction of crime and disorder in their area.

Gun control

In the wake of Dunblane and Hungerford, it is clear that only the strictest firearms laws can provide maximum safety. The Conservatives failed to offer the protection required. Labour led the call for an outright ban on all handguns in general civilian use. There will be legislation to allow individual MPs a free vote for a complete ban on all handguns.

Labour is the party of law and order in Britain today.'[1]

---

[1]   Extract from the Labour Party Manifesto.

Consultation papers

1.2   The new Labour Government took office on 1 May 1997, and wasted little time. By the autumn of 1997 the Home Office had produced a large number of consultation papers/documents, namely—
  (a) Tackling Youth Crime (September 1997);
  (b) Getting to Grips with Crime: A new framework for local action (September 1997);
  (c) Racial Violence and Harassment (September 1997);
  (d) Community Safety Orders (September 1997: the forerunner of the anti-social behaviour order);
  (e) New National and Local Focus on Youth Crime (October 1997);
  (f) Tackling Delays in the youth justice system (October 1997);
  (g) Community Protection Orders (November 1997: the forerunner of the sexual offender order).

The Government invited responses to documents (a), (e), and (f) above by 12 November 1997 and summaries of responses received were published in December 1997. Meanwhile both the White Paper 'No More Excuses—a New Approach to Tackling Youth Crime in England and Wales'[1] and the Crime and Disorder Bill itself had already been published. However, not all the changes in this Bill had been clearly signposted in advance. For example, the first mention of the home detention curfew license was an announcement in Parliament by the Home Secretary on 20 November.

---

[1]   Cm 3809.

1.3   The concerns raised in the consultation papers were not new. In June 1995 the Labour Party had published 'A Quiet Life, Tough Action on Criminal Neighbours', which first formulated the 'community safety order', and 'Tackling Youth Crime—Reforming Youth Justice' appeared in May 1996. The previous Conservative Government had shown a real interest in dealing with the problems of delays. In February 1997 a Home Office team led by Martin Narey had produced a 'Review of Delay in the Criminal Justice System'. In March 1997, the Conservative Government had published a Green Paper on 'Preventing Children Offending', many of the ideas in which seem to be echoed in the Crime and Disorder Bill. In the past, it had been the Conservative Party that had appeared to assume the label of 'the party of law and order'. In the 18 years of Conservative rule a whole range of new powers had been introduced in a seemingly endless stream of criminal justice statutes. The Police and Criminal Evidence Act 1984, the Public Order Act 1986, the Criminal Justice and Public Order Act 1994 are just three examples from the long list of criminal justice Acts. It is hardly surprising that the Conservative Party in Opposition did not oppose many of the provisions in the Crime and Disorder Bill.

THE WHITE PAPER

1.4 'No More Excuses—a New Approach to Tackling Youth Crime in England and Wales'[1] was published in November 1997. Detailed reference to the White Paper will be made throughout this guide, but in summary it set out that the reform programme aims to provide—
- (a) a clear strategy preventing offending and re-offending;
- (b) that offenders, and their parents, face up to their offending behaviour and take responsibility for it;
- (c) earlier, more effective intervention when young people first offend;
- (d) faster, more efficient procedures from arrest to sentence;
- (e) partnerships between all youth justice agencies to deliver a better, faster system.

The White Paper invited views by the end of March 1998 in response to two specific issues, namely the proposals for a protocol to support the statutory duty of youth justice agencies to have regard to the need to prevent offending; and the proposals for reform of the youth court. By then the Bill had completed its passage through the House of Lords.

---

[1] Cm 3809.

Concerns

1.5 Commentators were not slow to raise their concerns. Professor Ashworth commented that—

> 'The shower of consultation papers published in autumn 1997 prior to the Bill amounted to little more than tokenism, since the papers were thin on argument and analysis, gave extremely short time-limits for comment, and generally gave the impression of policies already firmly decided. Above all there is no recognition in the Bill or the preceding documents, that it is possible to pursue the right goals by the wrong means.'.[1]

Professor Rutherford drew attention to the Government's 'unduly narrow and instrumental view of the law in responding to crime' and wrote—

> 'In decrying the "excuse culture", the Government appears, by implication, to be prepared to discard common sense assumptions which guided youth justice policy and practice for much of the post-war era.'.[2]

Another example of the disappointment felt by many is the damning indictment of anti-social behaviour orders written jointly by six leading academics—

> '. . . the Government's latest legislative proposal is neither sensible nor carefully targeted . . . Blunderbuss solutions do not help, and serve only to politicise what are very real problems for those who live in poorer neighbourhoods.'.[3]

Dr David Thomas has pointed out a number of ways in which the Act is likely to cause difficulties in the courts,[4] but now that the Act has reached the statute book, there is a likely to be a period of monitoring and evaluation before it can be said with any certainty that the Act has failed to achieve that which the Government hoped.

---

1   1998 Criminal Law Review 81.
2   Rutherford, 'A Bill to be tough on crime' [1998] NLJ 13.
3   Ashworth, Gardner, Morgan, Smith, von Hirsch, Wasik, 'Neighbouring on the Oppressive' [1998] Criminal Justice, Vol 16, No 1, February 1998, p 7 (also at para 2.4).
4   See paras 3.8 and 5.44.

THE BILL'S JOURNEY THROUGH PARLIAMENT

The House of Lords

1.6   The Crime and Disorder Bill was published on 2 December 1997. It received its Second Reading in the House of Lords on 16 December, in a debate introduced by Lord Williams of Mostyn, Parliamentary Under-Secretary of State at the Home Office. He stressed that the Bill contained a substantial package of measures taking forward 12 manifesto commitments and set out its six main themes—

   (a) nipping youth crime in the bud;
   (b) combating anti-social behaviour and promoting local action against crime and disorder;
   (c) tackling racist crime;
   (d) expediting justice;
   (e) protecting the public from sexual, violent and drug-misusing offenders;
   (f) providing greater consistency and clarity in sentencing.[1]

---

1   HL Report, 16 December 1997, col 532.

1.7   The Committee stage in the House of Lords opened on 3 February 1998, and continued until 3 March. The Report stage began on 17 March, and the Bill had its Third Reading in the House of Lords on 31 March. Much of the technical work on the Bill was conducted in the Lords, and it grew from 96 to 103 clauses, with 85 Government amendments approved at Third Reading.

The House of Commons

1.8   The Bill was unopposed at Second Reading, and was considered in Committee from 28 April until 11 June. In Committee, it was agreed that the Scottish provisions would be considered at the end in order to allow another key element in the Government's legislative programme, the Scotland Bill, to complete its proceedings through the Commons first. The Opposition, which was led in Committee by Mr Clappison, made small headway given the Government's huge majority. In Mr Clappison's words—

   'The Government's steamrollering tendency means that they ignore every constructive piece of advice and practical criticism and pass bad legislation as a result.'.[1]

The Bill returned to the House of Commons on 22 June 1998. In six and a half hours of debate that day, the House debated just two clauses: Sir Norman Fowler's proposed football behaviour order (on an amendment which was eventually withdrawn, see para 1.13) and the reduction of the age of consent for homosexual sex, which was passed on a free vote by 336 to 129 votes (but see para 1.12).

[1]   HL SC B, 4 June 1998, col 696.

Return to the House of Lords

1.9   The Bill returned to the House of Lords on 22 July 1998.[1] Most Commons' amendments were carried without debate, with two exceptions. First, Lord Ackner argued strongly for the reintroduction of the clause recreating the Standing Advisory Council on Criminal Justice and the Penal System. However the majority of peers clearly felt that an advisory council should not be forced upon the Government, and Lord Ackner's amendment was defeated (see para 1.16). More contentiously Baroness Young moved a motion disagreeing with the Commons' amendment to reduce the age of consent. A heated debate resulted in a success for the motion (see para 1.12).

[1]   HL Report, 22 July 1998, col 918.

Royal Assent

1.10 The Bill received Royal Assent on 31 July 1998, the day Parliament rose for its summer recess.

MATTERS THAT FAILED TO REACH THE STATUTE BOOK

The age of consent

1.11 Amendments were tabled in the House of Commons at Report stage on 12 June to equalise the age of consent for homosexual and heterosexual activity at the age of 16. The clause's main proposer in the debate on 22 June was Ann Keen. She stressed that the purpose of the new clause was to make the age of consent the same for everyone, and was a simple question of equality. An important background to this was the litigation in *Sutherland and Morris v United Kingdom* in the European Commission on Human Rights. On 21 October 1997 the Government lodged with the European Court an undertaking reached with Mr Sutherland and Mr Morris by which they agreed to stay their proceedings. In return, the Government undertook—

    (i) at the 'earliest appropriate opportunity' to have a free vote in the House of Commons on the equalisation of the age of consent, and

    (ii) that if a majority of the House of Commons voted in favour of a reduction in the age of consent for homosexual acts to 16—

        'the government will bring forward legislation to implement the will of Parliament, such legislation to be introduced in time for the consideration of such legislation to have been completed by the end of the next Parliamentary session at the latest.'.[1]

[1]   See the speech of the Home Secretary in HC Report, 28 July 1998, col 180.

1.12 When questioned as to why the amendment was not introduced at a much earlier stage, the Home Secretary explained that it had been judged appropriate that the matter should first be debated in the House of Commons, and had it not been 'for the intervention of two sets of Northern Ireland legislation', there would have been ample time. On 22 June in a free vote, the House of Commons backed the amendments by 336 to 129 votes.[1] In the House of Lords, however, Baroness Young led a strong counter-attack, and the House of Commons' clause was defeated by 290 to 122 votes.[2] The Government thus faced the dilemma of whether to send the amendment back to the Lords and risk losing the whole Bill, or to withdraw the amendment. A factor weighing heavily with the Government was that the provisions of the Parliament Acts 1911 and 1949 are not available on Bills which begin their journey through Parliament in the House of Lords. The Home Secretary therefore proposed on 28 July[3] that the issue should be dealt with in separate legislation to be introduced in the House of Commons in the next Session, and the clause was dropped from the Bill.

1 HC Report, 22 June 1998, col 805.
2 HL Report, 22 July 1998, col 973.
3 HC Report, 28 July 1998, col 177.

Football behaviour orders

1.13 A clause proposing a new football behaviour order was proposed by Sir Norman Fowler, Shadow Home Secretary, during the Third Reading of the Bill in the House of Commons.[1] The debate on the clause took place whilst the World Cup was being held in France, and there was strong support for increasing the deterrent value of restriction orders, and widening police powers in relation to football hooligans. However, Sir Norman withdrew his amendment after the Home Secretary undertook to return to the subject at a later date. What was to become s 84 of the Act was added by an amendment to the Bill the next day (see para 5.47).

1 HC Report, 22 June 1998, col 710.

The Standing Advisory Council on Criminal Justice and the Penal System

1.14 Lord Ackner first proposed to reconstitute the old Advisory Council on the Penal System, which had operated in the 1960s and 1970s, in Committee[1] in the House of Lords, but withdrew the clause at that point ('intending *reculer pour mieux sauter* should that be necessary').[2] However, the clause was inserted into the Bill at the Third Reading in the House of Lords, when Lord Ackner's amendment was accepted by a majority of nine votes on a Division (114 to 105).[3] The amendment was supported by the Lord Chief Justice, the former Lord Chief Justice, seven Law Lords, two former Home Secretaries and many others. Only Lord Henley spoke against the motion.

1 HL Report, 3 March 1998, col 1126.
2 Ibid, col 1146.
3 HL Report, 31 March 1998, col 170.

1.15 The clause was removed from the Bill again in Committee in the House of Commons (on a division of 11 to 2 votes).[1] The Minister of State at the Home Office,

Mr Michael, explained that there now existed a wide range of advisory bodies, including the Criminal Justice Consultative Council, the Trial Issues Group, the Inspectorates of prisons and the probation service, the Law Commission, the National Audit Office and the Audit Commission. Two new bodies were being introduced in this Act (the Youth Justice Board and the Sentencing Advisory Panel) and the Government therefore considered this clause to be neither helpful nor necessary.

---

[1]   HC SC B, 28 April 1998, col 11.

1.16   When the Bill returned to the House of Lords on 22 July 1998, Lord Ackner argued strongly for the reintroduction of the clause. Using the Crime (Sentences) Act 1997, s 2, as an example, he concluded that—

> ' . . . the deeply depressing and worrying fact is that the Government, by a stubborn refusal to allow the provision of sound advice, so far from securing the safety of the public, are seriously prejudicing it . . .'.[1]

However, many peers, although supporting Lord Ackner in principle, did not feel that an advisory council should be forced upon the Government, and on a vote his amendment was defeated by 127 to 66 votes.

---

[1]   HL Report, 22 July 1998, col 923.

Automatic life sentences

1.17   In Committee in the House of Lords[1] there was a spirited attempt by Lord Windlesham to repeal the Crime (Sentences) Act 1997, s 2(5)(d), and to call attention to the 'irrationality and deep injustice of mandatory sentencing'.[2] He and many other peers were clearly strongly opposed to the whole section ('the most serious mistake that has been made in our criminal justice system for many years . . .'), but in the face of Government opposition, did not press for a division.

---

[1]   HL Report, 24 February 1998, col 599.
[2]   Ibid, col 613.

Offence of publishing telephone conversations

1.18   Lord Bridges moved an amendment in Committee in the House of Lords which would have made it an offence to publish the text of a clandestinely recorded telephone conversation.[1] Lord Bridges explained that this would mark the limits of acceptable behaviour in an area where clarity is needed. It would also make it clear to newspaper editors that they would be personally responsible for publishing illegal material. Lord Williams of Mostyn and Lord McIntosh of Haringey raised the difficulty that the amendment 'cuts across our implementation of the EC Telecoms Data Protection Directive', which must be implemented by 24 October 1998 (although there is a derogation in relation to Article 5 until October 2000). The amendment was defeated by 82 to 55 votes.[2]

---

[1]   HL Report, 12 February 1998, col 1310.
[2]   HL Report, 19 March 1998, col 830.

Judicial discretion to exclude young sexual offenders from the notification requirements

1.19 A clause was proposed by Baroness Mallalieu which would have given the judiciary an element of discretion as to whether to require an offender aged ten years or upwards to be required to register under the Sex Offenders Act 1997.[1] It was withdrawn when Lord Williams of Mostyn promised to look further at the matter.

---

[1]   HL Report, 12 February 1998, col 1351.

Drug supply offender protection order

1.20 A Conservative amendment moved on Committee would have introduced a drug supply offender protection order, which would have mirrored in many ways the sexual offender order (see CDA 1998, s 2, at para 2.14), but in relation to suppliers of illegal drugs. However, the clause was withdrawn after the Government gave it no support.[1]

---

[1]   HC SC B, 5 May 1998, col 194.

Increase in maximum sentences for intercourse with a girl under the age of 16

1.21 A clause to increase the maximum sentence for unlawful sexual intercourse with a girl under the age of 16 from two to seven years was read for the first time towards the end of Committee stage in the House of Commons.[1] This also was withdrawn when the Government undertook to review more generally the law on sexual offences.

---

[1]   HC SC B, 9 June 1998, col 817.

Cross-examination of rape victims

1.22 Baroness Anelay introduced a clause in Committee in the House of Lords which would have prevented a defendant charged with rape or indecent assault from asking questions of a complainant in the course of a trial.[1] It was opposed by Lord Ackner, amongst others, who thought that, whilst guidance should be given by the Court of Appeal or the Judicial Studies Board to help trial judges, a blanket statutory prohibition would be a denial of justice and contrary to Art 6(3)(d) of the European Convention on Human Rights (ECHR). The amendment was withdrawn. Another similar clause ('Complainant in rape cases') was read for the first time in Committee in the House of Commons.[2] If a defendant was not legally represented, or had ceased to have a legal representative during the proceedings, the court would have been required to appoint a legal representative to ask questions of the victim on his behalf. The Government had already pledged to give greater protection to victims in cases of serious sexual offences, and the clause was withdrawn.[3]

---

[1]   HL Report, 12 February 1998, col 1353.
[2]   HC SC B, 9 June 1998, col 820.
[3]   The Report of the Interdepartmental Working Group on the treatment of vulnerable or intimidated witnesses in the criminal justice system, 'Speaking up for Justice', was published in June 1998. The report contains 78 recommendations, and is currently being considered.

Rape

1.23　Lord Goodhart moved an amendment at the Report stage which would have made three changes in the law of rape, namely—

- (a) the defence of mistaken belief in consent where that mistake is not reasonable would have been removed;
- (b) the defendant's sexual history would have been put in issue when leave is given to cross-examine the complainant on her sexual history, and
- (c) the defendant would be given anonymity until convicted.

The purpose of the amendment was to raise the issues, and was withdrawn without a vote.[1]

---

[1]　HL Report, 19 March 1998, col 862.

Increase in maximum sentence for offences under the Offences against the Person Act 1861

1.24　A clause introduced in Committee in the House of Commons[1] would have increased the maximum sentence for offences of assault occasioning actual bodily harm, wounding and causing grievous bodily harm from the present level of five years to a new level of ten years. Mr Clappison relied on the decision of the Court of Appeal in *Hashi*[2] to show the inadequacy of the current law. However, Mr Michael stated that the Government were not convinced of the need for doubling maximum penalties—

> 'Provisional figures for 1997 show that, of 1,918 offenders sentenced to immediate custody for assault occasioning actual bodily harm, only six offenders—0.3 per cent of the total—received sentences approaching the maximum. Only 9 out of 2,030 offenders—0.4 per cent of the total—convicted for causing grievous bodily harm received sentences approaching the maximum.'[3]

In any case, the Government said that it was premature to change the maximum penalties in advance of decisions about the proposals in the Consultation Document 'Violence: Reforming the Offences against the Person Act 1861', which had been published in February 1998. The consultation period on the proposals ended only on 15 May 1998.

---

[1]　HC SC B, 9 June 1998, col 824.
[2]　*R v Abdi Guaid Hashi* (1995) 16 Cr App Rep (S) 121.
[3]　HC SC B, 9 June 1998, col 826.

Life imprisonment for indecent assault

1.25　Two other clauses introduced in Committee in the House of Commons[1] would have increased the maximum penalty for indecent assault on both men and women from ten years' imprisonment to life imprisonment. However, the Government responded that it was necessary to review not only the penalties, but also the offences, and the clauses were withdrawn.

---

[1]　HC SC B, 19 June 1998, col 827.

Detention of girls under the age of 18

1.26 An amendment was moved three times in the House of Lords (Second Reading, Report and at Third Reading)[1] by Lady Masham of Ilton to make it unlawful for girls under the age of 18 to be held with adults in prison. This was in order to bring the UK into line with the United Nations Convention on the Rights of the Child, Art 37, to which the UK Government had entered a reservation. Her amendment was defeated by 69 to 50 votes, with Lord Williams for the Government clearly reluctant to make any promises. In the House of Commons, the Liberal Democrats introduced a new clause read for the first time in Committee which would have made it unlawful for girls under the age of 18 to be held with adults in prison except in exceptional circumstances.[2] After the Minister of State stated that the Government did not believe that the clause was either necessary or the best way to address the needs of vulnerable female prisoners, it was withdrawn.

[1]   For a full discussion, see the debate on Report: HL Report, 3 March 1998, col 1115.
[2]   Ibid, col 835.

Increase in sentences for aggravation based on sexual orientation

1.27 This clause, again promoted by the Liberal Democrats in Committee,[1] provided that an offence was to be treated as aggravated if the offender had demonstrated towards the victim hostility based on the victim's actual or presumed sexual orientation. It was withdrawn after a serious debate on homophobic attacks.

[1]   HC SC B, 11 June 1998, col 840.

Prostitution by children and young persons

1.28 Lord Hylton proposed an amendment in the House of Lords which would have decriminalised soliciting for prostitution in the streets for girls under the age of 18, enabled emergency protection orders to be obtained for children found soliciting and increased the penalty for procuring a girl under the age of 21 from two to four years.[1]

[1]   HL Report, 12 February 1998, col 1325.

Pimping: increased protection for 16 and 17-year-old girls

1.29 Another clause introduced by the Liberal Democrats would have given greater protection to 16 and 17-year-old prostitutes. Mr Allan pointed out that—

> 'Home office figures show that between 1989 and 1996 there were 2,615 cautions and 1,880 convictions secured against children and young people for offences relating to prostitution. However, between 1989 and 1994 there were only six convictions against adults for procuring children for the purposes of prostitution.'.[1]

He argued that 16 and 17-year-olds are inadequately protected by the Sexual Offences Act 1956. However, in view of the minister's assurance that the Government was reviewing the area and took the points raised seriously, the clause was withdrawn.

[1]   HC SC B, 11 June 1998, col 855.

Increase in maximum sentence for offences involving indecent photographs of children

1.30 A new clause[1] read for the first time in Committee, would have increased the sentence for taking indecent photographs of children from three to five years' imprisonment. This also was dropped in view of the minister's commitment to a wider review of the subject.

---

[1]   HC SC B, 11 June 1998, col 858.

IMPLEMENTATION

1.31 The Crime and Disorder Act 1998 (Commencement No 1) Order 1998, SI 1998/1883, was made on 31 July 1998 (see Appendix 1). The Order brought into force a number of provisions on 1 August 1998. These deal with the power to appoint the members and a Chairman of the Youth Justice Board (see CDA 1998, s 41, Sch 2, para 1, and para 4.13), and to provide that certain things which may be done by a single justice of the peace may be done by a justices' clerk (see s 49, and para 4.27). The provisions relating to football spectators (see s 84, and para 5.47) came into force on 7 August 1998. The Crime and Disorder Act 1998 (Commencement No 2 and Transitional Provisions) Order 1998, SI 1998/2327, implements the majority of other provisions on 30 September 1998 (see Appendix). However, sexual offender orders (s 2, and para 2.14), police powers against truancy (s 16, and para 2.43) and face coverings (s 25, and para 2.56) and the changes to criminal procedures for indictable-only offences (ss 51–52, and para 4.32) will not be brought into force until December 1998. HO Circular 38/1998 sets out the time scale for implementation, and gives some details on the timing and geographical locations of the various pilot schemes: youth justice pilots, drug treatment and testing order pilots, piloting measures to reduce delay and TV link pilots. Anti-social behaviour orders will not be implemented until April 1999.

SCOTLAND

1.32 Finally, it should be noted that this is likely to have been the last criminal justice Bill containing legislation relating to Scottish criminal law to be debated in Westminster. From May 1999, such issues will be discussed in Holyrood. While it remains theoretically possible for Westminster to legislate on Scottish criminal law, the Home Secretary has made it clear that this is unlikely.[1] A study of this Act, where miscellaneous Scottish provisions are mixed up with provisions applying predominantly in England and Wales, suggests that devolution may help simplify the law.

---

[1]   HC Report, 28 July 1998, col 207.

---

2 Prevention of crime and disorder

INTRODUCTION

2.1 Part I of the Act, entitled 'Prevention of Crime and Disorder', comprises three chapters, covering England and Wales, Scotland and Great Britain respectively. It contains a wide range of measures designed to deal with some of the main social issues perceived by the Government to be of concern to the electorate: anti-social neighbours, paedophiles, inadequate parents and delinquent youths. Whether anti-social behaviour orders, sex offender orders, parenting orders, child safety orders and local child curfew orders are the right way to deal with these social concerns remains in dispute. Wide-ranging restrictive orders which need only be proved to the civil standard of proof, and breach of which may result in significant terms of imprisonment, have been challenged both in principle and in practice. Pilot schemes, which carefully and independently monitor these so-called preventative measures, are essential, and are to be carried out over the next 18 months. Many of the provisions in Pt I do not sit comfortably with existing police powers, while some seem so bureaucratic that the constituents about whom MPs are rightly concerned are more likely to rely on the older powers. The loose wording of many of the measures is deliberate, therefore it is disappointing that the Act does not contain a general statement in favour of the liberty of the subject or a general anti-discrimination section. The Human Rights Bill when enacted will doubtless be used to challenge many of the following provisions.

2.2 Another strand of Pt I imposes on local authorities a duty to develop a crime and disorder strategy. The provisions are again loosely-worded ('embryonic', in the words of Andrew Rutherford)[1] but should result in useful local 'crime audits' which may lead to properly targeted crime prevention initiatives. Alternatively, they may end up creating yet another costly bureaucracy diverting resources from the coal-face of crime prevention. Chapter II introduces anti-social behaviour orders and sex offender orders in Scotland, but not, interestingly, parenting orders, child safety orders, or local child curfew orders. Chapter III introduces a new police power throughout Great Britain to require the removal of masks.

---

[1] Rutherford, 'A Bill to be tough on crime' [1998] NLJ 13.

CHAPTER I: ENGLAND AND WALES: CRIME AND DISORDER: GENERAL

Anti-social behaviour orders

2.3 Section 1(1) gives a local council the right to apply to a magistrates' court for an anti-social behaviour order (ASBO) against individuals, aged ten years or over. The orders were proposed in the Consultation Paper II 'Community Safety Order', published in September 1997, and will be explained in greater detail by non-statutory guidance to be published in the autumn of 1998. Section 1(1) defines anti-social behaviour as acting 'in a manner that caused or was likely to cause harassment, alarm or distress to one or more persons not of the same household as himself'. The original Bill specified that two or more persons not in the same household must be caused the harassment, alarm or distress, but the Government accepted on Report that this should be amended to one or more.[1] The key controversy has concerned the exact type of behaviour to be dealt with. In Committee in the House of Lords, Lord Williams of Mostyn was at pains to repeat 'the important point' that the order was 'a prohibitory order. It requires the subject of it to do no more—I paraphrase bluntly—than to behave in a decent way to the fellow citizens of our country'.[2]

---

[1]   HL Report, 17 March 1998, col 579.
[2]   HL Report, 3 February 1998, col 514.

Opposition to ASBOs

2.4   Not everyone is so sanguine. In an article entitled 'Neighbouring on the Oppressive' published in the Howard League's magazine 'Criminal Justice', six leading academics[1] argued that the proposed orders should be abandoned. Highlighting the low standards of proof, the wide scope of the order and the disproportionate character of the penalty, they concluded that legislation should build instead on existing civil and criminal measure—

'The Government's latest legislative proposal is neither sensible nor carefully targeted. It takes sweepingly defined conduct within its ambit, grants local agencies virtually unlimited discretion to seek highly restrictive orders, jettisons fundamental legal protections for the grant of those orders, and authorises potentially draconian and wholly disproportionate penalties for violations of them. While the Government claims that this measure is aimed at those who terrorise their neighbours, its actual reach is far broader and covers a wide spectrum of conduct deemed 'anti-social', whether criminal or not. We think it unfortunate that one of the Government's first major proposals on criminal justice policy is of such a character.

Blunderbuss solutions do not help, and serve only to politicise what are very real problems for those who live in poorer neighbourhoods'.[2]

---

[1]   Professor Andrew Ashworth, Dr John Gardner, Professor Rod Morgan, Professor ATH Smith, Professor Andrew von Hirsch, Professor Martin Wasik.
[2]   [1998] Criminal Justice, Vol 16, No 1, February 1998, p 7, at p 7 and p 14.

Scope of proscribed behaviour

2.5   The scope of the proscribed behaviour was rigorously debated at various stages during the Bill's passage through Parliament. What behaviour will be included? Anti-social behaviour, it was noted, is defined 'entirely by reference to its effects'.[1] In the House of Lords, the clause was described as 'a dangerous catch-all',[2] and Lord Ackner questioned in Committee whether the test to be applied would be objective or subjective.[3] In Committee in the House of Commons, the Liberal Democrats unsuccessfully proposed amendments that would have provided for 'a test of reasonableness to ascertain whether behaviour was anti-social' and to ensure that the behaviour had to be 'serious' before an order was made.[4] The Home Secretary has said that the ASBO will 'tackle that serious, persistent, anti-social behaviour',[5] whereas the Minister of State in the Home Office, Mr Michael, caused concern with his repeated mention of 'sub-criminal behaviour'.[6] He explained that the 'purpose of the order is not to punish behaviour but to prevent it, and that there are three key elements'. First, the orders are intended to tackle persistent behaviour. Secondly, the cumulative effect on the victims will often be more important than each individual act. Thirdly, the orders are intended to be used for 'criminal or sub-criminal activity, not run-of-the-mill civil disputes between neighbours'.[7] The term 'sub-criminal' was described by one MP as—

> 'a term that we can never define, although the Minister thinks he knows what he means by it, and I hope that we think we know what he thinks he means by it'.[8]

A Conservative amendment would have restricted the type of behaviour to that which is covered by existing criminal or civil law. Time will tell whether behaviour not already caught within the definitions of existing offences, including the public order legislation, housing legislation and the Noise Act 1996, will be used in support of applications for ASBOs.

---

[1] HC SC B, 30 April 1998, col 60 (Mr Clappison).
[2] Lord Rodgers (leader of the Liberal Democrats) at HL Report, 2 February 1998, col 544.
[3] HL Report, 3 February 1998, col 516.
[4] HC SC B, 28 April 1998, col 19.
[5] HL Report, 8 April 1998, col 373.
[6] See for example HC SC B, 30 April 1998, col 66.
[7] HC SC B, 30 April 1998, col 47.
[8] Ibid, col 57 (Mr Malins).

2.6 The behaviour need not be intentional. Lord Goodhart proposed an amendment in the House of Lords which would have excluded the imposition of an ASBO on a person—

> 'if his acts are neither motivated by an intention to harass or cause alarm or distress to other persons nor likely to cause serious and justified alarm or distress to other persons.'.[1]

The Government's response was that one can rely on the discretion of local authorities, the police and the courts to ensure that unjustifiable orders are not made, but this was not good enough for Lord Goodhart—

> 'The level of conduct which triggers the order should in itself be high enough not to make it necessary in large numbers of cases to have to rely on the discretion of the courts.'.[2]

However, his amendment was defeated by 131 to 43 votes.

---

[1] HL Report, 17 March 1998, col 579.
[2] Ibid, col 585.

2.7 Although ASBOs will be available against anyone over the age of ten, the Government has stressed that the main target is not juveniles. A Liberal Democrat amendment proposing that the minimum age should be 16, ie, the age level that the Government set for equivalent orders in Scotland,[1] was not accepted. Baroness David moved an amendment in the House of Lords to prevent a local authority from making an application for an ASBO in respect of a person under the age of 18 without first receiving a report from a Youth Offending Team. She withdrew it having received an answer from the Government that although they were supportive of what the amendment was seeking to achieve they wanted to leave the position as flexible as possible and would therefore leave such matters to the published guidance, rather than include them in the Act.[2]

---

1   HL Report, 23 June 1998, col 867.
2   HL Report, 3 February 1998, col 552.

Definition of 'relevant authority'

2.8   Section 1(1) also defines the 'relevant authority' which may apply for an order as 'the council for the local government area or any chief officer of police any part of whose police area lies within that area'. Thus, either the police or the local authority may apply, though they must consult with each other (s 1(2)). The specification of 'by complaint' in s 1(3) makes it clear that the magistrates' court is acting in its civil capacity. If the magistrates find the conditions in s 1(1) are fulfilled, they may make an order 'which prohibits the defendant from doing anything described in the order' (s 1(4)). Opposition members in Parliament queried whether this wording laid down adequate guidance for magistrates.

Reasonable exceptions

2.9   Section 1(5), which was added by the House of Lords in Committee,[1] provides that the court shall disregard any act of the defendant which he shows was 'reasonable in the circumstances'. Lord Williams of Mostyn gave various examples, such as that of a charity worker collecting door to door, or an aircraft company flying over residential areas in permitted hours. Both of these might be 'offensive', but a sensible explanation ought to provide a defence. Lord Goodhart criticised the amendment which he felt should extend to trivial as well as reasonable acts, and because it puts the burden of proof on the defendant.[2] This concern was echoed in the House of Commons—

> 'In how many cases where the civil standard of proof is used does the burden of proof shift to the defendant rather than the prosecution or the applicant?'.[3]

---

1   HL Report, 3 February 1998, col 564.
2   Ibid, col 565.
3   HC SC B, 30 April 1998, col 103 (Mr Clappison).

ASBOs covering more than one area

2.10   Section 1(6) originally provided that the prohibitions must be necessary for the protection of people in the local government area from further anti-social acts by the defendant. The Government had at that point decided that if 'an application involved different areas, separate applications might be needed to prohibit the same type of behaviour in both areas'.[1] However, they then decided that to restrict the application of the order to a single local authority in every case, even where a single pattern of offending might spread to two or more adjoining areas, would be unnecessarily restrictive. Therefore an amendment was accepted in the House of Lords which allows a local authority to include adjoining areas to be included in an application as long as all relevant authorities have been consulted before an order is sought.[2] The subsection was further significantly amended in the House of Commons.[3]

---

[1]   HC SC B, 30 April 1998, col 97.
[2]   HL Report, 22 July 1998, col 930.
[3]   HL Report, 23 June 1998, col 880.

Duration of ASBO

2.11 Under s 1(7), an ASBO shall have effect for a period (not less than two years) specified in the order or until further order. Lord Williams of Mostyn responded to critics of this minimum, rather than maximum, time limit by stating that—

> 'The minimum duration is not a burden on any individual unless he or she wishes to restart the previous pattern of activity. . . . if a court does not believe that a case has been made out for the minimum period of time, it is better not to make an order at all.'.[1]

Section 1(8) provides for the variation or discharge of the order by further order, subject to s 1(9) which provides that the order shall not be discharged before two years unless with the consent of both parties. This consent requirement may lead to applications for judicial review from individuals seeking to vary or discharge an order made against them.

---

[1]   HL Report, 3 February 1998, col 572.

Breach of ASBO

2.12 Breach of the orders is dealt with in s 1(10). Building on the precedent set by the Protection from Harassment Act 1997, breach may result in a criminal penalty on summary conviction of imprisonment for not more than six months, or a fine not exceeding the statutory maximum, or both; and on conviction on indictment to imprisonment for not more than five years, or a fine, or both. Section 1(11) specifies that the court cannot make a conditional discharge for a breach of an order. These penalties make the order look far more like a criminal penalty than a civil order. The 'ferocity' of the sentencing power was described by Lord Thomas of Gresford as 'extraordinary'. He compared the maximum of five years' imprisonment to the maximum of six months' imprisonment for intentionally causing harassment, under the Criminal Justice and Public Order Act 1994—'when things were going pretty well over the top under the previous Government'.[1] Amendments in Committee would have reduced the penalties, and indeed the Liberal Democrats suggested that breaches should be dealt with only in civil courts as contempts of court. It seems likely that the ASBO will be treated in substance as a criminal sanction and must therefore conform with Art 6(3) of the European Convention on Human Rights (see *Schmautzer v Austria* (1995)).[2]

---

[1]   HL Report, 3 February 1998, col 600.
[2]   (1995) 21 EHRR 511.

2.13 How ASBOs will work in practice remains to be seen. Will they be as popular as some MPs suggest? What is the relationship with the Public Order Act 1986, ss 4 and 5, which require the criminal standard of proof? Will unhappy neighbours prefer the speedier option of reporting their neighbours to the police for breach of the peace? The Government has confirmed that legal aid will be available for anti-social behaviour orders and sex offender orders by an extension of the ABWOR scheme. There were many references in Parliament to the draft guidance on anti-social behaviour orders, but these seemed to give rise to more rather than less concern. For example, it became clear that proceedings concerning juveniles need not be in private, that local authorities may hire 'professional witnesses' (paid snoopers, commented one member),[1] and that the guidance to courts proceeding in the defendant's absence merely counsels that they 'should think carefully' before doing so.

---

[1]   HC SC B, 30 April 1998, col 66 (Mr Leigh).

Sex offender orders

2.14   Section 2 provides that a chief officer of police may apply to the magistrates' court for a sex offender order (SOO) in the area in which the alleged behaviour took place. These orders, which will prohibit the offender from 'doing anything described in the order', were first proposed as 'community protection orders' in a consultation paper of that name published in November 1997. The Bill was published before the end of the consultation period, and by then the name of the proposed orders had been changed. They should be seen in the context of the Sex Offenders Act (SOA) 1997, which requires notification of information to the police by persons who have committed certain sex offenders. Failure, without reasonable excuse, to comply with the notification requirements is a summary offence under that Act, as is the provision of false information. The notification requirements of SOA 1997 will continue to have effect during the currency of a SOO (s 2(5)).

Conditions

2.15   Two conditions must be fulfilled before the police officer may apply. First, the person must be a 'sex offender', defined in s 3(1) to include all those convicted or cautioned (or reprimanded or warned as a child or young person (see s 3(4)) of an offence to which SOA 1997, Pt I, applies). Equivalent offences committed abroad are also included (s 3(5), though s 3(6) sets out a procedure, and provides for rules of court, whereby a defendant may challenge by notice on the applicant that he has committed an act abroad which constituted an offence under that law). Secondly, the offender must have acted, since the relevant date, 'in such a way as to give reasonable cause to believe that an order under this section is necessary to protect the public from serious harm from him' (s 2(1)(b)). The section was originally drafted without reference to a relevant date, but this would probably have infringed the European Convention on Human Rights (ECHR), Art 7, since the section would have applied where the offence had been committed before the Act came into force. The 'relevant date' is therefore defined in s 3(2) as his date of conviction, or, if later, the date of commencement of s 2. The behaviour threshold, that the offender must have acted so as to give reasonable cause that an order is necessary to protect the public from serious harm, was challenged in Committee in both Houses of Parliament. However, Mr Michael stressed that—

> 'A sex offender order is a civil order, and that is its great strength. It will allow the police to intervene before a further offence is committed by someone who has committed a sex offence in the past. The idea is to stop him in his tracks when such behaviour by another person may be considered innocent.'.[1]

The 'true target' of the SOOs are paedophiles. It is worth considering the relationship of these orders with PACE 1984, s 25, which already gives a police officer the power to arrest someone if he has reasonable grounds for believing that the arrest is necessary to prevent them causing physical injury to any person or to protect a child or other vulnerable person from him.

---

[1]   HC SC B, 5 May 1998, col 173.

2.16   The specification of 'by complaint' in s 2(2) makes clear that the magistrates' court is acting in its civil capacity. Under s 2(3), the magistrates' court may make an order under this section 'which prohibits the defendant from doing anything described in the order'. These provisions are extraordinarily wide, limited simply by s 2(4) which provides that the prohibitions must be necessary for the protection of the 'public from serious harm from the defendant'. Lord Goodhart asked in Committee in the House of Lords what limits the Government envisaged, and continued—

> 'It surely cannot be right to make an order, for example, which prevents the subject of the order from going into a public place. That would amount to house arrest, which clearly would not be an acceptable application of the power to make an order.'.[1]

The answer may well lie, as Lord Goodhart and Lord Williams recognised, with the Human Rights Act when it comes into force. Section 2(3) will have to be interpreted as being compatible with the right to liberty under ECHR, Art 5. HO Circular 38/1998 states that guidance should be published in the autumn of 1998.

---

[1]   HL Report, 3 February 1998, col 617.

Duration of order

2.17   Section 2(5) provides that the order shall have effect for a minimum period of not less than five years. This was challenged in Committee in the House of Lords,[1] as was the requirement in s 2(7) which provides that, except with the consent of both parties, no SOO may be discharged within five years. Lord Goodhart stated that 'it is a bad principle that the police should have a right of veto on whether or not to discharge an order made by a court'.[2] Breach of the order is dealt with in s 2(8). If without reasonable excuse a person does anything which he is prohibited from doing by a sex offender order, it may result in a maximum penalty on summary conviction of imprisonment for not more than six months, or a fine not exceeding the statutory maximum, or both; and on conviction on indictment, imprisonment for not more than five years, or a fine, or both. As with the ASBO, a conditional discharge will not be an available penalty.

---

[1]   HL Report, 3 February 1998, col 620.
[2]   HL Report, 16 December 1997, col 587.

Appeals against orders

2.18   Section 4 allows for appeals against both ASBOs and SOOs. An appeal is to the Crown Court (even though these are civil orders), and any order made on appeal shall for the purposes of subsequent breach proceedings be treated as an order of the magistrates' court.

CRIME AND DISORDER STRATEGIES

2.19 The ideas behind the 1998 Act, ss 5–7, and s 17, are to be found in Ch 2 of the consultation document, 'Getting to Grips with Crime; A New Framework for Local Action', published on 17 September 1997. Although most commentators have welcomed these strategies, concern has been expressed that they should not be seen as ends in themselves, nor as the solution to all problems. Mr Malins asked in Committee in the House of Commons 'Are we not dealing with a very bureaucratic and cumbersome animal here, and will the financial resources be available for it?'[1] In response, the minister explained that the word 'strategy' rather than 'plan' had been used 'to demonstrate that it is not the document itself which is important.' and 'We want effective partnership, leading to a reduction in crime and disorder.'.[2] Sections 5–18 came into force on 30 September 1998.[3]

---

[1]   HC SC B, 7 May 1998, col 213.
[2]   Ibid, col 224.
[3]   The Crime and Disorder (Commencement No 2 and Transitional Provisions) Order 1998, SI 1998/2327 (see Appendix).

Authorities responsible for strategies

2.20 Section 5 defines the bodies responsible for the formulation of crime and disorder reduction strategies, and draws the distinction between those bodies which must be involved with the responsible authorities, and those that must simply be invited to become involved. Section 5(1) defines the responsible authorities as the local authorities (the unitary authority for the area, or if there is not a unitary authority, the district council and the county in which the district falls) and the police (every chief officer of police, part of whose police area lies within the area) for each local government area. These strategies are therefore district, not county based.

2.21 Police authorities, probation committees, health authorities and other bodies as defined by order of the Secretary of State must co-operate fully with the responsible authorities in developing and delivering the strategy (s 5(2)). Intriguingly, s 5(3) empowers the Secretary of State to require local authorities and the police to ensure that certain other organisations are 'invited' to contribute to the process. The Minster of State explained that these powers '. . . are likely to be used to ensure that the voluntary and business sectors are involved and those on whom it would not be appropriate to impose legal duties.'.[1]

---

[1]   HC SC B, 7 May 1998, col 220.

Formulation and implementation of strategies

2.22 Section 6 requires local authorities and the police to formulate and implement a strategy for reducing crime and disorder in their area, and stipulates a number of specific things which they must do in discharging this obligation. Section 6(2) spells out what the local authorities must do *before* they draw up the strategy, namely—

(a) carry out a review of the levels and patterns of crime and disorder in the area (taking due account of the knowledge and experience of persons in the area);

(b) prepare an analysis of the results of that review;

(c) publish in the area a report of the analysis (which it was explained in Parliament should include details of the entire process, including ownership of targets and performance against them);

(d) consult fully with the local community (obtain views, hold public meetings etc).

While the section says 'review' the more popular term in Parliament was 'audit'. Strategies will be expected to run for three years, but they must be kept under review during that period. The original 'Notes on Clauses' explained that—

> 'the clause aims to ensure that the strategies are developed on a broadly consistent basis across the whole of England and Wales (without being prescriptive as to the detail) and in particular that they take full account of the concerns of the local community, rather than relying solely on participating agencies' perceptions of local problems.'.

2.23 Baroness Kennedy moved an amendment to ensure that the crime and disorder strategy should take account also of the fear of crime and disorder in an area, but she withdrew it after the Solicitor-General, Lord Falconer, argued that—

> 'An obligation to reduce the fear of crime may well lead to any area experiencing a high fear of crime being given an artificially high priority simply so that the partnership could demonstrate that it was taking steps to combat the fear of crime. This could lead to an inappropriate diversion of resources, away from poor, high crime areas to affluent, low crime areas which can demonstrate a high fear of crime. I fear that if the provision is put on the face of the Bill there will be an inappropriate diversion of resources simply in order that the strategies appear to be achieving something.'.[1]

A Conservative amendment during Committee in the House of Commons would have specified that the strategy should specifically address 'the problem of drug abuse involving controlled drugs'. After a heated debate, the amendment was rejected by 9 votes to 8.[2]

---

[1] HL Report, 10 February 1998, col 1062.
[2] HC SC B, 7 May 1998, col 241.

2.24 Section 6(4) specifies that the strategy must include objectives, and long-term and short-term performance targets for measuring the extent to which the objectives are met. Section 6(5) details the way in which the strategy must be promulgated in the area and s 6(6) requires the local authorities and police to keep the strategy under review during its life time (successive periods of three years). Section 7 ('Supplemental') describes the reserve powers which the Secretary of State shall have to oversee the work done locally, and to call for reports from each area, as and when he sees fit. 'Notes on Clauses' say the aim of this 'is simply to provide a clear legal power for him to become involved if there is evidence that a particular strategy is failing'.

YOUTH CRIME AND DISORDER

Parenting orders

2.25 Details of parenting orders were first set out in the consultation document 'Tackling Youth Crime', published in September 1997, and were developed in the White Paper, 'No More Excuses'.[1] The Secretary of State, Mr O'Brien, said in Committee in the House of Commons that a parenting order—

> ' . . . is designed to help and support parents to control the behaviour of their children by requiring them to attend counselling and guidance sessions and, if necessary, to comply with specific requirements, . . . We believe that, until now, insufficient help or attention has been given to parents to change their children's behaviour.'.[2]

---

[1]   Cm 3809.

[2]   HC SC B, 7 May 1998, col 255.

2.26 Many people remain to be convinced of the effectiveness of parenting orders. Pilot schemes (allowed for in s 8(3)), which started on 30 September 1998 and will last for 18 months, will show whether they succeed in practice. The National Association of Probation Officers' briefing document commented that the existence of the orders will make little difference to the core causes of poor parenting, and may make things worse. The Bishop of Hereford summed up many people's concerns in the first debate in the House of Lords—

> 'I believe also that parenting orders are a doubtful method of coping with the problems that we face. By definition, they come into effect, if they work at all, too late in the day to prevent young people being caught up in bad company and acquiring bad habits. They seem to be contrary to the spirit of partnership, which is at the heart of the Children Act. The threat of financial penalties on parents who are often already poor, inadequate and sometimes in despair is unlikely to achieve very much which is positive.'.[1]

Lord Thomas of Gresford went further—

> 'The orders seem to be wonderfully idealistic. We have before us the template of the new Labour family where no doubt the mother smilingly greets her children as they come from school with her arms covered in flour from baking scones for their tea, and the father is ready to help with the homework, and so on—and if they are not, we shall jolly well make them so because we shall train them in the proper duties of how to be a mother and father.
>
> People are not like that. The puritanical, almost Cromwellian, zeal with which the order is introduced is typical of other measures which may be found within the Bill.'.[2]

---

[1]   HL Report, 16 December 1997, col 557 (Lord Bishop of Hereford).

[2]   HL Report, 10 February 1998, col 1071.

Scope of parenting orders

2.27 Section 8(1) provides that a court may make a parenting order where—

    (a) a child safety order is made (see s 11);

    (b) an ASBO or SOO is made in respect of a child or young person (see ss 1 and 2);

    (c) a child or young person is convicted of an offence;

    (d) a person is convicted of offences under the Education Act 1996, ss 443 or 444.

An amendment by Baroness Kennedy, concerned about the use of criminal sanctions to ensure school attendance, to omit para (d), was unsuccessful.[1]

---

[1]   HL Report, 10 February 1998, col 1068.

2.28 The order will consist of two elements (s 8(4)). The first imposes a requirement on parents to comply with the requirements specified in the order. These are those which the court considers desirable in the interests of preventing repetition or the commission of offences (s 8(7)). The White Paper suggested that these requirements might include that the parent(s) ensure the child's attendance at school or that one parent or another responsible adult be home at night to supervise him. These requirements may be set for a period not exceeding 12 months. The second is that the court can impose on the parent a requirement to attend counselling and guidance sessions for no more than once a week and up to three months. Mr O'Brien stressed in Committee that this part was a core element of the order. He had been convinced of the effectiveness of parenting orders during his visit to the USA as a member of the Home Affairs Committee.[1] However, where a parent has previously been made the subject of a parenting order, for example, with a different child or after a previous conviction for an offence, then the court may exercise its discretion about whether to include a counselling requirement (s 8(5)).

---

[1]   HC SC B, 7 May 1998, col 256.

Parenting orders: procedure

2.29 Section 9 sets out the procedural requirements which the court must take into account *before* making an order. It also allows for the order to be discharged or varied and provides for sanctions that will be available to the court should the parent or guardian fail to comply with the terms of the order. Where a child or young person under the age of 16 is convicted of a criminal offence and where the court is satisfied that it would be desirable in the interests of preventing the further commission of an offence by that child or young person, the court shall make a parenting order. If it does not, it must state its reasons in open court (s 9(1)). Baroness Kennedy proposed an amendment in Committee in the House of Lords to remove this subsection and the statutory presumption in favour of parenting orders[1] but withdrew it, commenting that pilot schemes should be used to establish whether parents would be prepared to accept these orders voluntarily before compulsion is involved.

---

[1]   HL Report, 10 February 1998, col 1078.

2.30 Under s 9(2), the court must consider information about the child's family circumstances and the likely effect of the orders. The requirements of the order must 'as far as practicable' avoid any conflict with the parent's religious beliefs, work or education (s 9(4)). An amendment that this protection should be extended to cover the child's religion or education as well as the parent's, was withdrawn after the Government opposed such protection, arguing that the court is already under a duty to consider the family circumstances (see s 9(2)).[1] The court must explain to the parent in ordinary language the effect of the order, its requirements, the consequences of failure to comply, and the power to review (s 9(3)). Under s 9(5), the court is empowered to discharge or vary the order, but such applications to vary can only be made by the parent or the responsible officer. If an application for discharge is dismissed, then no further application for the discharge may be made without the consent of the court that made the order (s 9(6)).

---

[1]   HC SC B, 7 May 1998, col 263.

Failure to comply

2.31 Under s 9(7), if the parent fails to comply with any requirement in the order, or with specified directions given by the responsible officer, he or she is liable on summary conviction to a fine not exceeding level 3 (currently £1,000) on the standard scale. This has proved contentious, since the breach results in a criminal conviction. The Government has explained that the normal route to prosecution would be from the responsible officer (a probation officer, social worker or member of a youth offending team, see s 8(8)), to the police, and then normal prosecuting procedures would be followed.

Appeals against parenting orders

2.32 Section 10 sets out the appeals procedure following three specific applications. It provides that an appeal against the making of a parenting order in proceedings where a child safety order is made shall be to the High Court. Where a parenting order is made in proceedings where an anti-social behaviour or sex offender order is made, the appeal shall lie to the Crown Court. The section describes the options available to the appeal court, and states that the Lord Chancellor may by order make provision as to the circumstances in which appeals may be made against decisions taken by courts (s 10(6)).

Child safety orders

2.33 Child safety orders were first mooted in the consultation paper 'Tackling Youth Crime', and the thinking behind them was developed further in Ch 5 of the White Paper 'No More Excuses—A new approach to tackling youth crime'.[1] They are not being introduced in Scotland. The purpose of the child safety order is to protect children under the age of ten from the risk of becoming involved in crime and to protect those who have already started to behave in an anti-social or criminal manner. However, it remains very unclear how these will fit in with existing provisions under the Children Act (CA) 1989, namely—
(a) contact, prohibited steps, residence and specific issue orders under s 8;
(b) care and supervision orders under s 31;
(c) education supervision orders under s 36;
(d) child assessment orders under s 43; and
(e) emergency protection orders under s 44.

Much remains uncertain. In the Government's words— 'we are anxious not be overly prescriptive in our approach'.[2] Pilot schemes (necessary under s 11(2)) will operate from autumn 1998 for 18 months. Further details on how the orders are intended to work is available in the draft guidance document, published by the Home Office.

_____

[1]   Cm 3809.
[2]   HC SC B, 7 May 1998, col 270.

_____

Conditions for application

2.34 Section 11(1) allows a local authority (in practice, a local authority social services department) to apply to a family proceedings magistrates' court (see s 11(5)) for a child safety order. This places the child for a set period under the supervision of the responsible officer (a social worker or member of a youth offending team: see s 11(8)) and requires the child to comply with such requirements as are specified. The applicant must be satisfied that one or more of the very wide conditions specified in s 11(3) are fulfilled—

   (a) the child must have committed an act which had he been over ten would have constituted an offence;
   (b) the order is 'necessary' to prevent the child committing such an act;
   (c) the child has contravened a ban imposed by a curfew notice;
   (d) the child has acted in a manner that has caused or was likely to cause harassment, alarm or distress to one or more persons not of the same household as himself.

Baroness Kennedy argued unsuccessfully that children should be supervised by social workers rather than members of the youth offending team because of the cultural differences in the method of operation between the criminal courts, even when they act in a civil capacity, and family courts.[1]

_____

[1]   HL Report, 10 February 1998, col 1101.

_____

2.35 Child safety orders can only be imposed on children under the age of ten, and there is no minimum age for an order. The Association of Directors of Social Services were quoted in Parliament as saying 'The order in practice criminalises the behaviour of children under ten'.[1] However, the absence of a minimum age was justified by the Government on the ground that local authorities have a discretionary power and will act reasonably. The maximum period permitted for a child safety order is normally three months, or, exceptionally, 12 months (s 11(4)). Under s 11(5), the requirements which the court may specify are those which the court considers desirable in the interests of—

   (a) securing that the child receives appropriate care, protection and support and is subject to proper control; or
   (b) preventing any repetition of the kind of behaviour which led to the child safety order being made.

_____

[1]   HC SC B, 7 May 1998, col 274.

_____

2.36 In the White Paper 'No More Excuses', the Government gave the following example (at p 15)—

'For example, an 8 year old girl found shoplifting with a group of older girls in the local shopping centre might be referred by the police to social services. The local authority could apply to the court for a child safety order. The order might require her to stay away from the shopping centre, not mix with the older girls and (with the agreement of the organisers) attend a local youth programme to make constructive use of her leisure time.'.

Child safety orders: procedure

2.37   Section 12 makes supplemental provisions for child safety orders. It sets out the procedural requirements which the court must take into account before making an order and allows for the order to be discharged or varied. Under s 12(1), the court must consider information about the child's family circumstances and the likely effect of the orders. The court must explain to the parent or guardian of the child in ordinary language the effect of the order, its requirements, the consequences if the child fails to comply, and the power to review (s 12(2)). The requirements of the order must 'as far as practicable' avoid any conflict with the parent's religious beliefs, or the child's education (s 12(3)). Under s 12(4), the court is empowered to discharge or vary the order. If an application for discharge is dismissed, then no further application for the discharge may be made without the consent of the court that made the order (s 12(5)). Where a child fails to comply with the requirements specified in the order, the court may discharge the order and may make the child subject to a care order under CA 1989, s 31(1)(a), or may make an order varying the order (s 12(6)). This subsection has caused some concern, especially since s 12(7) makes it clear that a care order can be made whether or not the conditions to make a care order under CA 1989, s 31(2) are fulfilled.[1] CA 1989 streamlined care procedures and made it clear that the welfare of the child is the paramount consideration. This new procedure provides a second route into care. However, the minister confirmed after a searching interchange with Mr Clappison that CA 1989, s 1, applies to the 1998 Act, s 12(6),[2] and that the child's welfare shall be the court's paramount consideration.

---

[1]   Ie that the child concerned is suffering, or is likely to suffer, significant harm or that the harm, or likelihood of harm, is attributable to the care given, or likely to be given to the child (if the order were not made) not being what it would be reasonable to expect a parent to give him; or that the child is beyond parental control.
[2]   HC SC B, 12 May 1998, col 290.

Appeals against child safety orders

2.38   Appeals against child safety orders, dealt with in s 13, go to the High Court. This follows the practice established by s 10(1)(a) where a parenting order is imposed in conjunction with a child safety order, and is in line with the usual arrangements for appeals from the family proceedings court.

Local child curfew schemes

2.39   Section 14 makes provision for the establishment by local authorities of Local Child Curfew Schemes (LCCS). These were proposed in the consultation paper 'Tackling Youth Crime', and in the White Paper 'No More Excuses—A New

Approach to tackling youth crime in England and Wales'. The introduction of these schemes has been opposed in principle and on practical grounds. In principle, it has been argued that it is inappropriate to deny basic freedom of movement to general sections of the public on the basis of the possible behaviour of a few individuals, and that there are already enough powers under CA 1989 to deal with individuals. In practice, it is not clear how the schemes will fit in with existing orders. For example, under CA 1989, ss 46 and 47, police and local authorities have the power to investigate children at risk and take them to a place of safety. Will blanket curfew orders add to the protection and welfare of children? In practice, it might prevent a child from seeing a relative who lives around the corner. However, a vote in the House of Lords to leave out the section was defeated by 89 to 20 votes. Even the White Paper seems vague about how they will work—

> 'For example, if young children were regularly congregating at night in the public spaces of a housing estate, making residents' lives intolerable through vandalism, pilfering and abusive behaviour, local residents *might* seek the help of the police. If normal policing methods did not work the local authority and police, after, consultation *might* decide to introduce a local child curfew for a ninety day period. (author's italics)'[1]

---

[1] Cm 3809, p 16.

Information to be included

2.40 The guidance for local child curfews[1] includes a checklist of information to be included in an application for a local child curfew scheme. This list (with references to paragraphs within the draft guidance) reveals that this will not be easy—

    (a) the nature and scale of the problem caused by unsupervised children engaged in anti-social or potentially criminal behaviour or an indication of why a local child curfew scheme should be approved (para 4.9);

    (b) initial consultation arrangements (para 4.10);

    (c) proposed consultation arrangements for a notice served under the scheme (para 4.11);

    (d) consultation arrangements for repeat curfews (para 4.12);

    (e) notification and publicity of the curfew notice (para 4.13);

    (f) evidence of appropriate inter-agency working (para 4.14);

    (g) an indication of how early and how late the curfew should operate (para 4.27);

    (h) ages of children subject to the curfew and whether different times should apply to different age groups (para 4.27);

    (i) the date of commencement of the scheme (para 4.19);

    (j) dealing with enforcement of the curfew (s 5);

    (k) a contact point (para 4.17).

---

[1] Home Office circular No 46/1998.

2.41 Under s 14(1) a local authority may make a LCCS under which it may issue a notice imposing a ban for a specified period not exceeding 90 days for the purpose of maintaining order. Before making the scheme, the local authority will have to consult with the police and 'such other persons or bodies as it considers appropriate' (s 14(3)). The Home Secretary has to approve or reject the scheme (s 14(4), (5)).

Baroness Kennedy, worried by the wide discretion which the section gives, proposed an amendment that the local authority would have to be satisfied that there were 'exceptional circumstances' before imposing a curfew.[1] A ban may apply to children of specified ages (under ten) being in a public place within a specified area during specified hours (9 pm to 6 am), otherwise than under the effective control of a parent or responsible adult (s 14(2)). Under s 14(6), a notice may specify different hours in relation to children of different ages. Baroness Anelay moved an amendment to remove this subsection, but the Government repeated their clarion call for flexibility.[2] The issue of publicity and notification is dealt with in s 14(7), and s 14(8) defines 'local authority' and 'public place'.[3]

---

[1]   HL Report, 10 February 1998, col 1107.
[2]   Ibid, col 1123.
[3]   'Public place' has the same meaning as in the Public Order Act 1986, Pt II, ie any highway and any place to which at that time 'the public or any section of the public has access, on payment or otherwise, as of right or by virtue of express or implied permission'.

Contravention of curfew notices

2.42   Under s 15, where a constable has reasonable cause to believe that a child is in contravention of a ban imposed by a curfew notice, he *shall* as soon as practicable, inform the local authority of the contravention and *may* remove the child to the child's place of residence, unless he has reasonable cause to believe the child would, if removed to that place, be likely to suffer significant harm. This has caused concern because children on the street may be avoiding an unsafe home, in which case, the Government has suggested, the police officer would be expected to take the child into police protection under CA 1989, s 46. Section 15(4) amends CA 1989, s 47, in order to ensure that any intervention by the local authority is timely. Any breach of a curfew notice automatically triggers a visit by the local authority to the child's home.

Removal of truants to designated premises etc

2.43   Section 16 was added in Committee at a late stage in the House of Commons,[1] after the recommendations of the social exclusion unit had been examined. The House of Lords agreed it without a division.[2] The Parliamentary Under-Secretary of State for the Home Department, Mr Mike O'Brien, introduced the measure by explaining the significance of the problem: over one million children take at least one day off a year from school without authority. The section gives the police a power to remove truants, but it is not a power of arrest or detention, nor does it make truancy a criminal offence. However, the police will be protected from being sued to the extent to which the power depends on their 'reasonable belief' (s 16(3)). They will be able to use such reasonable force as was necessary in all the circumstances. The child must be in a public place when apprehended. This includes private premises, such as shopping centres and arcades, to which the public have access.

---

[1]   See HC SC B, 9 June 1998, col 777.
[2]   HL Report, 22 July 1998, col 931.

2.44   Section 16 will only apply where a local authority has designated premises to which children or young persons may be removed (s 16(1)). In answer to a question, Mr O'Brien stated—

'The designated place might or might not be a school . . . It is not anticipated that the designated place will be a police station. The local authority will decide on the best place: it might be a social services department, or even a school where there are suitable facilities and staff able to deal with children who might have come from other schools.'.[1]

The power will be exercisable only with the authority of a police officer of superintendent rank or above for a specified period and a specified place (s 16(2)). Then, if a constable has reasonable cause to believe that the child is of compulsory school age and is absent from school without authority, he may remove the child to his school or to the designated premises. Opposition concerns, which included the problem of children educated at home (in accordance with the Education Act 1996, s 7), prompted the Government to promise that the Home Office and the Department for Education and Employment would issue guidance for the police and local authorities about the operation of the provisions, which will be implemented on 1 December 1998.

---

[1]   HC SC B, 9 June 1998, col 784.

MISCELLANEOUS AND SUPPLEMENTAL

Duty to consider crime and disorder implications

2.45   Section 17 was foreshadowed in Ch 2 of the consultation document 'Getting to Grips with Crime: A New Framework for Local Action', published in September 1997. In the words of the original Notes on Clauses—

'The aim is to reflect the reality that there are crime and/or disorder implications in decisions made across the full range of local authority services, and to correct the current situation under which these implications are often not recognised at the time decisions are taken, with highly expensive consequences.'

Section 17(2) states that the section applies to a local authority, a joint authority, a police authority, a National Parks authority and the Broads authority. The Common Council of the City of London is not a local authority as defined in the Local Government Act 1972, s 270(1). As s 17(3) was originally drafted, it meant that the duty to consider crime and disorder implications of all decisions applies to the Common Council only in its capacity as a police authority, and not in its capacity as a local authority. This unintended anomaly was amended in the Commons by the addition of the Common Council into s 17(3) and this was accepted without a division in the House of Lords.[1] To put upon the police authority a duty to exercise its various functions with regard to preventing crime and disorder was considered by Lord Thomas of Gresford (and doubtless many others) as 'a little otiose. If the police are not involved in preventing crime and disorder in their areas, what on earth are they doing?'[2] Lord Thomas of Gresford also moved an amendment in Committee in the House of Lords to insert a clause entitled 'Reasonable duty of Ministers of Crown to prevent crime and disorder'[3] to impose on central government the same general obligation to consider crime and disorder implications as are imposed on local authorities. Unsurprisingly, it met with no Government support.

1   HL Report, 22 July 1998, col 932.
2   HL Report, 10 February 1998, col 1068.
3   Ibid, col 1065.

Interpretation etc of Chapter I

2.46 Section 18 defines the meaning of various expressions used in the 1998 Act, Pt I, Ch I, and imposes certain requirements in relation to probation officers and others giving directions under a parenting order or providing supervision under a child safety order.

CHAPTER II: SCOTLAND

Anti-social behaviour orders

2.47 As with the English provisions, there has been considerable doubt expressed about anti-social behaviour orders (ASBOs) in Scotland. In the House of Lords, Lord Mackay of Drumadoon referred to Simon Collins's book *Anti-social behaviour and Housing Law* (1997) and the 1997 report of the House of Commons' Scottish Affairs Committee on the subject, neither of which had supported ASBOs. He was critical of the fact that the Report had not been mentioned in the consultation paper 'Community Safety Order' issued in September 1997. The Government promised more explanation in the guidance, then in its fourth draft,[1] but stressed that 'the document has no legal significance, but it is significant in terms of due process'.

1   HC SC B, 4 June 1998, col 729.

2.48 The details of the Scottish ASBO vary in many ways from the English model (see paras 2.3–2.14). The first is in relation to age. Section 19(1) provides that an order can only apply to those over the age of 16 (the age is ten in England). Opposition amendments in both Houses to reduce the age limit from 16 to 12 failed. In the House of Lords it was taken to a vote and defeated by 107 to 45 votes.[1] The Commons' amendment was withdrawn after the Minister for Home Affairs and Devolution, Scottish Office, Mr McLeish, explained that the Government did not propose reducing the age to 12 because of the distinctive system of children's panels in Scotland. Secondly, only the local authority can apply for an ASBO—the police cannot. Notes on Clauses explain that in Scotland, it is unprecedented for the police to apply direct to the courts. This seems curious given that it is the police who will apply for a sex offender order (see para 2.51). Thirdly, the definition of anti-social behaviour in s 19(1)(a) refers to conduct that 'caused or was likely to cause alarm or distress', without mention of harassment, unlike s 1(1).

1   HL Report, 10 February 1998, col 1008.

2.49 Under s 19(2) an application must be made by summary application to the sheriff within whose sheriffdom the alarm and distress took place. The sheriff will thus be acting in his civil capacity, and the behaviour complained of, and the need for the order, will have to be proved on the balance of probabilities. If the sheriff is satisfied that the conditions in s 19(1) are fulfilled he may make an order which prohibits the individual from doing anything described in the order (s 19(3)). An amendment in Committee in the House of Lords, suggested by the Law Society of Scotland, would have inserted 'must' instead of 'may', ie it would have removed the sheriff's discretion once the conditions for making the order were met, but it was withdrawn.[1] Another Conservative amendment in Committee in the House of Lords would have attached a power of arrest to allow the arrest of someone subject to an order if the officer deemed it appropriate to do so, but it was withdrawn when Lord Hardie suggested that it was unnecessary.[2] On a vote on Report, the amendment was defeated by 70 to 18 votes.[3] Lord Mackay of Drumadoon proposed an amendment in the Lords which would have allowed sheriffs to make interim orders, but this amendment was defeated by 76 to 20 votes.[4]

---

[1]   HL Report, 10 February 1998, col 1030.
[2]   Ibid, col 1036.
[3]   HL Report, 17 March 1998, col 674.
[4]   Ibid, col 667.

2.50   A later amendment was tabled at the request of Glasgow City Council in the House of Commons in Committee that sheriffs should be able to make 'any interim order as he considers appropriate' but this was withdrawn when the Government insisted that the amendment would allow the possibility of knee-jerk reactions in which insufficiently prepared matters might be brought too quickly to court.[1] The Opposition also proposed an amendment which would have given the sheriff additional powers to take action against the parents or other adult with whom the person habitually resides, but this was withdrawn after Mr McLeish explained that it was a fundamental principle of Scottish law that the parent should not be held responsible for the actions of the child.[2] Other unsuccessful amendments would have prohibited sheriffs from granting an ASBO if it were to cause an individual against whom it was granted exceptional hardship, or would stop them living in their own homes, or affect their religious activity, or prevent them attending school or result in discrimination.

---

[1]   HC SC B, 4 June 1998, col 739.
[2]   See the Kilbrandon Committee Report, 'Children and young persons in Scotland' (1964).

Sex offender orders

2.51   Section 20 allows a chief constable to apply to the sheriff for a civil order, a sex offender order (SOO). Originally both the police and local authorities would have had the power to make applications, but this was changed by Government amendments in the House of Lords in Committee giving the police sole authority.[1] Another amendment in Committee in the House of Commons attempted to give a local authority rather than the chief constable power to apply for a SOO. This was justified by explaining that the Faculty of Advocates had proposed that if a SOO was not dealt with as a criminal matter by the procurator fiscal, it should be dealt with as a civil matter by the local authority. In any case, it was argued that it would be inappropriate for the police to make applications. However, the amendment was withdrawn.[2]

---

[1]   For discussion see Lord Hardie—HL Report, 10 February 1998, col 1040.
[2]   HC SB B, 4 June 1998, col 743.

Procedural provisions with respect to orders

2.52   Section 21 makes various procedural provisions for ASBOs and SOOs in Scotland. Lord Mackay of Drumadoon proposed an amendment which would have obliged local authorities to maintain a register containing details of those against whom these orders are made. However, he withdrew it when Lord Hardie suggested that the register would fulfil no useful purpose and might contravene the European Convention on Human Rights.[1]

---

[1]   HL Report, 10 February 1998, col 1052.

Offences in connection with breach of orders

2.53   Section 22 makes breach of an ASBO or a SOO a criminal offence. Section 22(6), (7) applies the provisions to SOOs. Breaching a SOO in the course of committing a separate criminal offence (eg indecent assault of a child in a playground from which the accused had been banned) is an aggravating factor to be taken into account in the sentence for that criminal offence.

Anti-social behaviour as ground for eviction

2.54   Section 23 is designed to close loopholes, by extending the discretionary grounds for eviction in relation to secure tenancies contained in the Housing (Scotland) Act 1987, Sch 3 and in the Housing (Scotland) Act 1988, Sch 5. In both Houses, concern was expressed that the section gives landlords too wide a power. Current housing legislation already provides discretionary grounds for eviction where a house is used for criminal or immoral purposes. This section extends the provisions to cover criminal and anti-social acts committed in the locality of the house, and applies also to the activities of visitors to the house. An amendment was proposed that the actions of people visiting the house should be excluded. The Government agreed that the section should not be a 'charter for unscrupulous landlords', but suggested that the 'new measures will help to produce more harmonious communities'.[1] As is often the case in this Act, more guidance will be published in due course.

---

[1]   HC Report, 23 June 1998, col 891.

Noise-making equipment: police power of seizure

2.55   Section 24 was added late in Committee stage in the House of Commons[1] and should be read in connection with Sch 1, which adds a new s 54(2A) and a new Sch 2A to the Civic Government (Scotland) Act 1982. It implements one of the recommendations in the 1996 Scottish Affairs Committee report on housing and anti-social behaviour, namely that the police should have the statutory power to confiscate equipment where they have grounds to suspect that a noise offence has been committed under the 1982 Act. If a person causing a noise fails to stop when requested to do so by the police, the police will be able to take the noise-making equipment away and hold it for 28 days. After that period, the owner will be able to apply to get it back, but will have to meet whatever conditions are imposed by the police on its collection and to pay whatever charge the police consider reasonable to cover their costs. Where court proceedings are instituted, the equipment can be held until the end of the case. There is an appeals mechanism to ensure that the police do not act unreasonably in handling claims for the return of equipment.

---

[1]   HC SC B, June 1998, col 748.

CHAPTER III: GREAT BRITAIN

Powers to require removal of masks etc

2.56 Section 25 adds a new s 60(4A) (powers to stop and search in anticipation of violence) to the Criminal Justice and Public Order Act (CJPOA) 1994. Section 60 has already been amended by the Knives Act 1997, s 8, to allow a power to search for knives and offensive weapons whether or not the constable has grounds for suspecting that weapons are carried. Originally, a similar clause was proposed by Viscount Tenby, moving Lord Carnarvon's amendment in Committee in the House of Lords on 'Removal of Face Coverings'.[1] He was clearly thinking of hunt saboteurs and animal rights activists, but withdrew the amendment to give the Government more time to consider the finer details. The clause introduced late in Committee stage in the House of Commons[2] provoked significant debate over a rival opposition proposal covering a wider range of activities. The definition of mask or face coverings was particularly controversial, since the House was mindful of, for example, women who cover their faces for religious reasons.

---

[1] HL Report, 3 March 1998, col 1153.
[2] HC SC B, 9 June 1998, col 787.

2.57 CJPOA 1994, s 60(4A) allows a constable to 'require a person to remove any item which the constable reasonably believes that the person is wearing wholly or mainly for the purpose of concealing his identity'. This is a potentially far-reaching power and is therefore subject to the safeguard (already part of CJPOA 1994, s 60) that it is only exercisable where authorised by an officer of at least inspector rank, where he believes that there will be violence, or weapons will be carried. The power only lasts for 24 hours after authorisation.

Retention and disposal of things seized

2.58 Section 26 inserts CJPOA 1994, s 60A, authorising the retention and disposal of things seized under s 60, and provides for regulations to be made by the Secretary of State.

Power of arrest for failure to comply with requirement

2.59 Section 27(1) amends PACE 1984, s 24(2), to give a power of arrest where someone fails to comply with the requirement to removal of a mask, and s 27(2) extends a similar power of arrest to constables in Scotland. Sections 25–27 were all accepted without debate in House of Lords on 22 July 1998.[1] These measures will be implemented in December 1998.

---

[1] HL Report, 22 July 1998, col 933.

3 Criminal law

INTRODUCTION

3.1 Part II of the Crime and Disorder Act 1998 deals predominantly with racially aggravated offences. (It also contains miscellaneous provisions to remove the presumption that a child is *doli incapax* (s 34), allowing a court to draw inferences from the failure of a juvenile to give evidence or answer questions at trial, and to abolish the death penalty for piracy and treason (s 36).) All the sections in Pt II came into force on 30 September 1998.[1] Although Pt II creates new racially aggravated offences, it does not make illegal what is presently legal, but simply makes existing offences more serious. The Labour Party Manifesto said—

> 'We will create a new offence of racial harassment and a new crime of racially motivated violence to protect ethnic minorities from intimidation.'

In September 1997 a brief Consultation Document 'Racial Violence and Harassment' was published, seeking swift responses by the end of October. The Bill then introduced the bizarre division which now exists in the law. Section 82 states as a general principle that 'if an offence is racially aggravated, the court shall treat that fact as an aggravating factor' (see para 5.45). This is designed to give statutory expression to the decision in *R v Ribbans, Duggan and Ridley*,[2] yet it specifically does not apply to the offences contained in Pt II of the 1998 Act, where certain offences (mostly the less serious) become more serious offences, subject to higher maximum penalties, because of racial aggravation.

---

[1]   The Crime and Disorder Act 1998 (Commencement No 2 and Transitional Provisions) Order 1998, SI 1998/2327 (see Appendix).
[2]   16 Cr App Rep (S) 698; [1995] Crim LR 258.

3.2 Murder, manslaughter and offences under the Offences against the Person (OAPA) Act 1861, s 18, have not been affected by these redefinitions. The Government explained that these offences already carry a life sentence and that the sentence the Court imposes can therefore be adequately increased under s 82. However, this does not explain why they did not proceed along these lines with less serious offences, ie by simply raising the maximum sentence available. The stated view is that to mark the seriousness of the racially aggravated criminal act, the offence itself should become a more serious one.

Problems with application

3.3 The way in which these two different methods of dealing with racially aggravated offences interplay is going to cause significant problems in practice. For example, racial aggravation under OAPA 1861, s 18, will remain a matter for sentencing judges, but offences falling under s 20 of the 1861 Act will have to be decided by the jury. If the jury acquits a defendant of a racially aggravated offence but convicts him of a non-racially aggravated offence, the judge will be bound to pass sentence on that basis. If an offender is charged under s 18, however, there will be no alternative racially aggravated offence. But if there is an alternative charge under s 20, the jury may then have to be directed on the racial aggravation elements. A similar difficulty will arise under the Public Order Act (POA) 1986. Viscount Colville asked in Committee whether it will be possible for a jury to convict of a racially aggravated s 20 offence where the original indictment mentions only s 18.[1] He then moved a clause in the House of Lords specifically to allow a charge under OAPA 1861, s 18, or POA 1986, ss 2 or 3, to include a racially aggravated element, in order to allow for alternative verdicts.[2] The Government, however, did not accept the amendment. The Crown Prosecution Service will therefore have to decide at an early stage whether to include a second alternative count on the indictment in order to deal with this difficulty. If the racially aggravated offence is not on the indictment, the jury will not be able to convict the offender of it. Alternative verdicts are not available in the magistrates' courts, therefore prosecutors in those courts will have to consider adding more charges to the information.

---

[1]   HL Report, 12 February 1998, col 1282.
[2]   HL Report, 17 March 1998, col 699.

RACIALLY AGGRAVATED OFFENCES: ENGLAND AND WALES

Meaning of 'racially aggravated'

3.4   Section 28 provides a two part test to be applied in deciding whether an offence, listed under ss 29–32, is racially aggravated. The prosecution will be required to prove, beyond reasonable doubt, *either*—

(a) the existence of racial hostility at or immediately before the time the offence was committed, *or*

(b) that the offence was motivated by racial hostility.

The Government believed that many cases would slip through the net, unless the first part of this test was included. Section 28(1)(a) provides that the 'racial hostility' may occur at the time the offence is committed or immediately before or after the offence is committed. The original clause specified that the hostility should be 'based on the victim's membership of, or association with members of a racial group', which was designed to cover cases where a person is attacked because of their relationship with a member or members of a racial group. Thus the white boyfriend of a black woman may be the victim of a racially aggravated attack by a white offender if the attack was motivated by the victim's association with his girlfriend. The section was amended in Report in the House of Commons[1] (and accepted without debate in the House of Lords[2]) to cover hostility 'based on the victim's membership (or presumed membership of) a racial group', thereby ensuring that the perpetrator of racist attacks will not escape liability because of his ignorance about the victim's racial group. The definition of 'association with members of a racial group' is contained in s 28(2).

---

[1]   HC Report, 23 June 1998, col 892.
[2]   HC Report, 22 July 1998, col 934.

3.5   The second aspect of the test (s 28(1)(b)) is 'racist motivation', designed to cover cases where the prosecution can show beyond reasonable doubt that the basic offence was committed as a result—but not necessarily wholly as a result—of hostility towards members of a racial group. A racial group is defined for the purpose of this section by reference to race, colour, nationality (including citizenship) or ethnic or national origins (s 28(4)). This is the definition used in the Race Relations Act 1976 (s 3) and POA 1986 (s 17). It does not include religion, and there was some discussion in Parliament as to whether the Bill should be amended to include protection from religious persecution. The Home Secretary announced that there would be research into the scale and nature of religious discrimination. He added s 28(3) at a late stage to the Bill making it clear that people charged with these offences cannot claim that they are motivated by religious, not racial, hatred.[1] The Muslim Council of Britain responded to the amendment by saying that—

> 'We view this amendment as a small but significant first step towards the economic, social and political inclusion of the Muslim community in the national life.'.[2]

The reason given by the Home Secretary for not including religion in the definition of racial group, was that whether someone belongs to a racial group can be subject to an objective test, whereas it is more difficult to define whether someone is a member of a religious group, which involves a subjective as well as an objective test. The Opposition proposal to add 'religion' to the definition of racial group in s 28(4) was defeated by 268 to 146 votes.[3]

---

[1]   HC Report, 23 June 1998, col 894.

[2]   As quoted by the Home Secretary, ibid, col 895.

[3]   Ibid, col 903.

3.6   In the House of Lords, Baroness Flather moved an amendment to include a new clause entitled 'Racial aggravation: duty of prosecution'[1] to force on the prosecution a duty to bring evidence of racial aggravation before the court, in order to avoid inappropriate plea bargains and to encourage good practice. However, the amendment was withdrawn after doubts were raised about its workability.

---

[1]   HL Reports, 19 March 1998, col 923.

Racially aggravated assaults

3.7   Section 29 creates four new offences of racially aggravated assaults—
   (a) racially aggravated wounding;
   (b) racially aggravated grievous bodily harm;
   (c) racially aggravated actual bodily harm;
   (d) racially aggravated common assault.

The new offences occur if the offender commits an act which amounts to a common assault or an offence under OAPA 1861, ss 20 or 47 and there is evidence satisfying the racial aggravation test in the 1998 Act, s 28. An offender convicted of an offence under s 29(1)(a) (racially aggravated offence under the 1861 Act, s 20)) or s 29(1)(b) (racially aggravated offence under the 1861 Act, s 47)) will be liable on summary conviction to six months' imprisonment, (ie no increase in the statutory maximum) or the statutory maximum fine, or on indictment to seven years' imprisonment and/or an unlimited fine. The frequency with which sentencing judges make use of this increase at the top end of their sentencing powers should be monitored. An offender convicted of an offence under s 29(1)(c) will be liable on summary conviction to the current six months' imprisonment or to a fine not exceeding the statutory maximum, or on indictment to imprisonment for a term not exceeding two years or a fine, or both. Again, it will be worth monitoring whether magistrates' courts commit such offences to the Crown Court in order that the increased powers may be used.

Racially aggravated criminal damage

3.8   The Government accepted an amendment[1] proposed by Lord Dholakia to introduce an offence of racially aggravated criminal damage, which is now contained in CDA 1998, s 30. A person found guilty under this section will be liable on summary conviction to six months' imprisonment or to a fine not exceeding the statutory maximum or both; or on conviction on indictment to a term of 14 years' imprisonment or to a fine. It is not clear whether arson is included in the new offence. From a strict reading of s 30, it would appear that it is, since arson is an offence under the Criminal Damage Act 1971, s 1. However, arson currently has a maximum sentence of life imprisonment (see the 1971 Act, s 4). Thus it would appear that in the case of racially aggravated arson, the maximum penalty has been reduced to 14 years. Dr David Thomas has also pointed out that—

'. . . it would also follow that a court would be prevented from treating an offence charged as arson contrary to s 1(1) and 1(3) of the Criminal Damage Act 1971 as racially aggravated for the purposes of s 82.'.[2]

There is a serious risk that the Act will cause 'trouble, confusion and injustice'[3] in the courts.

---

[1]   HL Report, 31 March 1998, col 201.
[2]   (1998) Current Sentencing News, Issue 3, p 9.
[3]   HC SC B, 12 May 1998, col 324 (Mr Clappison).

Racially aggravated public order offences

3.9   Section 31 creates three racially aggravated offences based on the offences in POA, ss 4, 4A and 5, ie—
   (a)   racially aggravated fear or provocation of violence;
   (b)   racially aggravated intentional harassment, alarm or distress;
   (c)   racially aggravated harassment, alarm or distress.

Section 31(2), (3) sets out the powers of arrest, which mirror those available for the basic offences under the 1986 Act. Section 31(4) increases the maximum penalties as follows. In the case of an offence of racially aggravated fear or provocation of violence or racially aggravated intentional harassment, alarm or distress, a person shall be liable on summary conviction to six months' imprisonment and/or the statutory maximum fine; and on conviction on indictment, to two years' imprisonment and/or an unlimited fine. In the case of racially aggravated harassment, alarm or distress, which is a summary offence, the maximum sentence is raised from a level 3 fine (currently £1,000) to a level 4 fine (currently £2,500).

3.10   Section 31(6) provides for alternative verdicts for offences under s 31(1)(a) or (b) and allows a jury to find the defendant guilty of the basic offence under the 1986 Act, which is otherwise only triable in the magistrates' court if the racial aggravation is not proved. It should be noted that POA 1986, s 7(3), makes provision that on the trial on indictment of a person charged with violent disorder or affray, the jury may find him instead guilty of an offence under s 4, but there is no provision for a jury to find a person guilty of an offence under s 4A (Intentional harassment, alarm or distress).

3.11 Section 31(7) alters the test in s 28(1)(a) to take account of the requirements of the basic offence contained in POA 1986, s 5(1). As the Notes on Clauses explain, s 5 of the 1986 Act states that the defendant's actions will be an offence only when they are directed at a person who is 'likely to be caused harassment, alarm or distress'. Section 31(7) equates such a person with the 'victim' described in s 28.

Racially aggravated harassment etc

3.12 Section 32 creates two new offences of 'racially aggravated harassment'. It fulfils the Labour Party manifesto commitment and incorporates the existing offences from the Protection from Harassment Act (PHA) 1997. Under s 32(1) a person may be guilty of—

(a) a racially aggravated offence under PHA 1997, s 2 (harassment). This requires a 'course of conduct' which amounts to harassment. The maximum penalty on summary conviction is six months' imprisonment and/or a fine not exceeding the statutory maximum; and on indictment is two years' imprisonment and/or an unlimited fine (increased from the maximum of six months or a level 5 fine for the basic offence under the 1997 Act) (s 32(3)).

(b) a racially aggravated offence under PHA 1997, s 4 (putting people in fear of violence). This requires that the offender knows, or ought to know, that his course of conduct is likely to cause the victim to fear that violence will be used against him/her. The maximum penalty on summary conviction for this offence is six months' imprisonment and/or a fine not exceeding the statutory maximum; and on indictment is seven years' imprisonment and/or an unlimited fine (increasing the maximum from five years for the basic offence under the 1997 Act) (s 32(4)).

3.13 Section 32(2) amends PACE 1984, s 24(2), to include a power of arrest for an offence under s 32(1)(a). A similar power is not provided for the more serious harassment offence, as such a power applies automatically since the maximum sentence exceeds five years. Section 32(5), (6) deals with alternative verdicts. Section 32(7) incorporates the provision in PHA 1997, s 5, authorising a court to impose restraining orders on a person convicted of a harassment offence under this section. A person who breaches a restraining order without reasonable excuse is guilty of an offence and is liable on summary trial to six months' imprisonment and/or the statutory maximum fine; or on indictment to five years' imprisonment and/or an unlimited fine (see PHA 1997, s 5(6)).

RACIALLY AGGRAVATED OFFENCES: SCOTLAND

Racially aggravated offences

3.14 The Scottish Office consultation paper published in September 1997 on the need to introduce new measures to deal with racist crime won strong support from organisations representing ethnic minorities. The Government's response is contained in s 33, which introduces a new s 50A into the Criminal Law (Consolidation) (Scotland) Act 1995. It provides for an offence of racially aggravated harassment.

A person is guilty of an offence if he—

'(a) pursues a racially aggravated course of conduct which amounts to harassment of a person and—

    (i) is intended to amount to harassment of that person; or

    (ii) occurs in circumstances where it would appear to a reasonable person that it would amount to harassment of that person; or

(b) acts in a manner which is racially aggravated and which causes, or is intended to cause, a person alarm or distress.' (s 50A(1)).

3.15 The terminology used to describe 'racial aggravation' in Scotland differs from that used in England and Wales. In Scotland an offence is racially aggravated if—

(a) the offender evinces towards the person affected malice and ill-will based on that person's membership (or presumed membership) of a racial group, or

(b) the course of conduct or action is motivated (wholly or partly) by malice and ill-will towards members of a racial group based on their membership of that group (see s 50A(2) as inserted by s 33).

In the House of Lords, Lord Monson argued that the Scottish definition should be adopted in England and Wales as 'malice and ill-will' were less trivial than 'hostility'.[1] The levels of punishment specified under the new s 50A(5) are the same as for the English offence under s 32(1)(b) (putting people in fear of violence).

---

[1]   HL Report, 12 February 1998, col 1277.

3.16 In the new s 50A(6) 'conduct' is defined to include speech, whilst 'harassment' includes causing the person alarm or distress and 'racial group' excludes religion. An amendment to add religion to the definition was rejected by the Government on the grounds that—

'. . . to include religion would extend the scope of the offences considerably, and risk diluting the emphasis on race and diluting the emphasis on race and the strength of the message that the Bill sends to the victims of racial violence and harassment.'.[1]

The amendment was withdrawn, though Mrs Laing commented that—

'. . . it is unfortunate that the Government are not willing to send the further message that religious hatred is as intolerable as racial hatred.'.[2]

(See also the debate on this subject discussed at para 3.5.)

---

[1]   HC SC B, 4 June 1998, col 750.
[2]   Ibid, col 751.

MISCELLANEOUS

Abolition of refutable presumption that a child is doli incapax

3.17 The doctrine of *doli incapax* has meant that, until now, when a child over the age of ten, but under the age of 14, was to be prosecuted, the prosecution had to prove that the child had not only the *mens rea* for the relevant crime, but also that s/he knew that what s/he did was a wrong act and not merely an act of simple naughtiness or mischief. This requirement has been challenged in recent years, particularly since the murder of the toddler, James Bulger, by two 11-year-olds in 1993. In *C v DPP*[1] the House of Lords overruled an attempt by Sir John Laws in the Divisional Court in 1994 to abolish the presumption, saying that only Parliament could reconsider such a fundamental doctrine. The Government's proposal to abolish the presumption was set out in the consultation paper 'Tackling Youth Crime' and in the White Paper, 'No More Excuses', in the chapter entitled 'Reinforcing Responsibility'—

> 'To respond effectively to youth crime, we must stop making excuses for children who offend . . . '[2]

> '. . . the practical difficulties which the presumption presents for the prosecution can stop some children who should be prosecuted and punished for their offences from being convicted or from even coming to court.'.[3]

Thus s 34 simply abolishes the presumption that a child over the age of ten is incapable of committing an offence.

---

[1]   [1996] AC 1, [1995] 2 All ER 43, [1995] 2 WLR 383.
[2]   Cm 3809, para 4.1.
[3]   Ibid, para 4.4.

3.18   Many people have argued that the presumption should be preserved,[1] or at least should have been reversed rather than simply abolished. Lord Goodhart, supported by Baroness Mallalieu, moved an amendment in Committee in the House of Lords that it would be a 'defence for a child over ten to show on the balance of probabilities that he did not know that his action was seriously wrong',[2] but this was defeated by 105 to 32 votes.[3] The Government line remained forthright in the House of Commons, where the Minister of State, Mr Michael, spoke of 'the absurd doctrine of *doli incapax*, which presumes that those aged ten to 13 do not know right from wrong.'.[4]

---

[1]   See for example Mark Ashford's article in [1998] *Criminal Justice* Vol 16, No 1, p 16, which argues that children are not able to comprehend the complexity of the investigation and trial process. He suggests that if the Government had been determined to be radical, they should have raised the age of criminal responsibility to 14. Sue Bandali also argues for taking the presumption seriously as a recognition of the protection the law should afford children [1998] 37 *Howard Journal* 114.
[2]   HL Report, 12 February 1998, col 1316.
[3]   HL Report, 19 March 1998, col 840.
[4]   HC SC B, 30 April 1998, col 77.

Effect of child's silence at trial

3.19   Section 35 was introduced at the Third Reading of the Bill in the House of Lords on 31 March 1998 by Lord Williams of Mostyn. It amends the Criminal Justice and Public Order Act (CJPOA) 1994, s 35, in order to allow a court to draw inferences from the failure of a juvenile to give evidence or answer questions at trial. Lord Williams gave two reasons for the change. First, to achieve consistency with the intention to abolish the presumption of *doli incapax* (see paras 3.17–3.18), and secondly to achieve consistency with other sections (CJPOA 1994, ss 34, 36 and 37). There are no restrictions on drawing inferences from the failure of ten to 13-year-olds to mention facts when charged or questioned. In response to a question from Baroness Mallalieu he admitted that there had been no consultation on this clause.[1]

The Opposition parties were able to capitalise on the fact that the Labour party, having opposed and voted against the abolition of the right of silence for adults in 1994, have now as Government gone a stage further and have ended the right to silence for children.

---

[1]   HL 3R, 31 March 1998, col 207.

Abolition of death penalty for treason and piracy etc

3.20 Section 36 was introduced for the first time on Report in the House of Lords by Lord Archer of Sandwell—

> '. . . to remove from the statute book once and for all the practice of breaking a human being's neck on behalf of the community in time of peace.'[1]

> ' . . . to remove finally from the statute book the last remnants of capital punishment in time of peace.'.[2]

He explained that he was proposing to replace the death penalty with a mandatory life sentence because that was the alternative adopted in the case of murder and he wished to keep the argument simple: one anomaly should be dealt with at a time. He would support the abolition of the mandatory sentence in due course.[3] However, Lord Williams of Mostyn replied that—

> 'I am advised that the amendment would substitute a maximum of life imprisonment, not a mandatory life sentence. . . . we believe that a discretionary life sentence is appropriate.'.[4]

The clause was amended on Third Reading to insert a maximum penalty of life imprisonment for various other treason-like offences, and was not contested.

---

[1]   HL Report, 12 February 1998, col 1341.
[2]   HL Report, 19 March 1998, col 841.
[3]   Ibid, col 843.
[4]   Ibid, col 853.

4 Criminal Justice System

INTRODUCTION

4.1   Part III of the 1998 Act introduces reforms which were promised in the Labour Party's manifesto (see para 1.1). These ideas were developed in the White Paper 'No More Excuses—A New Approach to Tackling Youth Crime in England and Wales'—

> 'For too long there has been a lack of clear direction in the youth justice system. The Government will give the necessary leadership.'.[1]

An evaluation of the impact on the prevention of youth crime by the Youth Justice Board and youth offending teams will only be possible in a few years time. Part III also concentrates on ways of reducing delays in criminal justice procedures, relying very heavily on the 'Review of Delay in the Criminal Justice System: a Report', published in February 1997. The Report is known as the Narey Report, after the senior civil servant who was asked in October 1996 to conduct the review. Whilst public attention has been drawn in particular to some of the new orders found earlier in the Act, these provisions tucked away at the end of Pt III may have more impact in practice. They include—

(a) tighter time limits (ss 43–46);

(b) more powers delegated to single magistrates and justices' clerks (ss 48, 49);

(c) abolition of committal proceedings for indictable offences (s 51);

(d) the use of non-lawyer Crown Prosecution Service (CPS) staff in some cases (s 53);

(e) increased use of sureties/recognizances when granting bail (s 54); and

(f) the use of television links at preliminary hearings so that defendants remanded in custody do not necessarily appear in court in person (s 57).

---

[1]   Cm 3809, p 26.

YOUTH JUSTICE

Aim of the youth justice system

4.2   Section 37 establishes that 'the principal aim' of the youth justice system is to prevent offending by children and young persons. Section s 37(2) states that—

> 'In addition to any other duty to which they are subject, it shall be the duty of all persons and bodies carrying out functions in relation to the youth justice system to have regard to that aim.'.

The 'youth justice system' is defined in s 42(1) as 'the system of criminal justice in so far as it relates to children and young persons', and this duty is clearly additional to existing duties. In Committee in both the House of Lords and in the House of Commons, ministers were questioned about the implications of 'the principal aim'. Why has the youth justice system been put in a special position? The dangers involved in making one aim pre-eminent were raised by many speakers in both

Houses of Parliament. Lord Goodhart questioned why the welfare of the child had not been singled out[1] whilst Sir Robert Smith raised the issue of defence solicitors—

> 'The primary role of defence solicitors must be to serve their clients, to present their cases in the best possible light in court, and to advise them how to plead in the light of the evidence.'.[2]

A defence solicitor who believes that the best interest of his client may be served by an adjournment may also believe that avoiding this delay might reduce the risk of re-offending. An amendment which would have brought together three principal aims (preventing offending, protecting and advancing the legal interests of children and young persons and promoting their welfare) was rejected on the ground that what was required was clarity and simplicity. According to the Minister of State, Mr Michael, the section—

> ' . . . is intended to end both the uncertainty about what is expected of those who work for youth justice agencies, and the confusion about balancing the interests of the offender, the victim and the community.'.[3]

---

[1]   HL Report, 12 February 1998, col 1360.
[2]   HC SC B, 14 May 1998, col 370.
[3]   Ibid, col 371.

4.3   Despite the provision in the Children and Young Persons Act (CYPA) 1933, s 44, it would appear that the welfare of the child is no longer paramount. The minister argued that the principal aim would not interfere with other duties which may be set out in legislation, professional codes of practice or oaths of office. How this principal aim will work in practice remains to be seen. Moreover, the changes introduced in s 37 appear to be only the beginning of the story—

> 'The Government proposes that the aim of the youth justice system and the duty on youth justice practitioners should be supported by a fuller, non-statutory, set of objectives for youth justice agencies . . . The Government proposes that non-statutory objectives for the youth justice system should be supported by a more detailed protocol drawn up in consultation with the relevant agencies and associations.'.[1]

A Protocol is to be published in September 1998.

---

[1]   Cm 3809, p 8.

Local provision of Youth Justice Services

4.4   Section 38, based on ideas to be found in the consultation paper 'New National and Local Focus on Youth Crime',[1] imposes a duty on local authorities to secure the availability of youth justice services. They must act in co-operation with every police authority, probation committee and health authority in their area (s 38(2)). In Committee, the Government moved amendments to include chief officers of police as well as police authorities in recognition of the different functions of the chief officer and the police authority. The operational nature of decisions about the deployment of police officers to youth offending teams revealed that the original reference to police authorities, rather than chief officers, was deemed inadequate.

---

[1]   Published on 9 October 1997.

4.5   Section 38(3) was added by the Government in Committee in the House of Commons to allow a local authority to set up a pooled budget or common fund. This is designed to allow flexibility over funding. Clearly funding issues are key to the success of many initiatives but the Government did not wish to be over-specific—

> '. . . we will provide guidance to local authorities and other relevant agencies on how the fund should operate, in the light of guidance that we are developing on establishing youth offending teams.'.[1]

Members of the Committee welcomed the provision of a fund that would exist for a specific purpose, and would be outside the remit of any single statutory body. However, there were concerns about where this money would come from. The Government appeared not to share this concern believing that shared working may prove to be cheaper working.

---

[1]   HC SC B, 14 May 1998, col 380.

4.6   'Youth justice services' are defined in s 38 to include—
   (a) the provision of persons to act as appropriate adults to safeguard the interests of children and young people being interviewed by the police;
   (b) assessment and rehabilitation work associated with a warning (see s 66(2) and para 5.18);
   (c) remand and bail support while awaiting trial or sentence;
   (d) placement in local authority accommodation of those committed under CYPA 1969, s 23;
   (e) the provision of reports etc to criminal courts;
   (f) the provision of responsible officers in relation to the new parenting orders, child safety orders, reparation orders, and action plan orders;
   (g) the supervision of community sentences, probation or combined orders;
   (h) post release supervision;
   (i) the performance of functions carrying out detention and training orders (see ss 73–75 and para 5.29).

4.7   In Committee in the House of Commons, there was some discussion about the first of these listed services. The responsibility for arranging the provision of persons to act as responsible adults currently falls on the police, and will in future be co-ordinated by the youth offending team. Mr Michael stated that this would not undermine the requirement of independence. Another area of concern was the provision of services to deal with adolescent sex offenders, following the Chief Inspector of Probation's recent report highlighting the lack of any coherent national strategy in this area.[1] The minister confirmed that s 38 covered the provision of youth justice services for all offenders who are under the age of 18, including young sex offenders. The Secretary of State may by order amend the definition of youth justice services (s 38(4)). Section 114(3) specifies that such an order will only be made by statutory instrument subject to the affirmative resolution procedure.

---

[1]   Chief Inspector of Probation.

Youth offending teams

4.8   Section 39 requires local authorities with social services and education responsibilities to establish one or more youth offending teams (YOT) for their area, in partnership with the other relevant local agencies. Lord Hylton asked in Committee in the House of Lords why the teams should not be called youth justice teams, but Lord Williams assured him that—

'We believe that our new teams ought to focus on tackling youth offending.'.[1]

Section 39(2) allows neighbouring local authorities to co-operate in establishing teams and s 39(3) places a reciprocal duty on chief officers of police, probation and health authorities to participate in YOTs. For a discussion of s 39(4), which allows the local authority to set up a pooled budget or common fund, see para 4.5.

---

[1]   HL Report, 12 February 1998, col 1363.

4.9   Section 39(5) sets out the basic membership of a youth offending team. Each team must include at least one of each of the following: probation officer, social worker, police officer, education staff and health authority staff. In Committee in the House of Commons, amendments were considered to include specifically representatives of voluntary organisations, victims' organisations and ethnic minority communities in the team. However, the Government was reluctant to be too prescriptive, and s 39(6) simply allows a local authority to include those who it thinks 'appropriate'. The Act says nothing about who should head the team. The White Paper said simply—

'The Government remains of the view that it would be best to leave the appointment of managers of YOTs to local decision on the basis of merit, rather than prescribe that managers should come from one specific agency. However, the Task Force on Youth Justice has been asked to undertake further work on YOTs to ensure proper accountability for their work.'.[1]

The question of proper accountability is vital. The duties of YOTs are set out in s 39(7): to co-ordinate the provision of youth justice services and to carry out the functions assigned to the team in the youth justice plan (see para 4.13). A draft inter-departmental circular on establishing YOTs was issued by the Home Office, the Department of Health, the Welsh Office and the Department for Education and Employment on 29 June 1998. The circular will be revised following the first six months' experience of the youth justice pilot schemes.

---

[1]   Cm 3809, p 27.

Youth justice plans

4.10   Section 40 requires local authorities to formulate and implement an annual youth justice plan setting out how youth justice services are to be provided and funded and how their YOTs are to operate etc. This has to be done after consultation with every police authority, probation committee, health authority, and, where there are two tiers of local government, district council in their area (s 40(2)). Section 40(3) allows for co-ordination with the preventative work already undertaken by the local authority under the Children Act 1989, Sch 2, para 7(b), and set out in the children's services plan prepared by the local authority under para 1A of that Schedule. Section 40(4) requires each local authority to submit their youth justice plan to the Youth Justice Board (see para 4.13) and to publish it in accordance with the Secretary of State's directions.

4.11 Other than those provisions mentioned above, the Act says no more about youth justice plans. The Notes on Clauses were more helpful, however, stating—

> 'It is envisaged that, to oversee the formulation of the youth justice plan and the establishment and operation of YOTs, local authorities will use or establish a senior management steering group, probably at chief officer level and chaired by the local authority chief executive. As well as the local authority's social services and education departments, this group will include the other key local agencies—the police, the probation service and the health authority—and may involve others with a significant interest in local youth justice arrangements, such as youth court magistrates, justices' clerks and the Prison Service. These will be matters for local decision, subject to any guidance given by the Secretary of State (under s 42(3)).'.

4.12 The draft inter-departmental circular on establishing YOTs (see para 4.9) gives advice on formulating a youth justice plan. For example—

> '44.The preparation of the youth justice plan should be overseen by the chief officers' steering group and then submitted in draft to the local authority, police authority, probation committee and health authority for consideration and approval—either separately or through an inter-authority members' group. They should discuss any alteration of their agency's contribution under the plan with their chief executive or chief officer.
>
> 45.   Youth justice plans will need to be consistent with, and complementary to, other plans and strategies drawn up by the local agencies, including—
>
> —   the crime and disorder strategy, objectives and targets drawn up for each unitary authority or district council area;
>
> —   the children's services plan prepared by the local authority—this will set a key context for the delivery of youth justice services and the work of youth offending teams, because many of those dealt with by the teams will be children "in need" under the Children Act 1989;
>
> —   the annual policing plan issued by the police authority;
>
> —   the probation service annual plan;
>
> —   the Drug Action Team's annual action plan, submitted to the UK Anti-Drugs Co-ordinator in December—particularly in relation to plans for prevention work with young people most at risk of developing serious drug problems; the development of treatment for those committing drug-related crime; work to involve communities in collaborative responses to local drug problems; work to increase take-up rate of further education and employment; and provision of specific support services for young people under 25 with drug problems;
>
> —   the behaviour support plan drawn up by the local authority in its capacity as local education authority for dealing with pupils with behavioural difficulties, including persistent non-attenders and excluded pupils;
>
> —   the annual review prepared by the Area child protection committee; and

— any plan drawn up by the Youth Court User Group for tackling delays and operating fast tracking procedures for persistent (and other) young offenders.'.[1]

---

[1] Draft inter-departmental circular on establishing YOTs, issued by the Home Office, the Department of Health, the Welsh Office and the Department for Education and Employment on 29 June 1998.

Youth Justice Board

4.13 Section 41 establishes a Youth Justice Board (YJB) for England and Wales. It is a body corporate (s 41(1)), and not a crown servant (s 41(2)). It will have 10–12 members (s 41(3)), who will have 'extensive recent experience of the youth justice system' (s 41(4)). The 1998 Act, Sch 2, makes further provisions with respect to membership, employees, procedure, annual reports and expenses of the YJB. It does not specify specific professions or interests, but the functions of the YJB are set out in some detail in s 41(5). These will be to—

(a) monitor the operation of the youth justice system and the provision of youth justice services;

(b) advise the Secretary of State on—
    — the operation of that system and the provision of such services;
    — how the principal aim of that system might most effectively be pursued;
    — any national standards for such services or accommodation during custody he may see fit to set;
    — the steps which might be taken to prevent offending by children and young persons;

(c) monitor the extent to which that aim is being achieved and such standards met;

(d) obtain and publish relevant information;

(e) identify, make known and promote good practice in the operation of the youth justice system and the provision of youth justice services;

(f) make grants, with the approval of the Secretary of State to local authorities and other bodies in order to develop, or commission research into, good practice in working with young offenders;

(g) commission research themselves.

4.14 These last two functions contained in s 41(5)(g), (h) were developed after amendments agreed at Third Reading in the House of Lords.[1] Although the functions at the moment are limited to advising, monitoring, identifying good practice etc, the Government has suggested that in due course it may be given responsibility over secure facilities for young offenders. The Secretary of State may by order alter the functions of the Board under s 41(6) (only by statutory instrument subject to the affirmative resolution procedure (s 114(3)). Throughout the debates in Parliament, when challenged about the details of new provisions, the Government made reference to the role of the Board in developing consistency and good practice. For example, when dealing with criticisms of detention and training orders, Mr Michael said that—

> 'The youth justice board for England and Wales will examine the regimes in place . . . The management and oversight of the youth justice board will ensure that regimes and placements are appropriate.'.[2]

Later, when discussing secure accommodation for juveniles, he added that 'the Board will also help draw up national standards for such accommodation and the regimes provided there. It will monitor the extent to which the standards are met'.[3] The Government were keen to establish the YJB speedily. It came into operation on 30 September 1998, and s 41 came into force on 1 August 1998 for the purpose of making appointments to the Board. The first chairman is Lord Warner, who previously chaired the Youth Justice Task Force.

---

[1]   HL Report, 31 March 1998, col 223.
[2]   HC SC B, 2 June 1998, col 629.
[3]   Ibid, col 673.

4.15 In order to aid co-operation and effective monitoring, s 41(8) requires relevant authorities (defined in s 41(1) as local authorities, chief police officers and health authorities) to provide the YJB with relevant information, and to require a relevant authority to submit to the Board a report as and when required. These reports are not meant to be regular reports, but rather one-off reports designed to enable the Board to hold local agencies to account when there appear to be difficulties.

Time limits

4.16 Section 43 makes significant changes to the framework established by the Prosecution of Offences Act (POA) 1985, tightening the court's discretion to grant extensions of time. The measures are a response to the Manifesto commitment to 'halve the time it takes to get persistent young offenders from arrest to sentencing', and were proposed in the consultation paper 'Tackling Delays in the Youth Justice System and Reducing Remand Delays'. Section 43(1) substitutes POA 1985, s 22(2)(a), (b), to enable time limits to be set only in specific areas, or in relation to specified classes of proceedings or people, and to allow different time limits in relation to different areas, classes of proceedings or people. In practice, this will allow for tighter time limits to be set in juvenile cases, even in particular cases involving persistent young offenders. Testing of pilot schemes on time limits can also be carried out on a geographical basis.

4.17 Section 43(2) substitutes POA, s 22(3), allowing for more prescriptive criteria for granting extension to time limits than the present one. Lord Falconer explained that 'We believe that the criteria for extension need to be made more prescriptive for the new time limits regime to have any teeth.'.[1] Thus the court will not be able to grant an extension to a time limit unless one of the specified grounds for an extension exists. The original Bill specified as grounds illness or absence of the accused, a witness, judge or magistrates; *or* some other 'good and sufficient cause' *and* required that 'the prosecution has acted with all due diligence and expedition'. An amendment on Third Reading in the House of Lords introduced another specific reason to justify an extension, namely where the court orders a separate trial for a single defendant charged with more than one offence or for co-defendants jointly charged.

---

[1]   HL Report, 31 March 1998, col 225.

4.18 Section 43(3) amends POA, s 22(4), providing that the appropriate court should stay proceedings if time limits are breached. This allows for the re-institution of stayed proceedings. The existing effect of a breach of a statutory time limit is the effective acquittal of the defendant which the Government was determined to avoid (see s 45 and para 4.21). Another tightening up of the legislation appears in s 43(5)–(7), which amends POA 1985, s 22(6)–(8), to provide that time limits are automatically suspended at the point at which a defendant escapes or fails to appear, until he appears before the court when the time limit re-applies. This replaces the existing provision that time limits cease to have effect where the defendant escapes or fails to appear. Finally, s 43(8) inserts a new POA 1985, s 22(11ZA), to define the commencement of proceedings for the purposes of that section. Proceedings now begin when the accused is charged with an offence or when the information is laid charging him with an offence. Time limits can now be set under s 22 from that point until the start of trial. An Opposition clause would have required each Chief Crown Prosecutor to publish an annual report giving details of total number of prosecutions and the numbers stayed etc, but this was withdrawn.[1] The Government has made it clear that time limits will only be set after 'piloting and further consultation'[2] (though the target date for guidance under these provisions is summer 1999, with time limit pilots to run for 12 months from the autumn of 1999).[3]

---

[1]   HC SC B, 9 June 1998, col 815.
[2]   HL Report, 12 February, col 1371.
[3]   Home Office circular No 38/1998.

Additional time limits for persons under the age of 18

4.19 Section 44 inserts POA 1985, s 22A, allowing the Secretary of State to make regulations for young offenders. Time limits under POA 1985, s 22, begin to run from the time when the defendant is charged (see para 4.18). In the case of young offenders, the Government wishes to take the time of arrest as the point when time begins to run. The decision to take arrest as the starting point was made with reference to the Government's pledge to halve the time between arrest and sentencing for persistent young offenders. Opposition members highlighted the dangers of hasty decision making by the police, and also wondered whether the time limits would cause delays in the decision to arrest. Curiously the Government is keen to minimise inter-agency referrals on the question whether to charge or merely to warn in order to reduce delays.

4.20 POA 1985, s 22A(1) (as inserted) provides for the Secretary of State to make regulations setting time limits from arrest to first court appearance ('the initial stage') and from conviction to sentence. Thus time limits will be set in young offender cases from arrest to first court appearance, from then to the start of the trial, and from conviction to sentence. Section 22A(2) will allow the Secretary of State to make regulations to apply only to certain areas, or to certain categories of offenders. The Government has made it clear that this will be used to pilot the new time limits in certain areas in order to set tougher time limits in the case of persistent young offenders. Section 22A(3) forbids courts from extending time limits in these cases unless there is 'good and sufficient cause', and s 22A(3)(b) makes it clear that police inefficiency will not be grounds for an extension. Section 22A(4) provides that where the time limit for the first stage expires *before* the young person has been charged, he/she is not to be charged unless fresh evidence comes to light and if he/she is under arrest he/she must be released and any police bail must be discharged. This is designed to impose a clear sanction on police inefficiency, but keeps the possibility of reviving cases in appropriate circumstances. Section 22A(5) also provides sanctions for inefficiency occuring *after* the charge, in which case, proceedings will be stayed (subject to s 45, discussed at para 4.21). Section 22A(6), which suspends the initial time limit when a young person absconds, is designed to avoid penalising the police/prosecution for the young person's actions. The provisions on appeals in POA 1985, s 22(7)–(9) will now apply to this new section once the accused has been charged (s 22A(7)), while s 22A(8) makes it clear that decisions about granting or refusing extensions of time to the initial stage will not be relevant issues in appeals against conviction. Finally, s 22A(9) provides that references in the section to laying a charge include laying an information.

Re-instituting stayed proceedings

4.21 Section 45 inserts POA 1985, s 22B, in order to provide for a procedure for the reinstitution of proceedings stayed under s 22 or 22A where a statutory time limit has been breached. The previous sanction for non-compliance with time-limits was the effective acquittal of the defendant, but now proceedings may be re-instituted within three months (or such longer period as the court may allow). In most cases, the only safeguard against the abuse of this procedure is that proceedings can only be re-instituted on the direction of a 'person designated for the purpose by the Secretary of State' (see s 22B(2)(c)). The sanction on prosecution inefficiency is greatly weakened if the prosecution can so easily re-institute proceedings.

Date of first court appearance in bail cases

4.22 Section 46 inserts PACE 1984, s 47(3A), to ensure that where a defendant is bailed to appear in court, the date set for his appearance is the earliest possible occasion. This important cultural change was proposed in the Narey Report. Having reviewed simple procedures which would lead to more effective management and the speedier completion of all cases, including locating CPS staff in police stations, with a duty to telephone magistrates' courts each day to notify them of the type of hearing needed the next day for all those charged, the Report concluded that—

> 'Simple guilty plea cases should be completed, and, unless there were reporting requirements such as for pre-sentence reports, the defendant should be sentenced the day after being charged (or where a court is sitting, a day or so after that). This would achieve a very significant improvement on current practice, where even the simplest case does not generally appear in court for four weeks after charge.
>
> The number and proportion of cases which might be completed immediately is very large. Durham CPS have been discussing a similar initiative with Durham Constabulary and estimate that with this system about 6,300 cases (over two thirds) of the 9,000 completed each year at magistrates' courts could be completed at the first available court following charge.'.[1]

This change has profound implications. While no-one doubts the importance of speedy justice, many cases, particularly contested cases, need sufficient time to be prepared. The provision may lead to earlier first hearings, but an increasing number of adjournments. Placing CPS staff in police stations raises fundamental questions about the independence of the CPS. The measure is to be piloted in specified areas for six months, with a view to national implementation in the autumn of 1999.[2]

FUNCTIONS OF COURTS ETC

Powers of youth courts

4.23 Section 47 gives youth courts new powers intended to reduce delays. Section 47(1) allows the youth court to remit to the adult court any person who reaches his 18th birthday before trial, or after conviction and before sentence, and s 47(2)–(4), added at a late stage in the House of Commons,[1] makes clear that there is no appeal against such a remission, and that the adult court has the powers which it would have had if the case had started there.

1   HC Report, 23 June 1998, col 911.

4.24 Section 47(5) establishes a presumption against adjournments in the youth court, in effect reversing the decision in *Khan*[1] that—

> '. . . save in exceptional circumstances, the youth court which sends a young person for trial at the Crown Court should postpone sentence in respect of other, *ex hypothesi,* less serious offences, until after the more serious matter has been dealt with.'

In Committee, Mr Clappison said—

> 'The rule in the case of *Khan* was not some dramatic innovation in sentencing policy or a radical departure from what had happened previously. It was a restatement of what was often regarded as being accepted practice in both the youth and Crown courts.'.[2]

He argued that the subsection was unnecessary and that the Government was wrongly 'demonising' the decision in *Khan*. Mr Michael clearly disagreed. The effect of the queuing system, he said, is appalling practice. Section 47(6) inserts the Magistrates' Courts Act (MCA) 1980, s 24(1A), which allows the court, when committing a case to the Crown Court for trial, to commit for trial at the same time for any other related indictable offences. 'Related' is defined in MCA 1980, s 38A(6), as 'if, were they both to be prosecuted on indictment, the charges for them could be joined in the same indictment'. Related summary offences can already be committed under the Criminal Justice Act 1988, s 41. The new provision should ensure that where a case is committed to the Crown Court for trial, related offences are committed at the same time, and unrelated offences are dealt with in the youth court without delay under s 47(5).

1   *R v Khan*, (1994) Times, 24 March, 158 JP 760.
2   HC SC B, 14 May 1998, col 403.

4.25 Section 47(7) gives effect to recommendation 33 of the Narey Report that the requirement that there should be an hour's interval between sittings of the magistrates and Youth Court in a courtroom should be abolished. The Report suggests that—

'this inefficient arrangement, which was designed to protect juveniles
from contact with older defendants, seems generally to be regarded as
out of date and unnecessary'.[1]

Presumably it was also meant to show that proceedings involving children had a
different ethos to proceedings involving adults. The change therefore symbolises a new
culture, making 'no excuses' for young people who offend.

---

[1]   'Review of Delay in the Criminal Justice System: A Report', Home Office, February 1997, p 46.

Youth courts: power of stipendiary magistrates to sit alone

4.26 Section 48 amends CYPA 1933, Sch 2, to allow metropolitan stipendiary
magistrates to sit alone in youth courts. The Narey Report concluded that the use of
stipendiaries would lead to more effective case management, especially in difficult
cases—

'There is no doubt, based on the opinion of almost all court users, but
also from my own observations, that stipendiaries are vastly more
effective in managing the parties in any given case'.[1]

It is important to remember that Narey's brief was to look at ways of expediting cases.
There may of course be other good reasons for the CYPA 1933 requirements that a
youth court should consist of three members, including a man and a woman.
Section 39 deals only with metropolitan stipendiary magistrates since primary
legislation is not necessary to allow stipendiaries to sit alone elsewhere. This requires
simply an amendment to the Youth Courts (Constitution) Rules 1954, which the
Government intends to make. Both changes were implemented on 30 September
1998.[2] The number of stipendiary magistrates has grown rapidly in recent years, and
seems set to increase. If the lay magistracy is to be encouraged to survive, the time has
come for a fundamental re-examination of the role of stipendiaries.

---

[1]   'Review of Delay in the Criminal Justice System: A Report', Home Office, February 1997, p 25.
[2]   Home Office circular No 38/1998, The Crime and Disorder Act 1998 (Commencement No 2 and
Transitional Provisions) Order 1998, SI 1998/2327 (see Appendix).

Powers of magistrates' courts exercisable by single justice etc

4.27 Section 49 provides that various powers of the magistrates' court may be
exercised by a single magistrate and, even more importantly, allows the Lord
Chancellor to make provision—following consultation with the justices and justices'
clerk for an area—for any of the listed powers to be exercised by justices' clerks in
that area. The proposals stem from the Narey report—

'There is in my view a powerful argument for reinforcing the position of
the lay magistracy by giving to justices' clerks (and other senior staff to
whom they may delegate their powers) the responsibility for managing
cases. Some will argue that this would amount to redefining the
essentially judicial role of the lay magistracy and the administrative role
of court clerks and would diminish the role and status of magistrates.
I am quite certain that this would not be so. On the contrary, removing
administrative case management from magistrates' remit—enabling them
to concentrate on determining the bail or custody status of defendants

and deciding on guilt and sentencing, for which they are best qualified—would do much to increase the quality and attractiveness of the work of the magistracy and increase its efficiency.'.[1]

Section 49(1) lists many powers which a single magistrate may exercise alone. The original Bill also contained the power, where the mode of trial has been determined, to determine the mode of trial on an amended or an additional charge, and the power to adjourn an early administrative hearing and to remand the accused in custody or on bail, but these were withdrawn. Section 49(2)(a) allows the Lord Chancellor to amend the Magistrates' Courts Rules 1981, SI 1981/552, to authorise justices' clerks, subject to specified restrictions or conditions, to carry out the powers specified in s 49(1). Section 49(2)(b) allows the Lord Chancellor to make rules area by area, permitting the new arrangements to be piloted. Pilot schemes started on 30 September 1998 for six months, with a view to national implementation in the autumn of 1999.

---

[1] 'Review of Delay in the Criminal Justice System: A Report', Home Office, February 1997, p 26.

4.28 At Second Reading in the House of Lords the Lord Chief Justice raised his concern that the role of justices' clerks should not be allowed to take over the role of magistrates. There was a crucial distinction between judicial and non-judicial acts—

'. . . I regard it as vital that a clear and categorical distinction be preserved between the role of the justice as judicial decision maker and the role of the justices' clerk as objective, professional, legal adviser and, on occasion, administrator. There are some powers listed in [clause 40] which can quite unobjectionably be exercised by a justices' clerk . . . these are formal, administrative acts; they are not judicial acts. But some powers listed in the clause are quite different, for example in (f) to require—

"a medical report and, for that purpose, to remand the accused in custody or on bail"

To send a defendant to prison is a judicial act; it is not an order which anyone not exercising judicial authority should make, and it is certainly not a matter of administration. There should be no power to make rules which would enable a justices' clerk to make such an order.'.

The Lord Chief Justice went on to give other examples of inappropriate delegation—the clerk should not be able to give an indication of seriousness to the Probation Service or make decisions about separate or joint trials. To allow this would be to—

'erode the fundamental distinction between the justices and the justices' legal adviser and in the longer term—as I fear—signal the demise of the lay magistracy which would be an irreparable loss'.'[1]

Section 49(3) was added to the Bill at Third Reading in the House of Lords in order to limit the powers of clerks, to meet these concerns. Rules shall *not* authorise justices' clerks to—

(a) impose or vary bail conditions without the consent of both parties;
(b) give an indication of seriousness and when requesting a pre-sentence report;
(c) remand in custody for a medical report, or without the consent of both parties, to vary conditions of remand on bail for a medical report;
(d) impose reporting restrictions;

(e) give, vary or revoke orders for separate or joint trials without the consent of all parties.

---

[1]   HL Report, 16 December 1997, col 561.

4.29 Section 49(4) requires the Lord Chancellor to consult magistrates and justices' clerks before making rules under s 49(2). In Committee in the House of Lords Baroness Anelay moved an amendment which would have required the single magistrate to be approved by the bench chairmanship committee.[1] She withdrew her amendment after Lord Williams said that although justices and clerks should be suitably experienced and qualified, this should be a question of good practice and not be enforced by legislation.[2] In reply to a similar amendment in Committee in the House of Commons, the Government argued that this was unnecessary, as 'we can allow the good sense of the courts.'.[3]

---

[1]   HL Report, 12 February 1998, col 1372.
[2]   Ibid, col 1378.
[3]   HC SC B, 14 May 1998, col 409.

Early administrative hearings

4.30 Section 50 gives effect to the Narey Report recommendation that early administrative hearings conducted by clerks should be placed on a statutory footing—

> 'In some magistrates' courts early administrative hearings (EAHs), conducted by clerks, have been introduced so that the defendant can hear what the court expects from him in terms of obtaining legal representation and supplying the evidence to enable the court to consider a legal aid application. The Clerk also explains to the defendant the nature of the forthcoming proceedings and the implications of the charge against him. In some cases this prompts a guilty plea; where the case is contested, experience has shown that overcoming defendants' inertia in applying for legal aid helps to reduce the number of adjournments.
>
> The magistrates' court at Bexley, which is a pioneer in this field, claims that the introduction of EAHs in 1993 has reduced from 55% to less than 10% the proportion of cases failing to make progress at first appearance because the defendant needs, but has not obtained, legal advice . . . Uncertainty over the extent of powers for the police to bail a defendant to appear at an EAH, or for the clerk to extend the bail to the first substantive appearance, has discouraged many courts from adopting EAHs, and there is a strong case for legislating so as to put them on a proper footing.'.[1]

---

[1]   'Review of Delay in the Criminal Justice System: A Report', Home Office, February 1997, p 28.

4.31 Section 50(1) provides that a defendant's first court appearance may be conducted by a single justice, except where it is a preliminary hearing for an indictable only offence, in which case, s 51 applies. Section 50(2) sets out the procedure at such a hearing. The purpose of these hearings is simply to determine defendants' eligibility for legal aid, and to encourage them to obtain legal advice before the first full court hearing. The original Notes on Clauses explain somewhat confusingly that—

> '(Such hearings as not defined as early administrative hearings, although that expression is used in the side note)'

Section 50(3) allows the single justice to remand the accused in custody or on bail. Section 50(4), which provides that a justice's clerk may also exercise powers under this section, does not authorise the clerk to remand the accused in custody or to remand him on different bail conditions without the consent of both parties. Legal aid means representation under the Legal Aid Act 1988, Pt V (s 50(5)).[1] The section was implemented on 30 September 1998 (SI 1998/2327, see Appendix).

---

[1]   It was defined in the original Bill to include representation by way of advice and assistance under Pt III, or under LAA 1988, Pt V.

No committal proceedings for indictable-only offences

4.32   Section 51 introduces a new fast-track procedure for indictable offences, designed to give effect to another recommendation of the Narey Report—

> 'On average, indictable cases spend 87 days (more than 12 weeks) in the magistrates' courts before committal. I recommend that while either way cases should continue to start in the magistrates' court, those triable only on indictment should begin their life in the Crown Court . . .
>
> There are two reasons for starting indictable cases in the magistrates' court. The first is so that the court can establish that there is a case to answer. It is arguable that this was more important before the establishment of the CPS brought the police decision to prosecute under independent scrutiny. It is also arguable that it was more important for magistrates to consider whether there was a prima facie case in the days of Assizes and Quarter Sessions, when (since these were not in permanent session) a defendant might otherwise have had to wait some time before the charges against him could be considered by a court.
>
> The second reason is so that a decision as to venue can be made. But in cases triable only on indictment, no mode of trial decision is necessary. . .
>
> Starting the most serious cases in the Crown Court would lead to them being completed more promptly, provide a clear opportunity for a very early guilty plea and reduce prisoner escapes.'.[1]

A serious concern raised by this change is the risk that it changes the overall character of the work of Crown Court judges. Currently many preliminary procedures take place in the magistrates' court. Judges will, in future, be much more involved in 'case management' (including bail applications), which may limit the time they can give to presiding over trials.[2] Some concern was shown in the Commons for those who are not represented. An amendment proposed in Committee would have limited the fast-track procedure to those who were legally represented, or if unrepresented, were in effect unrepresented by choice.[3] This was instantly rejected by the Government who saw it as providing another opportunity for delay.

---

[1]   'Review of Delay in the Criminal Justice System', Home Office, February 1997.

[2]   See for example Baroness Anelay in HL Report, 24 February 1998, col 551, and Lord Thomas of Gresford at col 553.
[3]   HC SC B, 14 May 1998, col 419.

4.33 Section 51(1) provides that when an adult who is charged with an indictable-only offence appears before a magistrates' court, the court is to send him forthwith to the Crown Court for trial for that offence, and for any either-way or summary offence with which he is charged which fulfils the requisite conditions (s 51(11)), namely—

   (a) that it appears to the court to be related to the indictable-only offence, and
   (b) in the case of summary offences, it is punishable with imprisonment or involves disqualification from driving.

Section 51(2) provides that where such an adult is subsequently before the magistrates' court charged with an either-way offence or summary offence which fulfils the requisite conditions, the court may send him to the Crown Court for these offences. Section 51(3) provides that where, on the same occasion as an adult defendant's appearance on an indictable-only charge, another adult appears as co-defendant with him in respect of a related either-way offence, he too is to be sent forthwith to the Crown Court for trial for the either-way offence. If the other adult appears on a later occasion, the court has a discretion whether to send him to the Crown Court. When an adult is sent for trial under s 51(3) the court shall at the same time send him to the Crown Court for trial for an either-way offence or summary offence which fulfils the requisite conditions (s 51(4)). Section 51(5) gives the magistrates a discretion in the case of children and young people charged jointly with adults sent to the Crown Court under s 51(1) or (3) as to whether or not to send them to the Crown Court for trial. Where it does do so, it may at the same time send them to the Crown Court for trial for an either-way offence or summary offence which fulfils the requisite conditions (s 51(6)).

4.34 Section 51(7) requires the court to serve on the defendant and give to the Crown Court a copy of a notice specifying the offences for which he is being sent for trial and the place where he is to be tried. The notice is to indicate, where there are related offences and there is more than one indictable-only offence, to which of them the other offences are related (s 51(8)). The summary offences which are sent to the Crown Court for trial are to be adjourned *sine die* (s 51(9)). Section 51(10) sets out the factors to which the court is to have regard in selecting where the case is to be tried.

Provisions supplementing section 51

4.35 Section 52(1) makes provision for a person who is sent to the Crown Court under s 51 to be on bail or in custody (subject to the Bail Act 1976, s 4). Where a court decides to grant the defendant bail on condition that he provides one or more sureties, but is unable to release him because no surety is available and so fixes the amount in which a surety is to be bound subsequently with a view to forfeiting that sum if the defendant fails to surrender to custody, then the court shall remand the defendant in custody until the recognisance of the surety is entered into subsequently (s 52(2)).

4.36 Section 52(3) and (4) provides that where an offence of criminal damage falls to be treated as triable either-way or summarily depending on the value involved, it is to be treated as an indictable offence unless it is clear to the court, having regard to any representations, that the value does not exceed the relevant sum. Section 52(5) confers a power to adjourn and s 52(6) introduces CDA 1998, Sch 3—Procedure where persons are sent for trial under section 51. The provisions are modelled on the Criminal Justice Act 1987, s 4, for the case of serious fraud trials, and provide for regulations to be made by the Attorney General. These provide that where a person is sent for trial under s 51, copies of documents containing the evidence are to be served on the defendant and given to the relevant Crown Court. Schedule 3, para 5 (use of depositions as evidence) was added late in proceedings.[1]

---

[1]   HC SC B, 23 June 1998, col 930.

4.37 Schedule 3 seemed to provoke two main concerns in Committee in the House of Lords. First, shifting challenges to the Crown Court would inevitably increase costs. The Government denied that this would be a problem: the aim is to hold fewer such hearings and to constrain the opportunities for delay. The second concern was whether there was a risk that complainants in serious sexual cases might be required to give evidence both before the judge alone and at trial. This debate allowed the Lord Chancellor the opportunity to signpost his commitment to a fundamental review of rights of audience. Recognising that the result of these new provisions is that Crown Prosecutors and defence solicitors who can now handle these procedures in magistrates' courts will no longer be able to do so because they have been moved to the Crown Court, he said—

> 'As the Government outlined at the general election, we are not satisfied that the current restrictions on the exercise of rights of audience, in particular, for qualified lawyers working for the CPS, are in the public interest. Moreover, the existing procedures in the Courts and Legal Services Act 1990 for granting or extending rights of audience and rights to conduct litigation have proved to be unacceptably labyrinthine and slow . . .[1]

> A fundamental reshaping of the provisions in the 1990 Act is required. . . Parliament needs to be given an early opportunity to consider afresh the provisions required to widen rights of audience.'[2]

These sections will be piloted for 12 months from the winter of 1998–99, with a view to national implementation in the spring of 2000.[3]

---

[1]   HL Report, 24 February 1998, col 556.
[2]   Ibid, col 557.
[3]   Home Office circular No 38/1998.

MISCELLANEOUS

Crown Prosecution Service: powers of non-legal staff

4.38 Section 53 inserts POA 1985, s 7A, authorising the Director of Public Prosecutions (DPP) to designate members of the CPS who are not Crown Prosecutors to carry out certain tasks. Most importantly in relation to bail applications and the conduct of proceedings in magistrates' courts. This follows from the Narey Report which concluded that—

> 'The DPP should confer on lay staff the power of a Crown Prosecutor to review files.
>
> Non-lawyers employed by the CPS should be able to present uncontested cases in magistrates' courts.'

A safeguard is to be found in the new s 7A(7), which was added in Committee, that the DPP must set out in his Annual Report the criteria applied by the Director in determining whether to designate persons under this section, the training they undergo, and any general instructions given under s 7A(4). These measures were implemented on 30 September 1998, but the DPP's power will initially be exercised only in specified pilot areas (SI 1998/2327, see Appendix).

Bail: increased powers to require security or impose conditions

4.39 Section 54 gives the courts and the police increased powers to impose bail conditions. Section 54(1) amends the Bail Act 1976, s 3(5), relating to the powers of the courts and the police to require a person to give a security for his surrender to custody. It repeals the proviso that such a security may be required only if it appears that a person is 'unlikely to remain in Britain until the time appointed for him to surrender to custody'. Home Office circular 34/98 explains that—

> '. . . there may be cases where the court takes the view that an up-front payment, in the form of a security, of a relatively small amount would be more effective in securing the defendant's attendance than the availability of a surety with the means to enter into a recognizance for a more substantial sum . . . it is suggested that the security should usually be in the form of cash or a banker's draft to avoid problems of valuation, storage or conversion.'[1].

Section 54(2) inserts the Bail Act 1976, s 3(6)(e), stating that a defendant may be required to attend an interview with an authorised advocate or litigator. This condition may not be imposed by a police custody officer when granting police bail. According to the Home Office circular 34/98—

> 'If a defendant indicates that he does not wish to have legal representation, then it would clearly not be appropriate for the condition to be imposed. The new requirement can be imposed at any relevant stage of proceedings, including at an Early Administrative Hearing . . .'

---

[1]   Issued 10 August 1998.

Forfeiture of recognizances

4.40 Section 55 substitutes MCA 1980, s 120(1), (2), requiring the court to declare the immediate and automatic forfeiture of a recognizance where a defendant fails to answer bail. After declaring the recognizance to be forfeited, the court must issue a summons to the surety to appear before the court to explain why he should not pay the sum, whereupon the court has a discretion to decide whether the sum should be paid. If the surety fails to answer the summons, the court can proceed in his absence provided that it is satisfied that the summons has been correctly served. The Crown Court (Amendment) Rules 1998, SI 1998/2168, r 21A, came into force on

30 September 1998, making similar changes in respect of the forfeiture and estreatment of recognizances conditioned for the appearance of a defendant in the Crown Court (see Home Office circular 34/98). The Rules of the Supreme Court (Revision) 1965, SI 1965/1776, and the Criminal Appeal Rules 1968, SI 1968/1262 will similarly be amended.

Bail: restrictions in certain cases of homicide or rape

4.41 Section 56, which was added on Third Reading in the House of Lords, amends the Criminal Justice and Public Order Act (CJPOA) 1994, s 25, removing the total prohibition on the granting of bail to those charged with homicide or rape after previous convictions for such offences. It replaces the prohibition with a rebuttable reversal of the general presumption of bail. Lord Falconer said that the provision allows—

> '. . . some flexibility to prevent injustice, while ensuring that the protection of the public remains the primary concern and providing a tough additional safeguard against bad bail decisions in these particularly serious circumstances.'.[1]

The change caused considerable concern amongst Conservative MPs, especially when the minister suggested that the change was provoked by concerns that the existing provision fetters judicial discretion and infringes the European Convention on Human Rights.

---

[1]   HL Report, 31 March 1998, col 240.

Use of live television links at preliminary hearings

4.42 Every year a significant number of prisoners abscond from custody during their absence from prison to appear in court. During 1997 there were 78 escapes by escorted prisoners while in transit between courts and prisons and from court buildings, and 11 escapes from escort or court by young offenders in the year to March 1998. The 'Learmont Report'[1] had proposed the use of TV links where a defendant is held in custody, and this proposal was taken up both in the Narey Report and in the consultation paper 'Reducing Remand Delays'.[2] Whilst the Government has stressed the security issue, civil liberties were very much in the minds of some MPs—

> '. . . a statute which states that "the accused shall be treated as being present in the court" even though he is not, should worry anybody who is concerned about natural justice and traditional civil liberties.'.[3]

Liberty, the civil rights group, raised concerns about the need for communication between a defendant and his or her legal representative. In particular with television links, it would be impossible for a lawyer to go through documents with his or her client during the hearing. Conservative amendments at Committee stage would have disallowed television links at the plea before venue proceedings, when the mode of trial decision is taken, or in cases involving children or young people. A Liberal Democrat amendment would have given defendants an absolute right to prevent television links from taking place.[4]

---

1   *Review of Prison Service Security in England and Wales and the escapes from Parkhurst prison on Tuesday 3rd January 1995* (1995) HMSO, Cm 3020.
2   Published in October 1997.
3   HC SC B, 19 May 1998, col 486 (Mr Leigh).
4   Amendment No 422, see HC SC B, 19 May 1998, col 471.

4.43 Section 57(3) requires a magistrates' court, where it would be possible to conduct a particular hearing over a live TV link, to give its reasons if it decides not to do so. In the words of an Opposition member—

> 'the court gets a big nudge in favour of not allowing the defendant to attend in person.'.[1]

The aim is to pilot this in Bristol and Manchester to ascertain the problems and to ensure that they can be dealt with.[2] Pilot studies will allow for private and secure telephone links with lawyers and possibly during the hearings. Guidance will not be published until March 1999.

---

1   HC SC B, 19 May 1998, col 482 (Mr Clappison).
2   Bristol Prison and Eastwood Park will be linked to Bristol and Swindon Magistrates' Court, and Manchester Prison and Hindley YOI will be linked to Manchester City Magistrates' Court: see the announcement by Mr Michael in reply to a Parliamentary Question on 15 June 1998.

5 Dealing with offenders

INTRODUCTION

Sex offenders

5.1 Part IV of the Crime and Disorder Act (CDA) 1998 is entitled 'Dealing with Offenders'. The first chapter deals with England and Wales, and concentrates on three categories of offenders who have been in the public eye recently, namely sexual and violent offenders, drug dependent offenders and persistent young offenders. In recent years much debate has centred on the need to supervise sex offenders. The Criminal Justice Act (CJA) 1991, s 44, focused on this when it allowed a court to order that when a sex offender is released on license, the license should remain in force until the end of the sentence, and not merely until the three-quarters stage is reached. If the ex-prisoner were to be recalled they were then liable to be detained until the end of the sentence, and not merely until the three-quarters stage. This section is replaced by the 1998 Act, s 59. The Crime (Sentences) Act 1997, s 20, which the incoming Government decided not to implement, would have subjected sex offenders to even more rigorous post-release supervision. More recently, the Sex Offenders Act 1997 requires sex offenders, both convicted and cautioned, to register with the police. Much of the debate in Parliament consisted of party political point-scoring over whether the new Government is tougher/stronger or more lenient/weaker than its predecessor in dealing with sex offenders.

Drug dependent offenders

5.2 The introduction of drug treatment and testing orders was generally welcomed, and not seriously disputed in either House. The changes in relation to persistent young offenders were not subject to serious challenge, but perhaps this is due to people suspecting that the legislative changes are more apparent than real. Whether reprimands and warnings are applied differently to the old cautions remains to be seen. There is little evidence that the current cautioning system is inadequate, and the detention and training order may turn out to be another name for the secure training order. The 1998 Act provides a plethora of different orders, such as reparation orders (s 67) and action plan orders (s 69) introduced in Pt IV, to add to the 'preventative' orders of Pt I. The Government appears to believe that it is simpler to have a number of community orders, whilst there is just one custodial option. It might have been more straightforward to have a single community order for juveniles under which could be grouped alternative sanctions, especially as it is unclear how the various new options will fit into the sentencing tariff. Reparation orders and actions plans are going to be piloted over an 18 month period from October 1998, with a view to national implementation in 2000–2001. The results of these pilots must be carefully evaluated.

Sentencing guidelines

5.3 Part IV of the 1998 Act also imposes a statutory duty on the Court of Appeal to produce sentencing guidelines (s 80), and introduces the Sentencing Advisory Panel (s 81), which should be contrasted with the Standing Advisory Council on Criminal Justice and the Penal System, which Lord Ackner hoped to revive (see para 1.14). It is worth noting that the Government was totally opposed to Lord Ackner's proposed Council which would have provided advice across the board to the Government, yet it is committed to creating a not-dissimilar body simply to advise the Court of Appeal. The sentencing provision also provides increases in sentences for existing offences which are racially aggravated, which, as was noted at para 3.2, will work clumsily alongside the new racially aggravated offences introduced in Pt II.

Scotland

5.4   Chapter II relates to Scotland. Three of the changes introduced in England and Wales are introduced in Scotland, namely extended sentences for sex and violent offenders; drug treatment and testing orders; and increases in sentences for racially aggravated offences. However, there are some interesting variations in the way these changes are to be introduced in Scotland which are noted at paras 5.49–5.61.

SEXUAL OR VIOLENT OFFENDERS

Sentences extended for license purposes

5.5   Section 58 allows courts to extend sentences, for the purpose of requiring offenders to undergo a longer period of post-release supervision. The section applies when a court decides to impose a custodial sentence on a person who has committed either a sexual or violent offence (as defined in CJA 1991, s 31(1)), and where it is considered that the period for which the offender would otherwise be subject to post-release would be too short for the purpose of preventing the offender from committing further offences and for securing his rehabilitation (s 58(1)).

5.6   If an offender meets the criteria set out in the section, the court can impose an extended sentence, ie a custodial sentence the term of which is the aggregate of 'the custodial term' (the period that the court would have imposed other than under this section) and 'the extension period' (the period during which the offender is to be subject to a license). There was serious discussion in Parliament on this terminology. For example, in the House of Lords Lord Windlesham, supported by the Lord Chief Justice and Lord Ackner, asked how the description 'custodial sentence' could be used to cover a sentence, the extended part of which is not served in custody.[1] Lord Falconer insisted that it was a custodial sentence made up of a custodial term and an extension period.

---

[1]   HL Report, 24 February 1998, col 593.

5.7   An extended sentence may be applied to 'sex offenders' who receive any term of imprisonment, whereas for 'violent offenders', the court may not pass an extended sentence where the custodial term is less than four years (s 58(3)). Given that a life sentence is already available for those convicted of an offence under OAPA 1861, s 18, and that the maximum sentence for offences under OAPA 1861, s 20, is currently only five years, it would appear that the main targets of these extended sentences are not violent offenders, but rather sexual offenders. For sex offenders the maximum extension period is ten years, and for violent offenders it is five years (s 58(4)), though it must remain within the maximum penalty that is available for the offence in question (s 58(5)). Section 58(6) appears to indicate that the court must determine the length of the custodial term for the purpose of CJA 1991, s 2(2), in the normal way, ignoring the extension period that it is also considering. The maximum length of this extended supervision can then be extended up to ten years by order of the Secretary of State (s 58(7)).

Effect of extended sentences

5.8   Section 59 substitutes CJA 1991, s 44. This section currently provides the courts with a power to require a person convicted of a sexual offence to remain on license until the end of the sentence, rather than until the three-quarters point, which is when a license would otherwise expire. It has now been superseded by the 1998 Act to clarify which provisions in the 1991 Act apply to extended sentences, which elements of an extended sentence should be taken into account in doing so, and which provisions of the 1991 Act will not apply. It should mean that the same period of imprisonment will be available as immediately prior to the enactment of the 1998 Act, followed by a considerably longer period of post-release supervision, but the wording is extremely complex. For example, s 44(2) provides that CJA 1991, Pt II, except for ss 40 and 40A, shall have effect as if the term of the extended sentence did not include the extension period. In other words, when applying the provisions of Pt II of the 1991 Act to a person who has been given an extended sentence, the provisions should generally be applied as if the sentence comprised only the custodial term and no account should be taken of the extension period for these purposes—ie the offender will be released under the normal procedures set out in CJA 1991. However, those returned to prison under s 40 will find their period of extension taken into account. For discussion of s 40A, inserted into the 1991 Act by CDA 1998, s 105, see para 6.18.

5.9   The new CJA 1991, s 44(3), provides that when an offender who has been given an extended sentence is released on license under the 1991 Act, Pt II, the license shall remain in force until the end of the extension period, unless it is revoked during that period and the offender is recalled to prison. New s 44(4) applies in the (perhaps rare?) case of an offender who would have been released unconditionally, ie who had received a sentence of less than 12 months but whose sentence is extended. In this case, the offender will be released on license for whatever extension period the court adds to the custodial term. In other cases, the extension period begins on the date at which the offender would have been released unconditionally—ie the half-way point of the custodial term (s 44(5)). Section 44(6) does not apply to offenders given extended sentences under the 1991 Act, ss 33(3), 33A(1) and 46 (which are amended by s 104 of the 1998 Act), because at both the three-quarters point and at the half-way point the offender would continue to be subject to a license by virtue of the extension period. New s 44(7) provides that the question of whether the offender is a long-term or short-term prisoner will depend on the length of the term of extended sentence.

Re-release of prisoners serving extended sentences

5.10 Section 60 was added at Committee stage in the House of Commons, and inserts CJA 1991, s 44A, to ensure that short-term and long-term extended-sentence prisoners are eligible for the same consideration for release on license if recalled to prison. The section makes specific provision for extended-sentence prisoners who have been recalled to prison under CJA 1991, s 39. They may require the Secretary of State to refer their cases to the Parole Board at any time (s 44A(2)), though not within one year after an unsuccessful reference (s 44A(3)).

5.11 The Minister of State, Mr Michael, stressed that it is important that under s 44A(4) the Parole Board shall, if satisfied that it is no longer necessary for the protection of the public that a prisoner should be confined, 'direct' his release rather than 'recommend' it, as under existing provisions—

> 'It means that the consideration of extended-sentence recall cases will be undertaken by the parole board, which will take into account all such evidence as may be adduced before it and act in its judicial capacity as a tribunal. In other words, the proceedings will be oral, before which the offender would have the opportunity to present his case and, if appropriate, call witnesses to give evidence.'.[1]

The extra workload on the Parole Board may be significant, though the Financial Memorandum attached to the Bill suggested that additional costs to the Parole Board 'are expected to be minimal'. These provisions were implemented on 30 September 1998 (SI 1998/2327, see Appendix).

---

[1]   HC SC B, 19 May 1998, col 517; First and Second Reading and added to Bill: HC SC B, 9 June 1998, col 777.

OFFENDERS DEPENDENT ETC ON DRUGS

Drug treatment and testing orders

5.12 Section 61 provides that an offender aged 16 or over, who has been convicted of an offence for which the sentence is not fixed by law and who the court is satisfied misuses drugs, may be sentenced to a DTTO (s 61(2)). The court shall not make a DTTO unless it is satisfied that he is dependent on drugs or has a propensity to misuse them, *and* that his dependency or propensity requires and may be susceptible to treatment (s 61(5)). There is no need to establish a link between the offence under consideration and the offender's drug misuse. Such an order will be a community order within the meaning of CJA 1991, s 6, and will not be made unless the court has been notified that it can be implemented in the relevant area (s 61(3)). This later provision will allow piloting of the DTTO, planned for 18 months from September 1998, before it is introduced nationally.

5.13 The DTTO builds on the previous provision in the Powers of Criminal Courts Act 1973, Sch 1A, which allowed the courts to make it an additional requirement of a probation order that an offender undergo drug treatment. A Conservative amendment on Committee in the House of Commons would have reduced the age-limit to 12 (despite Lord Henley in the House of Lords having argued for a minimum age of 18), but the Government stated that this was neither necessary nor appropriate. The age limits of DTTOs are intended to be the same as those relating to probation orders. Younger offenders with drug problems can be required to undergo drug treatment under an action plan order (see s 69) or a supervision order under the Children and Young Persons Act (CYPA) 1969, s 12(2). The duration of a DTTO may be between six months and three years (s 61(2)), which also mirrors the length of a probation order. The court may order the offender to undergo a drug test, to which he or she must consent, to inform its sentencing decision (s 61(6)). Section 61(7) is another example of the wide power the Secretary of State is given to amend the length of the order.

Requirements and provisions to be included in orders

5.14 Section 62 provides that a DTTO will include—
(a) 'a treatment requirement', indicating whether the treatment will be residential or non-residential and specifying the treatment provider (see s 62(1)–(3)). The court will not comment on the nature of the treatment, as this is beyond its expertise;
(b) 'a testing requirement', specifying the minimum number of occasions per month that samples must be provided (s 62(4)–(5)). The offender will be required to keep in touch with his probation officer, and communicate the results of drug tests to him;
(c) 'a residence specification'—under s 62(6) the order will include a provision specifying the petty sessions area in which it appears to the court that the offender resides.

The supervision of the responsible probation officer will be limited to reporting to the court responsible for the order the offender's progress, any failure to comply with the order, and any decision as to whether to apply to the court for revocation or amendment of the order (s 62(8)).

Periodic reviews

5.15 Section 63 provides that the court will periodically (at least once a month) review the offender's progress on the basis of a written report by a probation officer. The offender and the probation officer will attend these hearings unless the court decides that because of satisfactory progress, subsequent reviews may take place on the basis of a report alone (s 63(7)). At a review hearing, the court may amend the order with the consent of the offender (s 63(3)), and if the offender refuses his consent to an amendment the court may revoke the order and re-sentence the offender for the offence for which the order was made (s 63(4)). Section 63(6) deals with persons under 18 being charged with what is for an adult an indictable only offence. It provides that if the court is re-sentencing under s 63(4), they may impose a fine of up to £5,000 and/or deal with him in any way that they could have done had he just been convicted of an offence punishable with six months' imprisonment. This was amended at a late stage in the House of Commons from a choice of 'one' of these options to 'either or both'.[1]

---

[1] HC Report, 23 June 1998, col 916.

Supplementary provisions as to orders

5.16 When a court decides to make a DTTO, it must explain the effect and consequences of it in ordinary language to the offender, and the offender must indicate his willingness to comply (s 64(1)). Section 64(2) and (3) were added late in proceedings in the House of Commons[1] to ensure that copies of the order and any subsequent amendments would be sent to any other relevant court, as well as to the offender, treatment provider and the responsible officer. Section 64(5) provides that CJA 1991, Sch 2, which deals with the enforcement of community orders, having been amended by the 1998 Act, Sch 4 (Enforcement etc of drug treatment and testing orders), will also apply to the enforcement of DTTOs.

[1]   HC Report, 23 June 1998, col 917.

YOUNG OFFENDERS: REPRIMANDS AND WARNINGS

5.17   The police have never been obliged to prosecute all offenders, but until now neither formal nor informal cautioning has been governed by statute. Concern over multiple cautioning led to the issue of Home Office circular No 18/94, which tightened up the guidance to the police. There is some evidence that the number of repeat cautions has since declined. New cautioning-plus schemes have also developed in many parts of the country. The White Paper 'No More Excuses' gave some examples—

> 'Thames Valley's scheme in Aylesbury which works with offenders who agree to co-operate rather than face charges. If the victim agrees, an offender will apologise face to face, and hear from the victim about the effects of crime. The programme is demanding for offenders and both victims and young offenders have found it worthwhile. More detailed research will be conducted, but Thames Valley's initial findings in terms of re-offending rates among young offenders who have participated in the project are promising.

> The Northamptonshire Diversion Unit: intervention packages are prepared following consultation with the offender and the victim(s) and tailored to the individual offender to address the offence and prevent re-offending. For example, a teenage boy who had caused damage to a church agreed to a package which included apologising to the church warden, gardening work in the church grounds, and paying a contribution towards the cost of repairing the damage.

> Both offenders and victims have benefited; the diversion unit reports that only 3% of offenders decline to co-operate; and 76% of victims are satisfied with the way the offences are resolved. Research conducted by Nene College estimated that the Unit's results were "consistent with the view that the Diversion Unit has played a significant part in reducing re-offending". The Unit estimates that the costs of a caution and referral to the Unit is less than 25% of the cost of disposal by prosecution.'[1]

The new system will be significantly different to these schemes. Most importantly, the warning will be given before and not after any referral to an inter-agency panel. There has been no clear analysis of the need for change. The pilot schemes are due to begin in October 1998 and to last for 18 months. It will be important that they monitor the due process implications of the system. Will decision-making be more invisible? Will it be unchallengeable, except by judicial review?[2]

[1]   Cmnd 3809, p 17.
[2]   See Home Office circular No 38/1998.

Reprimands and warnings

5.18 Section 65(1) sets out the basic criteria which must apply before a police officer can issue a reprimand or warning to a child or young person under the new system, as follows—

(a) a constable must have evidence that the child or young person has committed an offence;

(b) the constable must consider that if the offender was prosecuted there would be a realistic prospect of conviction;

(c) the offender must admit the offence;

(d) the offender must not have been previously convicted of an offence;

(e) the constable must be satisfied that it would not be in the public interest for the offender to be prosecuted.

These criteria are intended to ensure that reprimands and warnings are not given in inappropriate circumstances, but they have been criticised for being unduly rigid. The offender can be reprimanded if he has not been previously reprimanded or warned (s 65(2)); and warned if he has not been previously warned (though if the previous warning was more than two years earlier, another warning is possible: see s 65(3)). In no circumstances may a young person receive more than two warnings.

5.19 The warning or reprimand must take place in the police station, and if the offender is under 17, in the presence of an appropriate adult (s 65(5)). The constable must explain to the offender the full consequences of the warning or reprimand, in particular, that it may be cited in any subsequent criminal proceedings (see s 66(5)), and in the case of a warning, that the offender will be referred to the YOT (see para 5.21). Section 65(6) compels the Secretary of State to publish guidance on the circumstances in which reprimands and warnings can be given, the category of police officer who is entitled to give a warning or reprimand and the manner and form in which they should be given. In the House of Lords, there was an attempt to allow greater flexibility in granting second final warnings. Another amendment was introduced by Baroness David to provide that the warning should be given to the young offender after (rather than before) an assessment by a youth offending team.[1] Both options had been included in the consultation paper 'Tackling Youth Crime', but this was rejected.

---

[1]   HL Report, 24 February 1998, col 655.

5.20 In Committee in the House of Commons, Mr Michael was asked where informal cautions stood in the context of the new system. The Minister responded that the Government did not wish to be so prescriptive that the police were no longer able to give words of advice, but that all reprimands and warnings should be part of the formal system. 'I do not recognise the concept of an informal caution'.[1] He also stressed that—

> 'We use the term "final warning"—although it is just "warning" in the Bill—because we want to make it clear that it will normally be final.'.[2]

---

[1]   HC SC B, 21 May 1998, col 531.
[2]   Ibid, col 546.

Effect of reprimands and warnings

5.21 The consequences of receiving a reprimand or warning are set out in s 66, which is based on the proposals set out in the consultation paper 'Tackling Youth Crime' and in Ch 5 of the White Paper 'No more Excuses'. 'As soon as practicable' the offender will be referred to a YOT, which will assess the offender and, unless they consider it inappropriate, they will arrange for him to participate in a rehabilitation programme (s 66(2)). The Secretary of State is obliged to publish guidance as to the detail of rehabilitation programmes (s 66(3)), but it is understood that they will include group work, one-to-one work, family group conferencing, mentoring and reparation to victims, as well as supervised activities to improve school achievement and to encourage constructive use of leisure time. Unsurprisingly, some concern was expressed in Parliament about the level of bureaucracy involved. Unless there are exceptional circumstances, the option of the conditional discharge will not be available to a court sentencing the offender for a subsequent offence committed within two years of receiving a warning (s 66(4)).

YOUNG OFFENDERS: NON-CUSTODIAL ORDERS

Reparation orders

5.22 Section 67 introduces a new sentence, 'the reparation order', which requires a young offender (aged 10–17 inclusive) to make specific reparation to the victim. Although this is not clear from the wording of the statute, reparation will be in kind, rather than financial. The exact nature of the reparative activity will be specified in the order, though the White Paper suggests that—

> 'The reparation might involve writing a letter of apology, apologising to the victim in person, cleaning graffiti or repairing criminal damage.'.[1]

The order may specify that reparation be carried out either to the community at large or to a specified person or persons. Any person specified must be a person 'identified by the court as a victim of the offence or a person otherwise affected by it' (s 67(2)). Section 67(3) allows for the piloting of schemes. It will not be possible to combine a reparation order with a custodial sentence (s 67(4)(a)) or with a community service order, a combination order, a supervision order with requirements, an action plan order (s 67(4)(b)). Opposition MPs, echoing the concerns of the Magistrates' Association, questioned why reparation orders cannot be combined with community service orders or combination orders,[2] and were told that—

> 'reparation of one sort or another is already available as part of those orders[3] . . . It is . . . inappropriate to combine a compensation order with a reparation order, as it smacks too much of punishing the offender twice for the same offence. Given that the reparation order is likely to be used for offences at the lower end of the seriousness scale, it would be wrong to approach it in that way. In each case, the courts will decide whether financial reparation or reparation in kind is more suitable.'.[4]

The original Bill also specified that reparation orders could not be combined with a compensation order, but this was amended after comments such as 'reparation without the possibility of compensation is plain daft'.[5]

1   Cmnd 3809, para 4.14.
2   HC SC B, 21 May 1998, col 567.
3   Ibid, col 569.
4   Ibid, col 570.
5   Ibid, col 572 (Mr Clappison).

5.23 Section 67(5) sets the maximum limit of any reparative activity under the order at 24 hours in total. An Opposition amendment to double the maximum was rejected by the Government on the basis that a Saturday afternoon every week over a three month period was an appropriate maximum—the order should be implemented over a relatively short period in a focused way. It will not be made to any individual without that person's agreement, and it must be commensurate with the seriousness of the offence, or the combination of the offence and one or more offences associated with it (s 67(6)). Similarly it should not, as far as is practicable, conflict with the offender's religious beliefs, community order to which he is subject, educational or work commitments (s 67(7)). The court is under a duty to explain any reasons why it does not make a reparation order where it has power to do so (s 67(11)).

Reparation orders: supplemental

5.24 Section 68 imposes two procedural requirements before a reparation order can be made. First, the court must obtain a written report on the type of work which is suitable and indicate the attitude of the victim to the proposed requirements (s 68(1)). Secondly, the court must explain to the offender how the order will operate, and the consequences of breaching it (s 68(2)). Section 68(3) states that the procedure for dealing with breach, variation and discharge are set out in Sch 5 (Enforcement etc of reparation and action plan orders), which were significantly amended late in proceedings in the House of Commons.[1]

1   HC Report, 23 June 1998, col 932.

Action plan orders

5.25 Section 69 introduces another new community penalty, the action plan order (APO). It requires a young offender to comply with the requirements of a three month action plan designed to address his offending behaviour and to prevent further offending. This is similar to the old supervision orders with a condition of intermediate treatment under CYPA 1969, s 12, which continue to be available (see para 5.28). Supervision orders, according to the Government are 'less focused and last longer'.[1] The purpose of the action plan order is to tackle the causes of offending by providing a short, intensive and individually tailored programme combining punishment, rehabilitation and reparation and involving the young offender's parents. It will be available when a juvenile commits any offence which does not carry a mandatory sentence (s 69(1)). It will not be possible to combine an APO with a custodial sentence, or with a probation order, a community service order, a combination order, a supervision order or an attendance centre order (s 69(4)).

1   HC SC B, 21 May 1998, col 587.

5.26 Requirements in an APO, or directions given by a responsible officer, may include—

    (a) participation in specific activities;

    (b) attendance at specific meetings;

    (c) attendance at an attendance centre (if the offence in the case of an adult would have been punishable with imprisonment (see s 70(7));

    (d) avoidance of specific places;

    (e) educational arrangements;

    (f) reparation (subject to the conditions in ss 67–68);

    (g) attendance at a further court hearing (see s 70(3) and para 5.27).

These requirements should, as far as is practicable, not conflict with the offender's religious beliefs, or any community order to which he is subject, or his educational or work commitments (s 70(6)).

Action plan orders: supplemental

5.27 Before imposing an APO, the court must consider a written report from the local YOT, drawn up in consultation with the young offender and his or her family. This report will specify the requirements and benefits of the proposed APO, and the attitude of the offender's parents or guardian to the proposed requirements. Before making the order, the court must explain to the offender how the order will operate, and the consequences of breaching it (s 70(2)). If the court so requires, the offender will have to attend a further hearing, within 21 days of the order having been made, to review progress. The deadline for a further hearing had been 14 days in the consultation paper,[1] and in response to feedback it was extended to 21 days (see s 70(3)). An amendment in the House of Lords would have doubled the time of this review to 42 days, but was withdrawn when Lord Falconer insisted that six weeks would be far too long to wait to discover that the order was not working as successfully as had been anticipated. Section 70(5) states that the procedure for dealing with breach, variation and discharge are set out in Sch 5 (Enforcement etc of reparation and action plan orders).[2]

---

[1]   'Tackling Youth Crime', published 25 September 1997.

[2]   HC Report, 23 June 1998, col 932.

Supervision orders

5.28 Section 71 is designed to strengthen existing supervision orders in two ways (see CYPA 1969, ss 12A, 12AA, 13). First, it allows the courts to impose reparation to the victim or to the community as an additional requirement by amending the 1969 Act, s 12A (see s 71(1)). Secondly, s 71(4) substitutes the 1969 Act, s 12AA(6), widening the criteria under which a juvenile may be required to live in local authority non-secure accommodation for up to six months. Does the provision allow people to be put in local authority accommodation for offences which are not very serious? The Minister was asked to give examples of non-imprisonable offences which might lead a court to impose a residence requirement. He gave two, namely 'causing harassment, alarm or distress' under POA 1986, s 5, and 'the throwing of missiles, indecent or racial chanting or going on to the play area under ss 2, 3, or 4 of the Football Offences Act 1991'.[1] It should also be noted that s 71(5) disapplies CYPA 1969, s 13(2), which provided that courts could not place persons under 13 years old under the supervision of a probation officer, except on application by the local authority where the probation service is already involved with the child or their family. This is necessary because of the importance being given to YOTs (see CDA 1998, s 39(5), and para 4.8).

---

[1] HC SC B, 21 May 1998, col 592.

Breach of supervision requirements in supervision orders

5.29 Section 72 amends CYPA 1969, s 15, which deals with the variation and discharge of supervision orders. Under s 72(1), the following options are provided for dealing with a breach of a supervision order—

(a) a variation, under CYPA 1969, s 15(1);

(b) a fine up to £1,000; and/or

(c) an attendance centre order (CJA 1982, s 17) or a curfew order (CJA 1991, s 12);

(d) discharge of the supervision order, and re-sentence for the original offence; and

(e) where the original order is made by a Crown Court, commital of the offender by a youth court to the Crown Court.

Section 72(2) substitutes s 15(4)–(6) to allow the Crown Court to deal with breaches of Crown Court supervision orders. These provisions were implemented on 30 September 1998, though it is expected that the new residency requirements in s 71 will not come into effect until 1 April 1999 (SI 1998/2327, see Appendix). The new reparative conditions will await the outcome of the piloting of the reparation order (s 67(3)).

YOUNG OFFENDERS: DETENTION AND TRAINING ORDERS

Detention and training orders (DTOs)

5.30 These orders replace detention in a young offender institution for 15 to 17-year-olds, and secure training orders. Soon after the Government took office in 1997, it confirmed that it would be introducing the secure training order (itself the creation of the Criminal Justice and Public Order Act (CJPOA) 1994) and one secure training centre opened at Medway (close to Cookham Wood prison). DTOs were not mentioned in the three Consultation papers published in the autumn of 1997,[1] but the question of juvenile secure accommodation was referred to the Home Secretary's Youth Justice Task Force. Their second report, published in October 1997, looked at juvenile secure accommodation, and the White Paper 'No More Excuses' signalled a change in direction (pp 19–21)—

'— The present custodial accommodation is fragmented and regimes vary both in quality and cost

— Court's powers to remand young people to secure facilities are inadequate and inappropriate

— the sentencing framework can lead to arbitrary outcomes: the kind of institution in which the sentence is served is to a large extent determined by the powers under which the young person is sentenced rather than the needs of the young person; and

— the structure of sentences does not allow for sufficient emphasis to be placed on preventing offending or responding to progress.

. . . the Government intends to reform these chaotic and dysfunctional arrangements . . . It proposes to replace the sentences of detention in a YOI and the secure training order with a more constructive and flexible custodial sentence providing a clear focus on preventing offending.'.

---

[1]   See para 1.2.

5.31   Under s 73, a DTO will be the only available custodial sentence for 15 to 17-year-olds (subject to CYPA 1933, s 53 and CJA 1982, s 8) for any imprisonable offence serious enough to justify custody under CJA 1991, s 1. For 12 to 14-year-olds, the offence must be serious enough to justify custody under the 1991 Act *and* the offending must be persistent. For ten and 11-year-olds (if the Secretary of State uses his power to introduce DTOs for this age group), the order will only be available if additionally only custody would be sufficient to protect the public from further offending. The possibility that DTOs might be imposed on ten and 11-year-olds led to heated debates. An amendment proposed in the House of Lords would have restricted DTOs to those aged 12 and over—

'I do not believe that it is necessary for 11 to 12-year-olds. One could legislate for all sorts of things which might be possible in the future. One could imagine all sorts of strange things that one might introduce, on the possibility that they might be necessary at some future time. That does not seem an adequate reason for introducing them into Acts of Parliament.'.[1]

However, the amendment was defeated on a vote by 21 to 9 votes. The House also debated in Committee whether the 'trigger' for a DTO in the earliest age band should be protection of the public from 'serious harm', rather than from 'further offending'.

---

[1]   HL Report, 19 March 1998, col 921 (Baroness Hilton).

5.32   Section 73(3) explains that the DTO will comprise a period of detention and training, followed by a period of supervision: for more details see s 75(2) and para 5.34. Section 73(4) applies CJA 1991, ss 1–4, to DTOs, and s 73(5) provides that orders will range in length from a minimum of four months to a maximum of two years, with sentences of six, eight, ten, 12 and 18 months available inbetween. There were three reasons why the Government decided to propose these discrete periods. First it would be simpler and easier for the young person to comprehend, secondly it would allow their supervisors to produce a constructive sentence plan which is based on a fixed predetermined period, and finally to ensure that early release provisions rarely mean that an offender given a longer sentence serves a shorter period in custody than one who is given a shorter sentence.[1] However, it is likely to cause huge problems in practice, namely—

(a) courts will have to take account of time served on remand when they impose sentence, rather than the amount of time spent on remand being deducted from the time to be served in custody after sentence (see s 74(5));

(b) because of the statutory discount for guilty pleas—'courts will be forced either to create an exaggerated differential between offenders convicted of the same offence or to make no differentials at all';[2]

(c) more oddly still, the power of the Youth Court is not limited—the section allows magistrates to impose a sentence of up to 24 months. Mr Michael denied that this was a dramatic change—'In cases where the youth court felt that a custodial sentence of six months was inadequate, it would have to remit the case to the Crown Court for sentence. Such a restriction would be time-consuming and costly'.[3]

---

[1]   HC SC B, 21 May 1998, col 607.
[2]   Dr David Thomas QC, quoted at HC SC B, 21 May 1998, col 602 and again at HC SC B, 2 June 1998, col 613.
[3]   HC SC B, 21 May 1998, col 607.

Duties and powers of court

5.33 The aim of s 74 is to make the courts impose orders which are clear to the offender, but the requirement for sentencers to provide these explanations may well prove problematic. For example, under s 74(2) the court shall have the same power to pass consecutive DTOs 'as if they were sentences of imprisonment'. Since a magistrates' court can only sentence to a maximum aggregate term of 12 months (see MCA 1980, s 133(2)), it would appear that the youth court may sentence a young offender for concurrent sentences up to 24 months, but if the sentences are consecutive, the total may not exceed 12 months![1] Another difficulty arises from s 74(3) which provides that the maximum aggregate DTO is 24 months, with the result that where the combination of a number of consecutive sentences exceeds 24 months, 'the excess shall be treated as remitted' (s 74(4)). Dr Thomas's suggestion to remove s 74(4) was debated in Committee, but the Government remained unconvinced.[2]

---

[1]   See Current Sentencing Practice News, Issue 3, 1998, p 11 (DA Thomas QC).
[2]   HC SC B, 21 May 1998, col 605.

The period of detention and training

5.34 Section 75 deals with the length and place of detention and training. Under s 75(1) the DTO will be served in 'such secure accommodation as may be determined' by the Secretary of State, and he may delegate this responsibility to any other person. Under s 75(2) the period of detention and training under a detention and training order shall be one-half of the term of the order. However, s 75(3)–(5) make provision for earlier or later release. The Secretary of State may release an offender one or two months early, and, on application by the Secretary of State, a youth court can extend the length of detention as follows: by one month if the order was eight months or more, but less than 18 months, or by one or two months for orders of 18 months or longer. The involvement of the youth court in such extension is essential in order to comply with the European Convention on Human Rights, Art 5.

5.35 Section 75(7) defines 'secure accommodation' as—
(a) a secure training centre;
(b) a young offender institution;
(c) accommodation provided by a local authority for the purpose of restricting the liberty of children and young persons;
(d) accommodation provided for that purpose under s 82(5) of the Children Act 1989;

(e) such other accommodation provided for the purpose of restricting liberty as the Secretary of State may direct.

The vagueness of this last definition was severely challenged in Committee in the House of Commons,[1] though the Government staunchly defended its 'flexibility in the arrangements for young offenders sentenced to custody'.[2]

---

[1]   HC SC B, 2 June 1998, col 622.
[2]   Ibid, col 629.

The period of supervision

5.36 Section 76 requires that supervision will run from the end of the period of detention until the end of the order, unless the Secretary of State makes an order to the contrary. However, s 76(2) introduces an order-making power to shorten the supervision period. The Government views this as another example of flexibility, (though it will only be possible to shorten the period across the board for all offenders). Any such change will have to be made by statutory instrument, subject to the affirmative resolution procedure. Section 76(3) provides for the Secretary of State to determine the category of person to supervise the offender. The offender shall be given a notice specifying—

(a) the category of person responsible for his supervision (likely to be a member of the YOT: see para 4.8).

(b) any requirements with which he must comply (s 76(6)). The Government has made clear that 'normal requirements would include reporting to a supervising officer and attending counselling'.[1]

---

[1]   HC SC B, 2 June 1998, col 636.

Breaches of supervision requirements

5.37 Section 77 provides sanctions for breaches of the supervision requirement following release from custody under a DTO. Under s 77(1) a justice of the peace may issue an arrest warrant or a summons to bring to court an offender who appears to be in breach of any supervision requirement. The court has the power to impose a further period of custody (for up to three months or up to the end of the order whichever is shorter) or a fine of up to level 3 (currently £1,000: s 77(3)). Challenged on the appropriateness of fines for young offenders, the Government responded that fines were not 'ineffective' on youngsters, especially since young offenders are to have 'fast access to new deal opportunities'.[1]

---

[1]   HC SC B, 2 June 1998, col 637.

Offences during currency of order

5.38 Section 78 provides for the courts to impose a further period of detention on those who commit further imprisonable offences while they are subject to a DTO. This is irrespective of how the court deals with the offender for the new offence (s 78(2)). The period of detention can be up to the length of time between the new offence and the end of the DTO, and may be consecutive or concurrent to the sentence to be served for the new offence (s 78(3)).

Interaction with sentences of detention

5.39 Section 79 was added as the Bill came towards the end of its passage through the House of Commons on 23 June 1998. It sets out the arrangements that courts will have to follow when sentencing someone who is already under a custodial sentence to a further period of custody under the new DTO. It deals with situations in which, for example, a subsequent sentence is to run consecutively with the original sentence when that subsequent sentence is passed in either the custodial phase or post-release supervision of the original sentence (s 79(3)). It also deals with the circumstances in which an offender is re-sentenced because he or she has breached another order such as a community sentence, but has reached the age of 18 since the date of the original order (s 79(5)).

SENTENCING: GENERAL

Sentencing guidelines

5.40 A statutory duty upon the Court of Appeal to produce sentencing guidelines was one of the Government's manifesto commitments. The Court of Appeal has been producing an increasing number of guideline judgments in recent years. The main questions which arise from this new statutory duty concern how it will work in practice, and whether Parliament has given appropriate instructions to the Court. Section 80 provides that the Court of Appeal must consider whether to issue sentencing guidelines, or consider reviewing existing guidelines, where appropriate cases come before the court, or where they receive a proposal from the Sentencing Advisory Panel (SAP), established under s 81. References under CJA 1988, s 36, were added to s 80(1)(a) late in proceedings in the House of Commons in order to remove any doubt as to whether such cases are covered.[1] Guidelines shall 'if practicable' be included in the Court's judgment in the appeal (s 80(4)). Will this result in greater use of Practice Directions, or more delay in the giving of judgments? It is also unclear how the Court of Appeal is expected to interact with the SAP (see para 5.43).

---

[1]   HC Report, 23 June 1998, col 917.

5.41 Under s 80(2), the Court shall consider whether to frame guidelines—it is not required to issue them. Section 80(3) provides that where the court decides to frame or revise guidelines it shall have regard to—
   (a) the need to promote consistency in sentencing;
   (b) the sentences imposed by courts in England and Wales;
   (c) the cost and relative effectiveness of different sentences in preventing re-offending;
   (d) the need to promote public confidence in the criminal justice system;
   (e) the views of the SAP.

5.42 Unsurprisingly, the Government was much criticised for encouraging the courts to take cost into account. In the first debate in the House of Lords, the Lord Chief Justice, Lord Bingham said—
   'I have reservations about the reference to cost in [section 80(3)(c)], not because cost is unimportant or irrelevant but because the courts must

strive to find the right penalty even if it is expensive, rather than opting for the wrong penalty even though it is cheap.'.[1]

The Government's response was that CJA 1991, s 95, already imposes a duty on the Home Secretary to—

'. . . inform the courts about the financial implications of their decisions and that in many ways, the principle that the Court of Appeal and the Panel should consider that information complements that duty. It is right for the judiciary to be aware of the costs of the disposals that it uses.'.[2]

The Minister was questioned further: this clause, it was suggested, was not just about judges being aware of the different costs, but requires them to have regard to costs in framing guidelines—

'A departure, based on cost, from the right sentence can result in the wrong sentence. . . this clause on sentencing guidelines will tend to move us towards sausage machine, computerised justice in the long run.'.[3]

---

[1]   HL Report, 16 December 1997, col 560.
[2]   HC SC B, 2 June 1998, col 641 (Mr Michael).
[3]   Ibid, col 645 (Mr Malins).

The Sentencing Advisory Panel

5.43 Section 81 sets up a new Sentencing Advisory Panel to provide advice to the Court of Appeal. The Government explained in Committee that—

'The purpose of the advisory panel is to enable the criminal justice system to become more effective in its sentencing practice. . . The panel is intended to provide informed, well-researched and objective advice to the Court of Appeal . . .

It has been set up to promote consistency in sentencing by providing the Court of Appeal with additional tools which will assist in the framing or revision of guidelines. . . The panel may wish to commission research when the question of making a new guideline is raised by the Court of Appeal.'.[1]

This has caused concern about how the provisions will work in practice, and whether it will lead to extra paperwork, bureaucracy and cost.

---

[1]   HC SC B, 2 June 1998, col 650 (Mr Michael).

5.44 Section 81(2) provides that where the Court of Appeal decides to frame or to revise guidelines it shall notify the Panel. In Committee in the Commons, Dr David Thomas was quoted—

'It is not clear to me whether [s 81] requires the Court of Appeal, having notified the Sentencing Panel, to wait till it hears from the Sentencing Panel before it promulgates the guideline. It is clear that the Sentencing Panel will require some considerable time to report back to the Court of Appeal if it is to obtain and consider the views of other bodies in accordance with [s 81(4)]. I would suggest that [s 81] be amended by the addition of a further clause making it clear that the Court of Appeal is not obliged to wait for the report from the Sentencing Advisory Panel before proceeding with the guideline. Otherwise the process will be stultified.'.[1]

The Government's response was that it is anxious to avoid delays and therefore the court shall include guidelines 'where practicable'. Where this will result in 'unnecessary and unacceptable delay', it will be required instead to include the guidelines in the next appropriate judgment (s 80(6)). There will therefore be no obligation on the Court of Appeal to await the receipt of advice from the panel.

---

[1]   HC SC B, 2 June 1998, col 654.

Increase in sentences for racial aggravation

5.45   The courts have long treated racial aggravation as an aggravation in sentencing. Thus Lord Taylor said in *R v Ribbans, Duggan and Ridley*—

> 'It cannot be too strongly emphasised by this Court that where there is a racial element in an offence of violence, that is a gravely aggravating feature. There is no specific offence of racial violence although it has been suggested that there should be one. We take the view that it is perfectly possible for the court to deal with an offence of violence which has a proven racial element in it, in a way which makes clear that that aspect invests the offence with added gravity and therefore must be regarded as an aggravating feature.'.[1]

Section 82(2) puts this into statutory form. If an offence is racially aggravated, the court shall treat that fact as an aggravating factor, and shall so state in open court. However, s 82(1) makes clear that the section applies to all offences other than those contained in Pt II of the Act (see para 3.4). The interrelation of these different provisions will cause great difficulty in practice (see para 3.3). Moreover, s 82 gives no indication as to how the racial aggravation must be proved. It will presumably not be included in the indictment, and may not be raised until the sentencing stage of the trial is reached. The Scottish provisions discussed at para 5.61 are more helpful.

---

[1]   16 Cr App Rep (S) 698; [1995] Crim LR 258, 15 November 1994.

MISCELLANEOUS AND SUPPLEMENTAL

Power to make confiscation orders on committal for sentence

5.46   Section 83 was added late in Committee stage, and inserts CJA 1991, s 71(9A), in order to give the Crown Court the power to make confiscation orders under CJA 1988, Pt VI, on a committal for sentence, as well as in cases where the defendant is tried in that court.[1]

---

[1]   HC SC B, 9 June 1998, col 809.

Football spectators: failure to comply with reporting duty

5.47   Sir Norman Fowler (Shadow Home Secretary) had proposed a 'football behaviour order' during the Third Reading, but withdrew his amendment when the Government promised to return to the subject, which they did the next day. Section 84 was added to the Bill on 23 June 1998,[1] and increases the penalty for failing to report under a restriction order imposed under the Football Spectators Act 1989 from one to six months' imprisonment, or to a fine not exceeding level 5 (raised from level 3). Section 84(2) also makes failure to report in accordance with the order an arrestable offence under PACE 1984, s 24(2). This provision was implemented on 7 August 1998.

---

[1]   HC Report, 23 June 1998, col 861.

Interpretation of Ch I

5.48   Section 85(1) defines the meaning of various expressions used in Pt IV, Ch I, and s 85(2) imposes certain requirements in relation to persons providing supervision under an action plan order or a reparation order. Section 85(6) makes provision in relation to sentences under the Crime (Sentences) Act 1997: for the purposes of Pt IV, Ch I, a sentence falls to be imposed under ss 2(2), 3(2) or 4(2) of the 1997 Act if it is required by that provision and the court is not of the opinion there mentioned.

CHAPTER II: SCOTLAND

Sexual or violent offenders

Extended sentences for sexual and violent offenders

5.49   The Crime and Punishment (Scotland) Act 1997 made provision for the extended post-release supervision of violent and sexual offenders, but because the provisions were linked to early release arrangements which will not be introduced, they too will not be implemented. Instead, CDA 1998, s 86, inserts the Criminal Procedure (Scotland) Act 1995, s 210A. It provides that the court may impose an additional period of supervision (up to ten years in the case of a sexual offender and five years in the case of a violent offender (see s 210A(3)) where a determinate sentence or a sentence of four years or more is imposed. An amendment added by the Government in the House of Lords subtly changed the criteria in s 210A(1)(b) from—

> 'where the court considers that it is necessary to do so to protect the public from serious harm from the offender on his release'

to—

> 'where the court considers "that the period (if any) for which the offender would, apart from this section, be subject to a license would not be adequate for the purposes of protecting the public from serious harm from the offender"'.

Lord Hardie explained that the reference to the words 'on his release' were not entirely apt, since the prisoner may be released long before the extension period begins.'.[1]

---

[1]   HL Report, 31 March 1998, col 256.

5.50   Section 210A(5) sets the limits. The term of an extended sentence passed for a statutory offence shall not exceed the maximum term of imprisonment provided for in the statute in respect of that offence. When questioned in the House of Commons as to why there is any limit on the extended sentence, Mr McLeish explained—

> 'If it becomes clear with the operation of the legislation that a longer period is desirable in the case of violent offenders, the maximum may be increased up to the same level as for sex offenders by statutory instrument, subject to affirmative resolution.'.[1]

An Opposition amendment would have left out 'shall not' in s 210A(5) and inserted 'may', in order that the extension period should exceed the statutory maximum, but the amendment was withdrawn on the Government's insistence that the courts must operate within the framework laid down by Parliament.

---

[1]   HC Report, 23 June 1998, col 922.

5.51 The Government added an amendment in Committee requiring the court to obtain a pre-sentence report before an extended sentence could be imposed (see s 210A(4)). (No such express provision was necessary in relation to England and Wales since CJA 1991 already provides for this). Section 210A(7) allows the Secretary of State to extend the five year maximum extension period in the case of violent offences to ten years (similar to the provisions in England and Wales). This has to be by statutory instrument subject to the affirmative resolution procedure (s 210A(8)). Section 210A(9) provides that the provision does not apply retrospectively, and s 210A(10) includes a detailed list of sexual offences to which the provision applies.

Further provision as to extended sentences

5.52 Section 87 inserts the Prisoners and Criminal Proceedings (Scotland) Act 1993, s 26A, to take account of the provision in s 86 for extended sentences for sexual and violent offences. The existing arrangements for post-release supervision of long-term prisoners are contained in the 1993 Act, Pt I. The extension period of an extended sentence will be treated in the same way as a license under the 1993 Act. The Parole Board may set conditions for release (in the case of long-term prisoners) and make recommendations on recall and return to custody and re-release. In the case of long-term prisoners, the license period to which the offender would have been subject on release will be followed by the extension period (s 26A(5)). Short-term prisoners will be treated as long-term prisoners for all purposes, apart from release which will continue to be automatic at the half-way point of the custodial term.

Re-release of prisoners serving extended sentences

5.53 Section 88 inserts the Prisoners and Criminal Proceedings (Scotland) Act 1993, s 3A. It was added in Committee in the House of Commons, with Mr McLeish explaining that the provision was necessary to ensure compatibility with the European Convention on Human Rights. A prisoner who has been recalled to prison whilst serving an extended sentence, will be able to require the Secretary of State to refer his case to the Parole Board (s 3A(2)). The Board will act in a 'judicial capacity when reviewing the continued detention of recalled prisoners on extended sentences'.[1] This mirrors the English provision—CJA 1991, s 44A—inserted by CDA 1998, s 60 (see para 5.10).

---

[1]   HC SC B, 9 June 1998, col 763.

Offenders dependent etc on drugs

Drug treatment and testing orders

5.54 Section 89 inserts the Criminal Procedure (Scotland) Act 1995, s 234B, to provide for DTTOs in Scotland. The section parallels the provision relating to DTTOs in England and Wales (see s 61 and para 5.12). A Conservative amendment would have reduced the minimum age from 16 to 12,[1] but this was withdrawn after the Government argued that it was inappropriate since children under the age of 16 in Scotland are usually dealt with under the children's hearings system rather than by prosecution.[2] Another amendment that would have compelled the Secretary of State to publish a report on DTTOs every two years was also withdrawn.

---

[1]   HC SC B, 9 June 1998, col 769.
[2]   Ibid, col 770.

Requirements and provisions to be included in drug treatment and testing orders

5.55 Section 90 inserts the 1995 Act, s 234C, again mirroring the English requirements (see s 62 and para 5.14). A DTTO will include—

    (a) 'a treatment requirement', indicating whether the treatment will be residential or non-residential and specifying the treatment provider (see s 234C(1)–(2)). The court will not comment on the nature of the treatment, as this is beyond its expertise;

    (b) 'a testing requirement', specifying the minimum number of occasions per month that samples must be provided (s 234C(4)–(5)). The offender will be required to keep in touch with his probation officer, and communicate the results of drug tests to him;

    (c) 'a residence specification': under s 234C(6) the order will include a provision specifying the local authority in whose area the offender will reside. The supervision of the responsible probation officer will be limited to reporting on progress and failure to the court responsible for the order, and to deciding whether to apply to the court for revocation or amendment of the order (s 234C(8)).

Procedural matters relating to DTTOs

5.56 Section 91 inserts the 1995 Act, s 234D. This matches the requirements and provisions for England and Wales, as set out in s 64 (see para 5.16). The court must explain to the offender in ordinary language the effect and meaning of the requirements of the order, the consequences of failure to comply, and the powers of the court to review the order. The court must send a copy of the order to the offenders, the treatment provider, the child social worker of the local authority specified in the order, and, where it is not the appropriate court as defined in s 95, to the court responsible for reviewing the order.

Amendment and periodic review of DTTOs

5.57 Section 92 inserts two new sections into the 1995 Act. First, s 234E allows for the amendment of a DTTO on application by either the offender or the supervising officer. The court may, after hearing both parties, vary or revoke the order, provided any variation does not result in the length of the treatment and testing period falling out with the minimum or maximum period specified in s 234B(2)(a). Section s 234F provides that the court shall periodically (at monthly intervals) review the offender's progress at a review hearing. These provisions parallel the requirements for amendment and review of DTTOs in England and Wales (see s 63, and para 5.15).

Consequences of breach of DTTO

5.58 Section 93 inserts new ss 234G and 234H into the 1995 Act. It provides that in the event of a breach of a DTTO, a court may issue a citation requiring the offender to appear before the court or, if it considers it appropriate, issue a warrant for the arrest of the offender (s 234G(1)). If the offender has failed without reasonable cause to comply with any requirement of the order, the court may fine him or her, or vary or revoke the order (s 234G(2)). Where a court revokes a DTTO under this section, or under ss 234E and 234F, the court may use any of the sentencing options which would have been available at the time that the order was made (s 234H(1)). Before revoking a DTTO, a court is to have regard to the time the order has been in operation (s 234H(2)). Where a probation order and/or a restriction of liberty order is also in force, the court is to discharge the probation order and to revoke the restriction of liberty order (s 234H(3)). Section 93 is not reflected in the provisions relating to England and Wales for DTTOs, simply because those provisions concerning breach will, by virtue of Sch 4, be aligned to existing provisions (in CJA 1991, Sch 2) for breaches of community orders. Since there are no equivalent Scottish provisions for community orders, separate provision is needed to provide for the consequences of breach.

Combination of orders

5.59 Section 94(1) inserts new s 234J into the 1995 Act, providing that a court, if it considers it expedient to do so, may make concurrent DTTO and probation orders. Section 94(2) states that the provisions of CDA 1998, Sch 6—Drug treatment and testing orders: amendment of 1995 Act, (Pt I of which makes further provision in relation to the combination of DTTOs and Pt II of which makes provision in relation to appeals) shall have effect. This section again has no parallel in the provisions relating to England and Wales since there is already provision under CJA 1991, s 6(1), for the imposition of one or more concurrent community orders, and the definition of such orders has been expanded to include DTTOs.

Interpretation provision in relation to DTTOs

5.60 Section 95 simply defines 'the appropriate court' and 'local authority' and inserts a definition of 'DTTO' into the 1995 Act.

Racial aggravation

Offences racially aggravated

5.61 Section 96 provides that where racial aggravation is proved in respect of any offence, the court shall, on conviction, take the aggravation into account in determining the appropriate sentence. This follows the recommendation of a Scottish

Office consultation paper on the need to introduce new measures to deal with racist crime.[1] Section 96(1) provides that the section will apply where it is libelled in an indictment or specified in a complaint and proved to the satisfaction of the court that an offence has been racially aggravated. This appears somewhat clearer than its English counterpart (s 82), which is less specific about how the racial aggravation is to be proved (see para 5.45). Section 96(2) provides that an offence is racially aggravated for the purposes of this section if—

(a) at the time of committing the offence, or immediately before or after doing so, the offender evinces towards the victim (if any) of the offence malice and ill-will based on the victims' membership (or presumed membership) of a racial group; or

(b) the offence is motivated (wholly or partly) by malice and ill-will towards members of a racial group based on their membership of that group.

The section was amended, as was its English counterpart, to specify that membership includes association with members of that group (see para 3.4). Where the definition varies from its English equivalent is in the definition of racial aggravation to include 'malice and ill-will' (s 96(2)(b)): see further the discussion at para 3.15.

---

[1]   Published on 9 September 1997.

6 Miscellaneous and supplemental

INTRODUCTION

6.1   Part V is perhaps misleadingly entitled 'Miscellaneous and supplemental', since it contains two of the Act's most controversial provisions—first, changes in relation to remand accommodation for young people, described by one well-respected peer as 'perhaps the only wholly objectionable provision' in the Act (see para 6.5), and secondly, changes to early release provisions for short-term prisoners, who are now to be released subject to electronic monitoring, on a home detention curfew. As the detailed guidance already issued to the police, probation and prison services[1] makes clear, this is no miscellaneous or supplemental change. The Financial Memorandum attached to the original Bill suggested these changes alone are expected to cost up to £35 million a year, but should avoid the need for an estimated expenditure of up to £180 million a year on new prison places which would otherwise be necessary to accommodate the rising prison population. The last 16 sections of the Act may be more truly described as 'Miscellaneous and supplemental'.

---

[1]   Prison Service Instruction (PSI) 31/1998 is more than 30 pages long, including the Annexes.

REMANDS AND COMMITTALS

Remands and committals of children and young persons

6.2   Section 97 amends the Children and Young Persons Act (CYPA) 1969, s 23, allowing for the implementation of court-ordered secure remands, subject to certain criteria, for 12 to 16-year-olds. The section permits a court, if the necessary criteria are met, to remand a child of at least 12 years old directly to local authority secure accommodation (s 97(2)). It allows the Secretary of State to extend the provisions for court-ordered secure remands to any male and female age groups up to and including 16 years old. Organisations involved with young offenders are concerned that this power will be used to fill local authority places with the youngest offenders, thus 'condemning' more 15 and 16-year-olds to remain in the prison system, due to the lack of local authority secure accommodation.

6.3   Section 97(1) amends CYPA 1969, s 23(4), and s 97(3) inserts a new s 23(5A). These subsections were added on amendment as a safeguard to ensure that a child shall not be remanded into secure accommodation unless he is legally represented (or has been refused legal representation because it did not appear that his means were such that he required assistance, or because he refused or failed to apply for representation). Section 97(2) amends the 1969 Act, s 23(5), so that a court, if the necessary criteria are met, can remand a child of at least the age of 12 years old, or a young person of a prescribed description (as defined by s 97(4)), direct to local authority secure accommodation. Section 97(4) inserts a definition of 'prescribed description' into the 1969 Act, s 23(12), which includes an order-making power for the Secretary of State to set the definition! Section 20 of the Criminal Justice and Public Order Act (CJPOA) 1994, which has not been brought into force, is repealed and superseded by s 97(5) of the 1998 Act.

Remands and committals: alternative provision for 15 or 16-year-old boys

6.4   Section 98 makes alternative arrangement for the remand and committal of 15 and 16-year-old boys. These boys may be remanded to local authority secure accommodation, rather than prison, if they are adjudged by the court to meet the definition of vulnerability set out in s 98(3), which modifies CYPA 1969, s 23(4)–(5A), and where an accommodation place has been identified in advance. Those who do not meet the relevant criteria will be remanded to a remand centre or prison (new s 23(4)(b), (c)). The existing arrangement will continue until such time as 15 or 16-year-old boys fall within the 'prescribed description' of s 97. Much concern has focused in the last few years on the remand of 15 and 16-year-olds in prison, especially the shocking rates of suicides and self-harm amongst this age group.[1] In January 1998, 75 15-year-olds and 173 16-year-old boys were held in adult prisons (248 in all).[2] The Chief Inspector of Prisons published a thematic report on young offenders recommending that an independent chief inspector should be appointed to monitor the treatment of children throughout the youth justice system, and that the Prison Service should relinquish responsibility for all children under the age of 18.[3] This legislation is designed to signal a commitment to end prison remands, and offers what the Minister of State at the Home Office, Mr Michael, called—

> 'a grown up approach establishing the practical steps that need to be taken over time to implement a principle that cannot be acted on overnight.'.[4]

---

[1]   See for example the Howard League's campaigns reported in *Criminal Justice*.
[2]   Figures quoted by Mr Clappison, HC SC B, 2 June 1998, col 670.
[3]   Chief Inspector of Prisons, *Young Prisoners—a thematic review*, HMSO, 1997.
[4]   HC SC B, 2 June 1998, col 670.

6.5   Opposition members did not receive this with Mr Michael's equanimity. Lord Goodhart said during the Second Reading debate in the House of Lords that—

> '. . . it can be said that [section 98] contains what is perhaps the only wholly objectionable provision in the Bill. . . We believe that it is absolutely wrong to mix 15 and 16 year olds with adult prisoners.'.[1]

He reminded the House that the International Covenant on Civil and Political Rights, Art 10, requires accused juveniles to be separated from adults. The United Kingdom entered a reservation to that Article, but only where there is a lack of suitable alternative facilities or where the mixing of adults and juveniles is deemed to be mutually beneficial. The Opposition proposed an amendment in Committee that the Home Secretary should make an annual report to Parliament on the accommodation of offenders under the age of 17, but this proposal was rejected by the Government on the basis that the Youth Justice Board (see s 41 and para 4.13) which will be in place by October 1998, will monitor the performance and operation of the whole youth justice system, including the provision of secure accommodation for juveniles.

---

[1]   HL Report, 16 December 1997, col 589.

RELEASE AND RECALL OF PRISONERS

Power to release short-term prisoners on licence

6.6 Section 99 inserts the Criminal Justice Act (CJA) 1991, s 34A, providing a power to release short term prisoners (ie those serving up to four years) on a home detention curfew licence (HDCL). The curfew will be enforced by electronic monitoring, and will operate for up to two months (s 100(1)), in place of the final part of the sentence spent in custody. Opposition members capitalised on the Labour party's strong opposition to the previous Government's introduction of electronic tagging in 1991, comparing it with a Labour Home Secretary's statement in 1997 that—

> 'Tagging has a key role to play here. If prisoners who are serving short-term sentences are tagged towards the end of the custodial period of their nominal sentence, they can be given the opportunity to structure their lives more effectively and be swiftly brought back to prison if they breach the tagging conditions.'.[1]

Commenting on this statement, Mr Leigh asked in Committee 'Was that a conversion on the road to Damascus, or a conversion on the road from the Treasury? I suspect that it was the latter.'.[2]

---

[1] HC Report, 20 November 1997, col 454.
[2] HC SC B, 4 June 1998, col 685.

6.7 The Conservative party continued to oppose this section throughout the debates in Parliament—

> 'We oppose the early release of prisoners under the scheme. . . We want an extensive scheme for tagging to reinforce curfew orders, but it should be a proper sentence of the court. Courts could then decide to impose curfew orders as opposed to short-term custodial sentences where circumstances dictated that that would be beneficial. That is a better and more honest way to relieve pressure on the prison service, and to ease overcrowding. It is certainly a more appropriate use of tagging-based curfew sentences. . . We believe that, if the Government go ahead with the scheme, it will undermine public confidence in custodial sentences that are served up to only a quarter point of the original sentence, and in the use of tagging, which the public regard as a soft option to prison.'.[1]

The Government have, however, made it clear that they do not propose to release all prisoners under these provisions—

> 'The Prison Service will in each case conduct a risk assessment. If the prisoner fails it, he or she will continue to serve the sentence in prison until its halfway point, as now. . . the monitoring will be provided by private sector contractors, and there will be an invitation to tender in due course.'.[2]

In Committee, Mr O'Brien confirmed that the Government envisaged that 'between 45% and 60%—I suppose the working figure would be about half—of the relevant prisoners would pass the test.'.[3]

1   HC Report, 23 June 1998, col 925 (Mr Greenaway).
2   HC Report, 20 November 1997, col 455.
3   HC SC B, 4 June 1998, col 687.

6.8   The new s 34A(1) applies the new scheme to short-term prisoners serving three months or more. An Opposition amendment would have restricted eligibility to those serving six months or more rather than three months or more. They were concerned that public confidence will be undermined: under the provisions as enacted, a person sentenced to two and a half months may well serve longer than someone sentenced to three months, but Mr Michael replied that a home detention curfew will be a 'very rigorous regime' and—

> '. . . we should not make a totem of the length of time spent in prison.
> The objective of prison and the tagging regime is to punish and reform,
> and both sanctions will be in place.'.[1]

1   HC SC B, 4 June 1998, col 697.

6.9   Prisoners will not be eligible for home detention curfew if they are either serving extended sentences, recalled after temporary release, under a hospital order, or subject to deportation, in breach of a HDCL, or due for release within 14 days (s 34A(2)). This does not mean that all other prisoners will be released. The draft copy of the risk assessment guidance provides simply a 'presumption' in favour of release. There will be a two-stage process—first a standard assessment, and subsequently an enhanced procedure for those needing special attention. Under the enhanced procedure the prisoner will be considered by a board composed of the governor, a member of the through-care team (normally a seconded probation officer) and, usually, a member of the prison staff who has daily contact with the offender. The draft risk assessment specifies four reasons for not releasing the prisoner—

(a) an unacceptable risk to the victim or to members of the public;
(b) a pattern of offending which indicates an unacceptable risk of reoffending during the home detention curfew period;
(c) a probability of failure to comply with the conditions of the curfew;
(d) the lack of a suitable address.[1]

Originally the Government had said that sex offenders would be treated as other offenders. But on 31 March 1998 the Home Office announced that sex offenders would only be released on a home detention curfew in 'exceptional circumstances'. Amendments proposed in both the House of Lords[2] and in the Commons would have required the Home Secretary to publish the criteria used by the Prison Service to assess the suitability of prisoners for HDCL. However, the Government stated that whilst the criteria will be published, it would be more useful to retain the 'flexibility provided by non-statutory guidance, which can be amended in the light of experience'.

1   For more details see Annex D to Prison Service Instruction (PSI) 31/1998.
2   HL Report, 3 March 1998, col 1168.

6.10 The Secretary of State may release eligible prisoners once the 'requisite period is served' (new ss 34A(3), (4)). For sentences of three months but less than four months, the requisite period is 30 days; for sentences of four months but less than eight months it is one quarter of the sentence; for sentences of eight months or more, it is 60 days less than half the sentence. The new ss 34A(5), (6) allow the Secretary of State to amend (shorten or lengthen) the requisite period, and to extend it to those under the age of 18, subject to the affirmative resolution procedure. When the Government explained that they had no plans to amend the requisite period, Mr Clappison commented that—

> 'It seems another example of the Government's seeking a reserve power to do things that they have no intention of doing, and which would contradict what they are doing already.'.[1]

---

[1]   HC SC B, 4 June 1998, col 709.

6.11 Baroness David introduced an amendment in Committee which would have enabled prisoners under 16 to be eligible for the early release provisions set out in ss 99–103, without having to be electronically tagged. The Government reported that pilot schemes had started in Norfolk and Manchester on curfews for 10–15 year olds. These would not end until the summer of 1999, and therefore home detention curfews for juveniles would be delayed until after these pilots had been evaluated.[1] Meanwhile, the first releases on home detention curfew are expected to take place on 28 January 1999.[2]

---

[1]   HL Report, 3 March 1998, col 1171.
[2]   See Prison Service Instruction (PSI) No 31/1998, originally e-mailed to establishments on 23 June 1998 but issued on 10 July 1998, which sets out the funding arrangements and the details of the preparatory work that must be undertaken before full implementation.

Curfew condition to be included in licence

6.12 Section 100 inserts CJA 1991, ss 37A and 38A. They provide for the curfew conditions which must be met by a prisoner released on curfew under the new provisions of the 1991 Act, s 34A, inserted by the 1998 Act, s 99 (see para 6.6) and for the arrangements for recall to prison on breach. Section 37A(1)(a) requires the person to be curfewed to a specified place (which may be a probation hostel) for specified hours (at least nine hours a day (s 37A(2))). Despite a Government amendment in the House of Lords to allow prison governors, acting on behalf of the Secretary of State, to change the hours or place of curfew once the offender has started the home detention curfew licence period, there is no provision in the Act allowing this. Unnecessary recalls to prison could have been avoided where compliance with curfew conditions could be altered to accommodate changes in circumstances.

6.13 Section 38A, inserted by s 100(2), gives the Secretary of State the power to revoke a licence and recall the released person to prison if—
   (a) he has failed to comply with the curfew condition;
   (b) his whereabouts can no longer be electronically monitored at the place specified in the licence, or
   (c) it is necessary to protect the public from serious harm from him.

The latter two conditions were added in Committee in the House of Lords.[1] Opposition members in the House of Commons challenged the inclusion of the word 'serious' harm in the recall provisions as it meant that the threshold for recalling offenders was too high, but the Government was unconvinced.

---

[1]   HL Report, 3 March 1998, col 1167.

Early release: two or more sentences

6.14 Section 101 substitutes CJA 1991, s 51(2). It was introduced late in Committee stage,[1] when Mr Michael explained that—

> '. . . there are about 300 prisoners a year who are currently recalled for breach of licence, having been released from the custodial part of an earlier sentence, and who then receive a new custodial sentence. The new clause means that their new sentence will no longer be aggregated with the earlier one. In an estimated 80% of such cases sentenced in future, the offenders will serve a longer period in custody than under current procedures.'

The complexity of the provision caused one senior Opposition MP to say that '. . . to be blunt, I have no idea what is meant by the new clause'.[2] New s 51(2A) was added even later,[3] in order to clarify that where a suspended sentence is ordered to take effect, the sentence is deemed to be passed on the occasion when it is ordered to take effect.

---

[1]   HC SC B, 2 June 1998, col 611–612; brought up, read the first and second time and added to the Bill HC SC B, 9 June 1998, col 810.
[2]   HC SC B, 2 June 1998, col 614 (Mr Malins).
[3]   Official Report, 23 June 1998, col 929.

Restriction on consecutive sentences for released prisoners

6.15 Section 102 was also added in Committee.[1] It provides that a court sentencing a person to imprisonment shall not order the new sentence to be consecutive to any other sentence from which he has already been released.[2]

---

[1]   HC SC B, 9 June 1998, col 810.
[2]   See Home Office circular No 44/1998 (issued on 17 September) for detailed advice on sentence calculation.

Recall to prison of short–term prisoners

6.16 Section 103 provides for the procedures governing recall to prison for breach of licence conditions to be the same for short-term prisoners as they are for long-term prisoners. In effect, this section transfers all responsibility for revoking licences for both short and long-term prisoners from the courts to the Parole Board. When Lord Belstead congratulated the Government on this 'very substantial step forward', Lord Falconer entered the caveat that there are transitional provisions in Sch 9 which enable s 103 to be introduced later than other provisions in this part of the Act.[1] The Home Office have said that the provision will be implemented in early 2000.

---

[1]   HL Report, 3 March 1998, col 1173.

Release on licence following recall to prison

6.17 Section 104 provides that offenders who are released at the three-quarters stage of their sentence, having been recalled to prison, will be released again on licence, which will then run until the end of the sentence. While it may be useful that there is now some element of supervision following the offender's second release, the significance of this change may have to be explained in open court to offenders when they are first sentenced.

Release on licence following return to prison

6.18 Section 105 inserts CJA 1991, s 40A, which provides that offenders who return to prison under s 40 for 12 months or less will be made subject to a further three month supervision period following their release (s 40A(3)). This is the period considered necessary to draw up and implement an effective supervision plan. Offenders returned for periods of longer than 12 months are already subject to existing provisions for post-release in the 1991 Act.

MISCELLANEOUS

Pre-consolidation amendments

6.19 Section 106 introduces Sch 7 of the Act, which contains amendments to facilitate the consolidation of certain enactments. Schedule 7 consists of 17 pages of detailed amendments designed to clarify the law. The changes are the first step on the road to a sentencing code which can be introduced in a future session of Parliament.

Amendments to the Crime (Sentences) Act 1997 Act, Pt II, Ch I

6.20 Section 107(1) repeals the Crime (Sentences) Act 1997, ss 8, 10–27, which had sought to give statutory form to the previous Government's 'Honesty in Sentencing' policy. Section 9, which requires a court to credit time spent by a prisoner remanded in custody towards his sentence, is amended, largely to incorporate detailed provisions which were previously found within the repealed sections of the 1997 Act. New s 9A provides that the same rules on crediting periods of remand in custody should apply to those sentenced to detention in a young offender institution or in local authority accommodation (see s 107(5)).

Repeal of the Crime and Punishment (Scotland) Act 1997, Pt III, Ch I

6.21 Section 108 repeals the Crime and Punishment (Scotland) Act 1997, Pt III, Ch I, which dealt with the early release of prisoners.

Transitional provisions in relation to certain life prisoners

6.22 Section 109 was added in Committee in the House of Lords.[1] The Lord Advocate (Lord Hardie) explained that the amendment makes good an omission from the transitional provisions contained in the Crime and Punishment (Scotland) Act 1997, s 16(2), dealing with those sentenced for murder committed when they were under 18. This amendment aligns them with the earlier transitional provisions made for discretionary life prisoners contained in the Prisoners and Criminal Proceedings (Scotland) Act 1993 in order to avoid possible unfairness. The new s 16(3A)–(3C) provides that where a murderer under the age of 18 has been released by the Secretary of State under the pre-1997 Act procedures, he will be deemed to have served the designated part of his sentence for the purposes of the new procedures. That means that the Lord Justice General is not required to set a 'designated part' and arrangements thereby mirror the transitional arrangements made for discretionary life prisoners. It also provides that in any relevant case in which the Lord Justice General has made a certificate setting the designated part, it shall be disregarded.

---

[1]   HL Report, 3 March 1998, col 1179.

Calculation of period of detention at customs office etc where person previously detained

6.23 Section 110 was added late in Committee in the House of Commons,[1] and brings the powers of customs officers to detain and question suspects into line with those of the police in Scotland.

---

[1]   HC SC B, 9 June 1998, col 810.

Early release in Scotland: two or more sentences

6.24 Sections 111 and 112 insert new provisions into the Criminal Procedure (Scotland) Act 1995 to parallel changes to sentence calculation in Scotland with those being introduced in England and Wales. Again these sections were added late in Committee in the House of Commons.[1] It is not surprising that some Scottish members were unimpressed about this method of legislating for Scotland.

---

[1]   HC SC B, 9 June 1998, col 811.

Restriction on consecutive sentences for released prisoners: Scotland

6.25 Section 112 mirrors the provision relating to England and Wales (s 102), which was also added in Committee (see para 6.15). It provides that a court sentencing a person to imprisonment shall not order the new sentence to be consecutive to any sentence from which he has already been released.

Deputy authorising officer under the Police Act 1997, Pt III

6.26 Section 113 amends the Police Act 1997, Pt III, to allow Assistant Chief Constables, or their equivalents, in the National Criminal Intelligence Service or the National Crime Squad to be designated to authorise applications in the absence of the Directors General and their deputies. Section 113(2) was added in Committee to clarify ranks on promotion.[1] The section also allows the Commissioners of Customs and Excise to designate a deputy to act in the absence of the Chief Investigation Officer (National Investigation Service).

---

[1]   HC SC B, 4 June 1998, col 712.

SUPPLEMENTAL

Orders and regulations

6.27 Section 114 provides that any power of a Minister of the Crown to make an order or regulations under this Bill is exercisable by statutory instrument and includes the power to make such transitional provisions as appear necessary or expedient in connection with any provision made by order or by regulations. Whilst orders made under ss 5(2), (3) or 10(6) or regulations made under Sch 3 are subject only to the negative resolution procedure, s 114(3) provides an additional safeguard that orders under ss 38(5) (local provision of youth justice services), 41(6) (Youth Justice Board), 58(7) (sentences extended for licence purposes), 61(7) (drug treatment and testing orders), 73(2)(b)(ii) (detention and training orders) or 76(2) (the period of supervision under DTOs) have to be approved by the affirmative resolution procedure.

Disclosure of information

6.28 Section 115 provides a power, where except for this section there is none, to allow for the disclosure by any person, of information to relevant authorities or persons acting on their behalf, which is 'necessary or expedient for the purposes of any provision of this Act'. It was added to the Bill in the House of Lords, after Lady Hilton had raised concerns about the disclosure of personal information.[1] The police already have a common law power to disclose information for the prevention, detection and reduction of crime. The powers of other public bodies are less clear. In Committee in the House of Commons, Mr Michael explained—

> 'The approach which the Bill takes to tackling crime at its grass roots involves co-operation and partnership between agencies and partnerships both within and beyond the criminal justice system. . . Exchanging information is the life blood of these partnerships. . . The clause . . . is carefully drawn to provide a statutory authority for disclosure for those cases where none currently exists, so that the holder of the information has the say over what is disclosed and to meet the purposes of the Bill. . . It does not give anyone a power to demand disclosure, to override or interfere with any statutory or common law duty of confidence. . . nor does it create a data free-for-all which would have severe implications for civil liberties.[2]

---

[1] HL Report, 19 March 2998, col 937.
[2] HC SC B, 4 June 1998, col 713.

Transitory provisions[1]

6.29 Section 116 contains transitory provisions in relation to CJPOA 1994, ss 1–4, which are superseded by s 73(7)(b) of the 1998 Act. The order-making power is necessary to enable the Secretary of State to control demand for places in secure training centres, but will only be used if the demand for places exceeds the supply.[2] The transitional modifications specified in s 116(2) limit the power of courts to commit an offender who is subject to a secure training order, in the instance that a secure training centre place is not immediately available, to accommodation other than secure local authority accommodation specified in the warrant of commitment.

---

1   HC SC B, 4 June 1998, col 717.
2   See Home Office *Introductory Guide to the Crime and Disorder Act 1998.*

General interpretation[1]

6.30 Section 117 makes provision for the interpretation of certain expressions in the Act. Section 117(3) states that for the purposes of this Act, the age of a person is deemed to be the age which he or she appears to the court to be 'after considering any available evidence'.

---

1   HC SC B, 4 June 1998, col 717.

Provision for Northern Ireland

6.31 Section 118 makes provision for an Order in Council under the Northern Ireland Act 1974, Sch 1, para 1(1)(b), to enable certain sections to extend to Northern Ireland by means of a negative resolution order—
  (a) sex offender orders (ss 2–4)
  (b) abolition of the presumption that a child is *doli incapax* (s 34)
  (c) court arrangements for dealing with unrelated charges (s 47(5))
  (d) use of live court/prison TV links (s 57)
  (e) drug treatment and testing orders (ss 61–64)
  (f) interpretation of Pt IV, Ch I (s 85)

Minor and consequential amendments

6.32 Section 119 provides that the enactments mentioned in Sch 8 to the Act shall have effect, subject to the amendments there specified being minor amendments or consequential on the provisions of the Act.

Transitional provisions, savings and repeals

6.33 Section 120 provides for transitional provisions and savings specified in Sch 9, and for the repeals specified in Sch 10.

Short title, commencement and extent

6.34 Section 121 provides for the Act's short title, commencement and extent. It enables the Act to be brought into force on different days for different purposes or different areas, and sets out which provisions apply to Scotland, Northern Ireland, the Channel Islands and the Isle of Man. Subsections 121(9), (10) were added at the request of the Channel Islands and the Manx authorities and replace the death penalty for piracy with violence with a maximum penalty of life imprisonment.

SCHEDULES

6.35 The Act has ten Schedules, all of which have been mentioned in the appropriate place in the text of this guide—

Sch 1—Sch 2A to the Civic Government (Scotland) Act 1982 (see s 24(4) and para 2.55);

Sch 2—The Youth Justice Board: further provisions (see s 41(11) and para 4.13);

Sch 3—Procedure where persons are sent for trial under section 51 (see s 52(6) and para 4.37);

Sch 4—Enforcement etc of drug treatment and testing orders (see s 64(5) and para 5.16);

Sch 5—Enforcement etc of reparation and action plan orders (see s 68(3) and s 70(5), and paras 5.24 and 5.27);

Sch 6—Drug treatment and testing orders: amendment of the 1995 Act relating to a combination of orders (Pt I) and appeals (Pt II) (see s 94(2) and para 5.59);

Sch 7—Pre-consolidation amendments: powers of criminal courts (see s 106 and para 6.19);[1]

Sch 8—Minor and consequential amendments (see s 119 and para 6.32);[2]

Sch 9—Transitional provisions and savings (see s 120(1) and para 6.33);

Sch 10—Repeals (see s 120(2) and para 6.33).

---

[1] Introducing various minor amendments to Sch 7, Mr Michael made it clear that 'all the Government amendments to the schedule are simply further pre-consolidation amendments which are intended to correct minor anomalies in existing criminal justice legislation. That is intended to pave the way for a consolidation Bill in a future session that will bring together in a structured and coherent way all the existing legislation relating to the powers of the criminal court.' (HC SC B, 11 June 1998, col 862.)

[2] If anyone doubts the complexity of this legislation, they should read the six columns of amendments all added very late in proceedings. (HC Report, 23 June 1998, col 932.)

Appendix 1
Crime and Disorder Act 1998

Crime and Disorder Act 1998

(1998 c 37)

ARRANGEMENT OF SECTIONS

PART I
PREVENTION OF CRIME AND DISORDER

CHAPTER I
ENGLAND AND WALES

CHAPTER II
SCOTLAND

CHAPTER III

GREAT BRITAIN

PART II

CRIMINAL LAW

Racially-aggravated offences: England and Wales

Racially-aggravated offences: Scotland

Miscellaneous

PART III

CRIMINAL JUSTICE SYSTEM

Youth justice

Time limits etc

Functions of courts etc

Miscellaneous

PART IV
DEALING WITH OFFENDERS

CHAPTER I
ENGLAND AND WALES

CHAPTER II
SCOTLAND

An Act to make provision for preventing crime and disorder; to create certain racially-aggravated offences; to abolish the rebuttable presumption that a child is doli incapax and to make provision as to the effect of a child's failure to give evidence at his trial; to abolish the death penalty for treason and piracy; to make changes to the criminal justice system; to make further provision for dealing with offenders; to make further provision with respect to remands and committals for trial and the release and recall of prisoners; to amend Chapter I of Part II of the Crime (Sentences) Act 1997 and to repeal Chapter I of Part III of the Crime and Punishment (Scotland) Act 1997; to make amendments designed to facilitate, or otherwise desirable in connection with, the consolidation of certain enactments; and for connected purposes

[31 July 1998]

Parliamentary debates.

House of Commons:

2nd Reading 8 April 1998: 310 (Part 1) HC Official Report (6th series) col 370.

Committee Stage 28 April 1998-11 June 1998: HC Official Report SC B (Crime and Disorder Bill).

Remaining Stages 22, 23 June 1998: 314 HC Official Report (6th series) col 708.

Consideration of Lords Amendments 28 July 1998: 317 HC Official Report (6th series) col 176.

House of Lords:

2nd Reading 16 December 1997: 584 HL Official Report (5th series) col 532.

Committee Stage 3 February 1998: 585 HL Official Report (5th series) col 508; 10 February 1998: 585 HL Official Report (5th series) col 1000; 12 February 1998: 585 HL Official Report (5th series) col 1265; 24 February 1998: 586 HL Official Reports (5th series) col 548; 3 March 1998: 586 HL Official Report (5th series) col 1097.

Report Stage 17, 19 March 1998: 587 HL Official Report (5th series) col 575.

3rd Reading 31 March 1998: 588 HL Official Report (5th series) col 154.

Consideration of Commons Amendments 22 July 1998: 592 HL Official Report (5th series) col 976.

Commencement

As to the Commencement of this Act, see the Crime and Disorder Act 1998 (Commencement No 1) Order 1998, SI 1998/1883 and the Crime and Disorder Act 1998 (Commencement No 2 and Transitional Provisions) Order 1998, SI 1998/2327, as amended by SI 1998/2412.

PART I
PREVENTION OF CRIME AND DISORDER

CHAPTER I
ENGLAND AND WALES

Crime and disorder: general

1 Anti-social behaviour orders

(1)   An application for an order under this section may be made by a relevant authority if it appears to the authority that the following conditions are fulfilled with respect to any person aged 10 or over, namely—

      (a)   that the person has acted, since the commencement date, in an anti-social manner, that is to say, in a manner that caused or was likely to cause harassment, alarm or distress to one or more persons not of the same household as himself; and

(b) that such an order is necessary to protect persons in the local government area in which the harassment, alarm or distress was caused or was likely to be caused from further anti-social acts by him;

and in this section "relevant authority" means the council for the local government area or any chief officer of police any part of whose police area lies within that area.

(2) A relevant authority shall not make such an application without consulting each other relevant authority.

(3) Such an application shall be made by complaint to the magistrates' court whose commission area includes the place where it is alleged that the harassment, alarm or distress was caused or was likely to be caused.

(4) If, on such an application, it is proved that the conditions mentioned in subsection (1) above are fulfilled, the magistrates' court may make an order under this section (an "anti-social behaviour order") which prohibits the defendant from doing anything described in the order.

(5) For the purpose of determining whether the condition mentioned in subsection (1)(a) above is fulfilled, the court shall disregard any act of the defendant which he shows was reasonable in the circumstances.

(6) The prohibitions that may be imposed by an anti-social behaviour order are those necessary for the purpose of protecting from further anti-social acts by the defendant—

(a) persons in the local government area; and

(b) persons in any adjoining local government area specified in the application for the order;

and a relevant authority shall not specify an adjoining local government area in the application without consulting the council for that area and each chief officer of police any part of whose police area lies within that area.

(7) An anti-social behaviour order shall have effect for a period (not less than two years) specified in the order or until further order.

(8) Subject to subsection (9) below, the applicant or the defendant may apply by complaint to the court which made an anti-social behaviour order for it to be varied or discharged by a further order.

(9) Except with the consent of both parties, no anti-social behaviour order shall be discharged before the end of the period of two years beginning with the date of service of the order.

(10) If without reasonable excuse a person does anything which he is prohibited from doing by an anti-social behaviour order, he shall be liable—

(a) on summary conviction, to imprisonment for a term not exceeding six months or to a fine not exceeding the statutory maximum, or to both; or

(b) on conviction on indictment, to imprisonment for a term not exceeding five years or to a fine, or to both.

(11) Where a person is convicted of an offence under subsection (10) above, it shall not be open to the court by or before which he is so convicted to make an order under subsection (1)(b) (conditional discharge) of section 1A of the Powers of Criminal Courts Act 1973 ("the 1973 Act") in respect of the offence.

(12) In this section—

"the commencement date" means the date of the commencement of this section;

"local government area" means—

    (a)   in relation to England, a district or London borough, the City of London, the Isle of Wight and the Isles of Scilly;

    (b)   in relation to Wales, a county or county borough.

Definitions   For "chief officer of police" and "police area", see s 18(1); as to the City of London, see s 18(5); as to the age of a person, see s 117(3).
References   See paras 2.3–2.13.

2 Sex offender orders

(1)   If it appears to a chief officer of police that the following conditions are fulfilled with respect to any person in his police area, namely—

    (a)   that the person is a sex offender; and

    (b)   that the person has acted, since the relevant date, in such a way as to give reasonable cause to believe that an order under this section is necessary to protect the public from serious harm from him,

the chief officer may apply for an order under this section to be made in respect of the person.

(2)   Such an application shall be made by complaint to the magistrates' court whose commission area includes any place where it is alleged that the defendant acted in such a way as is mentioned in subsection (1)(b) above.

(3)   If, on such an application, it is proved that the conditions mentioned in subsection (1) above are fulfilled, the magistrates' court may make an order under this section (a "sex offender order") which prohibits the defendant from doing anything described in the order.

(4)   The prohibitions that may be imposed by a sex offender order are those necessary for the purpose of protecting the public from serious harm from the defendant.

(5)   A sex offender order shall have effect for a period (not less than five years) specified in the order or until further order; and while such an order has effect, Part I of the Sex Offenders Act 1997 shall have effect as if—

    (a)   the defendant were subject to the notification requirements of that Part; and

    (b)   in relation to the defendant, the relevant date (within the meaning of that Part) were the date of service of the order.

(6)   Subject to subsection (7) below, the applicant or the defendant may apply by complaint to the court which made a sex offender order for it to be varied or discharged by a further order.

(7)   Except with the consent of both parties, no sex offender order shall be discharged before the end of the period of five years beginning with the date of service of the order.

(8)   If without reasonable excuse a person does anything which he is prohibited from doing by a sex offender order, he shall be liable—

    (a)   on summary conviction, to imprisonment for a term not exceeding six months or to a fine not exceeding the statutory maximum, or to both; or

    (b)   on conviction on indictment, to imprisonment for a term not exceeding five years or to a fine, or to both.

(9)   Where a person is convicted of an offence under subsection (8) above, it shall not be open to the court by or before which he is so convicted to make an order

under subsection (1)(b) (conditional discharge) of section 1A of the 1973 Act in respect of the offence.

Definitions   For "sex offender", see s 3; for "the relevant date", see s 3(2)–(4); for "chief officer of police" and "police area", see s 18(1); as to protecting the public from serious harm, see, by virtue of s 18(2), the Criminal Justice Act 1991, s 31(3); for "commission area", see s 117(1).
References   See paras 2.14–2.17.

3 Sex offender orders: supplemental

(1)   In section 2 above and this section "sex offender" means a person who—
>   (a)   has been convicted of a sexual offence to which Part I of the Sex Offenders Act 1997 applies;
>   (b)   has been found not guilty of such an offence by reason of insanity, or found to be under a disability and to have done the act charged against him in respect of such an offence;
>   (c)   has been cautioned by a constable, in England and Wales or Northern Ireland, in respect of such an offence which, at the time when the caution was given, he had admitted; or
>   (d)   has been punished under the law in force in a country or territory outside the United Kingdom for an act which—
>   >   (i)   constituted an offence under that law; and
>   >   (ii)   would have constituted a sexual offence to which that Part applies if it had been done in any part of the United Kingdom.

(2)   In subsection (1) of section 2 above "the relevant date", in relation to a sex offender, means—
>   (a)   the date or, as the case may be, the latest date on which he has been convicted, found, cautioned or punished as mentioned in subsection (1) above; or
>   (b)   if later, the date of the commencement of that section.

(3)   Subsections (2) and (3) of section 6 of the Sex Offenders Act 1997 apply for the construction of references in subsections (1) and (2) above as they apply for the construction of references in Part I of that Act.

(4)   In subsections (1) and (2) above, any reference to a person having been cautioned shall be construed as including a reference to his having been reprimanded or warned (under section 65 below) as a child or young person.

(5)   An act punishable under the law in force in any country or territory outside the United Kingdom constitutes an offence under that law for the purposes of subsection (1) above, however it is described in that law.

(6)   Subject to subsection (7) below, the condition in subsection (1)(d)(i) above shall be taken to be satisfied unless, not later than rules of court may provide, the defendant serves on the applicant a notice—
>   (a)   stating that, on the facts as alleged with respect to the act in question, the condition is not in his opinion satisfied;
>   (b)   showing his grounds for that opinion; and
>   (c)   requiring the applicant to show that it is satisfied.

(7)   The court, if it thinks fit, may permit the defendant to require the applicant to show that the condition is satisfied without the prior service of a notice under subsection (6) above.

Definitions   By virtue of sub-s (3) above, for "convicted", see the Sex Offenders Act 1997, s 6(2); for "child" and "young person", see s 117(1), (3).
References   See para 2.14.

4 Appeals against orders

(1)   An appeal shall lie to the Crown Court against the making by a magistrates' court of an anti-social behaviour order or sex offender order.

(2)   On such an appeal the Crown Court—
  (a)   may make such orders as may be necessary to give effect to its determination of the appeal; and
  (b)   may also make such incidental or consequential orders as appear to it to be just.

(3)   Any order of the Crown Court made on an appeal under this section (other than one directing that an application be re-heard by a magistrates' court) shall, for the purposes of section 1(8) or 2(6) above, be treated as if it were an order of the magistrates' court from which the appeal was brought and not an order of the Crown Court.

Definitions   For "anti-social behaviour order", see s 1(4); for "sex offender order", see s 2(3).
References   See para 2.18.

Crime and disorder strategies

5 Authorities responsible for strategies

(1)   Subject to the provisions of this section, the functions conferred by section 6 below shall be exercisable in relation to each local government area by the responsible authorities, that is to say—
  (a)   the council for the area and, where the area is a district and the council is not a unitary authority, the council for the county which includes the district; and
  (b)   every chief officer of police any part of whose police area lies within the area.

(2)   In exercising those functions, the responsible authorities shall act in co-operation with the following persons and bodies, namely—
  (a)   every police authority any part of whose police area lies within the area;
  (b)   every probation committee or health authority any part of whose area lies within the area; and
  (c)   every person or body of a description which is for the time being prescribed by order of the Secretary of State under this subsection;
and it shall be the duty of those persons and bodies to co-operate in the exercise by the responsible authorities of those functions.

(3)   The responsible authorities shall also invite the participation in their exercise of those functions of at least one person or body of each description which is for the time being prescribed by order of the Secretary of State under this subsection.

(4)   In this section and sections 6 and 7 below "local government area" means—
  (a)   in relation to England, each district or London borough, the City of London, the Isle of Wight and the Isles of Scilly;
  (b)   in relation to Wales, each county or county borough.

Definitions   For "chief officer of police", "police area" and "police authority", see s 18(1); as to the City of London, see s 18(5); for "prescribed", see s 117(1).
References   See paras 2.19–2.21.

6 Formulation and implementation of strategies

(1)   The responsible authorities for a local government area shall, in accordance with the provisions of section 5 above and this section, formulate and implement, for each relevant period, a strategy for the reduction of crime and disorder in the area.

(2)   Before formulating a strategy, the responsible authorities shall—

    (a)   carry out a review of the levels and patterns of crime and disorder in the area (taking due account of the knowledge and experience of persons in the area);

    (b)   prepare an analysis of the results of that review;

    (c)   publish in the area a report of that analysis; and

    (d)   obtain the views on that report of persons or bodies in the area (including those of a description prescribed by order under section 5(3) above), whether by holding public meetings or otherwise.

(3)   In formulating a strategy, the responsible authorities shall have regard to the analysis prepared under subsection (2)(b) above and the views obtained under subsection (2)(d) above.

(4)   A strategy shall include—

    (a)   objectives to be pursued by the responsible authorities, by co-operating persons or bodies or, under agreements with the responsible authorities, by other persons or bodies; and

    (b)   long-term and short-term performance targets for measuring the extent to which such objectives are achieved.

(5)   After formulating a strategy, the responsible authorities shall publish in the area a document which includes details of—

    (a)   co-operating persons and bodies;

    (b)   the review carried out under subsection (2)(a) above;

    (c)   the report published under subsection (2)(c) above; and

    (d)   the strategy, including in particular—

        (i)   the objectives mentioned in subsection (4)(a) above and, in each case, the authorities, persons or bodies by whom they are to be pursued; and

        (ii)   the performance targets mentioned in subsection (4)(b) above.

(6)   While implementing a strategy, the responsible authorities shall keep it under review with a view to monitoring its effectiveness and making any changes to it that appear necessary or expedient.

(7)   In this section—

    "co-operating persons or bodies" means persons or bodies co-operating in the exercise of the responsible authorities' functions under this section;

    "relevant period" means—

    (a)   the period of three years beginning with such day as the Secretary of State may by order appoint; and

    (b)   each subsequent period of three years.

Definitions   For "the responsible authorities", see s 5(1); for "local government area", see s 5(4).
References   See paras 2.19, 2.22–2.24.

---

7 Supplemental

(1)   The responsible authorities for a local government area shall, whenever so required by the Secretary of State, submit to the Secretary of State a report on such matters connected with the exercise of their functions under section 6 above as may be specified in the requirement.

(2)   A requirement under subsection (1) above may specify the form in which a report is to be given.

(3)   The Secretary of State may arrange, or require the responsible authorities to arrange, for a report under subsection (1) above to be published in such manner as appears to him to be appropriate.

Definitions   For "the responsible authorities", see s 5(1); for "local government area", see s 5(4).
References   See para 2.24.

Youth crime and disorder

8 Parenting orders

(1)   This section applies where, in any court proceedings—
    (a)   a child safety order is made in respect of a child;
    (b)   an anti-social behaviour order or sex offender order is made in respect of a child or young person;
    (c)   a child or young person is convicted of an offence; or
    (d)   a person is convicted of an offence under section 443 (failure to comply with school attendance order) or section 444 (failure to secure regular attendance at school of registered pupil) of the Education Act 1996.

(2)   Subject to subsection (3) and section 9(1) below, if in the proceedings the court is satisfied that the relevant condition is fulfilled, it may make a parenting order in respect of a person who is a parent or guardian of the child or young person or, as the case may be, the person convicted of the offence under section 443 or 444 ("the parent").

(3)   A court shall not make a parenting order unless it has been notified by the Secretary of State that arrangements for implementing such orders are available in the area in which it appears to the court that the parent resides or will reside and the notice has not been withdrawn.

(4)   A parenting order is an order which requires the parent—
    (a)   to comply, for a period not exceeding twelve months, with such requirements as are specified in the order; and
    (b)   subject to subsection (5) below, to attend, for a concurrent period not exceeding three months and not more than once in any week, such counselling or guidance sessions as may be specified in directions given by the responsible officer;
and in this subsection "week" means a period of seven days beginning with a Sunday.

(5)   A parenting order may, but need not, include such a requirement as is mentioned in subsection (4)(b) above in any case where such an order has been made in respect of the parent on a previous occasion.

(6)   The relevant condition is that the parenting order would be desirable in the interests of preventing—
    (a)   in a case falling within paragraph (a) or (b) of subsection (1) above, any repetition of the kind of behaviour which led to the child safety order, anti-social behaviour order or sex offender order being made;
    (b)   in a case falling within paragraph (c) of that subsection, the commission of any further offence by the child or young person;
    (c)   in a case falling within paragraph (d) of that subsection, the commission of any further offence under section 443 or 444 of the Education Act 1996.

(7)   The requirements that may be specified under subsection (4)(a) above are those which the court considers desirable in the interests of preventing any such repetition or, as the case may be, the commission of any such further offence.

(8)   In this section and section 9 below "responsible officer", in relation to a parenting order, means one of the following who is specified in the order, namely—

    (a)   a probation officer;

    (b)   a social worker of a local authority social services department; and

    (c)   a member of a youth offending team.

Definitions   For "anti-social behaviour order", see s 1(4) of this Act; for "sex offender order", see s 2(3) of this Act; for "child safety order", see s 11(1); for "youth offending team", see s 117(1); for "child" and "young person", see s 117(1), (3).
References   See paras 2.27, 2.28.

9 Parenting orders: supplemental

(1)   Where a person under the age of 16 is convicted of an offence, the court by or before which he is so convicted—

    (a)   if it is satisfied that the relevant condition is fulfilled, shall make a parenting order; and

    (b)   if it is not so satisfied, shall state in open court that it is not and why it is not.

(2)   Before making a parenting order—

    (a)   in a case falling within paragraph (a) of subsection (1) of section 8 above;

    (b)   in a case falling within paragraph (b) or (c) of that subsection, where the person concerned is under the age of 16; or

    (c)   in a case falling within paragraph (d) of that subsection, where the person to whom the offence related is under that age,

a court shall obtain and consider information about the person's family circumstances and the likely effect of the order on those circumstances.

(3)   Before making a parenting order, a court shall explain to the parent in ordinary language—

    (a)   the effect of the order and of the requirements proposed to be included in it;

    (b) the consequences which may follow (under subsection (7) below) if he fails to comply with any of those requirements; and

    (c)   that the court has power (under subsection (5) below) to review the order on the application either of the parent or of the responsible officer.

(4)   Requirements specified in, and directions given under, a parenting order shall, as far as practicable, be such as to avoid—

    (a)   any conflict with the parent's religious beliefs; and

    (b)   any interference with the times, if any, at which he normally works or attends an educational establishment.

(5)   If while a parenting order is in force it appears to the court which made it, on the application of the responsible officer or the parent, that it is appropriate to make an order under this subsection, the court may make an order discharging the parenting order or varying it—

    (a)   by cancelling any provision included in it; or

    (b)   by inserting in it (either in addition to or in substitution for any of its provisions) any provision that could have been included in the order if the court had then had power to make it and were exercising the power.

(6)   Where an application under subsection (5) above for the discharge of a parenting order is dismissed, no further application for its discharge shall be made

under that subsection by any person except with the consent of the court which made the order.

(7)   If while a parenting order is in force the parent without reasonable excuse fails to comply with any requirement included in the order, or specified in directions given by the responsible officer, he shall be liable on summary conviction to a fine not exceeding level 3 on the standard scale.

Definitions   For "the parent", see s 8(2); for "parenting order", see s 8(4); for "the relevant condition", see s 8(6); for "responsible officer", see s 8(8).
References   See paras 2.29–2.31.

10 Appeals against parenting orders

(1)   An appeal shall lie—
  (a)   to the High Court against the making of a parenting order by virtue of paragraph (a) of subsection (1) of section 8 above; and
  (b)   to the Crown Court against the making of a parenting order by virtue of paragraph (b) of that subsection.

(2)   On an appeal under subsection (1) above the High Court or the Crown Court—
  (a)   may make such orders as may be necessary to give effect to its determination of the appeal; and
  (b)   may also make such incidental or consequential orders as appear to it to be just.

(3)   Any order of the High Court or the Crown Court made on an appeal under subsection (1) above (other than one directing that an application be re-heard by a magistrates' court) shall, for the purposes of subsections (5) to (7) of section 9 above, be treated as if it were an order of the court from which the appeal was brought and not an order of the High Court or the Crown Court.

(4)   A person in respect of whom a parenting order is made by virtue of section 8(1)(c) above shall have the same right of appeal against the making of the order as if—
  (a)   the offence that led to the making of the order were an offence committed by him; and
  (b)   the order were a sentence passed on him for the offence.

(5)   A person in respect of whom a parenting order is made by virtue of section 8(1)(d) above shall have the same right of appeal against the making of the order as if the order were a sentence passed on him for the offence that led to the making of the order.

(6)   The Lord Chancellor may by order make provision as to the circumstances in which appeals under subsection (1)(a) above may be made against decisions taken by courts on questions arising in connection with the transfer, or proposed transfer, of proceedings by virtue of any order under paragraph 2 of Schedule 11 (jurisdiction) to the Children Act 1989 ("the 1989 Act").

(7)   Except to the extent provided for in any order made under subsection (6) above, no appeal may be made against any decision of a kind mentioned in that subsection.

Definitions   For "parenting order", see s 8(4).
References   See para 2.32.

11 Child safety orders

(1)   Subject to subsection (2) below, if a magistrates' court, on the application of a local authority, is satisfied that one or more of the conditions specified in subsection (3) below are fulfilled with respect to a child under the age of 10, it may make an order (a "child safety order") which—

(a)   places the child, for a period (not exceeding the permitted maximum) specified in the order, under the supervision of the responsible officer; and

(b)   requires the child to comply with such requirements as are so specified.

(2)   A court shall not make a child safety order unless it has been notified by the Secretary of State that arrangements for implementing such orders are available in the area in which it appears that the child resides or will reside and the notice has not been withdrawn.

(3)   The conditions are—

(a)   that the child has committed an act which, if he had been aged 10 or over, would have constituted an offence;

(b)   that a child safety order is necessary for the purpose of preventing the commission by the child of such an act as is mentioned in paragraph (a) above;

(c)   that the child has contravened a ban imposed by a curfew notice; and

(d)   that the child has acted in a manner that caused or was likely to cause harassment, alarm or distress to one or more persons not of the same household as himself.

(4)   The maximum period permitted for the purposes of subsection (1)(a) above is three months or, where the court is satisfied that the circumstances of the case are exceptional, 12 months.

(5)   The requirements that may be specified under subsection (1)(b) above are those which the court considers desirable in the interests of—

(a)   securing that the child receives appropriate care, protection and support and is subject to proper control; or

(b)   preventing any repetition of the kind of behaviour which led to the child safety order being made.

(6)   Proceedings under this section or section 12 below shall be family proceedings for the purposes of the 1989 Act or section 65 of the Magistrates' Courts Act 1980 ("the 1980 Act"); and the standard of proof applicable to such proceedings shall be that applicable to civil proceedings.

(7)   In this section "local authority" has the same meaning as in the 1989 Act.

(8)   In this section and section 12 below, "responsible officer", in relation to a child safety order, means one of the following who is specified in the order, namely—

(a)   a social worker of a local authority social services department; and

(b)   a member of a youth offending team.

Definitions   For "curfew notice", see s 14(6); for "the 1980 Act", "the 1989 Act" and "youth offending team", see s 117(1); for "child", see s 117(1), (3).
References   See paras 2.34–2.36.

---

12 Child safety orders: supplemental

(1)   Before making a child safety order, a magistrates' court shall obtain and consider information about the child's family circumstances and the likely effect of the order on those circumstances.

(2)   Before making a child safety order, a magistrates' court shall explain to the parent or guardian of the child in ordinary language—

(a)   the effect of the order and of the requirements proposed to be included in it;

(b)   the consequences which may follow (under subsection (6) below) if the child fails to comply with any of those requirements; and

(c)   that the court has power (under subsection (4) below) to review the order on the application either of the parent or guardian or of the responsible officer.

(3)   Requirements included in a child safety order shall, as far as practicable, be such as to avoid—

(a)   any conflict with the parent's religious beliefs; and

(b)   any interference with the times, if any, at which the child normally attends school.

(4)   If while a child safety order is in force in respect of a child it appears to the court which made it, on the application of the responsible officer or a parent or guardian of the child, that it is appropriate to make an order under this subsection, the court may make an order discharging the child safety order or varying it—

(a)   by cancelling any provision included in it; or

(b)   by inserting in it (either in addition to or in substitution for any of its provisions) any provision that could have been included in the order if the court had then had power to make it and were exercising the power.

(5)   Where an application under subsection (4) above for the discharge of a child safety order is dismissed, no further application for its discharge shall be made under that subsection by any person except with the consent of the court which made the order.

(6)   Where a child safety order is in force and it is proved to the satisfaction of the court which made it or another magistrates' court acting for the same petty sessions area, on the application of the responsible officer, that the child has failed to comply with any requirement included in the order, the court—

(a)   may discharge the order and make in respect of him a care order under subsection (1)(a) of section 31 of the 1989 Act; or

(b)   may make an order varying the order—

(i)   by cancelling any provision included in it; or

(ii)   by inserting in it (either in addition to or in substitution for any of its provisions) any provision that could have been included in the order if the court had then had power to make it and were exercising the power.

(7)   Subsection (6)(a) above applies whether or not the court is satisfied that the conditions mentioned in section 31(2) of the 1989 Act are fulfilled.

Definitions   For "the parent", see s 8(2); for "child safety order", see s 11(1); for "responsible officer", see s 11(8); for "the 1989 Act" and "guardian", see s 117(1); for "child", see s 117(1), (3).
References   See para 2.37.

---

13 Appeals against child safety orders

(1)   An appeal shall lie to the High Court against the making by a magistrates' court of a child safety order; and on such an appeal the High Court—

(a)   may make such orders as may be necessary to give effect to its determination of the appeal; and

(b)   may also make such incidental or consequential orders as appear to it to be just.

(2) Any order of the High Court made on an appeal under this section (other than one directing that an application be re-heard by a magistrates' court) shall, for the purposes of subsections (4) to (6) of section 12 above, be treated as if it were an order of the magistrates' court from which the appeal was brought and not an order of the High Court.

(3) Subsections (6) and (7) of section 10 above shall apply for the purposes of subsection (1) above as they apply for the purposes of subsection (1)(a) of that section.

Definitions For "child safety order", see s 11(1).
References See para 2.38.

---

14 Local child curfew schemes

(1) A local authority may make a scheme (a "local child curfew scheme") for enabling the authority—
    (a) subject to and in accordance with the provisions of the scheme; and
    (b) if, after such consultation as is required by the scheme, the authority considers it necessary to do so for the purpose of maintaining order,

to give a notice imposing, for a specified period (not exceeding 90 days), a ban to which subsection (2) below applies.

(2) This subsection applies to a ban on children of specified ages (under 10) being in a public place within a specified area—
    (a) during specified hours (between 9 pm and 6 am); and
    (b) otherwise than under the effective control of a parent or a responsible person aged 18 or over.

(3) Before making a local child curfew scheme, a local authority shall consult—
    (a) every chief officer of police any part of whose police area lies within its area; and
    (b) such other persons or bodies as it considers appropriate.

(4) A local child curfew scheme shall be made under the common seal of the local authority and shall not have effect until it is confirmed by the Secretary of State.

(5) The Secretary of State—
    (a) may confirm, or refuse to confirm, a local child curfew scheme submitted under this section for confirmation; and
    (b) may fix the date on which such a scheme is to come into operation;

and if no date is so fixed, the scheme shall come into operation at the end of the period of one month beginning with the date of its confirmation.

(6) A notice given under a local child curfew scheme (a "curfew notice") may specify different hours in relation to children of different ages.

(7) A curfew notice shall be given—
    (a) by posting the notice in some conspicuous place or places within the specified area; and
    (b) in such other manner, if any, as appears to the local authority to be desirable for giving publicity to the notice.

(8) In this section—
    "local authority" means—
        (a) in relation to England, the council of a district or London borough, the Common Council of the City of London, the Council of the Isle of Wight and the Council of the Isles of Scilly;
        (b) in relation to Wales, the council of a county or county borough;

"public place" has the same meaning as in Part II of the Public Order Act 1986.

Definitions For "chief officer of police" and "police area", see s 117(1).
References See paras 2.39–2.41.

15 Contravention of curfew notices

(1)   Subsections (2) and (3) below apply where a constable has reasonable cause to believe that a child is in contravention of a ban imposed by a curfew notice.

(2)   The constable shall, as soon as practicable, inform the local authority for the area that the child has contravened the ban.

(3)   The constable may remove the child to the child's place of residence unless he has reasonable cause to believe that the child would, if removed to that place, be likely to suffer significant harm.

(4)   In subsection (1) of section 47 of the 1989 Act (local authority's duty to investigate)—

(a)   in paragraph (a), after sub-paragraph (ii) there shall be inserted the following sub-paragraph—

"(iii)   has contravened a ban imposed by a curfew notice within the meaning of Chapter I of Part I of the Crime and Disorder Act 1998; or"; and

(b)   at the end there shall be inserted the following paragraph—

"In the case of a child falling within paragraph (a)(iii) above, the enquiries shall be commenced as soon as practicable and, in any event, within 48 hours of the authority receiving the information."

Definitions In sub-ss (1)–(3) above, for "curfew notice", see s 14(6); for "the 1989 Act", see s 117(1); for "child", see s 117(1), (3). In the Children Act 1989, for "child", see s 105(1) thereof.
References See para 2.42.

16 Removal of truants to designated premises etc

(1)   This section applies where a local authority—

(a)   designates premises in a police area ("designated premises") as premises to which children and young persons of compulsory school age may be removed under this section; and

(b)   notifies the chief officer of police for that area of the designation.

(2)   A police officer of or above the rank of superintendent may direct that the powers conferred on a constable by subsection (3) below—

(a)   shall be exercisable as respects any area falling within the police area and specified in the direction; and

(b)   shall be so exercisable during a period so specified;

and references in that subsection to a specified area and a specified period shall be construed accordingly.

(3)   If a constable has reasonable cause to believe that a child or young person found by him in a public place in a specified area during a specified period—

(a)   is of compulsory school age; and

(b)   is absent from a school without lawful authority,

the constable may remove the child or young person to designated premises, or to the school from which he is so absent.

(4)   A child's or young person's absence from a school shall be taken to be without lawful authority unless it falls within subsection (3) (leave, sickness, unavoidable cause or day set apart for religious observance) of section 444 of the Education Act 1996.

(5)   In this section—
   "local authority" means—
   (a)   in relation to England, a county council, a district council whose district does not form part of an area that has a county council, a London borough council or the Common Council of the City of London;
   (b)   in relation to Wales, a county council or a county borough council;
   "public place" has the same meaning as in section 14 above;
   "school" has the same meaning as in the Education Act 1996.

Definitions   For "chief officer of police" and "police area", see s 18(1); for "child" and "young person", see s 117(1), (3).
References   See paras 2.43, 2.44.

Miscellaneous and supplemental

17 Duty to consider crime and disorder implications

(1)   Without prejudice to any other obligation imposed on it, it shall be the duty of each authority to which this section applies to exercise its various functions with due regard to the likely effect of the exercise of those functions on, and the need to do all that it reasonably can to prevent, crime and disorder in its area.

(2)   This section applies to a local authority, a joint authority, a police authority, a National Park authority and the Broads Authority.

(3)   In this section—
   "local authority" means a local authority within the meaning given by section 270(1) of the Local Government Act 1972 or the Common Council of the City of London;
   "joint authority" has the same meaning as in the Local Government Act 1985;
   "National Park authority" means an authority established under section 63 of the Environment Act 1995.

Definitions   For "police authority" see s 117(1).
References   See para 2.45.

18 Interpretation etc of Chapter I

(1)   In this Chapter—
   "anti-social behaviour order" has the meaning given by section 1(4) above;
   "chief officer of police" has the meaning given by section 101(1) of the Police Act 1996;
   "child safety order" has the meaning given by section 11(1) above;
   "curfew notice" has the meaning given by section 14(6) above;
   "local child curfew scheme" has the meaning given by section 14(1) above;
   "parenting order" has the meaning given by section 8(4) above;
   "police area" has the meaning given by section 1(2) of the Police Act 1996;
   "police authority" has the meaning given by section 101(1) of that Act;
   "responsible officer"—
   (a)   in relation to a parenting order, has the meaning given by section 8(8) above;

(b)   in relation to a child safety order, has the meaning given by section 11(8) above;

"sex offender order" has the meaning given by section 2(3) above.

(2)   In this Chapter, unless the contrary intention appears, expressions which are also used in Part I of the Criminal Justice Act 1991 ("the 1991 Act") have the same meanings as in that Part.

(3)   Where directions under a parenting order are to be given by a probation officer, the probation officer shall be an officer appointed for or assigned to the petty sessions area within which it appears to the court that the child or, as the case may be, the parent resides or will reside.

(4)   Where the supervision under a child safety order is to be provided, or directions under a parenting order are to be given, by—

(a)   a social worker of a local authority social services department; or

(b)   a member of a youth offending team,

the social worker or member shall be a social worker of, or a member of a youth offending team established by, the local authority within whose area it appears to the court that the child or, as the case may be, the parent resides or will reside.

(5)   For the purposes of this Chapter the Inner Temple and the Middle Temple form part of the City of London.

Definitions   For "youth offending team", see s 117(1); for "child", see s 117(1), (3).
References   See para 2.46.

CHAPTER II
SCOTLAND

19 Anti-social behaviour orders

(1)   A local authority may make an application for an order under this section if it appears to the authority that the following conditions are fulfilled with respect to any person of or over the age of 16, namely—

(a)   that the person has—

(i)   acted in an anti-social manner, that is to say, in a manner that caused or was likely to cause alarm or distress; or

(ii)   pursued a course of anti-social conduct, that is to say, pursued a course of conduct that caused or was likely to cause alarm or distress,

to one or more persons not of the same household as himself in the authority's area (and in this section "anti-social acts" and "anti-social conduct" shall be construed accordingly); and

(b)   that such an order is necessary to protect persons in the authority's area from further anti-social acts or conduct by him.

(2)   An application under subsection (1) above shall be made by summary application to the sheriff within whose sheriffdom the alarm or distress was alleged to have been caused or to have been likely to be caused.

(3)   On an application under subsection (1) above, the sheriff may, if he is satisfied that the conditions mentioned in that subsection are fulfilled, make an order under this section (an "anti-social behaviour order") which, for the purpose of protecting persons in the area of the local authority from further anti-social acts or conduct by the person against whom the order is sought, prohibits him from doing anything described in the order.

(4)   For the purpose of determining whether the condition mentioned in subsection (1)(a) is fulfilled, the sheriff shall disregard any act of the person in respect of whom the application is made which that person shows was reasonable in the circumstances.

(5)   This section does not apply in relation to anything done before the commencement of this section.

(6)   Nothing in this section shall prevent a local authority from instituting any legal proceedings otherwise than under this section against any person in relation to any anti-social act or conduct.

(7)   In this section "conduct" includes speech and a course of conduct must involve conduct on at least two occasions.

(8)   In this section and section 21 below "local authority" means a council constituted under section 2 of the Local Government etc (Scotland) Act 1994 and any reference to the area of such an authority is a reference to the local government area within the meaning of that Act for which it is so constituted.

Definitions   As to the age of a person, see s 117(3).
References   See paras 2.47–2.50.

---

20 Sex offender orders

(1)   An application for an order under this section may be made by a chief constable if it appears to him that the conditions mentioned in subsection (2) below are fulfilled with respect to any person in the area of his police force.

(2)   The conditions are—
    (a)   that the person in respect of whom the application for the order is made is—
        (i)   of or over the age of 16 years; and
        (ii)   a sex offender; and
    (b)   that the person has acted, since the relevant date, in such a way as to give reasonable cause to believe that an order under this section is necessary to protect the public from serious harm from him.

(3)   An application under subsection (1) above shall be made by summary application to the sheriff within whose sheriffdom the person is alleged to have acted as mentioned in subsection (2)(b) above.

(4)   On an application under subsection (1) above the sheriff may—
    (a)   pending the determination of the application, make any such interim order as he considers appropriate; and
    (b)   if he is satisfied that the conditions mentioned in subsection (2) above are fulfilled, make an order under this section ("a sex offender order") which prohibits the person in respect of whom it is made from doing anything described in the order.

(5)   The prohibitions that may be imposed by an order made under subsection (4) above are those necessary for the purpose of protecting the public from serious harm from the person in respect of whom the order is made.

(6)   While a sex offender order has effect, Part I of the Sex Offenders Act 1997 shall have effect as if—
    (a)   the person in respect of whom the order has been obtained were subject to the notification requirements of that Part; and
    (b)   in relation to that person, the relevant date (within the meaning of that Part) were the date on which the copy of the order was given or

delivered to that person in accordance with subsections (8) and (9) of section 21 below.

(7)   Section 3 above applies for the purposes of this section as it applies for the purposes of section 2 above with the following modifications—

(a)   any reference in that section to the defendant shall be construed as a reference to the person in respect of whom the order is sought; and

(b)   in subsection (2) of that section, the reference to subsection (1) of the said section 2 shall be construed as a reference to subsection (2)(b) of this section.

(8)   A constable may arrest without warrant a person whom he reasonably suspects of doing, or having done, anything prohibited by an order under subsection (4)(a) above or a sex offender order.

Definitions   As to the age of a person, see s 117(3).
References   See para 2.51.

21 Procedural provisions with respect to orders

(1)   Before making an application under—

(a)   section 19(1) above;

(b)   subsection (7)(b)(i) below,

the local authority shall consult the relevant chief constable.

(2)   Before making an application under section 20(1) above or subsection (7)(b)(i) below, the chief constable shall consult the local authority within whose area the person in respect of whom the order is sought is for the time being.

(3)   In subsection (1) above "relevant chief constable" means the chief constable of the police force maintained under the Police (Scotland) Act 1967 the area of which includes the area of the local authority making the application.

(4) ⋅ A failure to comply with subsection (1) or (2) above shall not affect the validity of an order made on any application to which either of those subsections applies.

(5)   A record of evidence shall be kept on any summary application under section 19 or 20 above or subsection (7)(b) below.

(6)   Subsections (7) to (9) below apply to anti-social behaviour orders and sex offender orders and subsections (8) and (9) below apply to an order made under section 20(4)(a) above.

(7)   An order to which this subsection applies—

(a)   shall have effect for a period specified in the order or indefinitely; and

(b)   may at any time be varied or revoked on a summary application by—

(i)   the local authority or, as the case may be, chief constable who obtained the order; or

(ii)   the person subject to the order.

(8)   The clerk of the court by which an order to which this subsection applies is made or varied shall cause a copy of the order as so made or varied to be—

(a)   given to the person named in the order; or

(b)   sent to the person so named by registered post or by the recorded delivery service.

(9)   An acknowledgement or certificate of delivery of a letter sent under subsection (8)(b) above issued by the Post Office shall be sufficient evidence of the delivery of the letter on the day specified in such acknowledgement or certificate.

(10)   Where an appeal is lodged against the determination of an application under section 19 or 20 above or subsection (7)(b) above, any order made on the application shall, without prejudice to the determination of an application under subsection (7)(b) above made after the lodging of the appeal, continue to have effect pending the disposal of the appeal.

Definitions   For "anti-social behaviour order", see s 19(3); for "sex offender order", see s 20(4)(b).
References   See para 2.52.

22   Offences in connection with breach of orders

(1)   Subject to subsection (3) below, if without reasonable excuse a person breaches an anti-social behaviour order by doing anything which he is prohibited from doing by the order, he shall be guilty of an offence and shall be liable—

    (a)   on summary conviction, to a term of imprisonment not exceeding six months or to a fine not exceeding the statutory maximum or to both; or

    (b)   on conviction on indictment, to imprisonment for a term not exceeding five years or to a fine or to both.

(2)   Subsection (3) applies where—

    (a)   the breach of the anti-social behaviour order referred to in subsection (1) above consists in the accused having acted in a manner prohibited by the order which constitutes a separate offence (in this section referred to as the "separate offence"); and

    (b)   the accused has been charged with that separate offence.

(3)   Where this subsection applies, the accused shall not be liable to be proceeded against for an offence under subsection (1) above but, subject to subsection (4) below, the court which sentences him for that separate offence shall, in determining the appropriate sentence or disposal for that offence, have regard to—

    (a)   the fact that the offence was committed by him while subject to an anti-social behaviour order;

    (b)   the number of such orders to which he was subject at the time of the commission of the offence;

    (c)   any previous conviction of the accused of an offence under subsection (1) above; and

    (d)   the extent to which the sentence or disposal in respect of any such previous conviction of the accused differed, by virtue of this subsection, from that which the court would have imposed but for this subsection.

(4)   The court shall not, under subsection (3) above, have regard to the fact that the separate offence was committed while the accused was subject to an anti-social behaviour order unless that fact is libelled in the indictment or, as the case may be, specified in the complaint.

(5)   The fact that the separate offence was committed while the accused was subject to an anti-social behaviour order shall, unless challenged—

    (a)   in the case of proceedings on indictment, by giving notice of a preliminary objection under paragraph (b) of section 72 of the Criminal Procedure (Scotland) Act 1995 ("the 1995 Act") or under that paragraph as applied by section 71(2) of that Act; or

    (b)   in summary proceedings, by preliminary objection before his plea is recorded,

be held as admitted.

(6)   Subject to subsection (7) below, subsections (1) to (5) above apply in relation to an order under section 20(4)(a) above and to a sex offender order as they apply in relation to an anti-social behaviour order.

(7)   Subsection (2) above as applied for the purposes of subsection (6) above shall have effect with the substitution of the words "at the time at which he committed" for the words "which constitutes".

Definitions   For "anti-social behaviour order", see s 19(3); for "sex offender order", see s 20(4)(b).
References   See para 2.53.

---

23 Anti-social behaviour as ground of eviction

(1)   Schedule 3 to the Housing (Scotland) Act 1987 (grounds of eviction in relation to secure tenancies) shall be amended in accordance with subsections (2) and (3) below.

(2)   For paragraph 2 there shall be substituted the following paragraph—

"2.—(1) The tenant, a person residing or lodging in the house with the tenant or a person visiting the house has been convicted of—
    (a)   using or allowing the house to be used for immoral or illegal purposes; or
    (b)   an offence punishable by imprisonment committed in, or in the locality of, the house.

    (2)   In sub-paragraph (1) above "tenant" includes any one of joint tenants and any sub-tenant."

(3)   For paragraph 7 there shall be substituted the following paragraph—

"7.—(1) The tenant, a person residing or lodging in the house with the tenant or a person visiting the house has—
    (a)   acted in an anti-social manner in relation to a person residing, visiting or otherwise engaging in lawful activity in the locality; or
    (b)   pursued a course of anti-social conduct in relation to such a person as is mentioned in head (a) above,

and it is not reasonable in all the circumstances that the landlord should be required to make other accommodation available to him.

    (2)   In sub-paragraph (1) above—
    "anti-social", in relation to an action or course of conduct, means causing or likely to cause alarm, distress, nuisance or annoyance;
    "conduct" includes speech and a course of conduct must involve conduct on at least two occasions; and
    "tenant" includes any one of joint tenants and any sub-tenant."

(4)   For Ground 15 in Schedule 5 to the Housing (Scotland) Act 1988 (eviction on ground of use of premises for immoral or illegal purposes etc) there shall be substituted the following—

"Ground 15

The tenant, a person residing or lodging in the house with the tenant or a person visiting the house has—
    (a)   been convicted of—
        (i)   using or allowing the house to be used for immoral or illegal purposes; or
        (ii)   an offence punishable by imprisonment committed in, or in the locality of, the house; or
    (b)   acted in an anti-social manner in relation to a person residing, visiting or otherwise engaging in lawful activity in the locality; or
    (c)   pursued a course of anti-social conduct in relation to such a person as is mentioned in head (b) above.

In this Ground "anti-social", in relation to an action or course of conduct, means causing or likely to cause alarm, distress, nuisance or annoyance, "conduct" includes speech and a course of conduct must involve conduct on at least two occasions and "tenant" includes any one of joint tenants."

(5) No person shall be liable to eviction under paragraph 2 or 7 of Schedule 3 to the Housing (Scotland) Act 1987 or Ground 15 in Schedule 5 to the Housing (Scotland) Act 1988 as substituted respectively by subsection (2), (3) and (4) above in respect of any act or conduct before the commencement of this section unless he would have been liable to be evicted under those paragraphs or, as the case may be, that Ground as they had effect before that substitution.

Definitions   In the Housing (Scotland) Act 1987, Sch 3, for "landlord" and "tenant", see s 82 of that Act (and note also as to "tenant", paras 2(2), 7(2) of that Schedule, as substituted by sub-ss (1)–(3) above); in the Housing (Scotland) Act 1988, Sch 5, for "house", see s 55(1) of that Act, and for "tenant", see s 55(1), (3) thereof (and note Ground 15 of Sch 5, as inserted by sub-s (4) above).
References   See para 2.54.

24 Noise-making equipment: police power of seizure

(1) The Civic Government (Scotland) Act 1982 shall be amended in accordance with this section.

(2) In section 54 (offence of playing instruments, etc), after subsection (2) there shall be inserted the following subsections—

"(2A) Where a constable reasonably suspects that an offence under subsection (1) above has been committed in relation to a musical instrument or in relation to such a device as is mentioned in paragraph (c) of that subsection, he may enter any premises on which he reasonably suspects that instrument or device to be and seize any such instrument or device he finds there.

(2B) A constable may use reasonable force in the exercise of the power conferred by subsection (2A) above.

(2C) Schedule 2A to this Act (which makes provision in relation to the retention and disposal of property seized under subsection (2A) above) shall have effect."

(3) In section 60 (powers of search and seizure)—
    (a) in subsection (5)—
        (i) after the words "Nothing in" there shall be inserted the words "section 54(2A) of this Act or"; and
        (ii) for the words from "which" to the end there shall be substituted the words "which is otherwise exercisable by a constable"; and
    (b) in subsection (6)—
        (i) in paragraph (a), for the words from "in pursuance" to the word "vessel" there shall be substituted the words—

"to enter and search—
        (i) any premises in pursuance of section 54(2A) of this Act or of subsection (1) above; or
        (ii) any vehicle or vessel in pursuance of the said subsection (1),"; and

        (ii) in paragraph (c), after "under" there shall be inserted the words "section 54(2A) of this Act or".

(4) After Schedule 2 there shall be inserted the Schedule set out in Schedule 1 to this Act.

References   See para 2.55.

CHAPTER III
GREAT BRITAIN

25 Powers to require removal of masks etc

(1)   After subsection (4) of section 60 (powers to stop and search in anticipation of violence) of the Criminal Justice and Public Order Act 1994 ("the 1994 Act") there shall be inserted the following subsection—

"(4A) This section also confers on any constable in uniform power—
>   (a)   to require any person to remove any item which the constable reasonably believes that person is wearing wholly or mainly for the purpose of concealing his identity;
>   (b)   to seize any item which the constable reasonably believes any person intends to wear wholly or mainly for that purpose."

(2)   In subsection (5) of that section, for the words "those powers" there shall be substituted the words "the powers conferred by subsection (4) above".

(3)   In subsection (8) of that section, for the words "to stop or (as the case may be) to stop the vehicle" there shall be substituted the following paragraphs—

>   "(a)   to stop, or to stop a vehicle; or
>   (b)   to remove an item worn by him,".

References   See paras 2.56, 2.57.

26 Retention and disposal of things seized

After section 60 of the 1994 Act there shall be inserted the following section—

"60A Retention and disposal of things seized under section 60

(1)   Any things seized by a constable under section 60 may be retained in accordance with regulations made by the Secretary of State under this section.

(2)   The Secretary of State may make regulations regulating the retention and safe keeping, and the disposal and destruction in prescribed circumstances, of such things.

(3)   Regulations under this section may make different provisions for different classes of things or for different circumstances.

(4)   The power to make regulations under this section shall be exercisable by statutory instrument which shall be subject to annulment in pursuance of a resolution of either House of Parliament."

References   See para 2.58.

27 Power of arrest for failure to comply with requirement

(1)   In section 24(2) (arrestable offences) of the Police and Criminal Evidence Act 1984 ("the 1984 Act"), after paragraph (n) there shall be inserted—

>   "(o)   an offence under section 60(8)(b) of the Criminal Justice and Public Order Act 1994 (failing to comply with requirement to remove mask etc);"

(2)   After section 60A of the 1994 Act there shall be inserted the following section—

"60B Arrest without warrant for offences under section 60: Scotland

In Scotland, where a constable reasonably believes that a person has committed or is committing an offence under section 60(8) he may arrest that person without warrant."

Definitions   For "the 1994 Act", see s 117(1).
References   See para 2.59.

PART II
CRIMINAL LAW

Racially-aggravated offences: England and Wales

28 Meaning of "racially aggravated"

(1)   An offence is racially aggravated for the purposes of sections 29 to 32 below if—

    (a)   at the time of committing the offence, or immediately before or after doing so, the offender demonstrates towards the victim of the offence hostility based on the victim's membership (or presumed membership) of a racial group; or

    (b)   the offence is motivated (wholly or partly) by hostility towards members of a racial group based on their membership of that group.

(2)   In subsection (1)(a) above—

    "membership", in relation to a racial group, includes association with members of that group;

    "presumed" means presumed by the offender.

(3)   It is immaterial for the purposes of paragraph (a) or (b) of subsection (1) above whether or not the offender's hostility is also based, to any extent, on—

    (a)   the fact or presumption that any person or group of persons belongs to any religious group; or

    (b)   any other factor not mentioned in that paragraph.

(4)   In this section "racial group" means a group of persons defined by reference to race, colour, nationality (including citizenship) or ethnic or national origins.

References   See paras 3.4, 3.5.

29 Racially-aggravated assaults

(1)   A person is guilty of an offence under this section if he commits—

    (a)   an offence under section 20 of the Offences Against the Person Act 1861 (malicious wounding or grievous bodily harm);

    (b)   an offence under section 47 of that Act (actual bodily harm); or

    (c)   common assault,

which is racially aggravated for the purposes of this section.

(2)   A person guilty of an offence falling within subsection (1)(a) or (b) above shall be liable—

    (a)   on summary conviction, to imprisonment for a term not exceeding six months or to a fine not exceeding the statutory maximum, or to both;

    (b)   on conviction on indictment, to imprisonment for a term not exceeding seven years or to a fine, or to both.

(3)   A person guilty of an offence falling within subsection (1)(c) above shall be liable—

(a)   on summary conviction, to imprisonment for a term not exceeding six months or to a fine not exceeding the statutory maximum, or to both;

(b)   on conviction on indictment, to imprisonment for a term not exceeding two years or to a fine, or to both.

Definitions   For "racially aggravated", see s 28.
References   See para 3.7.

30 Racially-aggravated criminal damage

(1)   A person is guilty of an offence under this section if he commits an offence under section 1(1) of the Criminal Damage Act 1971 (destroying or damaging property belonging to another) which is racially aggravated for the purposes of this section.

(2)   A person guilty of an offence under this section shall be liable—

(a)   on summary conviction, to imprisonment for a term not exceeding six months or to a fine not exceeding the statutory maximum, or to both;

(b)   on conviction on indictment, to imprisonment for a term not exceeding fourteen years or to a fine, or to both.

(3)   For the purposes of this section, section 28(1)(a) above shall have effect as if the person to whom the property belongs or is treated as belonging for the purposes of that Act were the victim of the offence.

Definitions   For "racially aggravated", see s 28 (and note sub-s (3) above).
References   See para 3.8.

31 Racially-aggravated public order offences

(1)   A person is guilty of an offence under this section if he commits—

(a)   an offence under section 4 of the Public Order Act 1986 (fear or provocation of violence);

(b)   an offence under section 4A of that Act (intentional harassment, alarm or distress); or

(c)   an offence under section 5 of that Act (harassment, alarm or distress),

which is racially aggravated for the purposes of this section.

(2)   A constable may arrest without warrant anyone whom he reasonably suspects to be committing an offence falling within subsection (1)(a) or (b) above.

(3)   A constable may arrest a person without warrant if—

(a)   he engages in conduct which a constable reasonably suspects to constitute an offence falling within subsection (1)(c) above;

(b)   he is warned by that constable to stop; and

(c)   he engages in further such conduct immediately or shortly after the warning.

The conduct mentioned in paragraph (a) above and the further conduct need not be of the same nature.

(4)   A person guilty of an offence falling within subsection (1)(a) or (b) above shall be liable—

(a)   on summary conviction, to imprisonment for a term not exceeding six months or to a fine not exceeding the statutory maximum, or to both;

(b)   on conviction on indictment, to imprisonment for a term not exceeding two years or to a fine, or to both.

(5)   A person guilty of an offence falling within subsection (1)(c) above shall be liable on summary conviction to a fine not exceeding level 4 on the standard scale.

(6)   If, on the trial on indictment of a person charged with an offence falling within subsection (1)(a) or (b) above, the jury find him not guilty of the offence charged, they may find him guilty of the basic offence mentioned in that provision.

(7)   For the purposes of subsection (1)(c) above, section 28(1)(a) above shall have effect as if the person likely to be caused harassment, alarm or distress were the victim of the offence.

Definitions   For "racially aggravated", see s 28 (and note sub-s (7) above).
References   See para 3.9–3.11.

---

32 Racially-aggravated harassment etc

(1)   A person is guilty of an offence under this section if he commits—
    (a)   an offence under section 2 of the Protection from Harassment Act 1997 (offence of harassment); or
    (b)   an offence under section 4 of that Act (putting people in fear of violence),
which is racially aggravated for the purposes of this section.

(2)   In section 24(2) of the 1984 Act (arrestable offences), after paragraph (o) there shall be inserted—

    "(p)   an offence falling within section 32(1)(a) of the Crime and Disorder Act 1998 (racially-aggravated harassment);".

(3)   A person guilty of an offence falling within subsection (1)(a) above shall be liable—
    (a)   on summary conviction, to imprisonment for a term not exceeding six months or to a fine not exceeding the statutory maximum, or to both;
    (b)   on conviction on indictment, to imprisonment for a term not exceeding two years or to a fine, or to both.

(4)   A person guilty of an offence falling within subsection (1)(b) above shall be liable—
    (a)   on summary conviction, to imprisonment for a term not exceeding six months or to a fine not exceeding the statutory maximum, or to both;
    (b)   on conviction on indictment, to imprisonment for a term not exceeding seven years or to a fine, or to both.

(5)   If, on the trial on indictment of a person charged with an offence falling within subsection (1)(a) above, the jury find him not guilty of the offence charged, they may find him guilty of the basic offence mentioned in that provision.

(6)   If, on the trial on indictment of a person charged with an offence falling within subsection (1)(b) above, the jury find him not guilty of the offence charged, they may find him guilty of an offence falling within subsection (1)(a) above.

(7)   Section 5 of the Protection from Harassment Act 1997 (restraining orders) shall have effect in relation to a person convicted of an offence under this section as if the reference in subsection (1) of that section to an offence under section 2 or 4 included a reference to an offence under this section.

Definitions   For "racially aggravated", see s 28.
References   See para 3.12.

Racially-aggravated offences: Scotland

33 Racially-aggravated offences

After section 50 of the Criminal Law (Consolidation) (Scotland) Act 1995 there shall be inserted the following section—

"Racially-aggravated harassment

50A Racially aggravated harassment

(1) A person is guilty of an offence under this section if he—
   (a) pursues a racially-aggravated course of conduct which amounts to harassment of a person and—
      (i) is intended to amount to harassment of that person; or
      (ii) occurs in circumstances where it would appear to a reasonable person that it would amount to harassment of that person; or
   (b) acts in a manner which is racially aggravated and which causes, or is intended to cause, a person alarm or distress.

(2) For the purposes of this section a course of conduct or an action is racially aggravated if—
   (a) immediately before, during or immediately after carrying out the course of conduct or action the offender evinces towards the person affected malice and ill-will based on that person's membership (or presumed membership) of a racial group; or
   (b) the course of conduct or action is motivated (wholly or partly) by malice and ill-will towards members of a racial group based on their membership of that group.

(3) In subsection (2)(a) above—
   "membership", in relation to a racial group, includes association with members of that group;
   "presumed" means presumed by the offender.

(4) It is immaterial for the purposes of paragraph (a) or (b) of subsection (2) above whether or not the offender's malice and ill-will is also based, to any extent, on—
   (a) the fact or presumption that any person or group of persons belongs to any religious group; or
   (b) any other factor not mentioned in that paragraph.

(5) A person who is guilty of an offence under this section shall—
   (a) on summary conviction, be liable to a fine not exceeding the statutory maximum, or imprisonment for a period not exceeding six months, or both such fine and such imprisonment; and
   (b) on conviction on indictment, be liable to a fine or to imprisonment for a period not exceeding seven years, or both such fine and such imprisonment.

(6) In this section—
   "conduct" includes speech;
   "harassment" of a person includes causing the person alarm or distress;
   "racial group" means a group of persons defined by reference to race, colour, nationality (including citizenship) or ethnic or national origins,

and a course of conduct must involve conduct on at least two occasions."

References   See paras 3.14–3.16.

Miscellaneous

34 Abolition of rebuttable presumption that a child is doli incapax

The rebuttable presumption of criminal law that a child aged 10 or over is incapable of committing an offence is hereby abolished.

Definitions   For "child", see s 117(1), (3).
References   See para 3.17.

35 Effect of child's silence at trial

In section 35 of the 1994 Act (effect of accused's silence at trial), the following provisions shall cease to have effect, namely—
    (a)   in subsection (1), the words "who has attained the age of fourteen years"; and
    (b)   subsection (6).

References   See para 3.19.

36 Abolition of death penalty for treason and piracy

    (1)   In section I of the Treason Act (Ireland) 1537 (practising any harm etc to, or slandering, the King, Queen or heirs apparent punishable as high treason), for the words "have and suffer such pains of death and" there shall be substituted the words "be liable to imprisonment for life and to such".

    (2)   In the following enactments, namely—
    (a)   section II of the Crown of Ireland Act 1542 (occasioning disturbance etc to the crown of Ireland punishable as high treason);
    (b)   section XII of the Act of Supremacy (Ireland) 1560 (penalties for maintaining or defending foreign authority);
    (c)   section 3 of the Treason Act 1702 (endeavouring to hinder the succession to the Crown etc punishable as high treason);
    (d)   section I of the Treason Act (Ireland) 1703 (which makes corresponding provision),

for the words "suffer pains of death" there shall be substituted the words "be liable to imprisonment for life".

    (3)   The following enactments shall cease to have effect, namely—
    (a)   the Treason Act 1790;
    (b)   the Treason Act 1795.

    (4)   In section 1 of the Treason Act 1814 (form of sentence in case of high treason), for the words "such person shall be hanged by the neck until such person be dead", there shall be substituted the words "such person shall be liable to imprisonment for life".

    (5)   In section 2 of the Piracy Act 1837 (punishment of piracy when murder is attempted), for the words "and being convicted thereof shall suffer death" there shall be substituted the words "and being convicted thereof shall be liable to imprisonment for life".

    (6)   The following enactments shall cease to have effect, namely—
    (a)   the Sentence of Death (Expectant Mothers) Act 1931; and
    (b)   sections 32 and 33 of the Criminal Justice Act (Northern Ireland) 1945 (which make corresponding provision).

References   See para 3.20.

PART III
CRIMINAL JUSTICE SYSTEM

Youth justice

37 Aim of the youth justice system

(1) It shall be the principal aim of the youth justice system to prevent offending by children and young persons.

(2) In addition to any other duty to which they are subject, it shall be the duty of all persons and bodies carrying out functions in relation to the youth justice system to have regard to that aim.

Definitions For "youth justice system", see s 42(1); for "children" and "young person", see s 117(1), (3).
References See paras 4.2, 4.3.

38 Local provision of youth justice services

(1) It shall be the duty of each local authority, acting in co-operation with the persons and bodies mentioned in subsection (2) below, to secure that, to such extent as is appropriate for their area, all youth justice services are available there.

(2) It shall be the duty of—
    (a) every chief officer of police or police authority any part of whose police area lies within the local authority's area; and
    (b) every probation committee or health authority any part of whose area lies within that area,
to co-operate in the discharge by the local authority of their duty under subsection (1) above.

(3) The local authority and every person or body mentioned in subsection (2) above shall have power to make payments towards expenditure incurred in the provision of youth justice services—
    (a) by making the payments directly; or
    (b) by contributing to a fund, established and maintained by the local authority, out of which the payments may be made.

(4) In this section and sections 39 to 41 below "youth justice services" means any of the following, namely—
    (a) the provision of persons to act as appropriate adults to safeguard the interests of children and young persons detained or questioned by police officers;
    (b) the assessment of children and young persons, and the provision for them of rehabilitation programmes, for the purposes of section 66(2) below;
    (c) the provision of support for children and young persons remanded or committed on bail while awaiting trial or sentence;
    (d) the placement in local authority accommodation of children and young persons remanded or committed to such accommodation under section 23 of the Children and Young Persons Act 1969 ("the 1969 Act");
    (e) the provision of reports or other information required by courts in criminal proceedings against children and young persons;
    (f) the provision of persons to act as responsible officers in relation to parenting orders, child safety orders, reparation orders and action plan orders;

(g) the supervision of young persons sentenced to a probation order, a community service order or a combination order;

(h) the supervision of children and young persons sentenced to a detention and training order or a supervision order;

(i) the post-release supervision of children and young persons under section 37(4A) or 65 of the 1991 Act or section 31 of the Crime (Sentences) Act 1997 ("the 1997 Act");

(j) the performance of functions under subsection (1) of section 75 below by such persons as may be authorised by the Secretary of State under that subsection.

(5) The Secretary of State may by order amend subsection (4) above so as to extend, restrict or otherwise alter the definition of "youth justice services" for the time being specified in that subsection.

Definitions For "chief officer of police" and "police authority", see s 42(1); for "local authority", see s 42(1), (2); for "the 1991 Act", see s 117(1); for "child" and "young person", see s 117(1), (3).
References See paras 4.4–4.7.

---

39 Youth offending teams

(1) Subject to subsection (2) below, it shall be the duty of each local authority, acting in co-operation with the persons and bodies mentioned in subsection (3) below, to establish for their area one or more youth offending teams.

(2) Two (or more) local authorities acting together may establish one or more youth offending teams for both (or all) their areas; and where they do so—

(a) any reference in the following provisions of this section (except subsection (4)(b)) to, or to the area of, the local authority or a particular local authority shall be construed accordingly, and

(b) the reference in subsection (4)(b) to the local authority shall be construed as a reference to one of the authorities.

(3) It shall be the duty of—

(a) every chief officer of police any part of whose police area lies within the local authority's area; and

(b) every probation committee or health authority any part of whose area lies within that area,

to co-operate in the discharge by the local authority of their duty under subsection (1) above.

(4) The local authority and every person or body mentioned in subsection (3) above shall have power to make payments towards expenditure incurred by, or for purposes connected with, youth offending teams—

(a) by making the payments directly; or

(b) by contributing to a fund, established and maintained by the local authority, out of which the payments may be made.

(5) A youth offending team shall include at least one of each of the following, namely—

(a) a probation officer;

(b) a social worker of a local authority social services department;

(c) a police officer;

(d) a person nominated by a health authority any part of whose area lies within the local authority's area;

(e) a person nominated by the chief education officer appointed by the local authority under section 532 of the Education Act 1996.

(6)   A youth offending team may also include such other persons as the local authority thinks appropriate after consulting the persons and bodies mentioned in subsection (3) above.

(7)   It shall be the duty of the youth offending team or teams established by a particular local authority—

    (a)   to co-ordinate the provision of youth justice services for all those in the authority's area who need them; and

    (b)   to carry out such functions as are assigned to the team or teams in the youth justice plan formulated by the authority under section 40(1) below.

Definitions   For "youth justice services", see s 38(4), (5); for "youth justice plan", see s 40; for "local authority", see s 42(1), (2); for "chief officer of police" see s 42(1); for "youth offending team", see s 117(1).
References   See paras 4.8, 4.9.

40 Youth justice plans

(1)   It shall be the duty of each local authority, after consultation with the relevant persons and bodies, to formulate and implement for each year a plan (a "youth justice plan") setting out—

    (a)   how youth justice services in their area are to be provided and funded; and

    (b)   how the youth offending team or teams established by them (whether alone or jointly with one or more other local authorities) are to be composed and funded, how they are to operate, and what functions they are to carry out.

(2)   In subsection (1) above "the relevant persons and bodies" means the persons and bodies mentioned in section 38(2) above and, where the local authority is a county council, any district councils whose districts form part of its area.

(3)   The functions assigned to a youth offending team under subsection (1)(b) above may include, in particular, functions under paragraph 7(b) of Schedule 2 to the 1989 Act (local authority's duty to take reasonable steps designed to encourage children and young persons not to commit offences).

(4)   A local authority shall submit their youth justice plan to the Board established under section 41 below, and shall publish it in such manner and by such date as the Secretary of State may direct.

Definitions   For "youth justice services", see s 38(4), (5); for "the Board", see s 41(1); for "local authority", see s 42(1), (2); for "the 1989 Act" and "youth offending team", see s 117(1).
References   See para 4.10.

41 The Youth Justice Board

(1)   There shall be a body corporate to be known as the Youth Justice Board for England and Wales ("the Board").

(2)   The Board shall not be regarded as the servant or agent of the Crown or as enjoying any status, immunity or privilege of the Crown; and the Board's property shall not be regarded as property of, or held on behalf of, the Crown.

(3)   The Board shall consist of 10, 11 or 12 members appointed by the Secretary of State.

(4)   The members of the Board shall include persons who appear to the Secretary of State to have extensive recent experience of the youth justice system.

(5)   The Board shall have the following functions, namely—
    (a)   to monitor the operation of the youth justice system and the provision of youth justice services;
    (b)   to advise the Secretary of State on the following matters, namely—
        (i)   the operation of that system and the provision of such services;
        (ii)   how the principal aim of that system might most effectively be pursued;
        (iii)   the content of any national standards he may see fit to set with respect to the provision of such services, or the accommodation in which children and young persons are kept in custody; and
        (iv)   the steps that might be taken to prevent offending by children and young persons;
    (c)   to monitor the extent to which that aim is being achieved and any such standards met;
    (d)   for the purposes of paragraphs (a), (b) and (c) above, to obtain information from relevant authorities;
    (e)   to publish information so obtained;
    (f)   to identify, to make known and to promote good practice in the following matters, namely—
        (i)   the operation of the youth justice system and the provision of youth justice services;
        (ii)   the prevention of offending by children and young persons; and
        (iii)   working with children and young persons who are or are at risk of becoming offenders;
    (g)   to make grants, with the approval of the Secretary of State, to local authorities or other bodies for them to develop such practice, or to commission research in connection with such practice; and
    (h)   themselves to commission research in connection with such practice.

(6)   The Secretary of State may by order—
    (a)   amend subsection (5) above so as to add to, subtract from or alter any of the functions of the Board for the time being specified in that subsection; or
    (b)   provide that any function of his which is exercisable in relation to the youth justice system shall be exercisable concurrently with the Board.

(7)   In carrying out their functions, the Board shall comply with any directions given by the Secretary of State and act in accordance with any guidance given by him.

(8)   A relevant authority—
    (a)   shall furnish to the Board any information required for the purposes of subsection (5)(a), (b) or (c) above; and
    (b)   whenever so required by the Board, shall submit to the Board a report on such matters connected with the discharge of their duties under the foregoing provisions of this Part as may be specified in the requirement.

 A requirement under paragraph (b) above may specify the form in which a report is to be given.

(9)   The Board may arrange, or require the relevant authority to arrange, for a report under subsection (8)(b) above to be published in such manner as appears to the Board to be appropriate.

(10)   In this section "relevant authority" means a local authority, a chief officer of police, a police authority, a probation committee and a health authority.

(11)   Schedule 2 to this Act (which makes further provision with respect to the Board) shall have effect.

Definitions For "youth justice services", see s 38(4), (5); for "chief officer of police", "police authority" and "youth justice system", see s 42(1); for "local authority", see s 42(1), (2); for "children" and "young person", see s 117(1), (3).
References See paras 4.13–4.15.

42 Supplementary provisions

(1)   In the foregoing provisions of this Part and this section—
    "chief officer of police" has the meaning given by section 101(1) of the
        Police Act 1996;
    "local authority" means—
        (a)   in relation to England, a county council, a district council whose
            district does not form part of an area that has a county council, a
            London borough council or the Common Council of the City of
            London;
        (b)   in relation to Wales, a county council or a county borough council;
    "police authority" has the meaning given by section 101(1) of the Police
        Act 1996;
    "youth justice system" means the system of criminal justice in so far as it
        relates to children and young persons.

(2)   For the purposes of those provisions, the Isles of Scilly form part of the county of Cornwall and the Inner Temple and the Middle Temple form part of the City of London.

(3)   In carrying out any of their duties under those provisions, a local authority, a police authority, a probation committee or a health authority shall act in accordance with any guidance given by the Secretary of State.

Definitions For "children" and "young person", see s 117(1), (3).
References See para 4.2.

Time limits etc

43 Time limits

(1)   In subsection (2) of section 22 (time limits in relation to criminal proceedings) of the Prosecution of Offences Act 1985 ("the 1985 Act"), for paragraphs (a) and (b) there shall be substituted the following paragraphs—
    "(a)   be made so as to apply only in relation to proceedings instituted in
            specified areas, or proceedings of, or against persons of, specified
            classes or descriptions;
        (b)   make different provision with respect to proceedings instituted in
            different areas, or different provision with respect to proceedings of,
            or against persons of, different classes or descriptions;".

(2)   For subsection (3) of that section there shall be substituted the following subsection—

    "(3)   The appropriate court may, at any time before the expiry of a time limit imposed by the regulations, extend, or further extend, that limit; but the court shall not do so unless it is satisfied—
        (a)   that the need for the extension is due to—
            (i)   the illness or absence of the accused, a necessary witness, a
                judge or a magistrate;
            (ii)   a postponement which is occasioned by the ordering by the
                court of separate trials in the case of two or more accused or
                two or more offences; or
            (iii)   some other good and sufficient cause; and

       (b)   that the prosecution has acted with all due diligence and expedition."

(3)   In subsection (4) of that section, for the words from "the accused" to the end there shall be substituted the words "the appropriate court shall stay the proceedings".

(4)   In subsection (6) of that section—

       (a)   for the word "Where" there shall be substituted the words "Subsection (6A) below applies where"; and

       (b)   for the words from "the overall time limit" to the end there shall be substituted the words "and is accordingly unlawfully at large for any period."

(5)   After that subsection there shall be inserted the following subsection—

"(6A) The following, namely—

       (a)   the period for which the person is unlawfully at large; and

       (b)   such additional period (if any) as the appropriate court may direct, having regard to the disruption of the prosecution occasioned by—

           (i)   the person's escape or failure to surrender; and

           (ii)   the length of the period mentioned in paragraph (a) above,

shall be disregarded, so far as the offence in question is concerned, for the purposes of the overall time limit which applies in his case in relation to the stage which the proceedings have reached at the time of the escape or, as the case may be, at the appointed time."

(6)   In subsection (7) of that section, after the words "time limit," there shall be inserted the words "or to give a direction under subsection (6A) above,".

(7)   In subsection (8) of that section, after the words "time limit" there shall be inserted the words ", or to give a direction under subsection (6A) above,".

(8)   After subsection (11) of that section there shall be inserted the following subsection—

"(11ZA)For the purposes of this section, proceedings for an offence shall be taken to begin when the accused is charged with the offence or, as the case may be, an information is laid charging him with the offence."

Definitions   For "the 1985 Act", see s 117(1); for "appropriate court" and "overall time limit", see the Prosecution of Offences Act 1985, s 22(11).
References   See paras 4.1, 4.16–4.18.

44 Additional time limits for persons under 18

After section 22 of the 1985 Act there shall be inserted the following section—

"22A Additional time limits for persons under 18

(1)   The Secretary of State may by regulations make provision—

       (a)   with respect to a person under the age of 18 at the time of his arrest in connection with an offence, as to the maximum period to be allowed for the completion of the stage beginning with his arrest and ending with the date fixed for his first appearance in court in connection with the offence ("the initial stage");

       (b)   with respect to a person convicted of an offence who was under that age at the time of his arrest for the offence or (where he was not arrested for it) the laying of the information charging him with it, as to the period within which the stage between his conviction and his being sentenced for the offence should be completed.

(2)   Subsection (2) of section 22 above applies for the purposes of regulations under subsection (1) above as if—

(a)   the reference in paragraph (d) to custody or overall time limits were a reference to time limits imposed by the regulations; and

(b)   the reference in paragraph (e) to proceedings instituted before the commencement of any provisions of the regulations were a reference to a stage begun before that commencement.

(3)   A magistrates' court may, at any time before the expiry of the time limit imposed by the regulations under subsection (1)(a) above ("the initial stage time limit"), extend, or further extend, that limit; but the court shall not do so unless it is satisfied—

(a)   that the need for the extension is due to some good and sufficient cause; and

(b)   that the investigation has been conducted, and (where applicable) the prosecution has acted, with all due diligence and expedition.

(4)   Where the initial stage time limit (whether as originally imposed or as extended or further extended under subsection (3) above) expires before the person arrested is charged with the offence, he shall not be charged with it unless further evidence relating to it is obtained, and—

(a)   if he is then under arrest, he shall be released;

(b)   if he is then on bail under Part IV of the Police and Criminal Evidence Act 1984, his bail (and any duty or conditions to which it is subject) shall be discharged.

(5)   Where the initial stage time limit (whether as originally imposed or as extended or further extended under subsection (3) above) expires after the person arrested is charged with the offence but before the date fixed for his first appearance in court in connection with it, the court shall stay the proceedings.

(6)   Where—

(a)   a person escapes from arrest; or

(b)   a person who has been released on bail under Part IV of the Police and Criminal Evidence Act 1984 fails to surrender himself at the appointed time,

and is accordingly unlawfully at large for any period, that period shall be disregarded, so far as the offence in question is concerned, for the purposes of the initial stage time limit.

(7)   Subsections (7) to (9) of section 22 above apply for the purposes of this section, at any time after the person arrested has been charged with the offence in question, as if any reference (however expressed) to a custody or overall time limit were a reference to the initial stage time limit.

(8)   Where a person is convicted of an offence in any proceedings, the exercise of the power conferred by subsection (3) above shall not be called into question in any appeal against that conviction.

(9)   Any reference in this section (however expressed) to a person being charged with an offence includes a reference to the laying of an information charging him with it."

Definitions   For "the 1985 Act", see s 117(1).
References   See paras 4.1, 4.19, 4.20.

45 Re-institution of stayed proceedings

After section 22A of the 1985 Act there shall be inserted the following section—

"22B Re-institution of proceedings stayed under section 22(4) or 22A(5)

(1)   This section applies where proceedings for an offence ("the original proceedings") are stayed by a court under section 22(4) or 22A(5) of this Act.

(2)   If—

(a)   in the case of proceedings conducted by the Director, the Director or a Chief Crown Prosecutor so directs;

(b)   in the case of proceedings conducted by the Director of the Serious Fraud Office, the Commissioners of Inland Revenue or the Commissioners of Customs and Excise, that Director or those Commissioners so direct; or

(c)   in the case of proceedings not conducted as mentioned in paragraph (a) or (b) above, a person designated for the purpose by the Secretary of State so directs,

fresh proceedings for the offence may be instituted within a period of three months (or such longer period as the court may allow) after the date on which the original proceedings were stayed by the court.

(3)   Fresh proceedings shall be instituted as follows—

(a)   where the original proceedings were stayed by the Crown Court, by preferring a bill of indictment;

(b)   where the original proceedings were stayed by a magistrates' court, by laying an information.

(4)   Fresh proceedings may be instituted in accordance with subsections (2) and (3)(b) above notwithstanding anything in section 127(1) of the Magistrates' Courts Act 1980 (limitation of time).

(5)   Where fresh proceedings are instituted, anything done in relation to the original proceedings shall be treated as done in relation to the fresh proceedings if the court so directs or it was done—

(a)   by the prosecutor in compliance or purported compliance with section 3, 4, 7 or 9 of the Criminal Procedure and Investigations Act 1996; or

(b)   by the accused in compliance or purported compliance with section 5 or 6 of that Act.

(6)   Where a person is convicted of an offence in fresh proceedings under this section, the institution of those proceedings shall not be called into question in any appeal against that conviction."

References   See paras 4.1, 4.21.

46 Date of first court appearance in bail cases

(1)   In subsection (3) of section 47 of the 1984 Act (bail after arrest), for the words "subsection (4)" there shall be substituted the words "subsections (3A) and (4)".

(2)   After that subsection there shall be inserted the following subsection—

"(3A)   Where a custody officer grants bail to a person subject to a duty to appear before a magistrates' court, he shall appoint for the appearance—

(a)   a date which is not later than the first sitting of the court after the person is charged with the offence; or

(b)   where he is informed by the clerk to the justices for the relevant petty sessions area that the appearance cannot be accommodated until a later date, that later date."

References   See paras 4.1, 4.22.

Functions of courts etc

47 Powers of youth courts

(1)   Where a person who appears or is brought before a youth court charged with an offence subsequently attains the age of 18, the youth court may, at any time—
   (a)   before the start of the trial; or
   (b)   after conviction and before sentence,

remit the person for trial or, as the case may be, for sentence to a magistrates' court (other than a youth court) acting for the same petty sessions area as the youth court.

In this subsection "the start of the trial" shall be construed in accordance with section 22(11B) of the 1985 Act.

(2)   Where a person is remitted under subsection (1) above—
   (a)   he shall have no right of appeal against the order of remission;
   (b)   the remitting court shall adjourn proceedings in relation to the offence; and
   (c)   subsections (3) and (4) below shall apply.

(3)   The following, namely—
   (a)   section 128 of the 1980 Act; and
   (b)   all other enactments (whenever passed) relating to remand or the granting of bail in criminal proceedings,

shall have effect in relation to the remitting court's power or duty to remand the person on the adjournment as if any reference to the court to or before which the person remanded is to be brought or appear after remand were a reference to the court to which he is being remitted ("the other court").

(4)   The other court may deal with the case in any way in which it would have power to deal with it if all proceedings relating to the offence which took place before the remitting court had taken place before the other court.

(5)   After subsection (3) of section 10 of the 1980 Act (adjournment of trial) there shall be inserted the following subsection—

"(3A)   A youth court shall not be required to adjourn any proceedings for an offence at any stage by reason only of the fact—
   (a)   that the court commits the accused for trial for another offence; or
   (b)   that the accused is charged with another offence."

(6)   After subsection (1) of section 24 of the 1980 Act (summary trial of information against child or young person for indictable offence) there shall be inserted the following subsection—

"(1A)   Where a magistrates' court—
   (a)   commits a person under the age of 18 for trial for an offence of homicide; or
   (b)   in a case falling within subsection (1)(a) above, commits such a person for trial for an offence,

the court may also commit him for trial for any other indictable offence with which he is charged at the same time if the charges for both offences could be joined in the same indictment."

(7)   In subsection (2) of section 47 (procedure in youth courts) of the Children and Young Persons Act 1933 ("the 1933 Act"), the words from the beginning to "court; and" shall cease to have effect.

Definitions   For "the 1980 Act" and "the 1985 Act", see s 117(1).
References   See paras 4.23–4.25.

48 The courts: power of stipendiary magistrates to sit alone

(1)　In paragraph 15 of Schedule 2 to the 1933 Act (constitution of youth courts)—

    (a)　in paragraph (a), after the word "shall", in the first place where it occurs, there shall be inserted the words "either consist of a metropolitan stipendiary magistrate sitting alone or" and the word "shall", in the other place where it occurs, shall cease to have effect;

    (b)　in paragraph (b), after the words "the chairman" there shall be inserted the words "(where applicable)"; and

    (c)　in paragraph (c), after the words "the other members" there shall be inserted the words "(where applicable)".

(2)　In paragraph 17 of that Schedule, the words "or, if a metropolitan stipendiary magistrate, may sit alone" shall cease to have effect.

Definitions　For "the 1933 Act", see s 117(1).
References　See paras 4.1, 4.26.

49 Powers of magistrates' courts exercisable by single justice etc

(1)　The following powers of a magistrates' court for any area may be exercised by a single justice of the peace for that area, namely—

    (a)　to extend bail or to impose or vary conditions of bail;

    (b)　to mark an information as withdrawn;

    (c)　to dismiss an information, or to discharge an accused in respect of an information, where no evidence is offered by the prosecution;

    (d)　to make an order for the payment of defence costs out of central funds;

    (e)　to request a pre-sentence report following a plea of guilty and, for that purpose, to give an indication of the seriousness of the offence;

    (f)　to request a medical report and, for that purpose, to remand the accused in custody or on bail;

    (g)　to remit an offender to another court for sentence;

    (h)　where a person has been granted police bail to appear at a magistrates' court, to appoint an earlier time for his appearance;

    (i)　to extend, with the consent of the accused, a custody time limit or an overall time limit;

    (j)　where a case is to be tried on indictment, to grant representation under Part V of the Legal Aid Act 1988 for purposes of the proceedings in the Crown Court;

    (k)　where an accused has been convicted of an offence, to order him to produce his driving licence;

    (l)　to give a direction prohibiting the publication of matters disclosed or exempted from disclosure in court;

    (m)　to give, vary or revoke directions for the conduct of a trial, including directions as to the following matters, namely—

        (i)　the timetable for the proceedings;

        (ii)　the attendance of the parties;

        (iii)　the service of documents (including summaries of any legal arguments relied on by the parties);

        (iv)　the manner in which evidence is to be given; and

    (n)　to give, vary or revoke orders for separate or joint trials in the case of two or more accused or two or more informations.

(2)　Without prejudice to the generality of subsection (1) of section 144 of the 1980 Act (rules of procedure)

    (a)　rules under that section may, subject to subsection (3) below, provide that any of the things which, by virtue of subsection (1) above, are authorised to be done by a single justice of the peace for any area may, subject to any specified restrictions or conditions, be done by a justices' clerk for that area; and

(b)   rules under that section which make such provision as is mentioned in paragraph (a) above may make different provision for different areas.

(3)   Rules under that section which make such provision as is mentioned in subsection (2) above shall not authorise a justices' clerk—

(a)   without the consent of the prosecutor and the accused, to extend bail on conditions other than those (if any) previously imposed, or to impose or vary conditions of bail;

(b)   to give an indication of the seriousness of an offence for the purposes of a pre-sentence report;

(c)   to remand the accused in custody for the purposes of a medical report or, without the consent of the prosecutor and the accused, to remand the accused on bail for those purposes on conditions other than those (if any) previously imposed;

(d)   to give a direction prohibiting the publication of matters disclosed or exempted from disclosure in court; or

(e)   without the consent of the parties, to give, vary or revoke orders for separate or joint trials in the case of two or more accused or two or more informations.

(4)   Before making any rules under that section which make such provision as is mentioned in subsection (2) above in relation to any area, the Lord Chancellor shall consult justices of the peace and justices' clerks for that area.

(5)   In this section and section 50 below "justices' clerk" has the same meaning as in section 144 of the 1980 Act.

Definitions   For "the 1980 Act", see s 117(1).
References   See paras 4.1, 4.27–4.29.

---

50 Early administrative hearings

(1)   Where a person ("the accused") has been charged with an offence at a police station, the magistrates' court before whom he appears or is brought for the first time in relation to the charge may, unless the accused falls to be dealt with under section 51 below, consist of a single justice.

(2)   At a hearing conducted by a single justice under this section—

(a)   the accused shall be asked whether he wishes to receive legal aid; and

(b)   if he indicates that he does, his eligibility for it shall be determined; and

(c)   if it is determined that he is eligible for it, the necessary arrangements or grant shall be made for him to obtain it.

(3)   At such a hearing the single justice—

(a)   may exercise, subject to subsection (2) above, such of his powers as a single justice as he thinks fit; and

(b)   on adjourning the hearing, may remand the accused in custody or on bail.

(4)   This section applies in relation to a justices' clerk as it applies in relation to a single justice; but nothing in subsection (3)(b) above authorises such a clerk to remand the accused in custody or, without the consent of the prosecutor and the accused, to remand the accused on bail on conditions other than those (if any) previously imposed.

(5)   In this section "legal aid" means representation under Part V of the Legal Aid Act 1988.

Definitions   For "justices' clerk", see s 49(5); for "the 1980 Act", see s 117(1).
References   See paras 4.30, 4.31.

---

51 No committal proceedings for indictable-only offences

(1)   Where an adult appears or is brought before a magistrates' court ("the court") charged with an offence triable only on indictment ("the indictable-only offence"), the court shall send him forthwith to the Crown Court for trial—
>   (a)   for that offence, and
>   (b)   for any either-way or summary offence with which he is charged which fulfils the requisite conditions (as set out in subsection (11) below).

(2)   Where an adult who has been sent for trial under subsection (1) above subsequently appears or is brought before a magistrates' court charged with an either-way or summary offence which fulfils the requisite conditions, the court may send him forthwith to the Crown Court for trial for the either-way or summary offence.

(3)   Where—
>   (a)   the court sends an adult for trial under subsection (1) above;
>   (b)   another adult appears or is brought before the court on the same or a subsequent occasion charged jointly with him with an either-way offence; and
>   (c)   that offence appears to the court to be related to the indictable-only offence,

the court shall where it is the same occasion, and may where it is a subsequent occasion, send the other adult forthwith to the Crown Court for trial for the either-way offence.

(4)   Where a court sends an adult for trial under subsection (3) above, it shall at the same time send him to the Crown Court for trial for any either-way or summary offence with which he is charged which fulfils the requisite conditions.

(5)   Where—
>   (a)   the court sends an adult for trial under subsection (1) or (3) above; and
>   (b)   a child or young person appears or is brought before the court on the same or a subsequent occasion charged jointly with the adult with an indictable offence for which the adult is sent for trial,

the court shall, if it considers it necessary in the interests of justice to do so, send the child or young person forthwith to the Crown Court for trial for the indictable offence.

(6)   Where a court sends a child or young person for trial under subsection (5) above, it may at the same time send him to the Crown Court for trial for any either-way or summary offence with which he is charged which fulfils the requisite conditions.

(7)   The court shall specify in a notice the offence or offences for which a person is sent for trial under this section and the place at which he is to be tried; and a copy of the notice shall be served on the accused and given to the Crown Court sitting at that place.

(8)   In a case where there is more than one indictable-only offence and the court includes an either-way or a summary offence in the notice under subsection (7) above, the court shall specify in that notice the indictable-only offence to which the

either-way offence or, as the case may be, the summary offence appears to the court to be related.

(9)   The trial of the information charging any summary offence for which a person is sent for trial under this section shall be treated as if the court had adjourned it under section 10 of the 1980 Act and had not fixed the time and place for its resumption.

(10)   In selecting the place of trial for the purpose of subsection (7) above, the court shall have regard to—

(a)   the convenience of the defence, the prosecution and the witnesses;
(b)   the desirability of expediting the trial; and
(c)   any direction given by or on behalf of the Lord Chief Justice with the concurrence of the Lord Chancellor under section 75(1) of the Supreme Court Act 1981.

(11)   An offence fulfils the requisite conditions if—

(a)   it appears to the court to be related to the indictable-only offence; and
(b)   in the case of a summary offence, it is punishable with imprisonment or involves obligatory or discretionary disqualification from driving.

(12)   For the purposes of this section—

(a)   "adult" means a person aged 18 or over, and references to an adult include references to a corporation;
(b)   "either-way offence" means an offence which, if committed by an adult, is triable either on indictment or summarily;
(c)   an either-way offence is related to an indictable-only offence if the charge for the either-way offence could be joined in the same indictment as the charge for the indictable-only offence;
(d)   a summary offence is related to an indictable-only offence if it arises out of circumstances which are the same as or connected with those giving rise to the indictable-only offence.

Definitions   For "the 1980 Act", see s 117(1); for "child" and "young person", see s 117(1), (3).
References   See paras 4.1, 4.32–4.34.

52 Provisions supplementing section 51

(1)   Subject to section 4 of the Bail Act 1976, section 41 of the 1980 Act, regulations under section 22 of the 1985 Act and section 25 of the 1994 Act, the court may send a person for trial under section 51 above—

(a)   in custody, that is to say, by committing him to custody there to be safely kept until delivered in due course of law; or
(b)   on bail in accordance with the Bail Act 1976, that is to say, by directing him to appear before the Crown Court for trial.

(2)   Where—

(a)   the person's release on bail under subsection (1)(b) above is conditional on his providing one or more sureties; and
(b)   in accordance with subsection (3) of section 8 of the Bail Act 1976, the court fixes the amount in which a surety is to be bound with a view to his entering into his recognisance subsequently in accordance with subsections (4) and (5) or (6) of that section,

the court shall in the meantime make an order such as is mentioned in subsection (1)(a) above.

(3)   The court shall treat as an indictable offence for the purposes of section 51 above an offence which is mentioned in the first column of Schedule 2 to the 1980 Act (offences for which the value involved is relevant to the mode of trial) unless it is

clear to the court, having regard to any representations made by the prosecutor or the accused, that the value involved does not exceed the relevant sum.

(4) In subsection (3) above "the value involved" and "the relevant sum" have the same meanings as in section 22 of the 1980 Act (certain offences triable either way to be tried summarily if value involved is small).

(5) A magistrates' court may adjourn any proceedings under section 51 above, and if it does so shall remand the accused.

(6) Schedule 3 to this Act (which makes further provision in relation to persons sent to the Crown Court for trial under section 51 above) shall have effect.

Definitions For "the 1980 Act", "the 1985 Act" and "the 1994 Act", see s 117(1).
References See paras 4.35, 4.36.

Miscellaneous

53 Crown Prosecution Service: powers of non-legal staff

For section 7A of the 1985 Act there shall be substituted the following section—

"7A Powers of non-legal staff

(1) The Director may designate, for the purposes of this section, members of the staff of the Crown Prosecution Service who are not Crown Prosecutors.

(2) Subject to such exceptions (if any) as may be specified in the designation, a person so designated shall have such of the following as may be so specified, namely—

    (a) the powers and rights of audience of a Crown Prosecutor in relation to—

        (i) applications for, or relating to, bail in criminal proceedings;

        (ii) the conduct of criminal proceedings in magistrates' courts other than trials;

    (b) the powers of such a Prosecutor in relation to the conduct of criminal proceedings not falling within paragraph (a)(ii) above.

(3) A person so designated shall exercise any such powers subject to instructions given to him by the Director.

(4) Any such instructions may be given so as to apply generally.

(5) For the purposes of this section—

    (a) "bail in criminal proceedings" has the same meaning as it would have in the Bail Act 1976 by virtue of the definition in section 1 of that Act if in that section "offence" did not include an offence to which subsection (6) below applies;

    (b) "criminal proceedings" does not include proceedings for an offence to which subsection (6) below applies; and

    (c) a trial begins with the opening of the prosecution case after the entry of a plea of not guilty and ends with the conviction or acquittal of the accused.

(6) This subsection applies to an offence if it is triable only on indictment, or is an offence—

    (a) for which the accused has elected to be tried by a jury;

    (b) which a magistrates' court has decided is more suitable to be so tried; or

    (c) in respect of which a notice of transfer has been given under section 4 of the Criminal Justice Act 1987 or section 53 of the Criminal Justice Act 1991.

(7)   Details of the following for any year, namely—
- (a)   the criteria applied by the Director in determining whether to designate persons under this section;
- (b)   the training undergone by persons so designated; and
- (c)   any general instructions given by the Director under subsection (4) above,

shall be set out in the Director's report under section 9 of this Act for that year."

Definitions   For "the 1985 Act", see s 117(1); for "Crown Prosecution Service", see the Prosecution of Offences Act 1985, s 1(1); for "Director", see s 15(1) of that Act; as to the conduct of proceedings, see s 15(3) of that Act.
References   See paras 4.1, 4.38.

54 Bail: increased powers to require security or impose conditions

(1)   In subsection (5) of section 3 of the Bail Act 1976 (general provisions as to bail), the words "If it appears that he is unlikely to remain in Great Britain until the time appointed for him to surrender to custody" shall cease to have effect.

(2)   In subsection (6) of that section, after paragraph (d) there shall be inserted the following paragraph—

"(e)   before the time appointed for him to surrender to custody, he attends an interview with an authorised advocate or authorised litigator, as defined by section 119(1) of the Courts and Legal Services Act 1990;".

(3)   In subsection (2) of section 3A of that Act (conditions of bail in the case of police bail), for the words "paragraph (d)" there shall be substituted the words "paragraph (d) or (e)".

Definitions   For "surrender to custody", see the Bail Act 1976, s 2(2).
References   See paras 4.1, 4.39.

55 Forfeiture of recognizances

For subsections (1) and (2) of section 120 of the 1980 Act (forfeiture of recognizances) there shall be substituted the following subsections—

"(1)   This section applies where—
- (a)   a recognizance to keep the peace or to be of good behaviour has been entered into before a magistrates' court; or
- (b)   any recognizance is conditioned for the appearance of a person before a magistrates' court, or for his doing any other thing connected with a proceeding before a magistrates' court.

(1A) If, in the case of a recognizance which is conditioned for the appearance of an accused before a magistrates' court, the accused fails to appear in accordance with the condition, the court shall—
- (a)   declare the recognizance to be forfeited;
- (b)   issue a summons directed to each person bound by the recognizance as surety, requiring him to appear before the court on a date specified in the summons to show cause why he should not be adjudged to pay the sum in which he is bound;

and on that date the court may proceed in the absence of any surety if it is satisfied that he has been served with the summons.

(2)   If, in any other case falling within subsection (1) above, the recognizance appears to the magistrates' court to be forfeited, the court may—
- (a)   declare the recognizance to be forfeited; and

141

    (b)   adjudge each person bound by it, whether as principal or surety, to pay the sum in which he is bound;

but in a case falling within subsection (1)(a) above, the court shall not declare the recognizance to be forfeited except by order made on complaint."

Definitions For "the 1980 Act", see s 117(1); for "magistrates' court", see the Magistrates' Courts Act 1980, s 148.
References See para 4.40.

56 Bail: restrictions in certain cases of homicide or rape

In subsection (1) of section 25 of the 1994 Act (no bail for defendants charged with or convicted of homicide or rape after previous conviction of such offences), for the words "shall not be granted bail in those proceedings" there shall be substituted the words "shall be granted bail in those proceedings only if the court or, as the case may be, the constable considering the grant of bail is satisfied that there are exceptional circumstances which justify it".

Definitions For "the 1994 Act", see s 117(1).
References See para 4.41.

57 Use of live television links at preliminary hearings

    (1)   In any proceedings for an offence, a court may, after hearing representations from the parties, direct that the accused shall be treated as being present in the court for any particular hearing before the start of the trial if, during that hearing—

    (a)   he is held in custody in a prison or other institution; and
    (b)   whether by means of a live television link or otherwise, he is able to see and hear the court and to be seen and heard by it.

    (2)   A court shall not give a direction under subsection (1) above unless—

    (a)   it has been notified by the Secretary of State that facilities are available for enabling persons held in custody in the institution in which the accused is or is to be so held to see and hear the court and to be seen and heard by it; and
    (b)   the notice has not been withdrawn.

    (3)   If in a case where it has power to do so a magistrates' court decides not to give a direction under subsection (1) above, it shall give its reasons for not doing so.

    (4)   In this section "the start of the trial" has the meaning given by subsection (11A) or (11B) of section 22 of the 1985 Act.

Definitions For "the 1985 Act", see s 117(1).
References See paras 4.1, 4.43.

PART IV
DEALING WITH OFFENDERS

CHAPTER I
ENGLAND AND WALES

Sexual or violent offenders

58 Sentences extended for licence purposes

    (1)   This section applies where a court which proposes to impose a custodial sentence for a sexual or violent offence considers that the period (if any) for which

the offender would, apart from this section, be subject to a licence would not be adequate for the purpose of preventing the commission by him of further offences and securing his rehabilitation.

(2)   Subject to subsections (3) to (5) below, the court may pass on the offender an extended sentence, that is to say, a custodial sentence the term of which is equal to the aggregate of—

      (a)   the term of the custodial sentence that the court would have imposed if it had passed a custodial sentence otherwise than under this section ("the custodial term"); and

      (b)   a further period ("the extension period") for which the offender is to be subject to a licence and which is of such length as the court considers necessary for the purpose mentioned in subsection (1) above.

(3)   Where the offence is a violent offence, the court shall not pass an extended sentence the custodial term of which is less than four years.

(4)   The extension period shall not exceed—

      (a)   ten years in the case of a sexual offence; and

      (b)   five years in the case of a violent offence.

(5)   The term of an extended sentence passed in respect of an offence shall not exceed the maximum term permitted for that offence.

(6)   Subsection (2) of section 2 of the 1991 Act (length of custodial sentences) shall apply as if the term of an extended sentence did not include the extension period.

(7)   The Secretary of State may by order amend paragraph (b) of subsection (4) above by substituting a different period, not exceeding ten years, for the period for the time being specified in that paragraph.

(8)   In this section—

      "licence" means a licence under Part II of the 1991 Act;

      "sexual offence" and "violent offence" have the same meanings as in Part I of that Act.

Definitions   For "the 1991 Act" and "custodial sentence", see s 117(1).
References   See paras 5.5–5.7.

59 Effect of extended sentences

For section 44 of the 1991 Act there shall be substituted the following section—

"44 Extended sentences for sexual or violent offenders

(1)   This section applies to a prisoner serving an extended sentence within the meaning of section 58 of the Crime and Disorder Act 1998.

(2)   Subject to the provisions of this section and section 51(2D) below, this Part, except sections 40 and 40A, shall have effect as if the term of the extended sentence did not include the extension period.

(3)   Where the prisoner is released on licence under this Part, the licence shall, subject to any revocation under section 39(1) or (2) above, remain in force until the end of the extension period.

(4)   Where, apart from this subsection, the prisoner would be released unconditionally—

      (a)   he shall be released on licence; and

      (b)   the licence shall, subject to any revocation under section 39(1) or (2) above, remain in force until the end of the extension period.

(5)   The extension period shall be taken to begin as follows—
    (a)   for the purposes of subsection (3) above, on the date given by section 37(1) above;
    (b)   for the purposes of subsection (4) above, on the date on which, apart from that subsection, the prisoner would have been released unconditionally.

(6)   Sections 33(3) and 33A(1) above and section 46 below shall not apply in relation to the prisoner.

(7)   For the purposes of sections 37(5) and 39(1) and (2) above the question whether the prisoner is a long-term or short-term prisoner shall be determined by reference to the term of the extended sentence.

(8)   In this section "extension period" has the same meaning as in section 58 of the Crime and Disorder Act 1998."

Definitions   For "the 1991 Act", see s 117; for "long-term prisoner" and "short-term prisoner", see the Criminal Justice Act 1991, ss 33(5), 51(1) (note that the prospective repeal of these sections by the Crime (Sentences) Act 1997, s 56(2), Sch 6, is itself repealed by ss 119, 120(2) of, Sch 8, para 139, Sch 10 to, this Act).
References   See paras 5.8, 5.9.

60 Re-release of prisoners serving extended sentences

After section 44 of the 1991 Act there shall be inserted the following section—

"44A Re-release of prisoners serving extended sentences

(1)   This section applies to a prisoner serving an extended sentence within the meaning of section 58 of the Crime and Disorder Act 1998 who is recalled to prison under section 39(1) or (2) above.

(2)   Subject to subsection (3) below, the prisoner may require the Secretary of State to refer his case to the Board at any time.

(3)   Where there has been a previous reference of the prisoner's case to the Board (whether under this section or section 39(4) above), the Secretary of State shall not be required to refer the case until after the end of the period of one year beginning with the disposal of that reference.

(4)   On a reference—
    (a)   under this section; or
    (b)   under section 39(4) above,
the Board shall direct the prisoner's release if satisfied that it is no longer necessary for the protection of the public that he should be confined (but not otherwise).

(5)   If the Board gives a direction under subsection (4) above it shall be the duty of the Secretary of State to release the prisoner on licence."

References   See paras 5.10. 5.11.

Offenders dependent etc on drugs

61 Drug treatment and testing orders

(1)   This section applies where a person aged 16 or over is convicted of an offence other than one for which the sentence—
    (a)   is fixed by law; or
    (b)   falls to be imposed under section 2(2), 3(2) or 4(2) of the 1997 Act.

(2)   Subject to the provisions of this section, the court by or before which the offender is convicted may make an order (a "drug treatment and testing order") which—

(a)   has effect for a period specified in the order of not less than six months nor more than three years ("the treatment and testing period"); and

(b)   includes the requirements and provisions mentioned in section 62 below.

(3)   A court shall not make a drug treatment and testing order unless it has been notified by the Secretary of State that arrangements for implementing such orders are available in the area proposed to be specified in the order and the notice has not been withdrawn.

(4)   A drug treatment and testing order shall be a community order for the purposes of Part I of the 1991 Act; and the provisions of that Part, which include provisions with respect to restrictions on imposing, and procedural requirements for, community sentences (sections 6 and 7), shall apply accordingly.

(5)   The court shall not make a drug treatment and testing order in respect of the offender unless it is satisfied—

(a)   that he is dependent on or has a propensity to misuse drugs; and

(b)   that his dependency or propensity is such as requires and may be susceptible to treatment.

(6)   For the purpose of ascertaining for the purposes of subsection (5) above whether the offender has any drug in his body, the court may by order require him to provide samples of such description as it may specify; but the court shall not make such an order unless the offender expresses his willingness to comply with its requirements.

(7)   The Secretary of State may by order amend subsection (2) above by substituting a different period for the minimum or maximum period for the time being specified in that subsection.

Definitions   For "the 1991 Act" and "the 1997 Act", see s 117(1); for "community sentence" see, by virtue of s 85(5), the Criminal Justice Act 1991, s 6(1).
References   See paras 5.12, 5.13.

62 Requirements and provisions to be included in orders

(1)   A drug treatment and testing order shall include a requirement ("the treatment requirement") that the offender shall submit, during the whole of the treatment and testing period, to treatment by or under the direction of a specified person having the necessary qualifications or experience ("the treatment provider") with a view to the reduction or elimination of the offender's dependency on or propensity to misuse drugs.

(2)   The required treatment for any particular period shall be—

(a)   treatment as a resident in such institution or place as may be specified in the order; or

(b)   treatment as a non-resident in or at such institution or place, and at such intervals, as may be so specified;

but the nature of the treatment shall not be specified in the order except as mentioned in paragraph (a) or (b) above.

(3)   A court shall not make a drug treatment and testing order unless it is satisfied that arrangements have been or can be made for the treatment intended to be specified in the order (including arrangements for the reception of the offender where he is to be required to submit to treatment as a resident).

(4)   A drug treatment and testing order shall include a requirement ("the testing requirement") that, for the purpose of ascertaining whether he has any drug in his body during the treatment and testing period, the offender shall provide during that period, at such times or in such circumstances as may (subject to the provisions of the order) be determined by the treatment provider, samples of such description as may be so determined.

(5)   The testing requirement shall specify for each month the minimum number of occasions on which samples are to be provided.

(6)   A drug treatment and testing order shall include a provision specifying the petty sessions area in which it appears to the court making the order that the offender resides or will reside.

(7)   A drug treatment and testing order shall—

    (a)   provide that, for the treatment and testing period, the offender shall be under the supervision of a responsible officer, that is to say, a probation officer appointed for or assigned to the petty sessions area specified in the order;

    (b)   require the offender to keep in touch with the responsible officer in accordance with such instructions as he may from time to time be given by that officer, and to notify him of any change of address; and

    (c)   provide that the results of the tests carried out on the samples provided by the offender in pursuance of the testing requirement shall be communicated to the responsible officer.

(8)   Supervision by the responsible officer shall be carried out to such extent only as may be necessary for the purpose of enabling him—

    (a)   to report on the offender's progress to the court responsible for the order;

    (b)   to report to that court any failure by the offender to comply with the requirements of the order; and

    (c)   to determine whether the circumstances are such that he should apply to that court for the revocation or amendment of the order.

(9)   In this section and sections 63 and 64 below, references to the court responsible for a drug treatment and testing order are references to—

    (a)   the court by which the order is made; or

    (b)   where another court is specified in the order in accordance with subsection (10) below, that court.

(10)   Where the area specified in a drug treatment and testing order made by a magistrates' court is not the area for which the court acts, the court may, if it thinks fit, include in the order provision specifying for the purposes of subsection (9) above a magistrates' court which acts for that area.

Definitions   For "drug treatment and testing order" and "the treatment and testing period", see s 61(2).
References   See para 5.14.

---

63 Periodic reviews

(1)   A drug treatment and testing order shall—

    (a)   provide for the order to be reviewed periodically at intervals of not less than one month;

    (b)   provide for each review of the order to be made, subject to subsection (7) below, at a hearing held for the purpose by the court responsible for the order (a "review hearing");

    (c)   require the offender to attend each review hearing;

(d)   provide for the responsible officer to make to the court, before each review, a report in writing on the offender's progress under the order; and

(e)   provide for each such report to include the test results communicated to the responsible officer under section 62(7)(c) above and the views of the treatment provider as to the treatment and testing of the offender.

(2)   At a review hearing the court, after considering the responsible officer's report, may amend any requirement or provision of the order.

(3)   The court—

(a)   shall not amend the treatment or testing requirement unless the offender expresses his willingness to comply with the requirement as amended;

(b)   shall not amend any provision of the order so as to reduce the treatment and testing period below the minimum specified in section 61(2) above, or to increase it above the maximum so specified; and

(c)   except with the consent of the offender, shall not amend any requirement or provision of the order while an appeal against the order is pending.

(4)   If the offender fails to express his willingness to comply with the treatment or testing requirement as proposed to be amended by the court, the court may—

(a)   revoke the order; and

(b)   deal with him, for the offence in respect of which the order was made, in any manner in which it could deal with him if he had just been convicted by the court of the offence.

(5)   In dealing with the offender under subsection (4)(b) above, the court—

(a)   shall take into account the extent to which the offender has complied with the requirements of the order; and

(b)   may impose a custodial sentence notwithstanding anything in section 1(2) of the 1991 Act.

(6)   Where the order was made by a magistrates' court in the case of an offender under the age of 18 years in respect of an offence triable only on indictment in the case of an adult, the court's power under subsection (4)(b) above shall be a power to do either or both of the following, namely—

(a)   to impose a fine not exceeding £5,000 for the offence in respect of which the order was made;

(b)   to deal with the offender for that offence in any way in which it could deal with him if it had just convicted him of an offence punishable with imprisonment for a term not exceeding six months;

and the reference in paragraph (b) above to an offence punishable with imprisonment shall be construed without regard to any prohibition or restriction imposed by or under any enactment on the imprisonment of young offenders.

(7)   If at a review hearing the court, after considering the responsible officer's report, is of the opinion that the offender's progress under the order is satisfactory, the court may so amend the order as to provide for each subsequent review to be made by the court without a hearing.

(8)   If at a review without a hearing the court, after considering the responsible officer's report, is of the opinion that the offender's progress under the order is no longer satisfactory, the court may require the offender to attend a hearing of the court at a specified time and place.

(9)   At that hearing the court, after considering that report, may—

(a)   exercise the powers conferred by this section as if the hearing were a review hearing; and

(b) so amend the order as to provide for each subsequent review to be made at a review hearing.

(10) In this section any reference to the court, in relation to a review without a hearing, shall be construed—

    (a) in the case of the Crown Court, as a reference to a judge of the court;

    (b) in the case of a magistrates' court, as a reference to a justice of the peace acting for the commission area for which the court acts.

Definitions For "drug treatment and testing order" and "treatment and testing period", see s 61(2); for "the treatment provider" and "the treatment requirement", see s 62(1); for "the testing requirement", see s 62(4); for "the responsible officer", see s 62(7); as to the court responsible for the order, see s 62(9), (10); for "custodial sentence" see, by virtue of s 85(5), the Criminal Justice Act 1991, s 31(1), as amended and repealed in part by ss 106, 119, 120(2) of, Sch 7, para 42, Sch 8, para 78(b), Sch 10 to, this Act; for "the 1991 Act" and "commission area", see s 117(1).
References See para 5.15.

---

64 Supplementary provisions as to orders

(1) Before making a drug treatment and testing order, a court shall explain to the offender in ordinary language—

    (a) the effect of the order and of the requirements proposed to be included in it;

    (b) the consequences which may follow (under Schedule 2 to the 1991 Act) if he fails to comply with any of those requirements;

    (c) that the order may be reviewed (under that Schedule) on the application either of the offender or of the responsible officer; and

    (d) that the order will be periodically reviewed at intervals as provided for in the order (by virtue of section 63 above);

and the court shall not make the order unless the offender expresses his willingness to comply with its requirements.

(2) Where, in the case of a drug treatment and testing order made by a magistrates' court, another magistrates' court is responsible for the order, the court making the order shall forthwith send copies of the order to the other court.

(3) Where a drug treatment and testing order is made or amended under section 63(2) above, the court responsible for the order shall forthwith or, in a case falling within subsection (2) above, as soon as reasonably practicable give copies of the order, or the order as amended, to a probation officer assigned to the court, and he shall give a copy—

    (a) to the offender;

    (b) to the treatment provider; and

    (c) to the responsible officer.

(4) Where a drug treatment and testing order has been made on an appeal brought from the Crown Court, or from the criminal division of the Court of Appeal, for the purposes of sections 62 and 63 above it shall be deemed to have been made by the Crown Court.

(5) Schedule 2 to the 1991 Act (enforcement etc of community orders) shall have effect subject to the amendments specified in Schedule 4 to this Act, being amendments for applying that Schedule to drug treatment and testing orders.

Definitions For "drug treatment and testing order", see s 61(2); for "the treatment provider", see s 62(1); for "the responsible officer", see s 62(7); as to the court responsible for the order, see s 62(9), (10); for "the 1991 Act", see s 117(1).
References See para 5.16.

Young offenders: reprimands and warnings

65 Reprimands and warnings

(1)   Subsections (2) to (5) below apply where—
  (a)   a constable has evidence that a child or young person ("the offender") has committed an offence;
  (b)   the constable considers that the evidence is such that, if the offender were prosecuted for the offence, there would be a realistic prospect of his being convicted;
  (c)   the offender admits to the constable that he committed the offence;
  (d)   the offender has not previously been convicted of an offence; and
  (e)   the constable is satisfied that it would not be in the public interest for the offender to be prosecuted.

(2)   Subject to subsection (4) below, the constable may reprimand the offender if the offender has not previously been reprimanded or warned.

(3)   The constable may warn the offender if—
  (a)   the offender has not previously been warned; or
  (b)   where the offender has previously been warned, the offence was committed more than two years after the date of the previous warning and the constable considers the offence to be not so serious as to require a charge to be brought;
but no person may be warned under paragraph (b) above more than once.

(4)   Where the offender has not been previously reprimanded, the constable shall warn rather than reprimand the offender if he considers the offence to be so serious as to require a warning.

(5)   The constable shall—
  (a)   give any reprimand or warning at a police station and, where the offender is under the age of 17, in the presence of an appropriate adult; and
  (b)   explain to the offender and, where he is under that age, the appropriate adult in ordinary language—
    (i)   in the case of a reprimand, the effect of subsection (5)(a) of section 66 below;
    (ii)   in the case of a warning, the effect of subsections (1), (2), (4) and (5)(b) and (c) of that section, and any guidance issued under subsection (3) of that section.

(6)   The Secretary of State shall publish, in such manner as he considers appropriate, guidance as to—
  (a)   the circumstances in which it is appropriate to give reprimands or warnings, including criteria for determining—
    (i)   for the purposes of subsection (3)(b) above, whether an offence is not so serious as to require a charge to be brought; and
    (ii)   for the purposes of subsection (4) above, whether an offence is so serious as to require a warning;
  (b)   the category of constable by whom reprimands and warnings may be given; and
  (c)   the form which reprimands and warnings are to take and the manner in which they are to be given and recorded.

(7)   In this section "appropriate adult", in relation to a child or young person, means—

(a) his parent or guardian or, if he is in the care of a local authority or voluntary organisation, a person representing that authority or organisation;

(b) a social worker of a local authority social services department;

(c) if no person falling within paragraph (a) or (b) above is available, any responsible person aged 18 or over who is not a police officer or a person employed by the police.

(8) No caution shall be given to a child or young person after the commencement of this section.

(9) Any reference (however expressed) in any enactment passed before or in the same Session as this Act to a person being cautioned shall be construed, in relation to any time after that commencement, as including a reference to a child or young person being reprimanded or warned.

Definitions For "child" and "young person", see s 117(1), (3).
References See paras 5.18–5.20.

66 Effect of reprimands and warnings

(1) Where a constable warns a person under section 65 above, he shall as soon as practicable refer the person to a youth offending team.

(2) A youth offending team—

(a) shall assess any person referred to them under subsection (1) above; and

(b) unless they consider it inappropriate to do so, shall arrange for him to participate in a rehabilitation programme.

(3) The Secretary of State shall publish, in such manner as he considers appropriate, guidance as to—

(a) what should be included in a rehabilitation programme arranged for a person under subsection (2) above;

(b) the manner in which any failure by a person to participate in such a programme is to be recorded; and

(c) the persons to whom any such failure is to be notified.

(4) Where a person who has been warned under section 65 above is convicted of an offence committed within two years of the warning, the court by or before which he is so convicted—

(a) shall not make an order under subsection (1)(b) (conditional discharge) of section 1A of the 1973 Act in respect of the offence unless it is of the opinion that there are exceptional circumstances relating to the offence or the offender which justify its doing so; and

(b) where it does so, shall state in open court that it is of that opinion and why it is.

(5) The following, namely—

(a) any reprimand of a person under section 65 above;

(b) any warning of a person under that section; and

(c) any report on a failure by a person to participate in a rehabilitation programme arranged for him under subsection (2) above,

may be cited in criminal proceedings in the same circumstances as a conviction of the person may be cited.

(6) In this section "rehabilitation programme" means a programme the purpose of which is to rehabilitate participants and to prevent them from re-offending.

Definitions For "the 1973 Act" and "youth offending team", see s 117(1).
References See para 5.21.

Young offenders: non-custodial orders

67 Reparation orders

(1)   This section applies where a child or young person is convicted of an offence other than one for which the sentence is fixed by law.

(2)   Subject to the provisions of this section and section 68 below, the court by or before which the offender is convicted may make an order (a "reparation order") which requires the offender to make reparation specified in the order—

    (a)   to a person or persons so specified; or

    (b)   to the community at large;

and any person so specified must be a person identified by the court as a victim of the offence or a person otherwise affected by it.

(3)   The court shall not make a reparation order unless it has been notified by the Secretary of State that arrangements for implementing such orders are available in the area proposed to be named in the order and the notice has not been withdrawn.

(4)   The court shall not make a reparation order in respect of the offender if it proposes—

    (a)   to pass on him a custodial sentence or a sentence under section 53(1) of the 1933 Act; or

    (b)   to make in respect of him a community service order, a combination order, a supervision order which includes requirements imposed in pursuance of sections 12 to 12C of the 1969 Act or an action plan order.

(5)   A reparation order shall not require the offender—

    (a)   to work for more than 24 hours in aggregate; or

    (b)   to make reparation to any person without the consent of that person.

(6)   Subject to subsection (5) above, requirements specified in a reparation order shall be such as in the opinion of the court are commensurate with seriousness of the offence, or the combination of the offence and one or more offences associated with it.

(7)   Requirements so specified shall, as far as practicable, be such as to avoid—

    (a)   any conflict with the offender's religious beliefs or with the requirements of any community order to which he may be subject; and

    (b)   any interference with the times, if any, at which the offender normally works or attends school or any other educational establishment.

(8)   Any reparation required by a reparation order—

    (a)   shall be made under the supervision of the responsible officer; and

    (b)   shall be made within a period of three months from the date of the making of the order.

(9)   A reparation order shall name the petty sessions area in which it appears to the court making the order, or to the court varying any provision included in the order in pursuance of this subsection, that the offender resides or will reside.

(10)   In this section "responsible officer", in relation to a reparation order, means one of the following who is specified in the order, namely—

    (a)   a probation officer;

    (b)   a social worker of a local authority social services department; and

    (c)   a member of a youth offending team.

(11)   The court shall give reasons if it does not make a reparation order in a case where it has power to do so.

Definitions   For "action plan order", see s 69(2); for "make reparation", see s 85(1); for "the 1933 Act", "the 1969 Act", "custodial sentence" and "youth offending team", see s 117(1); for "child" and "young person", see s 117(1), (3); for "combination order", "community order" and "supervision order" see, by virtue of s 85(5), the Criminal Justice Act 1991, s 31(1); as to an offence associated with another see, by virtue of s 85(5), s 31(2) of the 1991 Act.
References   See paras 5.2, 5.22, 5.23.

68 Reparation orders: supplemental

(1)   Before making a reparation order, a court shall obtain and consider a written report by a probation officer, a social worker of a local authority social services department or a member of a youth offending team, indicating—
>   (a)   the type of work that is suitable for the offender; and
>   (b)   the attitude of the victim or victims to the requirements proposed to be included in the order.

(2)   Before making a reparation order, a court shall explain to the offender in ordinary language—
>   (a)   the effect of the order and of the requirements proposed to be included in it;
>   (b)   the consequences which may follow (under Schedule 5 to this Act) if he fails to comply with any of those requirements; and
>   (c)   that the court has power (under that Schedule) to review the order on the application either of the offender or of the responsible officer.

(3)   Schedule 5 to this Act shall have effect for dealing with failure to comply with the requirements of reparation orders, for varying such orders and for discharging them with or without the substitution of other sentences.

Definitions   For "reparation order", see s 67(2); for "the responsible officer", see s 67(10); for "youth offending team", see s 117(1).
References   See para 5.24.

69 Action plan orders

(1)   This section applies where a child or young person is convicted of an offence other than one for which the sentence is fixed by law.

(2)   Subject to the provisions of this section and section 70 below, the court by or before which the offender is convicted may, if it is of the opinion that it is desirable to do so in the interests of securing his rehabilitation, or of preventing the commission by him of further offences, make an order (an "action plan order") which—
>   (a)   requires the offender, for a period of three months beginning with the date of the order, to comply with an action plan, that is to say, a series of requirements with respect to his actions and whereabouts during that period;
>   (b)   places the offender under the supervision for that period of the responsible officer; and
>   (c)   requires the offender to comply with any directions given by that officer with a view to the implementation of that plan.

(3)   The court shall not make an action plan order unless it has been notified by the Secretary of State that arrangements for implementing such orders are available in the area proposed to be named in the order and the notice has not been withdrawn.

(4)   The court shall not make an action plan order in respect of the offender if—
>   (a)   he is already the subject of such an order; or
>   (b)   the court proposes to pass on him a custodial sentence or a sentence under section 53(1) of the 1933 Act, or to make in respect of him a

probation order, a community service order, a combination order, a supervision order or an attendance centre order.

(5)   Requirements included in an action plan order, or directions given by a responsible officer, may require the offender to do all or any of the following things, namely—

(a)   to participate in activities specified in the requirements or directions at a time or times so specified;

(b)   to present himself to a person or persons specified in the requirements or directions at a place or places and at a time or times so specified;

(c)   to attend at an attendance centre specified in the requirements or directions for a number of hours so specified;

(d)   to stay away from a place or places specified in the requirements or directions;

(e)   to comply with any arrangements for his education specified in the requirements or directions;

(f)   to make reparation specified in the requirements or directions to a person or persons so specified or to the community at large; and

(g)   to attend any hearing fixed by the court under section 70(3) below.

(6)   Such requirements and directions shall, as far as practicable, be such as to avoid—

(a)   any conflict with the offender's religious beliefs or with the requirements of any other community order to which he may be subject; and

(b)   any interference with the times, if any, at which he normally works or attends school or any other educational establishment.

(7)   Subsection (5)(c) above does not apply unless the offence committed by the offender is punishable with imprisonment in the case of a person aged 21 or over.

(8)   A person shall not be specified in requirements or directions under subsection (5)(f) above unless—

(a)   he is identified by the court or, as the case may be, the responsible officer as a victim of the offence or a person otherwise affected by it; and

(b)   he consents to the reparation being made.

(9)   An action plan order shall name the petty sessions area in which it appears to the court making the order, or to the court varying any provision included in the order in pursuance of this subsection, that the offender resides or will reside.

(10)   In this section "responsible officer", in relation to an action plan order, means one of the following who is specified in the order, namely—

(a)   a probation officer;

(b)   a social worker of a local authority social services department; and

(c)   a member of a youth offending team.

(11)   An action plan order shall be a community order for the purposes of Part I of the 1991 Act; and the provisions of that Part, which include provisions with respect to restrictions on imposing, and procedural requirements for, community sentences (sections 6 and 7), shall apply accordingly.

Definitions   For "make reparation", see s 85(1); for "the 1933 Act", "the 1991 Act", "custodial sentence" and "youth offending team", see s 117(1); for "child" and "young person", see s 117(1), (3); for "community sentence" see, by virtue of s 85(5), the Criminal Justice Act 1991, s 6(1); for "community order" see, by virtue of the said s 85(5), s 6(4) of the 1991 Act, as amended and repealed in part by ss 119, 120(2) of, Sch 8, para 74, Sch 10 to, this Act; for "attendance centre order", "combination order" and "supervision order" see, by virtue of the said s 85(5), s 31(1) of the 1991 Act.
References   See paras 5.2, 5.25.

70 Action plan orders: supplemental

(1)   Before making an action plan order, a court shall obtain and consider—
   (a)   a written report by a probation officer, a social worker of a local authority social services department or a member of a youth offending team, indicating—
      (i)   the requirements proposed by that person to be included in the order;
      (ii)   the benefits to the offender that the proposed requirements are designed to achieve; and
      (iii)   the attitude of a parent or guardian of the offender to the proposed requirements; and
   (b)   where the offender is under the age of 16, information about the offender's family circumstances and the likely effect of the order on those circumstances.

(2)   Before making an action plan order, a court shall explain to the offender in ordinary language—
   (a)   the effect of the order and of the requirements proposed to be included in it;
   (b)   the consequences which may follow (under Schedule 5 to this Act) if he fails to comply with any of those requirements; and
   (c)   that the court has power (under that Schedule) to review the order on the application either of the offender or of the responsible officer.

(3)   Immediately after making an action plan order, a court may—
   (a)   fix a further hearing for a date not more than 21 days after the making of the order; and
   (b)   direct the responsible officer to make, at that hearing, a report as to the effectiveness of the order and the extent to which it has been implemented.

(4)   At a hearing fixed under subsection (3) above, the court—
   (a)   shall consider the responsible officer's report; and
   (b)   may, on the application of the responsible officer or the offender, vary the order—
      (i)   by cancelling any provision included in it; or
      (ii)   by inserting in it (either in addition to or in substitution for any of its provisions) any provision that the court could originally have included in it.

(5)   Schedule 5 to this Act shall have effect for dealing with failure to comply with the requirements of action plan orders, for varying such orders and for discharging them with or without the substitution of other sentences.

Definitions   For "action plan order", see s 69(2); for "the responsible officer", see s 67(10); for "youth offending team", see s 117(1).
References   See para 5.27.

---

71 Supervision orders

(1)   In subsection (3) of section 12A of the 1969 Act (young offenders), after paragraph (a) there shall be inserted the following paragraph—
      "(aa) to make reparation specified in the order to a person or persons so specified or to the community at large;".

(2)   In subsection (5) of that section, for the words "subsection (3)(a) or (b)" there shall be substituted the words "subsection (3)(a), (aa) or (b)".

(3)   In subsection (7) of that section, after paragraph (a) there shall be inserted the following paragraph—

> "(aa) any requirement to make reparation to any person unless that person—
>
> > (i)   is identified by the court as a victim of the offence or a person otherwise affected by it; and
> > (ii)   consents to the inclusion of the requirement; or".

(4)   In subsection (6) of section 12AA of the 1969 Act (requirement for young offender to live in local authority accommodation), for paragraphs (b) to (d) there shall be substituted the following paragraphs—

> "(b)   that order imposed—
>
> > (i)   a requirement under section 12, 12A or 12C of this Act; or
> > (ii)   a residence requirement;
>
> (c)   he fails to comply with that requirement, or is found guilty of an offence committed while that order was in force; and
>
> (d)   the court is satisfied that—
>
> > (i)   the failure to comply with the requirement, or the behaviour which constituted the offence, was due to a significant extent to the circumstances in which he was living; and
> > (ii)   the imposition of a residence requirement will assist in his rehabilitation;";

and for the words "the condition in paragraph (d)" there shall be substituted the words "sub-paragraph (i) of paragraph (d)".

(5)   In section 13 of the 1969 Act (selection of supervisor), subsection (2) shall cease to have effect.

Definitions   For "the 1969 Act", see s 117(1); for "a residence requirement", see the Children and Young Persons Act 1969, s 12AA(1).
References   See para 5.28.

72 Breach of requirements in supervision orders

(1)   In subsection (3) of section 15 of the 1969 Act (variation and discharge of supervision orders), for paragraphs (a) and (b) there shall be substituted the following paragraphs—

> "(a)   whether or not it also makes an order under subsection (1) above, may order him to pay a fine of an amount not exceeding £1,000, or make in respect of him—
>
> > (i)   subject to section 16A(1) of this Act, an order under section 17 of the Criminal Justice Act 1982 (attendance centre orders); or
> > (ii)   subject to section 16B of this Act, an order under section 12 of the Criminal Justice Act 1991 (curfew orders);
>
> (b)   if the supervision order was made by a relevant court, may discharge the order and deal with him, for the offence in respect of which the order was made, in any manner in which he could have been dealt with for that offence by the court which made the order if the order had not been made; or
>
> (c)   if the order was made by the Crown Court, may commit him in custody or release him on bail until he can be brought or appear before the Crown Court."

(2)   For subsections (4) to (6) of that section there shall be substituted the following subsections—

"(4) Where a court deals with a supervised person under subsection (3)(c) above, it shall send to the Crown Court a certificate signed by a justice of the peace giving—

    (a)   particulars of the supervised person's failure to comply with the requirement in question; and

    (b)   such other particulars of the case as may be desirable;

and a certificate purporting to be so signed shall be admissible as evidence of the failure before the Crown Court.

    (5)   Where—

    (a)   by virtue of subsection (3)(c) above the supervised person is brought or appears before the Crown Court; and

    (b)   it is proved to the satisfaction of the court that he has failed to comply with the requirement in question,

that court may deal with him, for the offence in respect of which the order was made, in any manner in which it could have dealt with him for that offence if it had not made the order.

    (6)   Where the Crown Court deals with a supervised person under subsection (5) above, it shall discharge the supervision order if it is still in force."

(3)   In subsections (7) and (8) of that section, for the words "or (4)" there shall be substituted the words "or (5)".

Definitions   For "the 1969 Act", "the 1982 Act" and "the 1991 Act", see s 117(1); for "supervision orders" and "supervised person", see the Children and Young Persons Act 1969, s 11, as amended by s 119 of, Sch 8, para 17 to, this Act; for "relevant court", see s 15(11) of the 1969 Act.
References   See para 5.29.

Young offenders: detention and training orders

73 Detention and training orders

(1)   Subject to section 53 of the 1933 Act, section 8 of the Criminal Justice Act 1982 ("the 1982 Act") and subsection (2) below, where—

    (a)   a child or young person ("the offender") is convicted of an offence which is punishable with imprisonment in the case of a person aged 21 or over; and

    (b)   the court is of the opinion that either or both of paragraphs (a) or (b) of subsection (2) of section 1 of the 1991 Act apply or the case falls within subsection (3) of that section,

the sentence that the court is to pass is a detention and training order.

(2)   A court shall not make a detention and training order—

    (a)   in the case of an offender under the age of 15 at the time of the conviction, unless it is of the opinion that he is a persistent offender;

    (b)   in the case of an offender under the age of 12 at that time, unless—

        (i)   it is of the opinion that only a custodial sentence would be adequate to protect the public from further offending by him; and

        (ii)   the offence was committed on or after such date as the Secretary of State may by order appoint.

(3)   A detention and training order is an order that the offender in respect of whom it is made shall be subject, for the term specified in the order, to a period of detention and training followed by a period of supervision.

(4)   A detention and training order shall be a custodial sentence for the purposes of Part I of the 1991 Act; and the provisions of sections 1 to 4 of that Act shall apply accordingly.

(5)   Subject to subsection (6) below, the term of a detention and training order shall be 4, 6, 8, 10, 12, 18 or 24 months.

(6)   The term of a detention and training order may not exceed the maximum term of imprisonment that the Crown Court could (in the case of an offender aged 21 or over) impose for the offence.

(7)   The following provisions, namely—

(a)   section 1B of the 1982 Act (detention in young offender institutions: special provision for offenders under 18); and

(b)   sections 1 to 4 of the 1994 Act (secure training orders),

which are superseded by this section and sections 74 to 78 below, shall cease to have effect.

Definitions   For "the 1933 Act", "the 1991 Act", "the 1994 Act" and "custodial sentence", see s 117(1); for "child" and "young person", see s 117(1), (3).
References   See paras 5.31, 5.32.

---

74 Duties and powers of court

(1)   On making a detention and training order in a case where subsection (2) of section 73 above applies, it shall be the duty of the court (in addition to the duty imposed by section 1(4) of the 1991 Act) to state in open court that it is of the opinion mentioned in paragraph (a) or, as the case may be, paragraphs (a) and (b)(i) of that subsection.

(2)   Subject to subsection (3) below, where—

(a)   an offender is convicted of more than one offence for which he is liable to a detention and training order; or

(b)   an offender who is subject to a detention and training order is convicted of one or more further offences for which he is liable to such an order,

the court shall have the same power to pass consecutive detention and training orders as if they were sentences of imprisonment.

(3)   A court shall not make in respect of an offender a detention and training order the effect of which would be that he would be subject to detention and training orders for a term which exceeds 24 months.

(4)   Where the term of the detention and training orders to which an offender would otherwise be subject exceeds 24 months, the excess shall be treated as remitted.

(5)   In determining the term of a detention and training order for an offence, the court shall take account of any period for which the offender has been remanded in custody in connection with the offence, or any other offence the charge for which was founded on the same facts or evidence.

(6)   The reference in subsection (5) above to an offender being remanded in custody is a reference to his being—

(a)   held in police detention;

(b)   remanded in or committed to custody by an order of a court;

(c)   remanded or committed to local authority accommodation under section 23 of the 1969 Act and placed and kept in secure accommodation; or

      (d)   remanded, admitted or removed to hospital under section 35, 36, 38 or 48 of the Mental Health Act 1983.

(7)   A person is in police detention for the purposes of subsection (6) above—

      (a)   at any time when he is in police detention for the purposes of the 1984 Act; and

      (b)   at any time when he is detained under section 14 of the Prevention of Terrorism (Temporary Provisions) Act 1989;

and in that subsection "secure accommodation" has the same meaning as in section 23 of the 1969 Act.

(8)   For the purpose of any reference in this section or sections 75 to 78 below to the term of a detention and training order, consecutive terms of such orders and terms of such orders which are wholly or partly concurrent shall be treated as a single term if—

      (a)   the orders were made on the same occasion; or

      (b)   where they were made on different occasions, the offender has not been released (by virtue of subsection (2), (3), (4) or (5) of section 75 below) at any time during the period beginning with the first and ending with the last of those occasions.

Definitions   For "offender", see s 73(1)(a); for "detention and training order", see s 73(3); for "sentence of imprisonment" see, by virtue of s 85(5), the Criminal Justice Act 1991, s 31(1); for "the 1969 Act", "the 1984 Act" and "the 1991 Act", see s 117(1).
References   See para 5.33.

75 The period of detention and training

(1)   An offender shall serve the period of detention and training under a detention and training order in such secure accommodation as may be determined by the Secretary of State or by such other person as may be authorised by him for that purpose.

(2)   Subject to subsections (3) to (5) below, the period of detention and training under a detention and training order shall be one-half of the term of the order.

(3)   The Secretary of State may at any time release the offender if he is satisfied that exceptional circumstances exist which justify the offender's release on compassionate grounds.

(4)   The Secretary of State may release the offender—

      (a)   in the case of an order for a term of 8 months or more but less than 18 months, one month before the half-way point of the term of the order; and

      (b)   in the case of an order for a term of 18 months or more, one month or two months before that point.

(5)   If the youth court so orders on an application made by the Secretary of State for the purpose, the Secretary of State shall release the offender—

      (a)   in the case of an order for a term of 8 months or more but less than 18 months, one month after the half-way point of the term of the order; and

      (b)   in the case of an order for a term of 18 months or more, one month or two months after that point.

(6)   An offender detained in pursuance of a detention and training order shall be deemed to be in legal custody.

(7)   In this section and sections 77 and 78 below "secure accommodation" means—

(a)   a secure training centre;
(b)   a young offender institution;
(c)   accommodation provided by a local authority for the purpose of restricting the liberty of children and young persons;
(d)   accommodation provided for that purpose under subsection (5) of section 82 of the 1989 Act (financial support by the Secretary of State); or
(e)   such other accommodation provided for the purpose of restricting liberty as the Secretary of State may direct.

Definitions   For "the offender", see s 73(1)(a); for "detention and training order", see s 73(3); for "the 1989 Act", see s 117(1); for "child" and "young person", see s 117(1), (3).
References   See paras 5.34, 5.35.

76 The period of supervision

(1)   The period of supervision of an offender who is subject to a detention and training order—
(a)   shall begin with the offender's release, whether at the half-way point of the term of the order or otherwise; and
(b)   subject to subsection (2) below, shall end when the term of the order ends.

(2)   The Secretary of State may by order provide that the period of supervision shall end at such point during the term of a detention and training order as may be specified in the order under this subsection.

(3)   During the period of supervision, the offender shall be under the supervision of—
(a)   a probation officer;
(b)   a social worker of a local authority social services department; or
(c)   a member of a youth offending team;
and the category of person to supervise the offender shall be determined from time to time by the Secretary of State.

(4)   Where the supervision is to be provided by a probation officer, the probation officer shall be an officer appointed for or assigned to the petty sessions area within which the offender resides for the time being.

(5)   Where the supervision is to be provided by—
(a)   a social worker of a local authority social services department; or
(b)   a member of a youth offending team,
the social worker or member shall be a social worker of, or a member of a youth offending team established by, the local authority within whose area the offender resides for the time being.

(6)   The offender shall be given a notice from the Secretary of State specifying—
(a)   the category of person for the time being responsible for his supervision; and
(b)   any requirements with which he must for the time being comply.

(7)   A notice under subsection (6) above shall be given to the offender—
(a)   before the commencement of the period of supervision; and
(b)   before any alteration in the matters specified in subsection (6)(a) or (b) above comes into effect.

Definitions   For "the offender", see s 73(1)(a); for "detention and training order", see s 73(3); for "youth offending team", see s 117(1).
References   See para 5.36.

77 Breaches of supervision requirements

(1)   Where a detention and training order is in force in respect of an offender and it appears on information to a justice of the peace acting for a relevant petty sessions area that the offender has failed to comply with requirements under section 76(6)(b) above, the justice—

(a)   may issue a summons requiring the offender to appear at the place and time specified in the summons before a youth court acting for the area; or

(b)   if the information is in writing and on oath, may issue a warrant for the offender's arrest requiring him to be brought before such a court.

(2)   For the purposes of this section a petty sessions area is a relevant petty sessions area in relation to a detention and training order if—

(a)   the order was made by a youth court acting for it; or

(b)   the offender resides in it for the time being.

(3)   If it is proved to the satisfaction of the youth court before which an offender appears or is brought under this section that he has failed to comply with requirements under section 76(6)(b) above, that court may—

(a)   order the offender to be detained, in such secure accommodation as the Secretary of State may determine, for such period, not exceeding the shorter of three months or the remainder of the term of the detention and training order, as the court may specify; or

(b)   impose on the offender a fine not exceeding level 3 on the standard scale.

(4)   An offender detained in pursuance of an order under subsection (3) above shall be deemed to be in legal custody; and a fine imposed under that subsection shall be deemed, for the purposes of any enactment, to be a sum adjudged to be paid by a conviction.

Definitions   For "the offender", see s 73(1)(a); for "detention and training order", see s 73(3); for "secure accommodation", see s 75(7).
References   See para 5.37.

---

78 Offences during currency of order

(1)   This section applies to a person subject to a detention and training order if—

(a)   after his release and before the date on which the term of the order ends, he commits an offence punishable with imprisonment in the case of a person aged 21 or over; and

(b)   whether before or after that date, he is convicted of that offence ("the new offence").

(2)   Subject to section 7(8) of the 1969 Act, the court by or before which a person to whom this section applies is convicted of the new offence may, whether or not it passes any other sentence on him, order him to be detained in such secure accommodation as the Secretary of State may determine for the whole or any part of the period which—

(a)   begins with the date of the court's order; and

(b)   is equal in length to the period between the date on which the new offence was committed and the date mentioned in subsection (1) above.

(3)   The period for which a person to whom this section applies is ordered under subsection (2) above to be detained in secure accommodation—

(a)   shall, as the court may direct, either be served before and be followed by, or be served concurrently with, any sentence imposed for the new offence; and

(b)   in either case, shall be disregarded in determining the appropriate length of that sentence.

(4)   Where the new offence is found to have been committed over a period of two or more days, or at some time during a period of two or more days, it shall be taken for the purposes of this section to have been committed on the last of those days.

(5)   A person detained in pursuance of an order under subsection (2) above shall be deemed to be in legal custody.

Definitions   For "detention and training order", see s 73(3); for "secure accommodation", see s 75(7); for "the 1969 Act", see s 117(1).
References   See para 5.38.

79 Interaction with sentences of detention

(1)   Where a court passes a sentence of detention in a young offender institution in the case of an offender who is subject to a detention and training order, the sentence shall take effect as follows—
    (a)   if the offender has been released by virtue of subsection (2), (3), (4) or (5) of section 75 above, at the beginning of the day on which it is passed;
    (b)   if not, either as mentioned in paragraph (a) above or, if the court so orders, at the time when the offender would otherwise be released by virtue of that subsection.

(2)   Where a court makes a detention and training order in the case of an offender who is subject to a sentence of detention in a young offender institution, the order shall take effect as follows—
    (a)   if the offender has been released under Part II of the 1991 Act, at the beginning of the day on which it is made;
    (b)   if not, either as mentioned in paragraph (a) above or, if the court so orders, at the time when the offender would otherwise be released under that Part.

(3)   Subject to subsection (4) below, where at any time an offender is subject concurrently—
    (a)   to a detention and training order; and
    (b)   to a sentence of detention in a young offender institution,
he shall be treated for the purposes of sections 75 to 78 above, section 1C of the 1982 Act and Part II of the 1991 Act as if he were subject only to the one of them that was imposed on the later occasion.

(4)   Nothing in subsection (3) above shall require the offender to be released in respect of either the order or the sentence unless and until he is required to be released in respect of each of them.

(5)   Where, by virtue of any enactment giving a court power to deal with a person in a manner in which a court on a previous occasion could have dealt with him, a detention and training order for any term is made in the case of a person who has attained the age of 18, the person shall be treated as if he had been sentenced to detention in a young offender institution for the same term.

Definitions   For "detention and training order", see s 73(3); for "the 1982 Act" and "the 1991 Act", see s 117(1).
References   See para 5.39.

Sentencing: general

80 Sentencing guidelines

(1)   This section applies where the Court—

     (a)   is seised of an appeal against, or a reference under section 36 of the Criminal Justice Act 1988 with respect to, the sentence passed for an offence; or

     (b)   receives a proposal under section 81 below in respect of a particular category of offence;

and in this section "the relevant category" means any category within which the offence falls or, as the case may be, the category to which the proposal relates.

(2)   The Court shall consider—

     (a)   whether to frame guidelines as to the sentencing of offenders for offences of the relevant category; or

     (b)   where such guidelines already exist, whether it would be appropriate to review them.

(3)   Where the Court decides to frame or revise such guidelines, the Court shall have regard to—

     (a)   the need to promote consistency in sentencing;

     (b)   the sentences imposed by courts in England and Wales for offences of the relevant category;

     (c)   the cost of different sentences and their relative effectiveness in preventing re-offending;

     (d)   the need to promote public confidence in the criminal justice system; and

     (e)   the views communicated to the Court, in accordance with section 81(4)(b) below, by the Sentencing Advisory Panel.

(4)   Guidelines framed or revised under this section shall include criteria for determining the seriousness of offences, including (where appropriate) criteria for determining the weight to be given to any previous convictions of offenders or any failures of theirs to respond to previous sentences.

(5)   In a case falling within subsection (1)(a) above, guidelines framed or revised under this section shall, if practicable, be included in the Court's judgment in the appeal.

(6)   Subject to subsection (5) above, guidelines framed or revised under this section shall be included in a judgment of the Court at the next appropriate opportunity (having regard to the relevant category of offence).

(7)   For the purposes of this section, the Court is seised of an appeal against a sentence if—

     (a)   the Court or a single judge has granted leave to appeal against the sentence under section 9 or 10 of the Criminal Appeal Act 1968; or

     (b)   in a case where the judge who passed the sentence granted a certificate of fitness for appeal under section 9 or 10 of that Act, notice of appeal has been given,

and (in either case) the appeal has not been abandoned or disposed of.

(8)   For the purposes of this section, the Court is seised of a reference under section 36 of the Criminal Justice Act 1988 if it has given leave under subsection (1) of that section and the reference has not been disposed of.

(9)   In this section and section 81 below—

     "the Court" means the criminal division of the Court of Appeal;

     "offence" means an indictable offence.

References   See paras 5.2, 5.40–5.42.

81 The Sentencing Advisory Panel

(1)   The Lord Chancellor, after consultation with the Secretary of State and the Lord Chief Justice, shall constitute a sentencing panel to be known as the Sentencing Advisory Panel ("the Panel") and appoint one of the members of the Panel to be its chairman.

(2)   Where, in a case falling within subsection (1)(a) of section 80 above, the Court decides to frame or revise guidelines under that section for a particular category of offence, the Court shall notify the Panel.

(3)   The Panel may at any time, and shall if directed to do so by the Secretary of State, propose to the Court that guidelines be framed or revised under section 80 above for a particular category of offence.

(4)   Where the Panel receives a notification under subsection (2) above or makes a proposal under subsection (3) above, the Panel shall—

- (a)   obtain and consider the views on the matters in issue of such persons or bodies as may be determined, after consultation with the Secretary of State and the Lord Chief Justice, by the Lord Chancellor;
- (b)   formulate its own views on those matters and communicate them to the Court; and
- (c)   furnish information to the Court as to the matters mentioned in section 80(3)(b) and (c) above.

(5)   The Lord Chancellor may pay to any member of the Panel such remuneration as he may determine.

Definitions   For "the Court" and "offence", see s 80(9).
References   See paras 5.2, 5.43, 5.44.

---

82 Increase in sentences for racial aggravation

(1)   This section applies where a court is considering the seriousness of an offence other than one under sections 29 to 32 above.

(2)   If the offence was racially aggravated, the court—

- (a)   shall treat that fact as an aggravating factor (that is to say, a factor that increases the seriousness of the offence); and
- (b)   shall state in open court that the offence was so aggravated.

(3)   Section 28 above applies for the purposes of this section as it applies for the purposes of sections 29 to 32 above.

References   See para 5.45.

Miscellaneous and supplemental

83 Power to make confiscation orders on committal for sentence

After subsection (9) of section 71 of the Criminal Justice Act 1988 (confiscation orders) there shall be inserted the following subsection—

> "(9A)   Where an offender is committed by a magistrates' court for sentence under section 38 or 38A of the Magistrates' Courts Act 1980 or section 56 of the Criminal Justice Act 1967, this section and sections 72 to 74C below shall have effect as if the offender had been convicted of the offence in the proceedings before the Crown Court and not in the proceedings before the magistrates' court."

Definitions   For "offence", see the Criminal Justice Act 1988, s 102(4).
References   See para 5.46.

84 Football spectators: failure to comply with reporting duty

(1)   In section 16(5) of the Football Spectators Act 1989 (penalties for failure to comply with reporting duty imposed by restriction order)—

    (a)   for the words "one month" there shall be substituted the words "six months"; and

    (b)   for the words "level 3" there shall be substituted the words "level 5".

(2)   In section 24(2) of the 1984 Act (arrestable offences), after paragraph (p) there shall be inserted—

    "(q)   an offence under section 16(4) of the Football Spectators Act 1989 (failure to comply with reporting duty imposed by restriction order)."

Definitions   For "the 1984 Act", see s 117(1).
References   See para 5.47.

85 Interpretation etc of Chapter I

(1)   In this Chapter—

    "action plan order" has the meaning given by section 69(2) above;

    "detention and training order" has the meaning given by section 73(3) above;

    "drug treatment and testing order" has the meaning given by section 61(2) above;

    "make reparation", in relation to an offender, means make reparation for the offence otherwise than by the payment of compensation;

    "reparation order" has the meaning given by section 67(2) above;

    "responsible officer"—

    (a)   in relation to a drug treatment and testing order, has the meaning given by section 62(7) above;

    (b)   in relation to a reparation order, has the meaning given by section 67(10) above; ·

    (c)   in relation to an action plan order, has the meaning given by section 69(10) above.

(2)   Where the supervision under a reparation order or action plan order is to be provided by a probation officer, the probation officer shall be an officer appointed for or assigned to the petty sessions area named in the order.

(3)   Where the supervision under a reparation order or action plan order is to be provided by—

    (a)   a social worker of a local authority social services department; or

    (b)   a member of a youth offending team,

the social worker or member shall be a social worker of, or a member of a youth offending team established by, the local authority within whose area it appears to the court that the child or young person resides or will reside.

(4)   In this Chapter, in relation to a drug treatment and testing order—

    "the treatment and testing period" has the meaning given by section 61(2) above;

    "the treatment provider" and "the treatment requirement" have the meanings given by subsection (1) of section 62 above;

"the testing requirement" has the meaning given by subsection (4) of that section.

(5)   In this Chapter, unless the contrary intention appears, expressions which are also used in Part I of the 1991 Act have the same meanings as in that Part.

(6)   For the purposes of this Chapter, a sentence falls to be imposed under section 2(2), 3(2) or 4(2) of the 1997 Act if it is required by that provision and the court is not of the opinion there mentioned.

Definitions   For "youth offending team", "the 1991 Act" and "the 1997 Act" see s 117(1); for "child" and "young person", see s 117(1), (3).
References   See para 5.48.

CHAPTER II
SCOTLAND

Sexual or violent offenders

86 Extended sentences for sex and violent offenders

(1)   After section 210 of the 1995 Act there shall be inserted the following section—

"210A Extended sentences for sex of a sexual or violent offenders

(1)   Where a person is convicted on indictment of a sexual or violent offence, the court may, if it—
  (a)   intends, in relation to—
      (i)   a sexual offence, to pass a determinate sentence of imprisonment; or
      (ii)   a violent offence, to pass such a sentence for a term of four years or more; and
  (b)   considers that the period (if any) for which the offender would, apart from this section, be subject to a licence would not be adequate for the purpose of protecting the public from serious harm from the offender,
pass an extended sentence on the offender.

(2)   An extended sentence is a sentence of imprisonment which is the aggregate of—
  (a)   the term of imprisonment ("the custodial term") which the court would have passed on the offender otherwise than by virtue of this section; and
  (b)   a further period ("the extension period") for which the offender is to be subject to a licence and which is, subject to the provisions of this section, of such length as the court considers necessary for the purpose mentioned in subsection (1)(b) above.

(3)   The extension period shall not exceed, in the case of—
  (a)   a sexual offence, ten years; and
  (b)   a violent offence, five years.

(4)   A court shall, before passing an extended sentence, consider a report by a relevant officer of a local authority about the offender and his circumstances and, if the court thinks it necessary, hear that officer.

(5)   The term of an extended sentence passed for a statutory offence shall not exceed the maximum term of imprisonment provided for in the statute in respect of that offence.

(6) Subject to subsection (5) above, a sheriff may pass an extended sentence which is the aggregate of a custodial term not exceeding the maximum term of imprisonment which he may impose and an extension period not exceeding three years.

(7) The Secretary of State may by order—

    (a) amend paragraph (b) of subsection (3) above by substituting a different period, not exceeding ten years, for the period for the time being specified in that paragraph; and

    (b) make such transitional provision as appears to him to be necessary or expedient in connection with the amendment.

(8) The power to make an order under subsection (7) above shall be exercisable by statutory instrument; but no such order shall be made unless a draft of the order has been laid before, and approved by a resolution of, each House of Parliament.

(9) An extended sentence shall not be imposed where the sexual or violent offence was committed before the commencement of section 86 of the Crime and Disorder Act 1998.

(10) For the purposes of this section—

    "licence" and "relevant officer" have the same meaning as in Part I of the Prisoners and Criminal Proceedings (Scotland) Act 1993;

    "sexual offence" means—

      (i) rape;

      (ii) clandestine injury to women;

      (iii) abduction of a woman or girl with intent to rape or ravish;

      (iv) assault with intent to rape or ravish;

      (v) indecent assault;

      (vi) lewd, indecent or libidinous behaviour or practices;

      (vii) shameless indecency;

      (viii) sodomy;

      (ix) an offence under section 170 of the Customs and Excise Management Act 1979 in relation to goods prohibited to be imported under section 42 of the Customs Consolidation Act 1876, but only where the prohibited goods include indecent photographs of persons;

      (x) an offence under section 52 of the Civic Government (Scotland) Act 1982 (taking and distribution of indecent images of children);

      (xi) an offence under section 52A of that Act (possession of indecent images of children);

      (xii) an offence under section 1 of the Criminal Law (Consolidation) (Scotland) Act 1995 (incest);

      (xiii) an offence under section 2 of that Act (intercourse with a stepchild);

      (xiv) an offence under section 3 of that Act (intercourse with child under 16 by person in position of trust);

      (xv) an offence under section 5 of that Act (unlawful intercourse with girl under 16);

      (xvi) an offence under section 6 of that Act (indecent behaviour towards girl between 12 and 16);

      (xvii) an offence under section 8 of that Act (abduction of girl under 18 for purposes of unlawful intercourse);

      (xviii) an offence under section 10 of that Act (person having parental responsibilities causing or encouraging sexual activity in relation to a girl under 16); and

(xix)   an offence under subsection (5) of section 13 of that Act (homosexual offences);
"imprisonment" includes—
    (i)   detention under section 207 of this Act; and
    (ii) detention under section 208 of this Act; and
"violent offence" means any offence (other than an offence which is a sexual offence within the meaning of this section) inferring personal violence.

(11)   Any reference in subsection (10) above to a sexual offence includes—

(a)   a reference to any attempt, conspiracy or incitement to commit that offence; and

(b)   except in the case of an offence in paragraphs (i) to (viii) of the definition of "sexual offence" in that subsection, a reference to aiding and abetting, counselling or procuring the commission of that offence."

(2)   In section 209 of the 1995 Act (supervised release orders), in subsection (1)—

(a)   after the word "convicted" there shall be inserted the words "on indictment";

(b)   after the words "an offence" there shall be inserted the words ", other than a sexual offence within the meaning of section 210A of this Act,"; and

(c)   the words "not less than twelve months but" shall cease to have effect.

Definitions   For "the 1995 Act", see s 117(2); for "local authority", "offence" and "sentence", see the Criminal Procedure (Scotland) Act 1995, s 307(1); for "court", see s 307(2) of that Act; for "relevant officer", see the Prisoners and Criminal Proceedings (Scotland) Act 1993, s 27(1).
References   See paras 5.49–5.51.

---

87 Further provision as to extended sentences

After section 26 of the Prisoners and Criminal Proceedings (Scotland) Act 1993 ("the 1993 Act") there shall be inserted the following section—

"Extended sentences

26A Extended sentences

(1)   This section applies to a prisoner who, on or after the date on which section 87 of the Crime and Disorder Act 1998 comes into force, has been made subject to an extended sentence within the meaning of section 210A of the 1995 Act (extended sentences).

(2)   Subject to the provisions of this section, this Part of this Act, except section 1A, shall apply in relation to extended sentences as if any reference to a sentence or term of imprisonment was a reference to the custodial term of an extended sentence.

(3)   Where a prisoner subject to an extended sentence is released on licence under this Part the licence shall, subject to any revocation under section 17 of this Act, remain in force until the end of the extension period.

(4)   Where, apart from this subsection, a prisoner subject to an extended sentence would be released unconditionally—

(a)   he shall be released on licence; and

(b)   the licence shall, subject to any revocation under section 17 of this Act, remain in force until the end of the extension period.

(5)   The extension period shall be taken to begin as follows—
    (a)   for the purposes of subsection (3) above, on the day following the date on which, had there been no extension period, the prisoner would have ceased to be on licence in respect of the custodial term;
    (b)   for the purposes of subsection (4) above, on the date on which, apart from that subsection, he would have been released unconditionally.

(6)   Subject to section 1A(c) of this Act and section 210A(3) of the 1995 Act and to any direction by the court which imposes an extended sentence, where a prisoner is subject to two or more extended sentences, the extension period which is taken to begin in accordance with subsection (5) above shall be the aggregate of the extension period of each of those sentences.

(7)   For the purposes of sections 12(3) and 17(1) of this Act, and subject to subsection (8) below, the question whether a prisoner is a long-term or short-term prisoner shall be determined by reference to the extended sentence.

(8)   Where a short-term prisoner serving an extended sentence in respect of a sexual offence is released on licence under subsection (4)(a) above, the provisions of section 17 of this Act shall apply to him as if he was a long-term prisoner.

(9)   In relation to a prisoner subject to an extended sentence, the reference in section 17(5) of this Act to his sentence shall be construed as a reference to the extended sentence.

(10) For the purposes of this section "custodial term", "extension period" and "imprisonment" shall have the same meaning as in section 210A of the 1995 Act.

(11) In section 1A(c) and section 16(1)(a) of this Act, the reference to the date on which a prisoner would have served his sentence in full shall mean, in relation to a prisoner subject to an extended sentence, the date on which the extended sentence, as originally imposed by the court, would expire."

Definitions   For "court", see the Prisoners and Criminal Proceedings (Scotland) Act 1993, s 27(1); for "long-term prisoner" and "short-term prisoner", see s 27(1)–(3) of that Act.
References   See para 5.52.

88 Re-release of prisoners serving extended sentences

After section 3 of the 1993 Act there shall be inserted the following section—

"3A Re-release of prisoners serving extended sentences

(1)   This section applies to a prisoner serving an extended sentence within the meaning of section 210A of the 1995 Act (extended sentences) who has been recalled to prison under section 17(1) of this Act.

(2)   Subject to subsection (3) below, a prisoner to whom this section applies may require the Secretary of State to refer his case to the Parole Board—
    (a)   where his case has previously been referred to the Parole Board under this section or section 17(3) of this Act, not less than one year following the disposal of that referral;
    (b)   in any other case, at any time.

(3)   Where a prisoner to whom this section applies is subject to another sentence which is not treated as a single sentence with the extended sentence, the Secretary of State shall not be required to refer his case to the Parole Board before he has served one half of that other sentence.

(4)   Where the case of a prisoner to whom this section applies is referred to the Parole Board under this section or section 17(3) of this Act, the Board shall, if it is satisfied that it is no longer necessary for the protection of the public from serious harm that the prisoner should be confined (but not otherwise), direct that he should be released.

(5)   If the Parole Board gives a direction under subsection (4) above, the Secretary of State shall release the prisoner on licence."

Definitions   For "the 1993 Act", see s 117(2); for "Parole Board", see the Prisoners and Criminal Proceedings (Scotland) Act 1993, s 27(1).
References   See para 5.53.

Offenders dependent etc on drugs

89 Drug treatment and testing orders

After section 234A of the 1995 Act there shall be inserted the following section—

"234B Drug treatment and testing order

(1)   This section applies where a person of 16 years of age or more is convicted of an offence, other than one for which the sentence is fixed by law, committed on or after the date on which section 89 of the Crime and Disorder Act 1998 comes into force.

(2)   Subject to the provisions of this section, the court by or before which the offender is convicted may, if it is of the opinion that it is expedient to do so instead of sentencing him, make an order (a "drug treatment and testing order") which shall—

    (a)   have effect for a period specified in the order of not less than six months nor more than three years ("the treatment and testing period"); and

    (b)   include the requirements and provisions mentioned in section 234C of this Act.

(3)   A court shall not make a drug treatment and testing order unless it—

    (a)   has been notified by the Secretary of State that arrangements for implementing such orders are available in the area of the local authority proposed to be specified in the order under section 234C(6) of this Act and the notice has not been withdrawn;

    (b)   has obtained a report by, and if necessary heard evidence from, an officer of the local authority in whose area the offender is resident about the offender and his circumstances; and

    (c)   is satisfied that—

        (i)   the offender is dependent on, or has a propensity to misuse, drugs;

        (ii)   his dependency or propensity is such as requires and is susceptible to treatment; and

        (iii)   he is a suitable person to be subject to such an order.

(4)   For the purpose of determining for the purposes of subsection (3)(c) above whether the offender has any drug in his body, the court may by order require him to provide samples of such description as it may specify.

(5)   A drug treatment and testing order or an order under subsection (4) above shall not be made unless the offender expresses his willingness to comply with its requirements.

(6)   The Secretary of State may by order—

(a) amend paragraph (a) of subsection (2) above by substituting a different period for the minimum or the maximum period for the time being specified in that paragraph; and

(b) make such transitional provisions as appear to him necessary or expedient in connection with any such amendment.

(7) The power to make an order under subsection (6) above shall be exercisable by statutory instrument; but no such order shall be made unless a draft of the order has been laid before and approved by resolution of each House of Parliament.

(8) A drug treatment and testing order shall be as nearly as may be in the form prescribed by Act of Adjournal."

Definitions For "the 1995 Act", see s 117(2); for "local authority", see the Criminal Procedure (Scotland) Act 1995, s 234K, as inserted by s 95(1); for "offence" and "sentence", see s 307(1) of the 1995 Act; for "court", see s 307(2) thereof; as to the age of a person, see s 307(7) thereof.
References See para 5.54.

90 Requirements and provisions to be included in drug treatment and testing orders

After section 234B of the 1995 Act there shall be inserted the following section—

"234C Requirements and provisions of drug treatment and testing orders

(1) A drug treatment and testing order shall include a requirement ("the treatment requirement") that the offender shall submit, during the whole of the treatment and testing period, to treatment by or under the direction of a specified person having the necessary qualifications or experience ("the treatment provider") with a view to the reduction or elimination of the offender's dependency on or propensity to misuse drugs.

(2) The required treatment for any particular period shall be—
(a) treatment as a resident in such institution or place as may be specified in the order; or
(b) treatment as a non-resident in or at such institution or place, and at such intervals, as may be so specified;
but the nature of the treatment shall not be specified in the order except as mentioned in paragraph (a) or (b) above.

(3) A court shall not make a drug treatment and testing order unless it is satisfied that arrangements have been made for the treatment intended to be specified in the order (including arrangements for the reception of the offender where he is required to submit to treatment as a resident).

(4) A drug treatment and testing order shall include a requirement ("the testing requirement") that, for the purpose of ascertaining whether he has any drug in his body during the treatment and testing period, the offender shall provide during that period, at such times and in such circumstances as may (subject to the provisions of the order) be determined by the treatment provider, samples of such description as may be so determined.

(5) The testing requirement shall specify for each month the minimum number of occasions on which samples are to be provided.

(6) A drug treatment and testing order shall specify the local authority in whose area the offender will reside when the order is in force and require that authority to appoint or assign an officer (a "supervising officer") for the purposes of subsections (7) and (8) below.

(7)   A drug treatment and testing order shall—
- (a)   provide that, for the treatment and testing period, the offender shall be under the supervision of a supervising officer;
- (b)   require the offender to keep in touch with the supervising officer in accordance with such instructions as he may from time to time be given by that officer, and to notify him of any change of address; and
- (c)   provide that the results of the tests carried out on the samples provided by the offender in pursuance of the testing requirement shall be communicated to the supervising officer.

(8)   Supervision by the supervising officer shall be carried out to such extent only as may be necessary for the purpose of enabling him—
- (a)   to report on the offender's progress to the appropriate court;
- (b)   to report to that court any failure by the offender to comply with the requirements of the order; and
- (c)   to determine whether the circumstances are such that he should apply to that court for the variation or revocation of the order."

Definitions   For "the 1995 Act", see s 117(2); for "drug treatment and testing order" and "the treatment and testing period", see the Criminal Procedure (Scotland) Act 1995, s 234B(2), as inserted by s 89; for "the appropriate court" and "local authority", see s 234K of the 1995 Act, as inserted by s 95(1) (note also as to "court", s 307(2) thereof).
References   See para 5.55.

91 Procedural matters relating to drug treatment and testing orders

After section 234C of the 1995 Act there shall be inserted the following section—

"234D Procedural matters relating to drug treatment and testing orders

(1)   Before making a drug treatment and testing order, a court shall explain to the offender in ordinary language—
- (a)   the effect of the order and of the requirements proposed to be included in it;
- (b)   the consequences which may follow under section 234G of this Act if he fails to comply with any of those requirements;
- (c)   that the court has power under section 234E of this Act to vary or revoke the order on the application of either the offender or the supervising officer; and
- (d)   that the order will be periodically reviewed at intervals provided for in the order.

(2)   Upon making a drug treatment and testing order the court shall—
- (a)   give, or send by registered post or the recorded delivery service, a copy of the order to the offender;
- (b)   send a copy of the order to the treatment provider;
- (c)   send a copy of the order to the chief social work officer of the local authority specified in the order in accordance with section 234C(6) of this Act; and
- (d)   where it is not the appropriate court, send a copy of the order (together with such documents and information relating to the case as are considered useful) to the clerk of the appropriate court.

(3)   Where a copy of a drug treatment and testing order has under subsection (2)(a) been sent by registered post or by the recorded delivery service, an acknowledgment or certificate of delivery of a letter containing a copy order issued by the Post Office shall be sufficient evidence of the delivery of the letter on the day specified in such acknowledgement or certificate."

Definitions   For "the 1995 Act", see s 117(2); for "drug treatment and testing order", see the Criminal Procedure (Scotland) Act 1995, s 234B(2), as inserted by s 89; for "the treatment provider", see s 234C(1) of that Act, as inserted by s 90; for "the appropriate court" and "local authority", see s 234K of the 1995 Act, as inserted by s 95(1) (note also as to "court", s 307(2) thereof).
References   See para 5.56.

92 Amendment and periodic review of drug treatment and testing orders

After section 234D of the 1995 Act there shall be inserted the following sections—

"234E Amendment of drug treatment and testing order

(1)   Where a drug treatment and testing order is in force either the offender or the supervising officer may apply to the appropriate court for variation or revocation of the order.

(2)   Where an application is made under subsection (1) above by the supervising officer, the court shall issue a citation requiring the offender to appear before the court.

(3)   On an application made under subsection (1) above and after hearing both the offender and the supervising officer, the court may by order, if it appears to it in the interests of justice to do so—

    (a)   vary the order by—
        (i)   amending or deleting any of its requirements or provisions;
        (ii)   inserting further requirements or provisions; or
        (iii)   subject to subsection (4) below, increasing or decreasing the treatment and testing period; or
    (b)   revoke the order.

(4)   The power conferred by subsection (3)(a)(iii) above shall not be exercised so as to increase the treatment and testing period above the maximum for the time being specified in section 234B(2)(a) of this Act, or to decrease it below the minimum so specified.

(5)   Where the court, on the application of the supervising officer, proposes to vary (otherwise than by deleting a requirement or provision) a drug treatment and testing order, sections 234B(5) and 234D(1) of this Act shall apply to the variation of such an order as they apply to the making of such an order.

(6)   If an offender fails to appear before the court after having been cited in accordance with subsection (2) above, the court may issue a warrant for his arrest.

234F Periodic review of drug treatment and testing order

(1)   A drug treatment and testing order shall—

    (a)   provide for the order to be reviewed periodically at intervals of not less than one month;
    (b)   provide for each review of the order to be made, subject to subsection (5) below, at a hearing held for the purpose by the appropriate court (a "review hearing");
    (c)   require the offender to attend each review hearing;
    (d)   provide for the supervising officer to make to the court, before each review, a report in writing on the offender's progress under the order; and
    (e)   provide for each such report to include the test results communicated to the supervising officer under section 234C(7)(c) of this Act and the views of the treatment provider as to the treatment and testing of the offender.

(2)   At a review hearing the court, after considering the supervising officer's report, may amend any requirement or provision of the order.

(3)   The court—

    (a)   shall not amend the treatment or testing requirement unless the offender expresses his willingness to comply with the requirement as amended;

    (b)   shall not amend any provision of the order so as reduce the treatment and testing period below the minimum specified in section 234B(2)(a) of this Act or to increase it above the maximum so specified; and

    (c)   except with the consent of the offender, shall not amend any requirement or provision of the order while an appeal against the order is pending.

(4)   If the offender fails to express his willingness to comply with the treatment or testing requirement as proposed to be amended by the court, the court may revoke the order.

(5)   If at a review hearing the court, after considering the supervising officer's report, is of the opinion that the offender's progress under the order is satisfactory, the court may so amend the order as to provide for each subsequent review to be made without a hearing.

(6)   A review without a hearing shall take place in chambers without the parties being present.

(7)   If at a review without a hearing the court, after considering the supervising officer's report, is of the opinion that the offender's progress is no longer satisfactory, the court may issue a warrant for the arrest of the offender or may, if it thinks fit, instead of issuing a warrant in the first instance, issue a citation requiring the offender to appear before that court as such time as may be specified in the citation.

(8)   Where an offender fails to attend—

    (a)   a review hearing in accordance with a requirement contained in a drug treatment and testing order; or

    (b)   a court at the time specified in a citation under subsection (7) above,

the court may issue a warrant for his arrest.

(9)   Where an offender attends the court at a time specified by a citation issued under subsection (7) above—

    (a)   the court may exercise the powers conferred by this section as if the court were conducting a review hearing; and

    (b)   so amend the order as to provide for each subsequent review to be made at a review hearing."

Definitions   For "the 1995 Act", see s 117(2); for "drug treatment and testing order" and "the treatment and testing period", see the Criminal Procedure (Scotland) Act 1995, s 234B(2), as inserted by s 89; for "the treatment provider" and "the treatment requirement", see s 234C(1) of that Act, as inserted by s 90; for "the testing requirement", see s 234C(4) of that Act, as so inserted; for "supervising officer", see s 234C(6) of that Act, as so inserted; for "the appropriate court", see s 234K of the 1995 Act, as inserted by s 95(1) (note also as to "court", s 307(2) thereof).
References   See para 5.57.

93 Consequences of breach of drug treatment and testing order

After section 234F of the 1995 Act there shall be inserted the following sections—

"234G Breach of drug treatment testing order

(1) If at any time when a drug treatment and testing is in force it appears to the appropriate court that the offender has failed to comply with any requirement of the order, the court may issue a citation requiring the offender to appear before the court at such time as may be specified in the citation or, if it appears to the court to be appropriate, it may issue a warrant for the arrest of the offender.

(2) If it is proved to the satisfaction of the appropriate court that the offender has failed without reasonable excuse to comply with any requirement of the order, the court may by order—

(a) without prejudice to the continuation in force of the order, impose a fine not exceeding level 3 on the standard scale;

(b) vary the order; or

(c) revoke the order.

(3) For the purposes of subsection (2) above, the evidence of one witness shall be sufficient evidence.

(4) A fine imposed under this section in respect of a failure to comply with the requirements of a drug treatment and testing order shall be deemed for the purposes of any enactment to be a sum adjudged to be paid by or in respect of a conviction or a penalty imposed on a person summarily convicted.

234H Disposal on revocation of drugs treatment and testing order

(1) Where the court revokes a drugs treatment and testing order under section 234E(3)(b), 234F(4) or 234G(2)(c) of this Act, it may dispose of the offender in any way which would have been competent at the time when the order was made.

(2) In disposing of an offender under subsection (1) above, the court shall have regard to the time for which the order has been in operation.

(3) Where the court revokes a drug treatment and testing order as mentioned in subsection (1) above and the offender is subject to—

(a) a probation order, by virtue of section 234J of this Act; or

(b) a restriction of liberty order, by virtue of section 245D of this Act; or

(c) a restriction of liberty order and a probation order, by virtue of the said section 245D,

the court shall, before disposing of the offender under subsection (1) above—

(i) where he is subject to a probation order, discharge that order;

(ii) where he is subject to a restriction of liberty order, revoke that order; and

(iii) where he is subject to both such orders, discharge the probation order and revoke the restriction of liberty order."

Definitions   For "the 1995 Act", see s 117(2); for "drug treatment and testing order", see the Criminal Procedure (Scotland) Act 1995, s 234B(2), as inserted by s 89; for "the appropriate court", see s 234K of the 1995 Act, as inserted by s 95(1) (note also as to "court", s 307(2) thereof); for "probation order", see s 307(1) of the 1995 Act.
References   See para 5.58.

---

94 Combination of orders

(1) After section 234H of the 1995 Act there shall be inserted the following section—

"234J Concurrent drug treatment and testing and probation orders

(1)   Notwithstanding sections 228(1) and 234B(2) of this Act, where the court considers it expedient that the offender should be subject to a drug treatment and testing order and to a probation order, it may make both such orders in respect of the offender.

(2)   In deciding whether it is expedient for it to exercise the power conferred by subsection (1) above, the court shall have regard to the circumstances, including the nature of the offence and the character of the offender and to the report submitted to it under section 234B(3)(b) of this Act.

(3)   Where the court makes both a drug treatment and testing order and a probation order by virtue of subsection (1) above, the clerk of the court shall send a copy of each of the orders to the following—
    (a)   the treatment provider within the meaning of section 234C(1);
    (b)   the officer of the local authority who is appointed or assigned to be the supervising officer under section 234C(6) of this Act; and
    (c)   if he would not otherwise receive a copy of the order, the officer of the local authority who is to supervise the probationer.

(4)   Where the offender by an act or omission fails to comply with a requirement of an order made by virtue of subsection (1) above—
    (a)   if the failure relates to a requirement contained in a probation order and is dealt with under section 232(2)(c) of this Act, the court may, in addition, exercise the power conferred by section 234G(2)(b) of this Act in relation to the drug treatment and testing order; and
    (b)   if the failure relates to a requirement contained in a drug treatment and testing order and is dealt with under section 234G(2)(b) of this Act, the court may, in addition, exercise the power conferred by section 232(2)(c) of this Act in relation to the probation order.

(5)   Where an offender by an act or omission fails to comply with both a requirement contained in a drug treatment and testing order and in a probation order to which he is subject by virtue of subsection (1) above, he may, without prejudice to subsection (4) above, be dealt with as respects that act or omission either under section 232(2) of this Act or under section 234G(2) of this Act but he shall not be liable to be otherwise dealt with in respect of that act or omission."

(2)   Schedule 6 to this Act (Part I of which makes further provision in relation to the combination of drug treatment and testing orders with other orders and Part II of which makes provision in relation to appeals) shall have effect.

Definitions   For "the 1995 Act", see s 117(2); for "drug treatment and testing order", see the Criminal Procedure (Scotland) Act 1995, s 234B(2), as inserted by s 89; for "local authority", see s 234K of the 1995 Act, as inserted by s 95(1); for "offence" and "probation order", see s 307(1) of the 1995 Act; as to "court", s 307(2) thereof.
References   See para 5.59.

95 Interpretation provision in relation to drug treatment and testing orders

(1)   After section 234J of the 1995 Act there shall be inserted the following section—

"234K Drug treatment and testing orders: interpretation

In sections 234B to 234J of this Act—
    "the appropriate court" means—
        (a)   where the drug treatment and testing order has been made by the High Court, that court;

      (b)   in any other case, the court having jurisdiction in the area of the local authority for the time being specified in the order under section 234C(6) of this Act, being a sheriff or district court according to whether the order has been made by a sheriff or district court, but in a case where an order has been made by a district court and there is no district court in that area, the sheriff court; and

    "local authority" means a council constituted under section 2 of the Local Government etc (Scotland) Act 1994 and any reference to the area of such an authority is a reference to the local government area within the meaning of that Act for which it is so constituted."

(2)   In section 307(1) of the 1995 Act (interpretation), after the definition of "diet" there shall be inserted the following definition—

    ""drug treatment and testing order" has the meaning assigned to it in section 234B(2) of this Act;".

Definitions   For "the 1995 Act", see s 117(2); for "drug treatment and testing order", see the Criminal Procedure (Scotland) Act 1995, s 234B(2), as inserted by s 89.
References   See para 5.60.

Racial aggravation

96 Offences racially aggravated

(1)   The provisions of this section shall apply where it is—
      (a)   libelled in an indictment; or
      (b)   specified in a complaint,
and, in either case, proved that an offence has been racially aggravated.

(2)   An offence is racially aggravated for the purposes of this section if—
      (a)   at the time of committing the offence, or immediately before or after doing so, the offender evinces towards the victim (if any) of the offence malice and ill-will based on the victim's membership (or presumed membership) of a racial group; or
      (b)   the offence is motivated (wholly or partly) by malice and ill-will towards members of a racial group based on their membership of that group,
and evidence from a single source shall be sufficient evidence to establish, for the purposes of this subsection, that an offence is racially aggravated.

(3)   In subsection (2)(a) above—
    "membership", in relation to a racial group, includes association with members of that group;
    "presumed" means presumed by the offender.

(4)   It is immaterial for the purposes of paragraph (a) or (b) of subsection (2) above whether or not the offender's malice and ill-will is also based, to any extent, on—
      (a)   the fact or presumption that any person or group of persons belongs to any religious group; or
      (b)   any other factor not mentioned in that paragraph.

(5)   Where this section applies, the court shall, on convicting a person, take the aggravation into account in determining the appropriate sentence.

(6)   In this section "racial group" means a group of persons defined by reference to race, colour, nationality (including citizenship) or ethnic or national origins.

References   See para 5.61.

PART V
MISCELLANEOUS AND SUPPLEMENTAL

Remands and committals

97 Remands and committals of children and young persons

(1)   In subsection (4) of section 23 of the 1969 Act (remands and committals to local authority accommodation), for the words "Subject to subsection (5) below," there shall be substituted the words "Subject to subsections (5) and (5A) below,".

(2)   In subsection (5) of that section, for the words "a young person who has attained the age of fifteen" there shall be substituted the words "a child who has attained the age of twelve, or a young person, who (in either case) is of a prescribed description".

(3)   After that subsection there shall be inserted the following subsection—

"(5A)   A court shall not impose a security requirement in respect of a child or young person who is not legally represented in the court unless—
(a)   he applied for legal aid and the application was refused on the ground that it did not appear his means were such that he required assistance; or
(b)   having been informed of his right to apply for legal aid and had the opportunity to do so, he refused or failed to apply."

(4)   In subsection (12) of that section, after the definition of "imprisonable offence" there shall be inserted the following definition—

""prescribed description" means a description prescribed by reference to age or sex or both by an order of the Secretary of State;".

(5)   Section 20 of the 1994 Act (which has not been brought into force and is superseded by this section) is hereby repealed.

Definitions   For "the 1969 Act" and "the 1994 Act", see s 117(1); for "security requirement", see the Children and Young Persons Act 1969, s 23(4), as amended by sub-s (1) above; for "court", see s 23(12) of that Act; for "child" and "young person", see s 70(1) of the 1969 Act.
References   See para 6.2. 6.3.

98 Remands and committals: alternative provision for 15 or 16 year old boys

(1)   Section 23 of the 1969 Act shall have effect with the modifications specified in subsections (2) to (6) below in relation to any male person who—
(a)   is of the age of 15 or 16; and
(b)   is not of a description prescribed for the purposes of subsection (5) of that section.

(2)   In subsection (1), immediately before the words "the remand" there shall be inserted the words "then, unless he is remanded to a remand centre or a prison in pursuance of subsection (4)(b) or (c) below,".

(3)   For subsections (4) to (5A) there shall be substituted the following subsections—

"(4)   Where a court, after consultation with a probation officer, a social worker of a local authority social services department or a member of a youth offending team, declares a person to be one to whom subsection (5) below applies—
(a)   it shall remand him to local authority accommodation and require him to be placed and kept in secure accommodation, if—
(i)   it also, after such consultation, declares him to be a person to whom subsection (5A) below applies; and
(ii)   it has been notified that secure accommodation is available for him;

> (b) it shall remand him to a remand centre, if paragraph (a) above does not apply and it has been notified that such a centre is available for the reception from the court of persons to whom subsection (5) below applies; and
>
> (c) it shall remand him to a prison, if neither paragraph (a) nor paragraph (b) above applies.

> (4A) A court shall not declare a person who is not legally represented in the court to be a person to whom subsection (5) below applies unless—
>
> (a) he applied for legal aid and the application was refused on the ground that it did not appear his means were such that he required assistance; or
>
> (b) having been informed of his right to apply for legal aid and had the opportunity to do so, he refused or failed to apply.

> (5) This subsection applies to a person who—
>
> (a) is charged with or has been convicted of a violent or sexual offence, or an offence punishable in the case of an adult with imprisonment for a term of fourteen years or more; or
>
> (b) has a recent history of absconding while remanded to local authority accommodation, and is charged with or has been convicted of an imprisonable offence alleged or found to have been committed while he was so remanded,
>
> if (in either case) the court is of opinion that only remanding him to a remand centre or prison, or to local authority accommodation with a requirement that he be placed and kept in secure accommodation, would be adequate to protect the public from serious harm from him.

> (5A) This subsection applies to a person if the court is of opinion that, by reason of his physical or emotional immaturity or a propensity of his to harm himself, it would be undesirable for him to be remanded to a remand centre or a prison."

(4) In subsection (6)—

> (a) for the words "imposes a security requirement in respect of a young person" there shall be substituted the words "declares a person to be one to whom subsection (5) above applies"; and
>
> (b) for the words "subsection (5) above" there shall be substituted the words "that subsection".

(5) In subsection (7), after the words "a security requirement" there shall be inserted the words "(that is to say, a requirement imposed under subsection (4)(a) above that the person be placed and kept in secure accommodation)".

(6) After subsection (9) there shall be inserted the following subsection—

> "(9A) Where a person is remanded to local authority accommodation without the imposition of a security requirement, a relevant court may, on the application of the designated authority, declare him to be a person to whom subsection (5) above applies; and on its doing so, subsection (4) above shall apply."

(7) Section 62 of the 1991 Act (which is superseded by this section) shall cease to have effect.

Definitions   For "the 1969 Act" and "the 1991 Act", see s 117(1); for "court", "imprisonable offence", "prescribed description", "relevant court", "secure accommodation", "violent offence" and "sexual offence", see the Children and Young Persons Act 1969, s 23(12), as amended by s 97(4) of this Act; for "local authority accommodation" and "youth offending team", see s 70(1) of the 1969 Act, as amended by s 119 of, Sch 8, para 23 to, this Act.
References   See paras 6.4, 6.5.

Release and recall of prisoners

99 Power to release short-term prisoners on licence

Immediately before section 35 of the 1991 Act there shall be inserted the following section—

"34A Power to release short-term prisoners on licence

(1)   Subject to subsection (2) below, subsection (3) below applies where a short-term prisoner aged 18 or over is serving a sentence of imprisonment for a term of three months or more.

(2)   Subsection (3) below does not apply where—
   (a)   the sentence is an extended sentence within the meaning of section 58 of the Crime and Disorder Act 1998;
   (b)   the sentence is for an offence under section 1 of the Prisoners (Return to Custody) Act 1995;
   (c)   the sentence was imposed under paragraph 3(1)(d) or 4(1)(d) of Schedule 2 to this Act in a case where the prisoner had failed to comply with a requirement of a curfew order;
   (d)   the prisoner is subject to a hospital order, hospital direction or transfer direction under section 37, 45A or 47 of the Mental Health Act 1983;
   (e)   the prisoner is liable to removal from the United Kingdom for the purposes of section 46 below;
   (f)   the prisoner has been released on licence under this section at any time and has been recalled to prison under section 38A(1)(a) below;
   (g)   the prisoner has been released on licence under this section or section 36 below during the currency of the sentence, and has been recalled to prison under section 39(1) or (2) below;
   (h)   the prisoner has been returned to prison under section 40 below at any time; or
   (j)   the interval between—
       (i)   the date on which the prisoner will have served the requisite period for the term of the sentence; and
       (ii)   the date on which he will have served one-half of the sentence,
   is less than 14 days.

(3)   After the prisoner has served the requisite period for the term of his sentence, the Secretary of State may, subject to section 37A below, release him on licence.

(4)   In this section "the requisite period" means—
   (a)   for a term of three months or more but less than four months, a period of 30 days;
   (b)   for a term of four months or more but less than eight months, a period equal to one-quarter of the term;
   (c)   for a term of eight months or more, a period that is 60 days less than one-half of the term.

(5)   The Secretary of State may by order made by statutory instrument—
   (a)   repeal the words "aged 18 or over" in subsection (1) above;
   (b)   amend the definition of "the requisite period" in subsection (4) above; and
   (c)   make such transitional provision as appears to him necessary or expedient in connection with the repeal or amendment.

(6)   No order shall be made under subsection (5) above unless a draft of the order has been laid before and approved by a resolution of each House of Parliament."

Definitions   For "the 1991 Act", see s 117(1); for "short-term prisoner", see the Criminal Justice Act 1991, s 33(5); for "sentence of imprisonment", see s 51(1) of that Act; (note that the prospective repeal of s 33(5), 51 of the 1991 Act by the Crime (Sentences) Act 1997, s 56(2), Sch 6, is itself repealed by ss 119, 120(2) of, Sch 8, para 139, Sch 10 to, this Act).
References   See paras 6.6–6.10.

100 Curfew condition to be included in licence

(1)   After section 37 of the 1991 Act there shall be inserted the following section—

"37A Curfew condition to be included in licence under section 34A

(1)   A person shall not be released under section 34A(3) above unless the licence includes a condition ("the curfew condition") which—
    (a)   requires the released person to remain, for periods for the time being specified in the condition, at a place for the time being so specified (which may be an approved probation hostel); and
    (b)   includes requirements for securing the electronic monitoring of his whereabouts during the periods for the time being so specified.

(2)   The curfew condition may specify different places or different periods for different days, but shall not specify periods which amount to less than 9 hours in any one day (excluding for this purpose the first and last days of the period for which the condition is in force).

(3)   The curfew condition shall remain in force until the date when the released person would (but for his release) have served one-half of his sentence.

(4)   The curfew condition shall include provision for making a person responsible for monitoring the released person's whereabouts during the periods for the time being specified in the condition; and a person who is made so responsible shall be of a description specified in an order made by the Secretary of State.

(5)   The power conferred by subsection (4) above—
    (a)   shall be exercisable by statutory instrument; and
    (b)   shall include power to make different provision for different cases or classes of case or for different areas.

(6)   Nothing in this section shall be taken to require the Secretary of State to ensure that arrangements are made for the electronic monitoring of released persons' whereabouts in any particular part of England and Wales.

(7)   In this section "approved probation hostel" has the same meaning as in the Probation Service Act 1993."

(2)   Immediately before section 39 of the 1991 Act there shall be inserted the following section—

"38A Breach of curfew condition

(1)   If it appears to the Secretary of State, as regards a person released on licence under section 34A(3) above—
    (a)   that he has failed to comply with the curfew condition;
    (b)   that his whereabouts can no longer be electronically monitored at the place for the time being specified in that condition; or

(c)   that it is necessary to do so in order to protect the public from serious harm from him,

the Secretary of State may, if the curfew condition is still in force, revoke the licence and recall the person to prison.

(2)   A person whose licence under section 34A(3) above is revoked under this section—

(a)   may make representations in writing with respect to the revocation;

(b)   on his return to prison, shall be informed of the reasons for the revocation and of his right to make representations.

(3)   The Secretary of State, after considering any representations made under subsection (2)(b) above or any other matters, may cancel a revocation under this section.

(4)   Where the revocation of a person's licence is cancelled under subsection (3) above, the person shall be treated for the purposes of sections 34A(2)(f) and 37(1B) above as if he had not been recalled to prison under this section.

(5)   On the revocation under this section of a person's licence under section 34A(3) above, he shall be liable to be detained in pursuance of his sentence and, if at large, shall be deemed to be unlawfully at large.

(6)   In this section "the curfew condition" has the same meaning as in section 37A above."

Definitions   For "the 1991 Act", see s 117(1); as to protecting the public from serious harm, see, by virtue of the Criminal Justice Act 1991, s 51(4), as amended by s 106 of, Sch 8, para 92 to, this Act, s 31(3) of that Act.
References   See paras 6.12, 6.13.

101 Early release: two or more sentences

(1)   For subsection (2) of section 51 of the 1991 Act (interpretation of Part II) there shall be substituted the following subsections—

"(2) For the purposes of any reference in this Part, however expressed, to the term of imprisonment to which a person has been sentenced or which, or part of which, he has served, consecutive terms and terms which are wholly or partly concurrent shall be treated as a single term if—

(a)   the sentences were passed on the same occasion; or

(b)   where they were passed on different occasions, the person has not been released under this Part at any time during the period beginning with the first and ending with the last of those occasions.

(2A) Where a suspended sentence of imprisonment is ordered to take effect, with or without any variation of the original term, the occasion on which that order is made shall be treated for the purposes of subsection (2) above as the occasion on which the sentence is passed.

(2B) Where a person has been sentenced to two or more terms of imprisonment which are wholly or partly concurrent and do not fall to be treated as a single term—

(a)   nothing in this Part shall require the Secretary of State to release him in respect of any of the terms unless and until the Secretary of State is required to release him in respect of each of the others;

(b)   nothing in this Part shall require the Secretary of State or the Board to consider his release in respect of any of the terms unless and until the Secretary of State or the Board is required to consider his release, or the Secretary of State is required to release him, in respect of each of the others;

(c)   on and after his release under this Part he shall be on licence for so long, and subject to such conditions, as is required by this Part in respect of any of the sentences; and

(d)   the date mentioned in section 40(1) above shall be taken to be that on which he would (but for his release) have served each of the sentences in full.

(2C) Where a person has been sentenced to one or more terms of imprisonment and to one or more life sentences (within the meaning of section 34 of the Crime (Sentences) Act 1997), nothing in this Part shall—

(a)   require the Secretary of State to release the person in respect of any of the terms unless and until the Secretary of State is required to release him in respect of each of the life sentences; or

(b)   require the Secretary of State or the Board to consider the person's release in respect of any of the terms unless and until the Secretary of State or the Board is required to consider his release in respect of each of the life sentences.

(2D) Subsections (2B) and (2C) above shall have effect as if the term of an extended sentence (within the meaning of section 58 of the Crime and Disorder Act 1998) included the extension period (within the meaning of that section)."

(2)   After subsection (3) of section 34 of the 1997 Act (interpretation of Chapter II) there shall be inserted the following subsection—

"(4)   Where a person has been sentenced to one or more life sentences and to one or more terms of imprisonment, nothing in this Chapter shall require the Secretary of State to release the person in respect of any of the life sentences unless and until the Secretary of State is required to release him in respect of each of the terms."

Definitions   For "the 1991 Act", see s 117(1); for "the Board", see the Criminal Justice Act 1991, s 51(1); for "life sentence", see the Crime (Sentences) Act 1997, s 34(2).
References   See para 6.14.

102 Restriction on consecutive sentences for released prisoners

(1)   A court sentencing a person to a term of imprisonment shall not order or direct that the term shall commence on the expiration of any other sentence of imprisonment from which he has been released under Part II of the 1991 Act.

(2)   Expressions used in this section shall be construed as if they were contained in that Part.

Definitions   For "the 1991 Act", see s 117(1); for "sentence of imprisonment", see, by virtue of sub-s (2) above, the Criminal Justice Act 1991, s 51(1); (note that the prospective repeal of that provision by the Crime (Sentences) Act 1997, s 56(2), Sch 6, is itself repealed by ss 119, 120(2) of, Sch 8, para 139, Sch 10 to, this Act).
References   See para 6.15.

103 Recall to prison of short-term prisoners

(1)   This section has effect for the purpose of securing that, subject to section 100(2) above, the circumstances in which prisoners released on licence under Part II of the 1991 Act may be recalled to prison are the same for short-term prisoners as for long-term prisoners.

(2)   Section 38 of the 1991 Act (breach of licence conditions by short-term prisoners) shall cease to have effect.

(3)   In subsection (1) of section 39 of the 1991 Act (recall of long-term prisoners while on licence), after the words "in the case of a" there shall be inserted the words "short-term or".

Definitions   For "the 1991 Act", see s 117(1).
References   See para 6.16.

104   Release on licence following recall to prison

(1)   In subsection (3) of section 33 of the 1991 Act (duty to release short-term and long-term prisoners), for the word "unconditionally" there shall be substituted the words "on licence".

(2)   After subsection (1) of section 37 of that Act (duration and conditions of licences) there shall be inserted the following subsection—

"(1A) Where a prisoner is released on licence under section 33(3) or (3A) above, subsection (1) above shall have effect as if for the reference to three-quarters of his sentence there were substituted a reference to the whole of that sentence."

Definitions   For "the 1991 Act", see s 117(1).
References   See para 6.17.

105   Release on licence following return to prison

After section 40 of the 1991 Act there shall be inserted the following section—

"40A   Release on licence following return to prison

(1)   This section applies (in place of sections 33, 33A, 37(1) and 39 above) where a court passes on a person a sentence of imprisonment which—
   (a)   includes, or consists of, an order under section 40 above; and
   (b)   is for a term of twelve months or less.

(2)   As soon as the person has served one-half of the sentence, it shall be the duty of the Secretary of State to release him on licence.

(3)   Where the person is so released, the licence shall remain in force for a period of three months.

(4)   If the person fails to comply with such conditions as may for the time being be specified in the licence, he shall be liable on summary conviction—
   (a)   to a fine not exceeding level 3 on the standard scale; or
   (b)   to a sentence of imprisonment for a term not exceeding the relevant period,
but not liable to be dealt with in any other way.

(5)   In subsection (4) above "the relevant period" means a period which is equal in length to the period between the date on which the failure occurred or began and the date of the expiry of the licence.

(6)   As soon as a person has served one-half of a sentence passed under subsection (4) above, it shall be the duty of the Secretary of State to release him, subject to the licence if it is still subsisting."

Definitions   For "the 1991 Act", see s 117(1); for "sentence of imprisonment", see the Criminal Justice Act 1991, s 81(1).
References   See para 6.18.

Miscellaneous

106 Pre-consolidation amendments

The enactments mentioned in Schedule 7 to this Act shall have effect subject to the amendments there specified, being amendments designed to facilitate, or otherwise desirable in connection with, the consolidation of certain enactments relating to the powers of courts to deal with offenders or defaulters.

References   See para 6.19.

107 Amendments to Chapter I of Part II of 1997 Act

(1)   Chapter I of Part II of the 1997 Act (which relates to the effect of determinate custodial sentences) shall be amended as follows.

(2)   Sections 8 and 10 to 27 are hereby repealed.

(3)   After subsection (7) of section 9 (crediting of periods of remand in custody) there shall be inserted the following subsection—

"(7A) Such rules may make such incidental, supplemental and consequential provisions as may appear to the Secretary of State to be necessary or expedient."

(4)   After subsection (10) of that section there shall be inserted the following subsections—

"(11) In this section "sentence of imprisonment" does not include a committal—
  (a)   in default of payment of any sum of money other than one adjudged to be paid by a conviction;
  (b)   for want of sufficient distress to satisfy any sum of money; or
  (c)   for failure to do or abstain from doing anything required to be done or left undone;
and cognate expressions shall be construed accordingly.

(12) For the purposes of any reference in this section, however expressed, to the term of imprisonment to which a person has been sentenced, consecutive terms and terms which are wholly or partly concurrent shall be treated as a single term if—
  (a)   the sentences were passed on the same occasion; or
  (b)   where they were passed on different occasions, the person has not been released under Part II of the 1991 Act at any time during the period beginning with the first and ending with the last of those occasions."

(5)   After that section there shall be inserted the following section—

"9A Provision supplementary to section 9

(1)   Section 9 above applies to—
  (a)   a sentence of detention in a young offender institution; and
  (b)   a determinate sentence of detention under section 53 of the Children and Young Persons Act 1933 ("the 1933 Act"),
as it applies to an equivalent sentence of imprisonment.

(2)   Section 9 above applies to—
  (a)   persons remanded or committed to local authority accommodation under section 23 of the Children and Young Persons Act 1969 ("the 1969 Act") and placed and kept in secure accommodation; and

(b)   persons remanded, admitted or removed to hospital under section 35, 36, 38 or 48 of the Mental Health Act 1983 ("the 1983 Act"),

as it applies to persons remanded in or committed to custody by an order of a court.

(3)   In this section "secure accommodation" has the same meaning as in section 23 of the 1969 Act."

Definitions   For "the 1997 Act", see s 117(1); for "the 1991 Act", see the Crime (Sentences) Act 1997, s 54(1).
References   See para 6.20.

108 Repeal of Chapter I of Part III of Crime and Punishment (Scotland) Act 1997

Chapter I of Part III of the Crime and Punishment (Scotland) Act 1997 (early release of prisoners) shall cease to have effect.

References   See para 6.21.

109 Transitional provisions in relation to certain life prisoners

(1)   Section 16 of the Crime and Punishment (Scotland) Act 1997 (designated life prisoners) shall have effect and shall be deemed always to have had effect with the amendments made by subsections (2) and (3) below.

(2)   In subsection (2), at the beginning there shall be inserted the words "Except in a case to which subsection (3A) or (3B) below applies,".

(3)   After subsection (3) there shall be inserted the following subsections—

"(3A)   This subsection applies in a case where a person—
   (a)   was sentenced, prior to 20 October 1997, in respect of a murder committed by him before he attained the age of 18 years; and
   (b)   has been released on licence, other than under section 3 of the 1993 Act, whether before or on that date.

(3B)   This subsection applies in a case where a person—
   (a)   was sentenced, prior to 20 October 1997, in respect of a murder committed by him before he attained the age of 18 years; and
   (b)   has been released on licence, other than under section 3 of the 1993 Act, after that date without his case having been considered under subsection (2) above.

(3C)   In a case to which subsection (3A) or (3B) applies, Part I of the 1993 Act shall apply as if the person were a designated life prisoner, within the meaning of section 2 of that Act, whose licence had been granted under subsection (4) of that section on his having served the designated part of his sentence."

(4)   Where, prior to the commencement of this section, a certificate has been issued under subsection (2) of section 16 of the Crime and Punishment (Scotland) Act 1997 in respect of a case to which subsection (3A) of that section applies, the certificate shall be disregarded.

Definitions   For "the 1993 Act", see s 117(2).
References   See para 6.22.

110 Calculation of period of detention at customs office etc where person previously detained

In section 24 of the Criminal Law (Consolidation) (Scotland) Act 1995 (detention and questioning by customs officers), in subsection (4)—

    (a)   for the words from "he" to "be" there shall be substituted the words "and is"; and

    (b)   after the word "detention" there shall be inserted the words ", the period of six hours mentioned in subsection (2) above shall be reduced by the length of that earlier detention".

References   See para 6.23.

111 Early release in Scotland: two or more sentences

(1)   After section 1 of the 1993 Act there shall be inserted the following section—

"1A Application to persons serving more than one sentence

Where a prisoner has been sentenced to two or more terms of imprisonment which are wholly or partly concurrent and do not fall to be treated as a single term by virtue of section 27(5) of this Act—

    (a)   nothing in this Part of this Act shall require the Secretary of State to release him in respect of any of the terms unless and until the Secretary of State is required to release him in respect of each of the other terms;

    (b)   nothing in this Part of this Act shall require the Secretary of State or the Parole Board to consider his release in respect of any of the terms unless and until the Secretary of State or the Parole Board is required to consider his release, or the Secretary of State is required to release him, in respect of each of the other terms; and

    (c)   where he is released on licence under this Part of this Act, he shall be on a single licence which—

        (i)   shall (unless revoked) remain in force until the date on which he would (but for his release) have served in full all the sentences in respect of which he has been so released; and

        (ii)   shall be subject to such conditions as may be specified or required by this Part of this Act in respect of any of the sentences."

(2)   After subsection (7) of section 16 of the 1993 Act (orders for return to prison on commission of further offence) there shall be inserted the following subsection—

"(8) Where a prisoner has been sentenced to two or more terms of imprisonment which are wholly or partly concurrent and do not fall to be treated as a single term by virtue of section 27(5) of this Act, the date mentioned in subsection (1)(a) above shall be taken to be that on which he would (but for his release) have served all of the sentences in full."

(3)   For subsection (5) of section 27 of the 1993 Act (interpretation of Part I) there shall be substituted the following subsection—

"(5) For the purposes of any reference, however expressed, in this Part of this Act to the term of imprisonment or other detention to which a person has been sentenced or which, or any part of which, he has served, consecutive terms and terms which are wholly or partly concurrent shall be treated as a single term if—

    (a)   the sentences were passed at the same time; or

    (b)   where the sentences were passed at different times, the person has not been released under this Part of this Act at any time during the period beginning with the passing of the first sentence and ending with the passing of the last."

(4) In sub-paragraph (1) of paragraph 6B of Schedule 6 to the 1993 Act (aggregation of old and new sentences)—

    (a)   for the words "a prisoner" there shall be substituted the words "an existing prisoner";

    (b)   the word "and" after head (a) shall cease to have effect;

    (c)   in head (b), for the words "that date" there shall be inserted the words "the date on which section 111 of the Crime and Disorder Act 1998 comes into force"; and

    (d)   after head (b) there shall be inserted the following—

"; and

    (c)   he has not at any time prior to the passing of the sentence or sentences mentioned in head (b) above been released from the sentence or sentences mentioned in head (a) above under the existing provisions."

(5) After that paragraph there shall be inserted the following paragraph—

"6C.—(1) This paragraph applies where—

    (a)   an existing prisoner was, at the relevant date, serving a sentence or sentences of imprisonment, on conviction of an offence, passed before that date;

    (b)   on or after the date on which section 111 of the Crime and Disorder Act 1998 comes into force he is, or has been, sentenced to a further term or terms of imprisonment on conviction of an offence, to be served wholly or partly concurrently with the sentence or sentences mentioned in head (a); and

    (c)   the sentences do not fall to be treated as a single term by virtue of paragraph 6B(2)(a) above.

(2) In a case to which this paragraph applies the Secretary of State shall not release, or be required to consider the release of, the prisoner unless and until the requirements for release, or for consideration of his release, of the new and the existing provisions are satisfied in relation to each sentence to which they respectively apply.

(3) In a case to which this paragraph applies the Parole Board shall not be required to consider the release of the prisoner unless and until the requirements for release, or for consideration for release, of the new and the existing provisions are satisfied in relation to each sentence to which they respectively apply.

(4) In a case to which this paragraph applies, where the prisoner is released on licence, he shall be on a single licence which—

    (a)   shall (unless revoked) remain in force until the later of—

        (i)   the date on which he would have been discharged from prison on remission of part of his sentence or sentences under the existing provisions if, after his release, he had not forfeited remission of any part of that sentence under those provisions; or

        (ii)   the date on which he would (but for his release) have served in full all the sentences in respect of which he was released on licence and which were imposed after the relevant date; and

    (b)   shall be deemed to be granted under the new provisions and, subject to sub-paragraph (5) below, those provisions so far as relating to conditions of licences, and recall or return to prison, shall apply as they apply in respect of a prisoner on licence in respect of a sentence passed after the relevant date.

(5) In the application of section 16 to a person whose licence is deemed to be granted under the new provisions by virtue of sub-paragraph (4)(b) above,

the reference to the original sentence (within the meaning of that section) shall be construed as a reference to the further term or terms mentioned in head (b) of sub-paragraph (1) above."

(6)   Subject to subsection (7) below, the amendments made by subsections (1) to (5) above apply where one or more of the sentences concerned was passed after the commencement of this section.

(7)   Where the terms of two or more sentences passed before the commencement of this section have been treated, by virtue of section 27(5) of, or paragraph 6B of Schedule 6 to, the 1993 Act, as a single term for the purposes of Part I of that Act, they shall continue to be so treated after that commencement.

(8)   In relation to a prisoner released on licence at any time under section 16(7)(b) of the 1993 Act, section 17(1)(a) of that Act shall have effect as if after the word "Act" there were inserted the words "or a short term prisoner has been released on licence by virtue of section 16(7)(b) of this Act".

Definitions   For "the 1993 Act", see s 117(2); for "Parole Board" and "short-term prisoner", see the Prisoners and Criminal Proceedings (Scotland) Act 1993, s 27(1); as to a term of imprisonment, see s 27(5) of that Act, as substituted by sub-s (3) above; for "existing prisoner", "existing provisions", "new provisions" and "relevant date", see Sch 6, para 1 to the 1993 Act.
References   See para 6.24.

112 Restriction on consecutive sentences for released prisoners: Scotland

After section 204 of the 1995 Act there shall be inserted the following section—

"204A Restriction on consecutive sentences for released prisoners

A court sentencing a person to imprisonment or other detention shall not order or direct that the term of imprisonment or detention shall commence on the expiration of any other such sentence from which he has been released at any time under the existing or new provisions within the meaning of Schedule 6 to the Prisoners and Criminal Proceedings (Scotland) Act 1993."

Definitions   For "the 1995 Act", see s 117(2); for "sentence", see the Criminal Procedure (Scotland) Act 1995, s 307(1); as to "court", see 307(2) thereof; for "existing provisions" and "new provisions", see the Prisoners and Criminal Proceedings (Scotland) Act 1993, Sch 6, para 1.
References   See paras 6.24, 6.25.

113 Deputy authorising officer under Part III of Police Act 1997

(1)   In subsection (1) of section 94 of the Police Act 1997 (authorisations given in absence of authorising officer), for the words "(f) or (g)" there shall be substituted the words "(f), (g) or (h)".

(2)   In subsection (3) of that section, for paragraphs (a) and (b) there shall be substituted the words "he holds the rank of assistant chief constable in that Service or Squad".

(3)   In subsection (4) of that section, the word "and" immediately preceding paragraph (c) shall cease to have effect and after that paragraph there shall be inserted the words

> "and
> (d)   in the case of an authorising officer within paragraph (h) of section 93(5), means the customs officer designated by the Commissioners of Customs and Excise to act in his absence for the purposes of this paragraph."

References   See para 6.26.

Supplemental

114 Orders and regulations

(1)   Any power of a Minister of the Crown to make an order or regulations under this Act—

    (a)   is exercisable by statutory instrument; and

    (b)   includes power to make such transitional provision as appears to him necessary or expedient in connection with any provision made by the order or regulations.

(2)   A statutory instrument containing an order under section 5(2) or (3) or 10(6) above, or regulations under paragraph 1 of Schedule 3 to this Act, shall be subject to annulment in pursuance of a resolution of either House of Parliament.

(3)   No order under section 38(5), 41(6), 58(7), 61(7), 73(2)(b)(ii) or 76(2) above shall be made unless a draft of the order has been laid before and approved by a resolution of each House of Parliament.

References   See para 6.27.

115 Disclosure of information

(1)   Any person who, apart from this subsection, would not have power to disclose information—

    (a)   to a relevant authority; or

    (b)   to a person acting on behalf of such an authority,

shall have power to do so in any case where the disclosure is necessary or expedient for the purposes of any provision of this Act.

(2)   In subsection (1) above "relevant authority" means—

    (a)   the chief officer of police for a police area in England and Wales;

    (b)   the chief constable of a police force maintained under the Police (Scotland) Act 1967;

    (c)   a police authority within the meaning given by section 101(1) of the Police Act 1996;

    (d)   a local authority, that is to say—

        (i)   in relation to England, a county council, a district council, a London borough council or the Common Council of the City of London;

        (ii)   in relation to Wales, a county council or a county borough council;

        (iii)   in relation to Scotland, a council constituted under section 2 of the Local Government etc (Scotland) Act 1994;

    (e)   a probation committee in England and Wales;

    (f)   a health authority.

References   See para 6.28.

116 Transitory provisions

(1)   The Secretary of State may by order provide that, in relation to any time before the commencement of section 73 above, a court shall not make an order under—

    (a)   section 1 of the 1994 Act (secure training orders); or

    (b)   subsection (3)(a) of section 4 of that Act (breaches of supervision requirements), unless it has been notified by the Secretary of State that accommodation at a secure training centre, or accommodation provided by a local authority for the purpose of restricting the liberty of children and young persons, is immediately available for the offender, and the notice has not been withdrawn.

(2)　An order under this section may provide that sections 2 and 4 of the 1994 Act shall have effect, in relation to any such time, as if—

    (a)　for subsections (2) and (3) of section 2 there were substituted the following subsection—

"(2)　Where accommodation for the offender at a secure training centre is not immediately available—

    (a)　the court shall commit the offender to accommodation provided by a local authority for the purpose of restricting the liberty of children and young persons until such time as accommodation for him at such a centre is available; and

    (b)　the period of detention in the centre under the order shall be reduced by the period spent by the offender in the accommodation so provided.";

    (b)　in subsection (5) of that section, for the words "subsections (2)(a)(ii) and (4)(b) apply" there were substituted the words "subsection (4)(b) applies";

    (c)　for subsection (8) of that section there were substituted the following subsection—

"(8)　In this section "local authority" has the same meaning as in the Children Act 1989."; and

    (d)　in subsection (4) of section 4, for the words "paragraphs (a), (b) and (c) of subsection (2) and subsections (5), (7) and (8) of section 2" there were substituted the words "paragraphs (a) and (b) of subsection (2) and subsections (7) and (8) of section 2".

(3)　In relation to any time before the commencement of section 73 above, section 4 of the 1994 Act shall have effect as if after subsection (4) there were inserted the following subsection—

"(4A)　A fine imposed under subsection (3)(b) above shall be deemed, for the purposes of any enactment, to be a sum adjudged to be paid by a conviction."

(4)　In relation to any time before the commencement of section 73 above, section 1B of the 1982 Act (special provision for offenders under 18) shall have effect as if—

    (a)　in subsection (4), immediately before the words "a total term" there were inserted the words "a term or (in the case of an offender to whom subsection (6) below applies)";

    (b)　in subsection (5)—

      (i)　immediately before the words "total term" there were inserted the words "term or (as the case may be)"; and

      (ii)　for the words "the term" there were substituted the word "it"; and

    (c)　for subsection (6) there were substituted the following subsection—

"(6)　This subsection applies to an offender sentenced to two or more terms of detention in a young offender institution which are consecutive or wholly or partly concurrent if—

    (a)　the sentences were passed on the same occasion; or

    (b)　where they were passed on different occasions, the offender has not been released under Part II of the Criminal Justice Act 1991 at any time during the period beginning with the first and ending with the last of those occasions;

and in subsections (4) and (5) above "the total term", in relation to such an offender, means the aggregate of those terms."

(5)   In this section "local authority" has the same meaning as in the 1989 Act.

Definitions   For "the 1982 Act", "the 1984 Act" and "the 1994 Act", see s 117(1); for "child" and "young person", see s 117(1), (3).
References   See para 6.29.

117 General interpretation

(1)   In this Act—
"the 1933 Act" means the Children and Young Persons Act 1933;
"the 1969 Act" means the Children and Young Persons Act 1969;
"the 1973 Act" means the Powers of Criminal Courts Act 1973;
"the 1980 Act" means the Magistrates' Courts Act 1980;
"the 1982 Act" means the Criminal Justice Act 1982;
"the 1984 Act" means the Police and Criminal Evidence Act 1984;
"the 1985 Act" means the Prosecution of Offences Act 1985;
"the 1989 Act" means the Children Act 1989;
"the 1991 Act" means the Criminal Justice Act 1991;
"the 1994 Act" means the Criminal Justice and Public Order Act 1994;
"the 1997 Act" means the Crime (Sentences) Act 1997;
"caution" has the same meaning as in Part V of the Police Act 1997;
"child" means a person under the age of 14,
"commission area" has the same meaning as in the Justices of the Peace Act 1997;
"custodial sentence" has the same meaning as in Part I of the 1991 Act;
"guardian" has the same meaning as in the 1933 Act;
"prescribed" means prescribed by an order made by the Secretary of State;
"young person" means a person who has attained the age of 14 and is under the age of 18;
"youth offending team" means a team established under section 39 above.

(2)   In this Act—
"the 1993 Act" means the Prisoners and Criminal Proceedings (Scotland) Act 1993; and
"the 1995 Act" means the Criminal Procedure (Scotland) Act 1995.

(3)   For the purposes of this Act, the age of a person shall be deemed to be that which it appears to the court to be after considering any available evidence.

References   See para 6.30.

118 Provision for Northern Ireland

An Order in Council under paragraph 1(1)(b) of Schedule 1 to the Northern Ireland Act 1974 (legislation for Northern Ireland in the interim period) which contains a statement that it is made only for purposes corresponding to those of sections 2 to 4, 34, 47(5), 57, 61 to 64 and 85 above—
(a)   shall not be subject to paragraph 1(4) and (5) of that Schedule (affirmative resolution of both Houses of Parliament); but
(b)   shall be subject to annulment in pursuance of a resolution of either House of Parliament.

References   See para 6.31.

119 Minor and consequential amendments

The enactments mentioned in Schedule 8 to this Act shall have effect subject to the amendments there specified, being minor amendments and amendments consequential on the provisions of this Act.

References   See para 6.32.

120 Transitional provisions, savings and repeals

(1)   The transitional provisions and savings contained in Schedule 9 to this Act shall have effect; but nothing in this subsection shall be taken as prejudicing the operation of sections 16 and 17 of the Interpretation Act 1978 (which relate to the effect of repeals).

(2)   The enactments specified in Schedule 10 to this Act, which include some that are spent, are hereby repealed to the extent specified in the third column of that Schedule.

References   See para 6.33.

121 Short title, commencement and extent

(1)   This Act may be cited as the Crime and Disorder Act 1998.

(2)   This Act, except this section, sections 109 and 111(8) above and paragraphs 55, 99 and 117 of Schedule 8 to this Act, shall come into force on such day as the Secretary of State may by order appoint; and different days may be appointed for different purposes or different areas.

(3)   Without prejudice to the provisions of Schedule 9 to this Act, an order under subsection (2) above may make such transitional provisions and savings as appear to the Secretary of State necessary or expedient in connection with any provision brought into force by the order.

(4)   Subject to subsections (5) to (12) below, this Act extends to England and Wales only.

(5)   The following provisions extend to Scotland only, namely—
  (a)   Chapter II of Part I;
  (b)   section 33;
  (c)   Chapter II of Part IV;
  (d)   sections 108 to 112 and 117(2); and
  (e)   paragraphs 55, 70, 71, 98 to 108, 115 to 124 and 140 to 143 of Schedule 8 and section 119 above so far as relating to those paragraphs.

(6)   The following provisions also extend to Scotland, namely—
  (a)   Chapter III of Part I;
  (b)   section 36(3) to (5);
  (c)   section 65(9);
  (d)   section 115;
  (e)   paragraph 3 of Schedule 3 to this Act and section 52(6) above so far as relating to that paragraph;
  (f)   paragraph 15 of Schedule 7 to this Act and section 106 above so far as relating to that paragraph;
  (g)   paragraphs 1, 7(1) and (3), 14(1) and (2), 35, 36, 45, 135, 136 and 138 of Schedule 8 to this Act and section 119 above so far as relating to those paragraphs; and
  (h)   this section.

(7)   Sections 36(1), (2)(a), (b) and (d) and (6)(b) and section 118 above extend to Northern Ireland only.

(8)   Section 36(3)(b), (4) and (5) above, paragraphs 7(1) and (3), 45, 135 and 138 of Schedule 8 to this Act, section 119 above so far as relating to those paragraphs and this section also extend to Northern Ireland.

(9)   Section 36(5) above, paragraphs 7(1) and (3), 45 and 134 of Schedule 8 to this Act, section 119 above so far as relating to those paragraphs and this section also extend to the Isle of Man.

(10)   Section 36(5) above, paragraphs 7(1) and (3), 45 and 135 of Schedule 8 to this Act, section 119 above so far as relating to those paragraphs and this section also extend to the Channel Islands.

(11)   The repeals in Schedule 10 to this Act, and section 120(2) above so far as relating to those repeals, have the same extent as the enactments on which the repeals operate.

(12)   Section 9(4) of the Repatriation of Prisoners Act 1984 (power to extend Act to Channel Islands and Isle of Man) applies to the amendments of that Act made by paragraphs 56 to 60 of Schedule 8 to this Act; and in Schedule 1 to the 1997 Act—
>   (a)   paragraph 14 (restricted transfers between the United Kingdom and the Channel Islands) as applied in relation to the Isle of Man; and
>   (b)   paragraph 19 (application of Schedule in relation to the Isle of Man),

apply to the amendments of that Schedule made by paragraph 135 of Schedule 8 to this Act.

References   See para 6.34.

SCHEDULES

SCHEDULE 1

Section 24(4)

SCHEDULE 2A TO THE CIVIC
GOVERNMENT (SCOTLAND) ACT 1982

"SCHEDULE 2A

Section 54(2C)

RETENTION AND DISPOSAL OF PROPERTY
SEIZED UNDER SECTION 54(2A) OF THIS ACT

Application

1.   This schedule applies to property seized under section 54(2A) of this Act.

Retention

2.—(1)   Subject to sub-paragraph (2) below, property to which this Schedule applies may be retained for a period of twenty-eight days beginning with the day on which it was seized.

(2)   Where proceedings for an offence are instituted within the period specified in sub-paragraph (1) above against any person, the property may be retained for a period beginning on the day on which it was seized and ending on the day when—
>   (a)   the prosecutor certifies that the property is not, or is no longer, required as a production in criminal proceedings or for any purpose relating to such proceedings;
>   (b)   the accused in such proceedings—

        (i)   is sentenced or otherwise dealt with for the offence; or

        (ii) is acquitted of the offence; or

  (c)   the proceedings are expressly abandoned by the prosecutor or are deserted *simpliciter.*

Arrangements for custody of property

3.—(1)   Subject to the proviso to section 17(3)(b) of the Police (Scotland) Act 1967 (duty to comply with instructions received from prosecutor), the chief constable shall, in accordance with the provisions of this Schedule, make such arrangements as he considers appropriate for the care, custody, return or disposal of property to which this Schedule applies.

(2)   Any reference in this Schedule to property being in the possession of, delivered by or disposed of by, the chief constable includes a reference to its being in the possession of, delivered by or disposed of by, another person under arrangements made under sub-paragraph (1) above.

Disposal

4.   Where the period of retention permitted by paragraph 2 above expires and the chief constable has reason to believe that the person from whom the property was seized is not the owner or the person having right to possession of it, he shall take reasonable steps to ascertain the identity of the owner or of the person with that right and to notify him of the procedures determined under paragraph 5(1) below.

5.—(1)   Subject to sub-paragraphs (5) and (6) below, the owner or any person having right to possession of any property to which this Schedule applies and which, at the expiry of the period of retention permitted by paragraph 2 above, is in the possession of the chief constable may at any time prior to its disposal under paragraph 6 below claim that property in accordance with such procedure as the chief constable may determine.

(2)   Subject to sub-paragraphs (3), (5) and (6) below, where the chief constable considers that the person making a claim in accordance with the procedure determined under sub-paragraph (1) above is the owner of the property or has a right to possession of it, he shall deliver the property to the claimant.

(3)   Subject to sub-paragraph (4) below, the chief constable may impose such conditions connected with the delivery to the claimant of property under sub-paragraph (2) above as he thinks fit and, without prejudice to that generality, such conditions may relate to the payment of such reasonable charges (including any reasonable expenses incurred in relation to the property by or on behalf of him) as he may determine.

(4)   No condition relating to the payment of any charge shall be imposed by the chief constable on the owner or person having right of possession of the property where he is satisfied that that person did not know, and had no reason to suspect, that the property to which this Schedule applies was likely to be used in a manner which gave rise to its seizure.

(5)   This paragraph does not apply where the period of retention expires in such manner as is mentioned in paragraph 2(2)(b)(i) above and the court by which he was convicted has made a suspended forfeiture order or a restraint order in respect of the property to which this Schedule applies.

(6)   This paragraph shall cease to apply where at any time—

  (a)   the property to which this Schedule applies—

        (i)   is seized under any other power available to a constable; or

        (ii) passes into the possession of the prosecutor; or

  (b)   proceedings for an offence are instituted, where the property to which this Schedule applies is required as a production.

6.—(1)   Where this sub-paragraph applies, the chief constable may—

  (a)   sell property to which this Schedule applies; or

  (b)   if in his opinion it would be impracticable to sell such property, dispose of it.

(2)   Sub-paragraph (1) above applies—
>   (a)   at any time after the expiry of the relevant period where, within that period—
>   >   (i)   no claim has been made under paragraph 5 above; or
>   >   (ii)   any such a claim which has been made has been rejected by the chief constable; and
>   (b)   where a claim has been made under paragraph 5 above and not determined within the relevant period, at any time after the rejection of that claim by the chief constable.

(3)   In sub-paragraph (2) above, the "relevant period" means a period of six months beginning with the day on which the period of retention permitted by paragraph 2 above expired.

(4)   Sections 71, 72 and 77(1) of this Act shall apply to a disposal under this paragraph as they apply to a disposal under section 68 of this Act.

Appeals

7.—(1)   A claimant under sub-paragraph (2) of paragraph 5 above may appeal to the sheriff against any decision of the chief constable made under that paragraph as respects the claim.

(2)   The previous owner of any property disposed of for value under paragraph 6 above may appeal to the sheriff against any decision of the chief constable made under section 72 of this Act as applied by sub-paragraph (4) of that paragraph.

(3)   Subsections (3) to (5) of section 76 of this Act shall apply to an appeal under this paragraph as they apply to an appeal under that section.

Interpretation

8.   In this Schedule—
>   "chief constable" means the chief constable for the police area in which the property to which this Schedule applies was seized, and includes a constable acting under the direction of the chief constable for the purposes of this Schedule;
>   "restraint order" shall be construed in accordance with section 28(1) of the Proceeds of Crime (Scotland) Act 1995;
>   "suspended forfeiture order" shall be construed in accordance with section 21(2) of that Act."

References   See paras 2.55, 6.35.

SCHEDULE 2

Section 41(11)

THE YOUTH JUSTICE BOARD: FURTHER PROVISIONS

Membership

1.   The Secretary of State shall appoint one of the members of the Board to be their chairman.

2.—(1)   Subject to the following provisions of this paragraph, a person shall hold and vacate office as a member of the Board, or as chairman of the Board, in accordance with the terms of his appointment.

(2)   An appointment as a member of the Board may be full-time or part-time.

(3)   The appointment of a person as a member of the Board, or as chairman of the Board, shall be for a fixed period of not longer than five years.

(4)   Subject to sub-paragraph (5) below, a person whose term of appointment as a member of the Board, or as chairman of the Board, expires shall be eligible for re-appointment.

(5)   No person may hold office as a member of the Board for a continuous period which is longer than ten years.

(6)   A person may at any time resign his office as a member of the Board, or as chairman of the Board, by notice in writing addressed to the Secretary of State.

(7)   The terms of appointment of a member of the Board, or the chairman of the Board, may provide for his removal from office (without cause being assigned) on notice from the Secretary of State of such length as may be specified in those terms, subject (if those terms so provide) to compensation from the Secretary of State; and in any such case the Secretary of State may remove that member from office in accordance with those terms.

(8)   Where—

    (a)   the terms of appointment of a member of the Board, or the chairman of the Board, provide for compensation on his removal from office in pursuance of sub-paragraph (7) above; and

    (b)   the member or chairman is removed from office in pursuance of that sub-paragraph,

the Board shall pay to him compensation of such amount, and on such terms, as the Secretary of State may with the approval of the Treasury determine.

(9)   The Secretary of State may also at any time remove a person from office as a member of the Board if satisfied—

    (a)   that he has without reasonable excuse failed to discharge his functions as a member for a continuous period of three months beginning not earlier than six months before that time;

    (b)   that he has been convicted of a criminal offence;

    (c)   that a bankruptcy order has been made against him, or his estate has been sequestrated, or he has made a composition or arrangement with, or granted a trust deed for, his creditors; or

    (d)   that he is unable or unfit to discharge his functions as a member.

(10)   The Secretary of State shall remove a member of the Board, or the chairman of the Board, from office in pursuance of this paragraph by declaring his office as a member of the Board to be vacant and notifying that fact in such manner as the Secretary of State thinks fit; and the office shall then become vacant.

(11)   If the chairman of the Board ceases to be a member of the Board he shall also cease to be chairman.

Members and employees

3.—(1)   The Board shall—

    (a)   pay to members of the Board such remuneration;

    (b)   pay to or in respect of members of the Board any such allowances, fees, expenses and gratuities; and

    (c)   pay towards the provision of pensions to or in respect of members of the Board any such sums,

as the Board are required to pay by or in accordance with directions given by the Secretary of State.

(2)   Where a member of the Board was, immediately before becoming a member, a participant in a scheme under section 1 of the Superannuation Act 1972, the Minister for the Civil Service may determine that his term of office as a member shall be treated for the purposes of the scheme as if it were service in the employment or office by reference to which he was a participant in the scheme; and his rights under the scheme shall not be affected by sub-paragraph (1)(c) above.

(3)   Where—

    (a)   a person ceases to hold office as a member of the Board otherwise than on the expiry of his term of appointment; and

    (b)   it appears to the Secretary of State that there are special circumstances which make it right for him to receive compensation,

the Secretary of State may direct the Board to make to the person a payment of such amount as the Secretary of State may determine.

4.—(1) The Board may appoint a chief executive and such other employees as the Board think fit, subject to the consent of the Secretary of State as to their number and terms and conditions of service.

(2) The Board shall—

    (a)   pay to employees of the Board such remuneration; and

    (b)   pay to or in respect of employees of the Board any such allowances, fees, expenses and gratuities,

as the Board may, with the consent of the Secretary of State, determine.

(3) Employment by the Board shall be included among the kinds of employment to which a scheme under section 1 of the Superannuation Act 1972 may apply.

5. The Board shall pay to the Minister for the Civil Service, at such times as he may direct, such sums as he may determine in respect of any increase attributable to paragraph 3(2) or 4(3) above in the sums payable out of money provided by Parliament under the Superannuation Act 1972.

House of Commons disqualification

6. In Part II of Schedule 1 to the House of Commons Disqualification Act 1975 (bodies of which all members are disqualified), there shall be inserted at the appropriate place the following entry—

"The Youth Justice Board for England and Wales".

Procedure

7.—(1) The arrangements for the procedure of the Board (including the quorum for meetings) shall be such as the Board may determine.

(2) The validity of any proceedings of the Board (or of any committee of the Board) shall not be affected by—

    (a)   any vacancy among the members of the Board or in the office of chairman of the Board; or

    (b)   any defect in the appointment of any person as a member of the Board or as chairman of the Board.

Annual reports and accounts

8.—(1) As soon as possible after the end of each financial year of the Board, the Board shall send to the Secretary of State a report on the discharge of their functions during that year.

(2) The Secretary of State shall lay before each House of Parliament, and cause to be published, a copy of every report sent to him under this paragraph.

9.—(1) The Board shall—

    (a)   keep proper accounts and proper records in relation to the accounts; and

    (b)   prepare a statement of accounts in respect of each financial year of the Board.

(2) The statement of accounts shall contain such information and shall be in such form as the Secretary of State may, with the consent of the Treasury, direct.

(3) The Board shall send a copy of the statement of accounts to the Secretary of State and to the Comptroller and Auditor General within such period after the end of the financial year to which the statement relates as the Secretary of State may direct.

(4) The Comptroller and Auditor General shall—

    (a)   examine, certify and report on the statement of accounts; and

    (b)   lay a copy of the statement of accounts and of his report before each House of Parliament.

10. For the purposes of this Schedule the Board's financial year shall be the period of twelve months ending with 31st March; but the first financial year of the Board shall be the period beginning with the date of establishment of the Board and ending with the first 31st March which falls at least six months after that date.

Expenses

11. The Secretary of State shall out of money provided by Parliament pay to the Board such sums towards their expenses as he may determine.

Definitions For "the Board", see s 41(1).
References See paras 4.13, 6.35.

SCHEDULE 3

Section 52(6)

PROCEDURE WHERE PERSONS ARE SENT FOR TRIAL UNDER SECTION 51

Regulations

1.—(1) The Attorney General shall by regulations provide that, where a person is sent for trial under section 51 of this Act on any charge or charges, copies of the documents containing the evidence on which the charge or charges are based shall, on or before the relevant date—
   (a) be served on that person; and
   (b) be given to the Crown Court sitting at the place specified in the notice under subsection (7) of that section.

(2) In sub-paragraph (1) above "the relevant date" means the date prescribed by the regulations.

Applications for dismissal

2.—(1) A person who is sent for trial under section 51 of this Act on any charge or charges may, at any time—
   (a) after he is served with copies of the documents containing the evidence on which the charge or charges are based; and
   (b) before he is arraigned (and whether or not an indictment has been preferred against him),

apply orally or in writing to the Crown Court sitting at the place specified in the notice under subsection (7) of that section for the charge, or any of the charges, in the case to be dismissed.

(2) The judge shall dismiss a charge (and accordingly quash any count relating to it in any indictment preferred against the applicant) which is the subject of any such application if it appears to him that the evidence against the applicant would not be sufficient for a jury properly to convict him.

(3) No oral application may be made under sub-paragraph (1) above unless the applicant has given to the Crown Court sitting at the place in question written notice of his intention to make the application.

(4) Oral evidence may be given on such an application only with the leave of the judge or by his order; and the judge shall give leave or make an order only if it appears to him, having regard to any matters stated in the application for leave, that the interests of justice require him to do so.

(5) If the judge gives leave permitting, or makes an order requiring, a person to give oral evidence, but that person does not do so, the judge may disregard any document indicating the evidence that he might have given.

(6) If the charge, or any of the charges, against the applicant is dismissed—
   (a) no further proceedings may be brought on the dismissed charge or charges except by means of the preferment of a voluntary bill of indictment; and
   (b) unless the applicant is in custody otherwise than on the dismissed charge or charges, he shall be discharged.

(7) Crown Court Rules may make provision for the purposes of this paragraph and, without prejudice to the generality of this sub-paragraph, may make provision—
   (a) as to the time or stage in the proceedings at which anything required to be done is to be done (unless the court grants leave to do it at some other time or stage);

(b)   as to the contents and form of notices or other documents;

(c)   as to the manner in which evidence is to be submitted; and

(d)   as to persons to be served with notices or other material.

Reporting restrictions

3.—(1) Except as provided by this paragraph, it shall not be lawful—

(a)   to publish in Great Britain a written report of an application under paragraph 2(1) above; or

(b)   to include in a relevant programme for reception in Great Britain a report of such an application,

if (in either case) the report contains any matter other than that permitted by this paragraph.

(2) An order that sub-paragraph (1) above shall not apply to reports of an application under paragraph 2(1) above may be made by the judge dealing with the application.

(3) Where in the case of two or more accused one of them objects to the making of an order under sub-paragraph (2) above, the judge shall make the order if, and only if, he is satisfied, after hearing the representations of the accused, that it is in the interests of justice to do so.

(4) An order under sub-paragraph (2) above shall not apply to reports of proceedings under sub-paragraph (3) above, but any decision of the court to make or not to make such an order may be contained in reports published or included in a relevant programme before the time authorised by sub-paragraph (5) below.

(5) It shall not be unlawful under this paragraph to publish or include in a relevant programme a report of an application under paragraph 2(1) above containing any matter other than that permitted by sub-paragraph (8) below where the application is successful.

(6) Where—

(a)   two or more persons were jointly charged; and

(b)   applications under paragraph 2(1) above are made by more than one of them,

sub-paragraph (5) above shall have effect as if for the words "the application is" there were substituted the words "all the applications are".

(7) It shall not be unlawful under this paragraph to publish or include in a relevant programme a report of an unsuccessful application at the conclusion of the trial of the person charged, or of the last of the persons charged to be tried.

(8) The following matters may be contained in a report published or included in a relevant programme without an order under sub-paragraph (2) above before the time authorised by sub-paragraphs (5) and (6) above, that is to say—

(a)   the identity of the court and the name of the judge;

(b)   the names, ages, home addresses and occupations of the accused and witnesses;

(c)   the offence or offences, or a summary of them, with which the accused is or are charged;

(d)   the names of counsel and solicitors engaged in the proceedings;

(e)   where the proceedings are adjourned, the date and place to which they are adjourned;

(f)   the arrangements as to bail;

(g)   whether legal aid was granted to the accused or any of the accused.

(9) The addresses that may be published or included in a relevant programme under sub-paragraph (8) above are addresses—

(a)   at any relevant time; and

(b)   at the time of their publication or inclusion in a relevant programme.

(10) If a report is published or included in a relevant programme in contravention of this paragraph, the following persons, that is to say—

(a)   in the case of a publication of a written report as part of a newspaper or periodical, any proprietor, editor or publisher of the newspaper or periodical;

(b)   in the case of a publication of a written report otherwise than as part of a newspaper or periodical, the person who publishes it;

(c)   in the case of the inclusion of a report in a relevant programme, any body corporate which is engaged in providing the service in which the programme is included and any person having functions in relation to the programme corresponding to those of the editor of a newspaper;

shall be liable on summary conviction to a fine not exceeding level 5 on the standard scale.

(11) Proceedings for an offence under this paragraph shall not, in England and Wales, be instituted otherwise than by or with the consent of the Attorney General.

(12) Sub-paragraph (1) above shall be in addition to, and not in derogation from, the provisions of any other enactment with respect to the publication of reports of court proceedings.

(13) In this paragraph—
"publish", in relation to a report, means publish the report, either by itself or as part of a newspaper or periodical, for distribution to the public;
"relevant programme" means a programme included in a programme service (within the meaning of the Broadcasting Act 1990);
"relevant time" means a time when events giving rise to the charges to which the proceedings relate occurred.

Power of justice to take depositions etc

4.—(1) Sub-paragraph (2) below applies where a justice of the peace for any commission area is satisfied that—
    (a)   any person in England and Wales ("the witness") is likely to be able to make on behalf of the prosecutor a written statement containing material evidence, or produce on behalf of the prosecutor a document or other exhibit likely to be material evidence, for the purposes of proceedings for an offence for which a person has been sent for trial under section 51 of this Act by a magistrates' court for that area; and
    (b)   the witness will not voluntarily make the statement or produce the document or other exhibit.

(2) In such a case the justice shall issue a summons directed to the witness requiring him to attend before a justice at the time and place appointed in the summons, and to have his evidence taken as a deposition or to produce the document or other exhibit.

(3) If a justice of the peace is satisfied by evidence on oath of the matters mentioned in sub-paragraph (1) above, and also that it is probable that a summons under sub-paragraph (2) above would not procure the result required by it, the justice may instead of issuing a summons issue a warrant to arrest the witness and to bring him before a justice at the time and place specified in the warrant.

(4) A summons may also be issued under sub-paragraph (2) above if the justice is satisfied that the witness is outside the British Islands, but no warrant may be issued under sub-paragraph (3) above unless the justice is satisfied by evidence on oath that the witness is in England and Wales.

(5) If—
    (a)   the witness fails to attend before a justice in answer to a summons under this paragraph;
    (b)   the justice is satisfied by evidence on oath that the witness is likely to be able to make a statement or produce a document or other exhibit as mentioned in sub-paragraph (1)(a) above;
    (c)   it is proved on oath, or in such other manner as may be prescribed, that he has been duly served with the summons and that a reasonable sum has been paid or tendered to him for costs and expenses; and
    (d)   it appears to the justice that there is no just excuse for the failure,

the justice may issue a warrant to arrest the witness and to bring him before a justice at the time and place specified in the warrant.

(6) Where—
    (a)   a summons is issued under sub-paragraph (2) above or a warrant is issued under sub-paragraph (3) or (5) above; and
    (b)   the summons or warrant is issued with a view to securing that the witness has his evidence taken as a deposition,

the time appointed in the summons or specified in the warrant shall be such as to enable the evidence to be taken as a deposition before the relevant date.

(7) If any person attending or brought before a justice in pursuance of this paragraph refuses without just excuse to have his evidence taken as a deposition, or to produce the document or other exhibit, the justice may do one or both of the following—

    (a)   commit him to custody until the expiration of such period not exceeding one month as may be specified in the summons or warrant or until he sooner has his evidence taken as a deposition or produces the document or other exhibit;

    (b)   impose on him a fine not exceeding £2,500.

(8) A fine imposed under sub-paragraph (7) above shall be deemed, for the purposes of any enactment, to be a sum adjudged to be paid by a conviction.

(9) If in pursuance of this paragraph a person has his evidence taken as a deposition, the clerk of the justice concerned shall as soon as is reasonably practicable send a copy of the deposition to the prosecutor and the Crown Court.

(10) If in pursuance of this paragraph a person produces an exhibit which is a document, the clerk of the justice concerned shall as soon as is reasonably practicable send a copy of the document to the prosecutor and the Crown Court.

(11) If in pursuance of this paragraph a person produces an exhibit which is not a document, the clerk of the justice concerned shall as soon as is reasonably practicable inform the prosecutor and the Crown Court of that fact and of the nature of the exhibit.

(12) In this paragraph—

    "prescribed" means prescribed by rules made under section 144 of the 1980 Act;

    "the relevant date" has the meaning given by paragraph 1(2) above.

Use of depositions as evidence

5.—(1) Subject to sub-paragraph (3) below, sub-paragraph (2) below applies where in pursuance of paragraph 4 above a person has his evidence taken as a deposition.

(2) Where this sub-paragraph applies the deposition may without further proof be read as evidence on the trial of the accused, whether for an offence for which he was sent for trial under section 51 of this Act or for any other offence arising out of the same transaction or set of circumstances.

(3) Sub-paragraph (2) above does not apply if—

    (a)   it is proved that the deposition was not signed by the justice by whom it purports to have been signed;

    (b)   the court of trial at its discretion orders that sub-paragraph (2) above shall not apply; or

    (c)   a party to the proceedings objects to sub-paragraph (2) above applying.

(4) If a party to the proceedings objects to sub-paragraph (2) applying the court of trial may order that the objection shall have no effect if the court considers it to be in the interests of justice so to order.

Power of Crown Court to deal with summary offence

6.—(1) This paragraph applies where a magistrates' court has sent a person for trial under section 51 of this Act for offences which include a summary offence.

(2) If the person is convicted on the indictment, the Crown Court shall consider whether the summary offence is related to the offence that is triable only on indictment or, as the case may be, any of the offences that are so triable.

(3) If it considers that the summary offence is so related, the court shall state to the person the substance of the offence and ask him whether he pleads guilty or not guilty.

(4) If the person pleads guilty, the Crown Court shall convict him, but may deal with him in respect of the summary offence only in a manner in which a magistrates' court could have dealt with him.

(5) If he does not plead guilty, the powers of the Crown Court shall cease in respect of the summary offence except as provided by sub-paragraph (6) below.

(6) If the prosecution inform the court that they would not desire to submit evidence on the charge relating to the summary offence, the court shall dismiss it.

(7) The Crown Court shall inform the clerk of the magistrates' court of the outcome of any proceedings under this paragraph.

(8) If the summary offence is one to which section 40 of the Criminal Justice Act 1988 applies, the Crown Court may exercise in relation to the offence the power conferred by that section; but where the person is tried on indictment for such an offence, the functions of the Crown Court under this paragraph in relation to the offence shall cease.

(9) Where the Court of Appeal allows an appeal against conviction of an indictable-only offence which is related to a summary offence of which the appellant was convicted under this paragraph—
   (a)   it shall set aside his conviction of the summary offence and give the clerk of the magistrates' court notice that it has done so; and
   (b)   it may direct that no further proceedings in relation to the offence are to be undertaken;

and the proceedings before the Crown Court in relation to the offence shall thereafter be disregarded for all purposes.

(10) A notice under sub-paragraph (9) above shall include particulars of any direction given under paragraph (b) of that sub-paragraph in relation to the offence.

(11) The references to the clerk of the magistrates' court in this paragraph shall be construed in accordance with section 141 of the 1980 Act.

(12) An offence is related to another offence for the purposes of this paragraph if it arises out of circumstances which are the same as or connected with those giving rise to the other offence.

Procedure where no indictable-only offence remains

7.—(1) Subject to paragraph 13 below, this paragraph applies where—
   (a)   a person has been sent for trial under section 51 of this Act but has not been arraigned; and
   (b)   the person is charged on an indictment which (following amendment of the indictment, or as a result of an application under paragraph 2 above, or for any other reason) includes no offence that is triable only on indictment.

(2) Everything that the Crown Court is required to do under the following provisions of this paragraph must be done with the accused present in court.

(3) The court shall cause to be read to the accused each count of the indictment that charges an offence triable either way.

(4) The court shall then explain to the accused in ordinary language that, in relation to each of those offences, he may indicate whether (if it were to proceed to trial) he would plead guilty or not guilty, and that if he indicates that he would plead guilty the court must proceed as mentioned in sub-paragraph (6) below.

(5) The court shall then ask the accused whether (if the offence in question were to proceed to trial) he would plead guilty or not guilty.

(6) If the accused indicates that he would plead guilty the court shall proceed as if he had been arraigned on the count in question and had pleaded guilty.

(7) If the accused indicates that he would plead not guilty, or fails to indicate how he would plead, the court shall consider whether the offence is more suitable for summary trial or for trial on indictment.

(8) Subject to sub-paragraph (6) above, the following shall not for any purpose be taken to constitute the taking of a plea—
   (a)   asking the accused under this paragraph whether (if the offence were to proceed to trial) he would plead guilty or not guilty;
   (b)   an indication by the accused under this paragraph of how he would plead.

8.—(1) Subject to paragraph 13 below, this paragraph applies in a case where—

    (a)   a person has been sent for trial under section 51 of this Act but has not been arraigned;

    (b)   he is charged on an indictment which (following amendment of the indictment, or as a result of an application under paragraph 2 above, or for any other reason) includes no offence that is triable only on indictment;

    (c)   he is represented by a legal representative;

    (d)   the Crown Court considers that by reason of his disorderly conduct before the court it is not practicable for proceedings under paragraph 7 above to be conducted in his presence; and

    (e)   the court considers that it should proceed in his absence.

(2)   In such a case—

    (a)   the court shall cause to be read to the representative each count of the indictment that charges an offence triable either way;

    (b)   the court shall ask the representative whether (if the offence in question were to proceed to trial) the accused would plead guilty or not guilty;

    (c)   if the representative indicates that the accused would plead guilty the court shall proceed as if the accused had been arraigned on the count in question and had pleaded guilty;

    (d)   if the representative indicates that the accused would plead not guilty, or fails to indicate how the accused would plead, the court shall consider whether the offence is more suitable for summary trial or for trial on indictment.

(3)   Subject to sub-paragraph (2)(c) above, the following shall not for any purpose be taken to constitute the taking of a plea—

    (a)   asking the representative under this section whether (if the offence were to proceed to trial) the accused would plead guilty or not guilty;

    (b)   an indication by the representative under this paragraph of how the accused would plead.

9.—(1) This paragraph applies where the Crown Court is required by paragraph 7(7) or 8(2)(d) above to consider the question whether an offence is more suitable for summary trial or for trial on indictment.

(2)   Before considering the question, the court shall afford first the prosecutor and then the accused an opportunity to make representations as to which mode of trial would be more suitable.

(3)   In considering the question, the court shall have regard to—

    (a)   any representations made by the prosecutor or the accused;

    (b)   the nature of the case;

    (c)   whether the circumstances make the offence one of a serious character;

    (d)   whether the punishment which a magistrates' court would have power to impose for it would be adequate; and

    (e)   any other circumstances which appear to the court to make it more suitable for the offence to be dealt tried in one way rather than the other.

10.—(1) This paragraph applies (unless excluded by paragraph 15 below) where the Crown Court considers that an offence is more suitable for summary trial.

(2)   The court shall explain to the accused in ordinary language—

    (a)   that it appears to the court more suitable for him to be tried summarily for the offence, and that he can either consent to be so tried or, of if he wishes, be tried by a jury; and

    (b)   that if he is tried summarily and is convicted by the magistrates' court, he may be committed for sentence to the Crown Court under section 38 of the 1980 Act if the convicting court is of such opinion as is mentioned in subsection (2) of that section.

(3)   After explaining to the accused as provided by sub-paragraph (2) above the court shall ask him whether he wishes to be tried summarily or by a jury, and—

    (a)   if he indicates that he wishes to be tried summarily, shall remit him for trial to a magistrates' court acting for the place where he was sent to the Crown Court for trial;

    (b)   if he does not give such an indication, shall retain its functions in relation to the offence and proceed accordingly.

11. If the Crown Court considers that an offence is more suitable for trial on indictment, the court—

    (a)   shall tell the accused that it has decided that it is more suitable for him to be tried for the offence by a jury; and

    (b)   shall retain its functions in relation to the offence and proceed accordingly.

12.—(1) Where the prosecution is being carried on by the Attorney General, the Solicitor General or the Director of Public Prosecutions and he applies for an offence which may be tried on indictment to be so tried—

    (a)   sub-paragraphs (4) to (8) of paragraph 7, sub-paragraphs (2)(b) to (d) and (3) of paragraph 8 and paragraphs 9 to 11 above shall not apply; and

    (b)   the Crown Court shall retain its functions in relation to the offence and proceed accordingly.

(2) The power of the Director of Public Prosecutions under this paragraph to apply for an offence to be tried on indictment shall not be exercised except with the consent of the Attorney General.

13.—(1) This paragraph applies, in place of paragraphs 7 to 12 above, in the case of a child or young person who—

    (a)   has been sent for trial under section 51 of this Act but has not been arraigned; and

    (b)   is charged on an indictment which (following amendment of the indictment, or as a result of an application under paragraph 2 above, or for any other reason) includes no offence that is triable only on indictment.

(2) The Crown Court shall remit the child or young person for trial to a magistrates' court acting for the place where he was sent to the Crown Court for trial unless—

    (a)   he is charged with such an offence as is mentioned in subsection (2) of section 53 of the 1933 Act (punishment of certain grave crimes) and the Crown Court considers that if he is found guilty of the offence it ought to be possible to sentence him in pursuance of subsection (3) of that section; or

    (b)   he is charged jointly with an adult with an offence triable either way and the Crown Court considers it necessary in the interests of justice that they both be tried for the offence in the Crown Court.

(3) In sub-paragraph (2) above "adult" has the same meaning as in section 51 of this Act.

Procedure for determining whether offences of criminal damage etc are summary offences

14.—(1) This paragraph applies where the Crown Court has to determine, for the purposes of this Schedule, whether an offence which is listed in the first column of Schedule 2 to the 1980 Act (offences for which the value involved is relevant to the mode of trial) is a summary offence.

(2) The court shall have regard to any representations made by the prosecutor or the accused.

(3) If it appears clear to the court that the value involved does not exceed the relevant sum, it shall treat the offence as a summary offence.

(4) If it appears clear to the court that the value involved exceeds the relevant sum, it shall treat the offence as an indictable offence.

(5) If it appears to the court for any reason not clear whether the value involved does or does not exceed the relevant sum, the court shall ask the accused whether he wishes the offence to be treated as a summary offence.

(6) Where sub-paragraph (5) above applies—

    (a)   if the accused indicates that he wishes the offence to be treated as a summary offence, the court shall so treat it;

    (b)   if the accused does not give such an indication, the court shall treat the offence as an indictable offence.

(7) In this paragraph "the value involved" and "the relevant sum" have the same meanings as in section 22 of the 1980 Act (certain offences triable either way to be tried summarily if value involved is small).

Power of Crown Court, with consent of legally-represented accused, to proceed in his absence

15.—(1) The Crown Court may proceed in the absence of the accused in accordance with such of the provisions of paragraphs 9 to 14 above as are applicable in the circumstances if—

    (a)   the accused is represented by a legal representative who signifies to the court the accused's consent to the proceedings in question being conducted in his absence; and

    (b)   the court is satisfied that there is good reason for proceeding in the absence of the accused.

(2) Sub-paragraph (1) above is subject to the following provisions of this paragraph which apply where the court exercises the power conferred by that sub-paragraph.

(3) If, where the court has considered as required by paragraph 7(7) or 8(2)(d) above, it appears to the court that an offence is more suitable for summary trial, paragraph 10 above shall not apply and—

    (a)   if the legal representative indicates that the accused wishes to be tried summarily, the court shall remit the accused for trial to a magistrates' court acting for the place where he was sent to the Crown Court for trial;

    (b)   if the legal representative does not give such an indication, the court shall retain its functions and proceed accordingly.

(4) If, where the court has considered as required by paragraph 7(7) or 8(2)(d) above, it appears to the court that an offence is more suitable for trial on indictment, paragraph 11 above shall apply with the omission of paragraph (a).

(5) Where paragraph 14 above applies and it appears to the court for any reason not clear whether the value involved does or does not exceed the relevant sum, sub-paragraphs (5) and (6) of that paragraph shall not apply and—

    (a)   the court shall ask the legal representative whether the accused wishes the offence to be treated as a summary offence;

    (b)   if the legal representative indicates that the accused wishes the offence to be treated as a summary offence, the court shall so treat it;

    (c)   if the legal representative does not give such an indication, the court shall treat the offence as an indictable offence.

Definitions   For "the 1933 Act", "the 1980 Act" and "commission area" and "prescribed", see s 117(1); for "child" and "young person", see s 117(1), (3).
References   See paras 4.36, 4.37, 6.35.

SCHEDULE 4

Section 64(5)

ENFORCEMENT ETC OF DRUG TREATMENT AND TESTING ORDERS

Preliminary

1.—Schedule 2 to the 1991 Act (enforcement etc of community orders) shall be amended as follows.

Meaning of "relevant order" etc

2.—(1) In sub-paragraph (1) of paragraph 1 (preliminary)—

    (a)   after the words "a probation order," there shall be inserted the words "a drug treatment and testing order,"; and

    (b)   in paragraph (a), for the words "probation or community service order" there shall be substituted the words "probation, community service or drug treatment and testing order".

(2) After sub-paragraph (3) of that paragraph there shall be inserted the following sub-paragraph—

    "(4)   In this Schedule, references to the court responsible for a drug treatment and testing order shall be construed in accordance with section 62(9) of the Crime and Disorder Act 1998."

Breach of requirements of order

3.—In sub-paragraph (2) of paragraph 2 (issue of summons or warrant), for the words "before a magistrates' court acting for the petty sessions area concerned" there shall be substituted the following paragraphs—

> "(a) except where the relevant order is a drug treatment and testing order, before a magistrates' court acting for the petty sessions area concerned;
>
> (b) in the excepted case, before the court responsible for the order."

4. In sub-paragraph (1) of paragraph 4 (powers of Crown Court), after the word "Where" there shall be inserted the words "under paragraph 2 or".

5. In sub-paragraph (2) of paragraph 5 (exclusions), for the words "is required by a probation order to submit to treatment for his mental condition, or his dependency on drugs or alcohol," there shall be substituted the following paragraphs—

> "(a) is required by a probation order to submit to treatment for his mental condition, or his dependency on or propensity to misuse drugs or alcohol; or
>
> (b) is required by a drug treatment and testing order to submit to treatment for his dependency on or propensity to misuse drugs,".

Revocation of order

6.—(1) In sub-paragraph (1) of paragraph 7 (revocation of order by magistrates' court), after the words "the petty sessions area concerned" there shall be inserted the words "or, where the relevant order is a drug treatment and testing order for which a magistrates' court is responsible, to that court".

(2) In sub-paragraph (3) of that paragraph—
> (a) after the words "a probation order" there shall be inserted the words "or drug treatment and testing order"; and
>
> (b) after the word "supervision" there shall be inserted the words "or, as the case may be, treatment".

7.—(1) After sub-paragraph (1) of paragraph 8 (revocation of order by Crown Court) there shall be inserted the following sub-paragraph—

> "(1A) This paragraph also applies where—
> (a) a drug treatment and testing order made by the Crown Court is in force in respect of an offender; and
>
> (b) the offender or the responsible officer applies to the Crown Court for the order to be revoked or for the offender to be dealt with in some other manner for the offence in respect of which the order was made."

(2) In sub-paragraph (3) of that paragraph—
> (a) after the words "a probation order" there shall be inserted the words "or drug treatment and testing order"; and
>
> (b) after the word "supervision" there shall be inserted the words "or, as the case may be, treatment".

8. In sub-paragraph (1) of paragraph 9 (revocation of order following custodial sentence), for paragraph (a) there shall be substituted the following paragraph—

> "(a) an offender in respect of whom a relevant order is in force is convicted of an offence—
> (i) by a magistrates' court other than a magistrates' court acting for the petty sessions area concerned; or
>
> (ii) where the relevant order is a drug treatment and testing order, by a magistrates' court which is not responsible for the order; and".

Amendment of order

9. In sub-paragraph (1) of paragraph 12 (amendment by reason of change of residence), after the words "a relevant order" there shall be inserted the words "(other than a drug treatment and testing order)".

10. After paragraph 14 there shall be inserted the following paragraph—

"Amendment of drug treatment and testing order

14A.—(1) Without prejudice to the provisions of section 63(2), (7) and (9) of the Crime and Disorder Act 1998, the court responsible for a drug treatment and testing order may by order—

    (a) vary or cancel any of the requirements or provisions of the order on an application by the responsible officer under sub-paragraph (2) or (3)(a) or (b) below; or

    (b) amend the order on an application by that officer under sub-paragraph (3)(c) below.

(2) Where the treatment provider is of the opinion that the treatment or testing requirement of the order should be varied or cancelled—

    (a) he shall make a report in writing to that effect to the responsible officer; and

    (b) that officer shall apply to the court for the variation or cancellation of the requirement.

(3) Where the responsible officer is of the opinion—

    (a) that the treatment or testing requirement of the order should be so varied as to specify a different treatment provider;

    (b) that any other requirement of the order, or a provision of the order, should be varied or cancelled; or

    (c) that the order should be so amended as to provide for each subsequent review under section 63 of the Crime and Disorder Act 1998 to be made without a hearing instead of at a review hearing, or vice versa,

he shall apply to the court for the variation or cancellation of the requirement or provision or the amendment of the order.

(4) The court—

    (a) shall not amend the treatment or testing requirement unless the offender expresses his willingness to comply with the requirement as amended; and

    (b) shall not amend any provision of the order so as to reduce the treatment and testing period below the minimum specified in section 61(2) of the Crime and Disorder Act 1998 or to increase it above the maximum so specified.

(5) If the offender fails to express his willingness to comply with the treatment or testing requirement as proposed to be amended by the court, the court may—

    (a) revoke the order; and

    (b) deal with him, for the offence in respect of which the order was made, in any manner in which it could deal with him if he had just been convicted by the court of the offence.

(6) In dealing with the offender under sub-paragraph (5)(b) above, the court—

    (a) shall take into account the extent to which the offender has complied with the requirements of the order; and

    (b) may impose a custodial sentence notwithstanding anything in section 1(2) of this Act.

(7) Paragraph 6A above shall apply for the purposes of this paragraph as it applies for the purposes of paragraph 3 above, but as if for the words "paragraph 3(1)(d) above" there were substituted the words "paragraph 14A(5)(b) below".

(8) In this paragraph—

"review hearing" has the same meaning as in section 63 of the Crime and Disorder Act 1998;

"the treatment requirement" and "the testing requirement" have the same meanings as in Chapter I of Part IV of that Act."

11. In paragraph 16 (order not to be amended pending appeal), after the words "paragraph 13 or 15 above" there shall be inserted the words "or, except with the consent of the offender, under paragraph 14A above".

12.—(1) In sub-paragraph (1) of paragraph 18 (notification of amended order), after the words "a relevant order" there shall be inserted the words "(other than a drug treatment and testing order)".

(2)   After that sub-paragraph there shall be inserted the following sub-paragraph—

"(1A) On the making under this Part of this Schedule of an order amending a drug treatment and testing order, the clerk to the court shall forthwith give copies of the amending order to the responsible officer."

(3)   In sub-paragraph (2) of that paragraph, after the words "sub-paragraph (1)" there shall be inserted the words "or (1A)".

Definitions   For "the 1991 Act", see s 117(1); for "drug treatment and testing order", see the Criminal Justice Act 1991, s 31(1), as amended by s 119 of, Sch 8, para 78(c) to, this Act; for "custodial sentence" see the said s 31(1) as amended and repealed in part by ss 106, 119, 120(2) of, Sch 7, para 42, Sch 8, para 78(b), Sch 10 to, this Act; for "relevant order", see Sch 2, para 1(1) to the 1991 Act.
References   See paras 5.16, 6.35.

SCHEDULE 5

Sections 68(3) and 70(5)

ENFORCEMENT ETC OF REPARATION
AND ACTION PLAN ORDERS

Preliminary

1.   In this Schedule—

"the appropriate court", in relation to a reparation order or action plan order, means the youth court acting for the petty sessions area for the time being named in the order in pursuance of section 67(9) or, as the case may be, section 69(9) of this Act;

"local authority accommodation" means accommodation provided by or on behalf of a local authority (within the meaning of the 1989 Act).

General power to discharge or vary order

2.—(1)   If while a reparation order or action plan order is in force in respect of an offender it appears to the appropriate court, on the application of the responsible officer or the offender, that it is appropriate to make an order under this sub-paragraph, the court may make an order discharging the reparation order or action plan order or varying it—

(a)   by cancelling any provision included in it; or

(b)   by inserting in it (either in addition to or in substitution for any of its provisions) any provision that could have been included in the order if the court had then had power to make it and were exercising the power.

(2)   Where an application under this paragraph for the discharge of a reparation order or action plan order is dismissed, no further application for its discharge shall be made under this paragraph by any person except with the consent of the appropriate court.

Failure to comply with order

3.—(1)   This paragraph applies where a reparation order or action plan order is in force and it is proved to the satisfaction of the appropriate court, on the application of the responsible officer, that the offender has failed to comply with any requirement included in the order.

(2)   The court—

(a)   whether or not it also makes an order under paragraph 2 above, may order the offender to pay a fine of an amount not exceeding £1,000, or make an attendance centre order or curfew order in respect of him; or

(b)   if the reparation order or action plan order was made by a youth court, may discharge the order and deal with him, for the offence in respect of which the order was made, in any manner in which he could have been dealt with for that offence by the court which made the order if the order had not been made; or

(c)   if the reparation order or action plan order was made by the Crown Court, may commit him in custody or release him on bail until he can be brought or appear before the Crown Court.

(3) For the purposes of sub-paragraph (2)(b) and (c) above, a reparation order or action plan order made on appeal from a decision of a magistrates' court or the Crown Court shall be treated as if it had been made by a magistrates' court or the Crown Court, as the case may be.

(4) Where a court deals with an offender under sub-paragraph (2)(c) above, it shall send to the Crown Court a certificate signed by a justice of the peace giving—

   (a)   particulars of the offender's failure to comply with the requirement in question; and

   (b)   such other particulars of the case as may be desirable;

and a certificate purporting to be so signed shall be admissible as evidence of the failure before the Crown Court.

(5) Where—

   (a)   by virtue of sub-paragraph (2)(c) above the offender is brought or appears before the Crown Court; and

   (b)   it is proved to the satisfaction of the court that he has failed to comply with the requirement in question,

that court may deal with him, for the offence in respect of which the order was made, in any manner in which it could have dealt with him for that offence if it had not made the order.

(6) Where the Crown Court deals with an offender under sub-paragraph (5) above, it shall revoke the reparation order or action plan order if it is still in force.

(7) A fine imposed under this paragraph shall be deemed, for the purposes of any enactment, to be a sum adjudged to be paid by a conviction.

(8) In dealing with an offender under this paragraph, a court shall take into account the extent to which he has complied with the requirements of the reparation order or action plan order.

Presence of offender in court, remands etc

4.—(1) Where the responsible officer makes an application under paragraph 2 or 3 above to the appropriate court, he may bring the offender before the court and, subject to sub-paragraph (9) below, the court shall not make an order under that paragraph unless the offender is present before it.

(2) Without prejudice to any power to issue a summons or warrant apart from this sub-paragraph, the court to which an application under paragraph 2 or 3 above is made may issue a summons or warrant for the purpose of securing the attendance of the offender before it.

(3) Subsections (3) and (4) of section 55 of the 1980 Act (which among other things restrict the circumstances in which a warrant may be issued) shall apply with the necessary modifications to a warrant under sub-paragraph (2) above as they apply to a warrant under that section and as if in subsection (3) after the word "summons" there were inserted the words "cannot be served or".

(4) Where the offender is arrested in pursuance of a warrant under sub-paragraph (2) above and cannot be brought immediately before the appropriate court, the person in whose custody he is—

   (a)   may make arrangements for his detention in a place of safety for a period of not more than 72 hours from the time of the arrest (and it shall be lawful for him to be detained in pursuance of the arrangements); and

   (b)   shall within that period bring him before a youth court.

(5) Where an offender is, under sub-paragraph (4) above, brought before a youth court other than the appropriate court, that court may—

   (a)   direct that he be released forthwith; or

   (b)   subject to sub-paragraph (6) below, remand him to local authority accommodation.

(6) Where the offender is aged 18 or over at the time when he is brought before the court, he shall not be remanded to local authority accommodation but may instead be remanded—

   (a)   to a remand centre, if the court has been notified that such a centre is available for the reception of persons under this sub-paragraph; or

   (b)   to a prison, if it has not been so notified.

(7)   Where an application is made to a court under paragraph 2(1) above, the court may remand (or further remand) the offender to local authority accommodation if—

  (a)   a warrant has been issued under sub-paragraph (2) of this paragraph for the purpose of securing the attendance of the offender before the court; or

  (b)   the court considers that remanding (or further remanding) him will enable information to be obtained which is likely to assist the court in deciding whether and, if so, how to exercise its powers under paragraph 2(1) above.

(8)   A court remanding an offender to local authority accommodation under this paragraph shall designate, as the authority who are to receive him, the local authority for the area in which the offender resides or, where it appears to the court that he does not reside in the area of a local authority, the local authority—

  (a)   specified by the court; and

  (b)   in whose area the offence or an offence associated with it was committed.

(9)   A court may make an order under paragraph 2 above in the absence of the offender if the effect of the order is one or more of the following, that is to say—

  (a)   discharging the reparation order or action plan order;

  (b)   cancelling a requirement included in the reparation order or action plan order;

  (c)   altering in the reparation order or action plan order the name of any area;

  (d)   changing the responsible officer.

Supplemental

5.—(1)   The provisions of section 17 of the 1982 Act (attendance centre orders) shall apply for the purposes of paragraph 3(2)(a) above but as if—

  (a)   in subsection (1), for the words from "has power" to "probation order" there were substituted the words "considers it appropriate to make an attendance centre order in respect of any person in pursuance of paragraph 3(2) of Schedule 5 to the Crime and Disorder Act 1998"; and

  (b)   subsection (13) were omitted.

(2)   Sections 18 and 19 of the 1982 Act (discharge and variation of attendance centre order and breach of attendance centre orders or attendance centre rules) shall also apply for the purposes of that paragraph but as if there were omitted—

  (a)   from subsection (4A) of section 18 and subsections (3) and (5) of section 19, the words ", for the offence in respect of which the order was made," and "for that offence"; and

  (b)   from subsection (4B) of section 18 and subsection (6) of section 19, the words "for an offence".

(3)   The provisions of section 12 of the 1991 Act (curfew orders) shall apply for the purposes of paragraph 3(2)(a) above but as if—

  (a)   in subsection (1), for the words from the beginning to "before which he is convicted" there were substituted the words "Where a court considers it appropriate to make a curfew order in respect of any person in pursuance of paragraph 3(2)(a) of Schedule 5 to the Crime and Disorder Act 1998, the court"; and

  (b)   in subsection (8), for the words "on conviction" there were substituted the words "on the date on which his failure to comply with a requirement included in the reparation order or action plan order was proved to the court".

(4)   Schedule 2 to the 1991 Act (enforcement etc of community orders), so far as relating to curfew orders, shall also apply for the purposes of that paragraph but as if—

  (a)   the power conferred on the magistrates' court by each of paragraphs 3(1)(d) and 7(2)(a)(ii) to deal with the offender for the offence in respect of which the order was made were a power to deal with the offender, for his failure to comply with a requirement included in the reparation order or action plan order, in any manner in which the appropriate court could deal with him for that failure to comply if it had just been proved to the satisfaction of that court;

  (b)   the power conferred on the Crown Court by paragraph 4(1)(d) to deal with the offender for the offence in respect of which the order was made were a power to deal with the offender, for his failure to comply with such a requirement, in any manner in which that court could deal with him for that failure to comply if it had just been proved to its satisfaction;

(c)   the reference in paragraph 7(1)(b) to the offence in respect of which the order was made were a reference to the failure to comply in respect of which the curfew order was made; and

(d)   the power conferred on the Crown Court by paragraph 8(2)(b) to deal with the offender for the offence in respect of which the order was made were a power to deal with the offender, for his failure to comply with a requirement included in the reparation order or action plan order, in any manner in which the appropriate court (if that order was made by a magistrates' court) or the Crown Court (if that order was made by the Crown Court) could deal with him for that failure to comply if it had just been proved to the satisfaction of that court.

(5)   For the purposes of the provisions mentioned in sub-paragraph (4)(a) and (d) above, as applied by that sub-paragraph, if the reparation order or action plan order is no longer in force the appropriate court's powers shall be determined on the assumption that it is still in force.

(6)   If while an application to the appropriate court in pursuance of paragraph 2 or 3 above is pending the offender attains the age of 18 years, the court shall, subject to paragraph 4(6) above, deal with the application as if he had not attained that age.

(7)   The offender may appeal to the Crown Court against—

(a)   any order made under paragraphs 2 or 3 above, except an order made or which could have been made in his absence (by virtue of paragraph 4(9) above);

(b)   the dismissal of an application under paragraph 2 above to discharge a reparation order or action plan order.

Definitions   For "the 1980 Act", "the 1982 Act", "the 1989 Act" and "the 1991 Act", see s 117(1); for "reparation order", see s 67(2); for "action plan order", see s 69(2); for "the responsible officer", see s 67(10) (in relation to a reparation order) and s 69(10) (in relation to an action plan order); for "attendance centre order" and "curfew order" see, by virtue of s 85(5), the Criminal Justice Act 1991, s 31(1). **References**   See paras 5.24, 5.27, 6.35.

SCHEDULE 6

Section 94(2)

DRUG TREATMENT AND TESTING ORDERS: AMENDMENT OF THE 1995 ACT

PART I
AMENDMENTS RELATING TO COMBINATION OF ORDERS

1.—In section 228(1) (probation orders), for the words "section 245D" there shall be substituted the words "sections 234J and 245D".

2.—(1) Section 232 (failure to comply with requirements of probation orders) shall be amended as follows.

(2)   In subsection (3A)—

(a)   for the words "a restriction of liberty order" there shall be substituted—

"(a)   a restriction of liberty order; or
(b)   a restriction of liberty order and a drug treatment and testing order,"; and

(b)   at the end there shall be added the words "or, as the case may be, the restriction of liberty order and the drug treatment and testing order."

(3)   After that subsection there shall be inserted the following subsection—

"(3B) Where the court intends to sentence an offender under subsection (2)(b) above and the offender is by virtue of section 234J of this Act subject to a drug treatment and testing order, it shall, before sentencing the offender under that paragraph, revoke the drug treatment and testing order."

3.   For section 245D there shall be substituted the following section—

"245D Combination of restriction of liberty order with other orders

(1) Subsection (3) applies where the court—
  - (a) intends to make a restriction of liberty order under section 245A(1) of this Act; and
  - (b) considers it expedient that the offender should also be subject to a probation order made under section 228(1) of this Act or to a drug treatment and testing order made under section 234B(2) of this Act or to both such orders.

(2) In deciding whether it is expedient to make a probation order or a drug treatment and testing order by virtue of paragraph (b) of subsection (1) above, the court shall—
  - (a) have regard to the circumstances, including the nature of the offence and the character of the offender; and
  - (b) obtain a report as to the circumstances and character of the offender.

(3) Where this subsection applies, the court, notwithstanding sections 228(1), 234B(2) and 245A(1) of this Act, may make a restriction of liberty order and either or both of a probation order and a drug treatment and testing order.

(4) Where the court makes a restriction of liberty order and a probation order by virtue of subsection (3) above, the clerk of the court shall send a copy of each order to—
  - (a) any person responsible for monitoring the offender's compliance with the restriction of liberty order; and
  - (b) the officer of the local authority who is to supervise the probationer.

(5) Where the court makes a restriction of liberty order and a drug treatment and testing order by virtue of subsection (3) above, the clerk of the court shall send a copy of each order to—
  - (a) any person responsible for monitoring the offender's compliance with the restriction of liberty order;
  - (b) the treatment provider, within the meaning of section 234C(1) of this Act; and
  - (c) the officer of the local authority who is appointed or assigned to be the supervising officer under section 234C(6) of this Act.

(6) Where the court makes a restriction of liberty order, a probation order and a drug treatment and testing order the clerk of the court shall send copies of each of the orders to the persons mentioned—
  - (a) in subsection (4) above;
  - (b) in paragraph (b) of subsection (5) above; and
  - (c) in paragraph (c) of that subsection, if that person would not otherwise receive such copies.

(7) Where the offender by an act or omission fails to comply with a requirement of an order made by virtue of subsection (3) above—
  - (a) if the failure relates to a requirement contained in a probation order and is dealt with under section 232(2)(c) of this Act, the court may, in addition, exercise the powers conferred by section 234G(2)(b) of this Act in relation to a drug treatment and testing order to which the offender is subject by virtue of subsection (3) above and by section 245F(2) of this Act in relation to the restriction of liberty order;
  - (b) if the failure relates to a requirement contained in a drug treatment and testing order and is dealt with under section 234G(2)(b) of this Act, the court may, in addition, exercise the powers conferred by section 232(2)(c) of this Act in relation to a probation order to which the offender is subject by virtue of subsection (3) above and by section 245F(2)(b) of this Act in relation to the restriction of liberty order; and
  - (c) if the failure relates to a requirement contained in a restriction of liberty order and is dealt with under section 245F(2)(b) of this Act, the court may, in addition, exercise the powers conferred by section 232(2)(c) of this Act in relation to a probation order and by section 234G(2)(b) of this Act in relation to a drug treatment and testing order to which, in either case, the offender is subject by virtue of subsection (3) above.

(8)   In any case to which this subsection applies, the offender may, without prejudice to subsection (7) above, be dealt with as respects that case under section 232(2) or, as the case may be, section 234G or section 245F(2) of this Act but he shall not be liable to be otherwise dealt with as respects that case.

(9)   Subsection (8) applies in a case where—
  (a)   the offender by an act or omission fails to comply with both a requirement contained in a restriction of liberty order and in a probation order to which he is subject by virtue of subsection (3) above;
  (b)   the offender by an act or omission fails to comply with both a requirement contained in a restriction of liberty order and in a drug treatment and testing order to which he is subject by virtue of subsection (3) above;
  (c)   the offender by an act or omission fails to comply with a requirement contained in each of a restriction of liberty order, a probation order and a drug treatment and testing order to which he is subject by virtue of subsection (3) above."

4.—(1) Section 245G (disposal on revocation of restriction of liberty order) shall be amended as follows.

(2) In subsection (2), for the words from "by" to the end there shall be substituted the words "by virtue of section 245D(3) of this Act, subject to a probation order or a drug treatment and testing order or to both such orders, it shall, before disposing the offender under subsection (1) above—
  (a)   where he is subject to a probation order, discharge that order;
  (b)   where he is subject to a drug treatment and testing order, revoke that order; and
  (c)   where he is subject to both such orders, discharge the probation order and revoke the drug treatment and testing order."

(3) After subsection (2) there shall be added—

  "(3)   Where the court orders a probation order discharged or a drug treatment and testing order revoked the clerk of the court shall forthwith give copies of that order to the persons mentioned in subsection (4) or, as the case may be, (5) of section 245D of this Act.

  (4)   Where the court orders a probation order discharged and a drug treatment and testing order revoked, the clerk of the court shall forthwith give copies of that order to the persons mentioned in section 245D(6) of this Act."

Definitions   For "the 1995 Act", see s 117(2); for "drug treatment and testing order", "local authority", "offence", "probationer", "probation order" and "sentence", see the Criminal Procedure (Scotland) Act 1995, s 307(1), as amended (definition "drug treatment and testing order" inserted) by s 95(2).
References   See paras 5.59, 6.35.

PART II
AMENDMENTS RELATING TO APPEALS

5. In section 106 (solemn appeals), in paragraph (d), after the words "probation order" there shall be inserted the words ", drug treatment and testing order".

6.—(1) Section 108 (right of appeal of prosecutor) shall be amended as follows.

(2) In subsection (1), after paragraph (d) there shall be inserted the following paragraph—

  "(dd) a drug treatment and testing order;"

(3) In subsection (2)(b)(iii), for the word "or", where it first occurs, there shall be substituted the word "to".

7.—(1) Section 175 (appeals in summary cases) shall be amended as follows.

(2) In subsection (2)(c), after the words "probation order" there shall be inserted the words ", drug treatment and testing order".

(3) In subsection (4), after paragraph (d) there shall be inserted the following paragraph—

"(dd) a drug treatment and testing order;".

(4) In subsection (4A)(b)(iii), for the word "or", where it first occurs, there shall be substituted the word "to".

Definitions   For "drug treatment and testing order", see the Criminal Procedure (Scotland) Act 1995, s 307(1), as amended by s 95(2).
References   See paras 5.59, 6.35.

SCHEDULE 7

Section 106

PRE-CONSOLIDATION AMENDMENTS: POWERS OF CRIMINAL COURTS

Children and Young Persons Act 1933 (c 12)

1.—(1) In subsection (1A) of section 55 of the 1933 Act (power to order parent or guardian to pay fine etc), in paragraph a), for the words "section 15(2A)" there shall be substituted the words "section 15(3)(a)".

(2) For paragraph (b) of that subsection there shall be substituted the following paragraphs—

"(b) a court would impose a fine on a child or young person under section 19(3) of the Criminal Justice Act 1982 (breach of attendance centre order or attendance centre rules); or

(bb) a court would impose a fine on a child or young person under paragraph 3(1)(a) or 4(1)(a) of Schedule 2 to the Criminal Justice Act 1991 (breach of requirement of a relevant order (within the meaning given by that Schedule) or of a combination order);".

(3) After subsection (5) of that section there shall be added the following subsection—

"(6) In relation to any other child or young person, references in this section to his parent shall be construed in accordance with section 1 of the Family Law Reform Act 1987."

Criminal Justice Act 1967 (c 80)

2.—(1) In subsection (1)(b)(i) of section 56 of the Criminal Justice Act 1967 (committal for sentence for offences tried summarily), for the words from "section 93" to "34 to 36" there shall be substituted the words "section 34, 35 or 36".

(2) In subsection (2) of that section, for the words from "section 8(6)" to the end there shall be substituted the words "section 1B(5) of the Powers of Criminal Courts Act 1973 (conditionally discharged person convicted of further offence) and section 24(2) of that Act (offender convicted during operational period of suspended sentence)."

(3) Subsection (3) of that section shall cease to have effect.

(4) For subsection (5) of that section there shall be substituted the following subsections—

"(5) Where under subsection (1) above a magistrates' court commits a person to be dealt with by the Crown Court in respect of an offence, the Crown Court may after inquiring into the circumstances of the case deal with him in any way in which the magistrates' court could deal with him if it had just convicted him of the offence.

(5A) Subsection (5) above does not apply where under subsection (1) above a magistrates' court commits a person to be dealt with by the Crown Court in respect of a suspended sentence, but in such a case the powers under section 23 of the Powers of Criminal Courts Act 1973 (power of court to deal with suspended sentence) shall be exercisable by the Crown Court.

(5B) Without prejudice to subsections (5) and (5A) above, where under subsection (1) above or any enactment to which this section applies a magistrates' court commits a person to be dealt with by the Crown Court, any duty or power which, apart from this subsection, would fall to be discharged or exercised by the magistrates' court shall not be discharged or exercised by that court but shall instead be discharged or may instead be exercised by the Crown Court.

(5C)   Where under subsection (1) above a magistrates' court commits a person to be dealt with by the Crown Court in respect of an offence triable only on indictment in the case of an adult (being an offence which was tried summarily because of the offender's being under 18 years of age), the Crown Court's powers under subsection (5) above in respect of the offender after he attains the age of 18 years shall be powers to do either or both of the following—

    (a)   to impose a fine not exceeding £5,000;

    (b)   to deal with the offender in respect of the offence in any way in which the magistrates' court could deal with him if it had just convicted him of an offence punishable with imprisonment for a term not exceeding six months.

(5D)   For the purposes of this section the age of an offender shall be deemed to be that which it appears to the court to be after considering any available evidence."

(5)   Subsection (13) of that section shall cease to have effect.

Children and Young Persons Act 1969 (c 54)

3.   After subsection (8) of section 7 of the 1969 Act (alterations in treatment of young offenders etc) there shall be added the following subsection—

"(9)   The reference in subsection (8) above to a person's parent shall be construed in accordance with section 1 of the Family Law Reform Act 1987 (and not in accordance with section 70(1A) of this Act)."

4.   In section 12 of the 1969 Act (power to include requirements in supervision orders), after subsection (3) there shall be added the following subsection—

"(4)   Directions given by the supervisor by virtue of subsection (2)(b) or (c) above shall, as far as practicable, be such as to avoid—

    (a)   any conflict with the offender's religious beliefs or with the requirements of any other community order (within the meaning of Part I of the Criminal Justice Act 1991) to which he may be subject; and

    (b)   any interference with the times, if any, at which he normally works or attends school or any other educational establishment."

5.—(1)   In subsection (1) of section 12B of the 1969 Act (power to include in supervision order requirements as to mental treatment)—

    (a)   for the words "medical practitioner", in the first place where they occur, there shall be substituted the words "registered medical practitioner";

    (b)   for the words "his detention in pursuance of a hospital order under Part III" there shall be substituted the words "the making of a hospital order or guardianship order within the meaning";

    (c)   in paragraph (a), for the words "fully registered medical practitioner" there shall be substituted the words "registered medical practitioner";

    (d)   after that paragraph there shall be inserted the following paragraph—

"(aa) treatment by or under the direction of a chartered psychologist specified in the order;";

    (e)   in paragraph (b), for the words "a place" there shall be substituted the words "an institution or place"; and

    (f)   in paragraph (c), for the words "the said Act of 1983" there shall be substituted the words "the Mental Health Act 1983".

(2)   After that subsection there shall be inserted the following subsection—

"(1A) In subsection (1) of this section "registered medical practitioner" means a fully registered person within the meaning of the Medical Act 1983 and "chartered psychologist" means a person for the time being listed in the British Psychological Society's Register of Chartered Psychologists."

(3)   After subsection (2) of that section there shall be added the following subsection—

"(3) Subsections (2) and (3) of section 54 of the Mental Health Act 1983 shall have effect with respect to proof for the purposes of subsection (1) above of a supervised person's mental condition as they have effect with respect to proof of an offender's mental condition for the purposes of section 37(2)(a) of that Act."

6 In section 16(11) of the 1969 Act (provisions supplementary to section 15), the words "seventeen or" shall cease to have effect.

7.—(1) In subsection (1)(a) of section 16A of the 1969 Act (application of sections 17 to 19 of Criminal Justice Act 1982), for the words "section 15(2A) or (4)" there shall be substituted the words "section 15(3)(a)".

(2) In subsection (2)(b) of that section—
    (a) in sub-paragraph (i), after the word "from" there shall be inserted the words "subsection (4A) of section 18 and"; and
    (b) in sub-paragraph (ii), for the words "subsection (6)" there shall be substituted the words "subsection (4B) of section 18 and subsection (6) of section 19".

8. In section 34(1)(c) of the 1969 Act (power of Secretary of State to amend references to young person), the words "7(7), 7(8)," shall cease to have effect.

9. Section 69(5) of the 1969 Act (power to include in commencement order certain consequential provisions) shall cease to have effect.

10. In section 70 of the 1969 Act (interpretation), for subsections (1A) and (1B) there shall be substituted the following subsections—

"(1A) In the case of a child or young person—
    (a) whose father and mother were not married to each other at the time of his birth, and
    (b) with respect to whom a residence order is in force in favour of the father,
any reference in this Act to the parent of the child or young person includes (unless the contrary intention appears) a reference to the father.

(1B) In subsection (1A) of this section, the reference to a child or young person whose father and mother were not married to each other at the time of his birth shall be construed in accordance with section 1 of the Family Law Reform Act 1987 and "residence order" has the meaning given by section 8(1) of the Children Act 1989."

11. In Schedule 6 to the 1969 Act (repeals), the entries relating to sections 55, 56(1) and 59(1) of the 1933 Act (which entries have never come into force or are spent) are hereby repealed.

Criminal Justice Act 1972 (c 71)

12. Section 49 of the Criminal Justice Act 1972 (community service order in lieu of warrant of commitment for failure to pay fine etc) shall cease to have effect.

Powers of Criminal Courts Act 1973 (c 62)

13.—(1)In subsection (6) of section 1 of the 1973 Act (deferment of sentence), for the words "13(1), (2) and (5)" there shall be substituted the words "13(1) to (3) and (5)".

(2) In subsection (8) of that section, for paragraph (a) there shall be substituted the following paragraph—

    "(a) is power to deal with him, in respect of the offence for which passing of sentence has been deferred, in any way in which the court which deferred passing sentence could have dealt with him; and".

14.—(1) In subsection (9) of section 1B of the 1973 Act (commission of further offence by person conditionally discharged), for the words from "those which" to the end there shall be substituted the words

"powers to do either or both of the following—
    (a) to impose a fine not exceeding £5,000 for the offence in respect of which the order was made;
    (b) to deal with the offender for that offence in any way in which a magistrates' court could deal with him if it had just convicted him of an offence punishable with imprisonment for a term not exceeding six months."

(2) Subsection (10) of that section (which is superseded by provision inserted by this Schedule in section 57 of the 1973 Act) shall cease to have effect.

15. In section 1C(1) of the 1973 Act (effect of absolute or conditional discharge)
- (a) in paragraph (a), for the words "the following provisions" there shall be substituted the words "section 1B"; and
- (b) paragraph (b) and the word "and" immediately preceding it shall cease to have effect.

16. In section 2(1) of the 1973 Act (probation orders), the words from "For the purposes" to "available evidence" (which are superseded by provision inserted by this Schedule in section 57 of the 1973 Act) shall cease to have effect.

17. Section 11 of the 1973 Act (which is superseded by the paragraph 8A inserted by this Schedule in Schedule 2 to the 1991 Act) shall cease to have effect.

18.—(1) For subsection (2) of section 12 of the 1973 Act (supplementary provision as to probation and discharge) there shall be substituted the following subsection—

"(2) Where an order for conditional discharge has been made on appeal, for the purposes of this Act it shall be deemed—
- (a) if it was made on an appeal brought from a magistrates' court, to have been made by that magistrates' court;
- (b) if it was made on an appeal brought from the Crown Court or from the criminal division of the Court of Appeal, to have been made by the Crown Court."

(2) In subsection (3) of that section, for the words from "any question whether a probationer" to "period of conditional discharge," there shall be substituted the words "any question whether any person in whose case an order for conditional discharge has been made has been convicted of an offence committed during the period of conditional discharge".

(3) For subsection (4) of that section there shall be substituted the following subsection—

"(4) Nothing in section 1A of this Act shall be construed as preventing a court, on discharging an offender absolutely or conditionally in respect of any offence, from making an order for costs against the offender or imposing any disqualification on him or from making in respect of the offence an order under section 35 or 43 of this Act or section 28 of the Theft Act 1968."

19.—(1) In subsection (1) of section 14 of the 1973 Act (community service orders in respect of convicted persons), after the word "imprisonment", in the first place where it occurs, there shall be inserted the words "(not being an offence the sentence for which is fixed by law or falls to be imposed under section 2(2), 3(2) or 4(2) of the Crime (Sentences) Act 1997)".

(2) In that subsection, after the words "young offenders" there shall be inserted the words "; and for the purposes of this subsection a sentence falls to be imposed under section 2(2), 3(2) or 4(2) of the Crime (Sentences) Act 1997 if it is required by that provision and the court is not of the opinion there mentioned".

(3) In subsection (7) of that section, for the words "paragraph (b)(i) or (ii)" there shall be substituted the words "paragraph (b)".

(4) Subsection (8) of that section shall cease to have effect.

20. For subsection (3) of section 15 of the 1973 Act (obligations of person subject to community service order) there shall be substituted the following subsection—

"(3) The instructions given by the relevant officer under this section shall, as far as practicable, be such as to avoid—
- (a) any conflict with the offender's religious beliefs or with the requirements of any other community order (within the meaning of Part I of the Criminal Justice Act 1991) to which he may be subject; and
- (b) any interference with the times, if any, at which he normally works or attends school or any other educational establishment."

21. In section 21(3)(b) of the 1973 Act (meaning of "sentence of imprisonment" for purposes of restriction on imposing sentences of imprisonment on persons not legally

represented), after the words "contempt of court" there shall be inserted the words "or any kindred offence".

22. In subsection (3) of section 22 of the 1973 Act (suspended sentences of imprisonment)—

    (a)   for the words "make a probation order in his case in respect of another offence" there shall be substituted the words "impose a community sentence in his case in respect of that offence or any other offence"; and

    (b)   at the end there shall be inserted the words "; and in this subsection "community sentence" has the same meaning as in Part I of the Criminal Justice Act 1991."

23.—(1) In section 31 of the 1973 Act (powers etc of Crown Court in relation to fines and forfeited recognizances), the following provisions shall cease to have effect—

    (a)   in subsection (3A), the words "Subject to subsections (3B) and (3C) below,";

    (b)   subsections (3B) and (3C); and

    (c)   in subsection (4), the words "4 or".

(2) In subsection (6) of that section—

    (a)   the words "about committal by a magistrates' court to the Crown Court" shall cease to have effect; and

    (b)   after the words "dealt with him" there shall be inserted the words "or could deal with him".

(3) In subsection (8) of that section, for the words "(2) to (3C)" there shall be substituted the words "(2) to (3A)".

24.—(1) In subsection (2) of section 32 of the 1973 Act (enforcement etc of fines imposed and recognizances forfeited by Crown Court), for the words "section 85(1)" there shall be substituted the words "section 85(2)".

(2) In subsection (3) of that section, after the words "to the Crown Court" there shall be inserted the words "(except the reference in subsection (1)(b) above)".

(3) For subsection (4) of that section there shall be substituted the following subsection—

    "(4) A magistrates' court shall not, under section 85(1) or 120 of the Magistrates' Courts Act 1980 as applied by subsection (1) above, remit the whole or any part of a fine imposed by, or sum due under a recognizance forfeited by—

        (a)   the Crown Court,

        (b)   the criminal division of the Court of Appeal, or

        (c)   the House of Lords on appeal from that division, without the consent of the Crown Court."

(4) Subsection (5) of that section shall cease to have effect.

25.—In section 46 of the 1973 Act (reports of probation officers), after subsection (2) there shall be added the following subsection—

    "(3) For the purposes of this section—

        (a)   references to an offender's parent shall be construed in accordance with section 1 of the Family Law Reform Act 1987; and

        (b)   "guardian" has the same meaning as in the Children and Young Persons Act 1933."

26.—(1) For subsection (5) of section 57 of the 1973 Act (interpretation) there shall be substituted the following subsection—

    "(5) Where a compensation order or supervision order has been made on appeal, for the purposes of this Act (except section 26(5)) it shall be deemed—

        (a)   if it was made on an appeal brought from a magistrates' court, to have been made by that magistrates' court;

        (b)   if it was made on an appeal brought from the Crown Court or from the criminal division of the Court of Appeal, to have been made by the Crown Court."

(2) After subsection (6) of that section there shall be added the following subsection—

"(7)   For the purposes of any provision of this Act which requires the determination of the age of a person by the court, his age shall be deemed to be that which it appears to the court to be after considering any available evidence."

27.—(1) In paragraph 2 of Schedule 1A to the 1973 Act (additional requirements in probation orders), for sub-paragraph (7) there shall be substituted the following sub-paragraph—

"(7)   Instructions given by a probation officer under sub-paragraph (4) or (6) above shall, as far as practicable, be such as to avoid—
  (a)   any conflict with the offender's religious beliefs or with the requirements of any other community order (within the meaning of Part I of the Criminal Justice Act 1991) to which he may be subject; and
  (b)   any interference with the times, if any, at which he normally works or attends school or any other educational establishment."

(2)   In paragraph 3 of that Schedule, for sub-paragraph (4) there shall be substituted the following sub-paragraph—

"(4)   Instructions given by a probation officer under sub-paragraph (3) above shall, as far as practicable, be such as to avoid—
  (a)   any conflict with the offender's religious beliefs or with the requirements of any other community order (within the meaning of Part I of the Criminal Justice Act 1991) to which he may be subject; and
  (b)   any interference with the times, if any, at which he normally works or attends school or any other educational establishment."

(3)   In paragraph 5 of that Schedule, for the words "duly qualified medical practitioner", wherever they occur, there shall be substituted the words "registered medical practitioner".

(4)   In that paragraph (both as amended by subsection (3) of section 38 of the 1997 Act and so far as that paragraph has effect without that amendment), in sub-paragraph (4), after the words "have been" there shall be inserted the words "or can be".

(5)   In sub-paragraph (10) of that paragraph, before the definition of "chartered psychologist" there shall be inserted the following definition—

""registered medical practitioner" means a fully registered person within the meaning of the Medical Act 1983;".

(6)   In paragraph 6 of that Schedule (both as amended by subsection (4) of section 38 of the 1997 Act and so far as that paragraph has effect without that amendment), in sub-paragraph (4), after the words "have been" there shall be inserted the words "or can be".

(7)   Sub-paragraph (7) of that paragraph shall cease to have effect.

Magistrates' Courts Act 1980 (c 43)

28.—In section 30(2)(a) of the 1980 Act (remand for medical examination), for the words "duly qualified medical practitioner" there shall be substituted the words "registered medical practitioner".

29.—(1) In subsection (2) of section 38 of the 1980 Act (committal for sentence on summary trial of offence triable either way), the words ", in accordance with section 56 of the Criminal Justice Act 1967," shall cease to have effect.

(2)   After that subsection there shall be inserted the following subsection—

"(2A)   Where the court commits a person under subsection (2) above, section 56 of the Criminal Justice Act 1967 (which enables a magistrates' court, where it commits a person under this section in respect of an offence, also to commit him to the Crown Court to be dealt with in respect of certain other offences) shall apply accordingly."

30.—(1) In subsection (2) of section 38A of the 1980 Act (committal for sentence on indication of guilty plea to offence triable either way), the words ", in accordance with section 56 of the Criminal Justice Act 1967," shall cease to have effect.

(2)   In subsection (5) of that section, for the words "the court might have dealt with him" there shall be substituted the words "the magistrates' court could deal with him if it had just convicted him of the offence".

(3) After that subsection there shall be inserted the following subsection—

"(5A) Where the court commits a person under subsection (2) above, section 56 of the Criminal Justice Act 1967 (which enables a magistrates' court, where it commits a person under this section in respect of an offence, also to commit him to the Crown Court to be dealt with in respect of certain other offences) shall apply accordingly."

31. In section 39(6)(b) of the 1980 Act (cases where magistrates' court may remit offender to another such court for sentence), for the words "section 34 or 36" there shall be substituted the words "section 34, 35 or 36".

32. In section 85(1)(a) of the 1980 Act (power to remit fine), for the words "section 74" there shall be substituted the words "section 77".

Criminal Justice Act 1982 (c 48)

33. In section 3(1) of the 1982 Act (restriction on imposing custodial sentences on persons under 21 not legally represented)—
> (a) in paragraph (a), the words "under section 1A above" shall cease to have effect;
> (b) in paragraph (c), for the words "section 8(2)" there shall be substituted the words "section 8(1) or (2)"; and
> (c) in paragraph (d), for the words "section 53(2)" there shall be substituted the words "section 53(1) or (3)".

34.—(1) In subsection (3) of section 13 of the 1982 Act (conversion of sentence of detention in a young offender institution to sentence of imprisonment), for the words "section 15 below" there shall be substituted the words "section 65 of the Criminal Justice Act 1991 (supervision of young offenders after release)".

(2) In subsection (6) of that section, for the words "section 8(2)" there shall be substituted the words "section 8(1) or (2)".

35. In subsection (2) of section 16 of the 1982 Act (meaning of "attendance centre"), for the words from "of orders made" to the end there shall be substituted the words "of orders made under section 17 below."

36.—(1) In subsection (1) of section 17 of the 1982 Act (attendance centre orders), for the words "Subject to subsections (3) and (4) below," there shall be substituted the words "Where a person under 21 years of age is convicted by or before a court of an offence punishable with imprisonment (not being an offence the sentence for which is fixed by law or falls to be imposed under section 2(2), 3(2) or 4(2) of the Crime (Sentences) Act 1997), or".

(2) In that subsection, for paragraph (a) there shall be substituted the following paragraph—
> "(a) would have power, but for section 1 above, to commit a person under 21 years of age to prison in default of payment of any sum of money or for failing to do or abstain from doing anything required to be done or left undone, or".

(3) In that subsection, in paragraph (b), for the words "any such person" there shall be substituted the words "a person under 21 years of age" and after that paragraph there shall be inserted the following paragraph—
> "(bb)has power to deal with a person under 16 years of age under that Part of that Schedule for failure to comply with any of the requirements of a curfew order, or".

(4) After that subsection there shall be inserted the following subsection—

"(1A) For the purposes of subsection (1) above—
> (a) the reference to an offence punishable with imprisonment shall be construed without regard to any prohibition or restriction imposed by or under any enactment on the imprisonment of young offenders; and
> (b) a sentence falls to be imposed under section 2(2), 3(2) or 4(2) of the Crime (Sentences) Act 1997 if it is required by that provision and the court is not of the opinion there mentioned."

(5) For subsection (8) of that section there shall be substituted the following subsection—

"(8)   The times at which an offender is required to attend at an attendance centre shall, as far as practicable, be such as to avoid—

(a)   any conflict with the offender's religious beliefs or with the requirements of any other community order (within the meaning of Part I of the Criminal Justice Act 1991) to which he may be subject; and

(b)   any interference with the times, if any, at which he normally works or attends school or any other educational establishment."

37.—(1) In section 18 of the 1982 Act (discharge and variation of attendance centre orders), for subsection (4A) there shall be substituted the following subsections—

"(4A) Any power conferred by this section—

(a)   on a magistrates' court to discharge an attendance centre order made by such a court, or

(b)   on the Crown Court to discharge an attendance centre order made by the Crown Court,

includes power to deal with the offender, for the offence in respect of which the order was made, in any manner in which he could have been dealt with for that offence by the court which made the order if the order had not been made.

(4B)   A person sentenced by a magistrates' court under subsection (4A) above for an offence may appeal to the Crown Court against the sentence."

(2)   Subsection (7) of that section shall cease to have effect.

(3)   In that section, after subsection (9) there shall be added the following subsections—

"(10)   Where an offender has been ordered to attend at an attendance centre in default of the payment of a sum of money or for such a failure or abstention as is mentioned in section 17(1)(a) above, subsection (4A) above shall have effect in relation to the order as if the words ", for the offence in respect of which the order was made," and "for that offence" were omitted.

(11)   Where an attendance centre order has been made on appeal, for the purposes of this section it shall be deemed—

(a)   if it was made on an appeal brought from a magistrates' court, to have been made by that magistrates' court;

(b)   if it was made on an appeal brought from the Crown Court or from the criminal division of the Court of Appeal, to have been made by the Crown Court;

and subsection (4A) above shall have effect in relation to an attendance centre order made on appeal as if the words "if the order had not been made" were omitted."

38.—(1) In subsection (1) of section 19 of the 1982 Act (breaches of attendance centre orders or attendance centre rules), for the words "has been made" there shall be substituted the words "is in force".

(2)   In subsection (5) of that section, after the word "failed" there shall be inserted the words "without reasonable excuse".

(3)   After subsection (7) of that section there shall be added the following subsections—

"(8)   Where an offender has been ordered to attend at an attendance centre in default of the payment of a sum of money or for such a failure or abstention as is mentioned in section 17(1)(a) above, subsections (3) and (5) above shall have effect in relation to the order as if the words ", for the offence in respect of which the order was made," and "for that offence" were omitted.

(9)   Where an attendance centre order has been made on appeal, for the purposes of this section it shall be deemed—

(a)   if it was made on an appeal brought from a magistrates' court, to have been made by that magistrates' court;

(b)   if it was made on an appeal brought from the Crown Court or from the criminal division of the Court of Appeal, to have been made by the Crown Court;

and, in relation to an attendance centre order made on appeal, subsection (3)(a) above shall have effect as if the words "if the order had not been made" were omitted and subsection (5) above shall have effect as if the words "if it had not made the order" were omitted."

Criminal Justice Act 1988 (c 33)

39. Paragraph 40 of Schedule 15 to the Criminal Justice Act 1988 (minor and consequential amendments) shall cease to have effect.

Criminal Justice Act 1991 (c 53)

40. In section 11 of the 1991 Act (orders combining probation and community service), after subsection (1) there shall be inserted the following subsection—

"(1A) The reference in subsection (1) above to an offence punishable with imprisonment shall be construed without regard to any prohibition or restriction imposed by or under any enactment on the imprisonment of young offenders."

41.—(1) In subsection (5)(c) of section 12 of the 1991 Act (curfew orders), for the words "supervising officer" there shall be substituted the words "responsible officer".

(2) After subsection (6A) of that section there shall be inserted the following subsection—

"(6B) The court by which a curfew order is made shall give a copy of the order to the offender and to the person responsible for monitoring the offender's whereabouts during the curfew periods specified in the order."

(3) After subsection (7) of that section there shall be added the following subsection—

"(8) References in this section to the offender's being under the age of sixteen years are references to his being under that age on conviction."

42. In section 31(1) of the 1991 Act (interpretation of Part I), in paragraph (b) of the definition of "custodial sentence", for the words "section 53" there shall be substituted the words "section 53(3)".

43.—(1) In subsection (3) of section 40 of the 1991 Act (convictions during currency of original sentences), for the words from "for sentence" to the end there shall be substituted the words "to be dealt with under subsection (3A) below".

(2) After that subsection there shall be inserted the following subsections—

"(3A) Where a person is committed to the Crown Court under subsection (3) above, the Crown Court may order him to be returned to prison for the whole or any part of the period which—
(a) begins with the date of the order; and
(b) is equal in length to the period between the date on which the new offence was committed and the date mentioned in subsection (1) above.

(3B) Subsection (3)(b) above shall not be taken to confer on the magistrates' court a power to commit the person to the Crown Court for sentence for the new offence, but this is without prejudice to any such power conferred on the magistrates' court by any other enactment."

(3) In subsection (4) of that section, for the words "subsection (2)" there shall be substituted the words "subsection (2) or (3A)".

44. In each of subsections (3)(b) and (4)(a) of section 57 of the 1991 Act (responsibility of parent or guardian for financial penalties), for the words "section 35(4)(a)" there shall be substituted the words "section 35(4)".

45. In section 58 of the 1991 Act (binding over of parent or guardian), after subsection (8) there shall be added the following subsection—

"(9) For the purposes of this section—
(a) "guardian" has the same meaning as in the 1933 Act; and
(b) taking "care" of a person includes giving him protection and guidance and "control" includes discipline."

46.—(1) In paragraph 1 of Schedule 2 to the 1991 Act (enforcement etc of community orders), after sub-paragraph (4) there shall be added the following sub-paragraph—

"(5) Where a probation order, community service order, combination order or curfew order has been made on appeal, for the purposes of this Schedule it shall be deemed—

(a)   if it was made on an appeal brought from a magistrates' court, to have been made by a magistrates' court;

(b)   if it was made on an appeal brought from the Crown Court or from the criminal division of the Court of Appeal, to have been made by the Crown Court."

(2)   In each of paragraphs 3(1) and 4(1) of that Schedule, for paragraph (c) there shall be substituted the following paragraph—

"(c)   where—
  (i)   the relevant order is a probation order and the offender is under the age of twenty-one years, or
  (ii)   the relevant order is a curfew order and the offender is under the age of sixteen years,

and the court has been notified as required by subsection (1) of section 17 of the 1982 Act, it may (subject to paragraph 6(6) below) make in respect of him an order under that section (attendance centre orders); or".

(3)   In paragraph 4(1) of that Schedule—
  (a)   after the word "failed" there shall be inserted the words "without reasonable excuse"; and
  (b)   in paragraph (d), for the words "by or before the court" there shall be substituted the words "before the Crown Court".

(4)   In paragraph 6 of that Schedule, in sub-paragraph (1), for the words "or (b)" there shall be substituted the words ", (b) or (c)".

(5)   After sub-paragraph (3) of that paragraph there shall be inserted the following sub-paragraph—

"(3A)   A community service order shall not be made under paragraph 3(1)(b) or 4(1)(b) above in respect of a person who is under the age of sixteen years."

(6)   For sub-paragraph (5) of that paragraph there shall be substituted the following sub-paragraph—

"(5)   Where the provisions of this Schedule have effect as mentioned in sub-paragraph (4) above in relation to a community service order under paragraph 3(1)(b) or 4(1)(b) above—
  (a)   the power conferred on the court by each of paragraphs 3(1)(d) and 4(1)(d) above and paragraph 7(2)(a)(ii) below to deal with the offender for the offence in respect of which the order was made shall be construed as a power to deal with the offender, for his failure to comply with the original order, in any manner in which the court could deal with him if that failure to comply had just been proved to the satisfaction of the court;
  (b)   the reference in paragraph 7(1)(b) below to the offence in respect of which the order was made shall be construed as a reference to the failure to comply in respect of which the order was made; and
  (c)   the power conferred on the court by paragraph 8(2)(b) below to deal with the offender for the offence in respect of which the order was made shall be construed as a power to deal with the offender, for his failure to comply with the original order, in any manner in which the court which made the original order could deal with him if that failure had just been proved to the satisfaction of that court;

and in this sub-paragraph "the original order" means the relevant order the failure to comply with whose requirements led to the making of the community service order under paragraph 3(1)(b) or 4(1)(b)."

(7)   After sub-paragraph (5) of that paragraph there shall be added the following sub-paragraph—

"(6)   The provisions of sections 17 to 19 of the 1982 Act (making, discharge, variation and breach of attendance centre order) shall apply for the purposes of paragraphs 3(1)(c) and 4(1)(c) above but as if there were omitted—
  (a)   subsection (13) of section 17;

    (b) from subsection (4A) of section 18 and subsections (3) and (5) of section 19, the words ", for the offence in respect of which the order was made," and "for that offence"."

(8) After paragraph 6 of that Schedule there shall be inserted the following paragraph—

"6A.—(1) Where a relevant order was made by a magistrates' court in the case of an offender under 18 years of age in respect of an offence triable only on indictment in the case of an adult, any powers exercisable under paragraph 3(1)(d) above by that or any other court in respect of the offender after he has attained the age of 18 years shall be powers to do either or both of the following—

    (a) to impose a fine not exceeding £5,000 for the offence in respect of which the order was made;

    (b) to deal with the offender for that offence in any way in which a magistrates' court could deal with him if it had just convicted him of an offence punishable with imprisonment for a term not exceeding six months.

(2)   In sub-paragraph (1)(b) above any reference to an offence punishable with imprisonment shall be construed without regard to any prohibition or restriction imposed by or under any enactment on the imprisonment of young offenders."

(9) In paragraph 7(5) of that Schedule, after the word "above" there shall be inserted the words "for an offence".

(10) In paragraph 8(2) of that Schedule, for paragraph (b) there shall be substituted the following paragraph—

"(b) revoke the order and deal with the offender, for the offence in respect of which the order was made, in any manner in which the court which made the order could deal with him if he had just been convicted of that offence by or before the court which made the order."

(11) After paragraph 8 of that Schedule there shall be inserted the following paragraph—

"8A.—(1) This paragraph applies where a probation order is in force in respect of any offender and on the application of the offender or the responsible officer it appears to a magistrates' court acting for the petty sessions area concerned that, having regard to circumstances which have arisen since the order was made, it would be in the interests of justice—

    (a) for the probation order to be revoked; and

    (b) for an order to be made under section 1A(1)(b) of the 1973 Act discharging the offender conditionally for the offence for which the probation order was made.

(2)   No application may be made under paragraph 7 above for a probation order to be revoked and replaced with an order for conditional discharge under section 1A(1)(b) of the 1973 Act; but otherwise nothing in this paragraph shall affect the operation of paragraphs 7 and 8 above.

(3)   Where this paragraph applies and the probation order was made by a magistrates' court—

    (a) the magistrates' court dealing with the application may revoke the probation order and make an order under section 1A(1)(b) of the 1973 Act discharging the offender in respect of the offence for which the probation order was made, subject to the condition that he commits no offence during the period specified in the order under section 1A(1)(b); and

    (b) the period specified in the order under section 1A(1)(b) shall be the period beginning with the making of that order and ending with the date when the probation period specified in the probation order would have ended.

(4)   Where this paragraph applies and the probation order was made by the Crown Court, the magistrates' court may send the application to the Crown Court to be heard by that court, and if it does so shall also send to the Crown Court such particulars of the case as may be desirable.

(5)   Where an application under this paragraph is heard by the Crown Court by virtue of sub-paragraph (4) above—

(a) the Crown Court may revoke the probation order and make an order under section 1A(1)(b) of the 1973 Act discharging the offender in respect of the offence for which the probation order was made, subject to the condition that he commits no offence during the period specified in the order under section 1A(1)(b); and

(b) the period specified in the order under section 1A(1)(b) shall be the period beginning with the making of that order and ending with the date when the probation period specified in the probation order would have ended.

(6) For the purposes of sub-paragraphs (3) and (5) above, subsection (1) of section 1A of the 1973 Act shall apply as if—

(a) for the words from the beginning to "may make an order either" there were substituted the words "Where paragraph 8A of Schedule 2 to the Criminal Justice Act 1991 applies, the court which under sub-paragraph (3) or (5) of that paragraph has power to dispose of the application may (subject to the provisions of that sub-paragraph) make an order in respect of the offender"; and

(b) paragraph (a) of that subsection were omitted.

(7) An application under this paragraph may be heard in the offender's absence if—

(a) the application is made by the responsible officer; and

(b) that officer produces to the court a statement by the offender that he understands the effect of an order for conditional discharge and consents to the making of the application;

and where the application is so heard section 1A(3) of the 1973 Act shall not apply.

(8) No application may be made under this paragraph while an appeal against the probation order is pending.

(9) Without prejudice to paragraph 11 below, on the making of an order under section 1A(1)(b) of the 1973 Act by virtue of this paragraph the court shall forthwith give copies of the order to the responsible officer, and the responsible officer shall give a copy to the offender.

(10) Each of sections 1(11), 2(9) and 66(4) of the Crime and Disorder Act 1998 (which prevent a court from making an order for conditional discharge in certain cases) shall have effect as if the reference to the court by or before which a person is convicted of an offence there mentioned included a reference to a court dealing with an application under this paragraph in respect of the offence."

(12) After paragraph 11 of that Schedule there shall be inserted the following paragraphs—

"11A. Paragraph 6A above shall apply for the purposes of paragraphs 7 and 8 above as it applies for the purposes of paragraph 3 above, but as if in paragraph 6A(1) for the words "powers exercisable under paragraph 3(1)(d) above" there were substituted the words "powers to deal with the offender which are exercisable under paragraph 7(2)(a)(ii) or 8(2)(b) below".

11B. Where under this Part of this Schedule a relevant order is revoked and replaced by an order for conditional discharge under section 1A(1)(b) of the 1973 Act and—

(a) the order for conditional discharge is not made in the circumstances mentioned in section 1B(9) of the 1973 Act (order made by magistrates' court in the case of an offender under eighteen in respect of offence triable only on indictment in the case of an adult), but

(b) the relevant order was made in those circumstances,

section 1B(9) of the 1973 Act shall apply as if the order for conditional discharge had been made in those circumstances."

Crime (Sentences) Act 1997 (c 43)

47. Section 1 of the 1997 Act (conditions relating to mandatory and minimum custodial sentences) shall cease to have effect.

48.—(1) In subsection (2) of section 3 of the 1997 Act (minimum of seven years for third class A drug trafficking offence)—

(a) for the words "specific circumstances" there shall be substituted the words "particular circumstances"; and

(b)   for the words "the prescribed custodial sentence unjust" there shall be substituted the words "it unjust to do so".

(2)   In subsection (3) of that section, for the words "specific circumstances" there shall be substituted the words "particular circumstances".

49.—(1) In subsection (2) of section 4 of the 1997 Act (minimum of three years for third domestic burglary)—

(a)   for the words "specific circumstances" there shall be substituted the words "particular circumstances"; and

(b)   for the words "the prescribed custodial sentence unjust" there shall be substituted the words "it unjust to do so".

(2)   In subsection (3) of that section, for the words "specific circumstances" there shall be substituted the words "particular circumstances".

50.—(1) In subsection (2)(a) of section 35 of the 1997 Act (community sentences for fine defaulters), for the words "and (11)" there shall be substituted the words ", (10) and (11)".

(2)   In subsection (5) of that section, paragraph (c) shall cease to have effect.

(3)   In that subsection, the word "and" at the end of paragraph (d) shall cease to have effect and after paragraph (e) there shall be added the following paragraphs—

"(f)   the reference in paragraph 7(1)(b) of that Schedule to the offence in respect of which the order was made shall be construed as a reference to the default in respect of which the order was made;

(g)   the power conferred by paragraph 7(2)(a)(ii) of that Schedule to deal with an offender for the offence in respect of which the order was made shall be construed as a power to deal with the person in respect of whom the order was made for his default in paying the sum in question; and

(h)   paragraph 8(2)(b) of that Schedule shall not apply."

(4)   In subsection (7) of that section, for the words "section 12(5)" there shall be substituted the words "section 12(6)".

(5)   In subsection (8) of that section, the word "and" at the end of paragraph (a) shall cease to have effect and after paragraph (b) there shall be added the following paragraphs—

"(c)   the reference in paragraph 7(1)(b) of that Schedule to the offence in respect of which the order was made shall be construed as a reference to the default in respect of which the order was made;

(d)   the power conferred by paragraph 7(2)(a)(ii) of that Schedule to deal with an offender for the offence in respect of which the order was made shall be construed as a power to deal with the person in respect of whom the order was made for his default in paying the sum in question; and

(e)   paragraph 8(2)(b) of that Schedule shall not apply."

(6)   In subsection (10) of that section, for the words "subsection (2)(b)" there shall be substituted the words "subsection (2)(a) or (b)".

51.—(1) In subsection (3) of section 37 of the 1997 Act (community sentences for persistent petty offenders—

(a)   in paragraph (a), for the words "(4) and (6)" there shall be substituted the words "(4), (5A) and (6)"; and

(b)   in paragraph (b), for the words "(5) and (6)" there shall be substituted the words "(5), (5A) and (6)".

(2)   For subsections (4) and (5) of that section there shall be substituted the following subsections—

"(4)   In this section "community service order" has the same meaning as in the 1973 Act and—

(a)   section 14(2) of that Act; and

(b)   so far as applicable, the other provisions of that Act relating to community service orders and the provisions of Part I of the 1991 Act so relating,

shall have effect in relation to an order under subsection (3)(a) above as they have effect in relation to a community service order made under the 1973 Act in respect of an offender.

(5)　　In this section "curfew order" has the same meaning as in Part I of the 1991 Act and—

    (a)　　section 12(6) of that Act; and

    (b)　　so far as applicable, the other provisions of that Part relating to curfew orders,

shall have effect in relation to an order under subsection (3)(b) above as they have effect in relation to a curfew order made under that Act in respect of an offender.

(5A)　　A court shall not make an order under subsection (3)(a) or (b) above in respect of a person who on conviction is under 16."

52. In section 50 of the 1997 Act (disclosure of pre-sentence reports), after subsection (6) there shall be added the following subsection—

"(7)　　In this section "guardian" has the same meaning as in the 1933 Act."

53. In section 54 of the 1997 Act (general interpretation), after subsection (3) there shall be added the following subsection—

"(4)　　For the purposes of any provision of this Act which requires the determination of the age of a person by the court, his age shall be deemed to be that which it appears to the court to be after considering any available evidence."

54. In section 55(2) of the 1997 Act (interpretation of minor and consequential amendments), for the words "in any case where" (in both places where they occur) there shall be substituted the word "and".

Definitions　　For "the 1933 Act", "the 1969 Act", "the 1973 Act", "the 1980 Act", "the 1982 Act", "the 1991 Act" and "the 1997 Act", see s 117(1). In the Children and Young Persons Act 1933, for "child" and "young person", see s 107(1) thereof. In the Criminal Justice Act 1967, for "suspended sentence", "offence punishable with imprisonment" and "any other enactment", see s 104 thereof. In the Children and Young Persons Act 1969, for "supervised person" and "supervisor", see s 11 thereof, as amended by s 119, Sch 8, para 17 of this Act; for "child" and "young person", see s 70(1) thereof; for "residence order", see s 70(1B) thereof, as inserted by para 10 above. For "order for conditional discharge" and "period of conditional discharge", see the Powers of Criminal Courts Act 1973, s 1A(2); for "compensation order", "court" and "supervision order", see s 57(1) of that Act; as to imprisonment and offences punishable by imprisonment, see s 57(2)-(4) of that Act; for "registered medical practitioner", see Sch 1A(10) to the 1973 Act, as inserted by para 27(5) above. In the Magistrates' Courts Act 1980, for "magistrates' court", see s 148 thereof. In the Criminal Justice Act 1982, for "attendance centre" and "attendance centre order", see ss 16(2), 17(2) thereof, as amended, in the case of s 16(2), by para 35 above. In the Criminal Justice Act 1991, for "curfew order", "custodial sentence", "combination order" and "responsible officer", see s 31(1) thereof, as amended and repealed in part (definition "custodial sentence"), by ss 119, 120(2) of, Sch 8, para 78(b), Sch 10 to, this Act; for "relevant order", see Sch 2, para 1(1) to that Act.

References　　See paras 6.19, 6.35.

SCHEDULE 8

Section 119

MINOR AND CONSEQUENTIAL AMENDMENTS

Children and Young Persons Act 1933 (c 12)

1. In subsection (4A) of section 49 of the 1933 Act (restrictions on reports of proceedings), for paragraph (e) there shall be substituted the following paragraph—

"(e)　　where a detention and training order is made, the enforcement of any requirements imposed under section 76(6)(b) of the Crime and Disorder Act 1998."

2. In subsection (1A) of section 55 of the 1933 Act (power of court to order parent or guardian to pay fine imposed on child or young person), after paragraph (c) there shall be inserted the words

"or

    (d)　　a court would impose a fine on a child or young person under section 77(3) of the Crime and Disorder Act 1998 (breach of requirements of supervision under detention and training order) or paragraph 3 of Schedule 5 to that Act (breach of requirements of reparation order or action plan order),".

3. After subsection (1) of section 56 of the 1933 Act (powers of other courts to remit young offenders to youth courts) there shall be inserted the following subsection—

"(1A) References in subsection (1) above to an offender's being committed for trial include references to his being sent for trial under section 51 of the Crime and Disorder Act 1998."

4. In section 58 of that Act (power of Secretary of State to send certain young offenders to approved schools), for the words "subsection (2)", in both places where they occur, there shall be substituted the words "subsection (3)".

Administration of Justice (Miscellaneous Provisions) Act 1933 (c 36)

5.—(1) In subsection (2) of section 2 of the Administration of Justice (Miscellaneous Provisions) Act 1933 (procedure for indictment of offenders)—
(a) after paragraph (ab) there shall be inserted the following paragraph—

"(ac) the person charged has been sent for trial for the offence under section 51 (no committal proceedings for indictable-only offences) of the Crime and Disorder Act 1998 ("the 1998 Act"); or"; and
(b) after paragraph (b) there shall be inserted the words

"or
(c) the bill is preferred under section 22B(3)(a) of the Prosecution of Offences Act 1985."

(2) After paragraph (iA) of the proviso to that subsection there shall be inserted the following paragraph—

"(iB) in a case to which paragraph (ac) above applies, the bill of indictment may include, either in substitution for or in addition to any count charging an offence specified in the notice under section 51(7) of the 1998 Act, any counts founded on material which, in pursuance of regulations made under paragraph 1 of Schedule 3 to that Act, was served on the person charged, being counts which may be lawfully joined in the same indictment;".

Prison Act 1952 (c 52)

6. In subsection (1) of section 43 of the Prison Act 1952 (which enables certain institutions for young offenders to be provided and applies provisions of the Act to them), for paragraph (d) there shall be substituted the following paragraph—

"(d) secure training centres, that is to say places in which offenders in respect of whom detention and training orders have been made under section 73 of the Crime and Disorder Act 1998 may be detained and given training and education and prepared for their release."

7.—(1) In subsection (1) of section 49 of that Act (persons unlawfully at large), for the words from "imprisonment" to "secure training centre" there shall be substituted the words "imprisonment or custody for life or ordered to be detained in secure accommodation or in a young offenders institution".

(2) In subsection (2) of that section—
(a) for the words from "imprisonment" to "secure training centre" there shall be substituted the words "imprisonment, or ordered to be detained in secure accommodation or in a young offenders institution"; and
(b) for the words from "in a prison" to "secure training centre" there shall be substituted the words "in a prison or remand centre, in secure accommodation or in a young offenders institution".

(3) After subsection (4) of that section there shall be inserted the following subsection—

"(5) In this section "secure accommodation" means—
(a) a young offender institution;
(b) a secure training centre; or
(c) any other accommodation that is secure accommodation within the meaning given by section 75(7) of the Crime and Disorder Act 1998 (detention and training orders)."

Criminal Procedure (Attendance of Witnesses) Act 1965 (c 69)

8. In subsection (4) of section 2 of the Criminal Procedure (Attendance of Witnesses) Act 1965 (issue of witness summons on application to Crown Court), after the words "committed for trial" there shall be inserted the words ", or sent for trial under section 51 of the Crime and Disorder Act 1998,".

Criminal Justice Act 1967 (c 80)

9.—(1)In subsection (2) of section 56 of the Criminal Justice Act 1967 (committal for sentence for offences tried summarily)—

    (a)   for the words "sections 37, 38 and 38A" there shall be substituted the words "sections 38 and 38A"; and

    (b)   for the words "section 17(3) of the Crime (Sentences) Act 1997 (committal for breach of conditions of release supervision order)" there shall be substituted the words "section 40(3)(b) of the Criminal Justice Act 1991 (committal for sentence for offence committed during currency of original sentence)".

(2) Subsection (6) of that section shall cease to have effect.

10. In subsection (5) of section 67 of that Act (computation of sentences of imprisonment or detention passed in England and Wales)—

    (a)   in paragraph (b), for the words "section 53(2)" there shall be substituted the words "section 53(3)"; and

    (b)   paragraph (c) shall cease to have effect.

11. At the end of subsection (2) of section 104 of that Act (general provisions as to interpretation) there shall be inserted the words

    "if—

    (a)   the sentences were passed on the same occasion; or

    (b)   where they were passed on different occasions, the person has not been released under Part II of the Criminal Justice Act 1991 at any time during the period beginning with the first and ending with the last of those occasions."

Criminal Appeal Act 1968 (c 19)

12. In subsection (2) of section 9 of the Criminal Appeal Act 1968 (appeal against sentence following conviction on indictment), after the words "for either way offence)" there shall be inserted the words "or paragraph 6 of Schedule 3 to the Crime and Disorder Act 1998 (power of Crown Court to deal with summary offence where person sent for trial for indictable-only offence)".

13.—(1) In subsection (2) of section 10 of that Act (appeal against sentence in other cases dealt with at Crown Court), the words "(other than a supervision order within the meaning of that Part)" shall cease to have effect.

(2) In subsection (3) of that section, after paragraph (c) there shall be inserted the following paragraph—

    "(cc) where the court makes such an order with regard to him as is mentioned in section 40(3A) of the Criminal Justice Act 1991."

Firearms Act 1968 (c 27)

14.—(1) In subsection (2) of section 21 of the Firearms Act 1968 (possession of firearms by persons previously convicted of crime), after the words "a secure training order" there shall be inserted the words "or a detention and training order".

(2) In subsection (2A) of that section, after paragraph (b) there shall be inserted the following paragraph—

    "(c) in the case of a person who has been subject to a detention and training order—

       (i)   the date on which he is released from detention under the order;

       (ii) the date on which he is released from detention ordered under section 77 of the Crime and Disorder Act 1998; or

      (iii) the date of the half-way point of the term of the order, whichever is the later."

15. In subsection (1) of section 52 of that Act (forfeiture and disposal of firearms), for the words "secure training order" there shall be substituted the words "detention and training order".

Children and Young Persons Act 1969 (c 54)

16. In subsection (8) of section 7 of the 1969 Act (alterations in treatment of young offenders etc), for the words from "person guilty" to "were begun" there shall be substituted the words "child or young person guilty of an offence".

17. In section 11 of the 1969 Act (supervision orders), for the words "a local authority designated by the order or of a probation officer" there shall be substituted the following paragraphs—

"(a) a local authority designated by the order;
(b) a probation officer; or
(c) a member of a youth offending team,"

18. Section 12D of the 1969 Act (duty of court to state in certain cases that requirement in place of custodial sentence) shall cease to have effect.

19. After subsection (3) of section 13 of the 1969 Act (selection of supervisor) there shall be inserted the following subsection—

"(4) Where a provision of a supervision order places a person under the supervision of a member of a youth offending team, the supervisor shall be a member of a team established by the local authority within whose area it appears to the court that the supervised person resides or will reside."

20.—(1) In subsection (8) of section 16 of the 1969 Act (provisions supplementary to section (15), after the words "under the preceding section" there shall be inserted the words "by a relevant court (within the meaning of that section)".

(2) Subsection (10) of that section shall cease to have effect.

21. After section 16A of the 1969 Act there shall be inserted the following section—

"16B Application of section 12 of Criminal Justice Act 1991 etc

(1) The provisions of section 12 of the Criminal Justice Act 1991 (curfew orders) shall apply for the purposes of section 15(3)(a) of this Act but as if—
(a) in subsection (1), for the words from the beginning to "before which he is convicted" there were substituted the words "Where a court considers it appropriate to make a curfew order in respect of any person in pursuance of section 15(3)(a) of the Children and Young Persons Act 1969, the court"; and
(b) in subsection (8), for the words "on conviction" there were substituted the words "on the date on which his failure to comply with a requirement included in the supervision order was proved to the court".

(2) Schedule 2 to the Criminal Justice Act 1991 (enforcement etc of community orders), so far as relating to curfew orders, shall also apply for the purposes of that section but as if—
(a) the power conferred on the magistrates' court by each of paragraphs 3(1)(d) and 7(2)(a)(ii) to deal with the offender for the offence in respect of which the order was made were a power to deal with the offender, for his failure to comply with a requirement included in the supervision order, in any manner in which the relevant court could deal with him for that failure to comply if it had just been proved to the satisfaction of that court;
(b) the power conferred on the Crown Court by paragraph 4(1)(d) to deal with the offender for the offence in respect of which the order was made were a power to deal with the offender, for his failure to comply with such a requirement, in any manner in which that court could deal with him for that failure to comply if it had just been proved to its satisfaction;
(c) the reference in paragraph 7(1)(b) to the offence in respect of which the order was made were a reference to the failure to comply in respect of which the curfew order was made; and
(d) the power conferred on the Crown Court by paragraph 8(2)(b) to deal with the offender for the offence in respect of which the order was made were a

power to deal with the offender, for his failure to comply with a requirement included in the supervision order, in any manner in which the relevant court (if that order was made by a magistrates' court) or the Crown Court (if that order was made by the Crown Court) could deal with him for that failure to comply if it had just been proved to the satisfaction of that court.

(3)   For the purposes of the provisions mentioned in subsection (2)(a) and (d) above, as applied by that subsection, if the supervision order is no longer in force the relevant court's powers shall be determined on the assumption that it is still in force.

(4)   In this section "relevant court" has the same meaning as in section 15 above."

22. In subsection (14) of section 23 of the 1969 Act (remands and committals to local authority accommodation), paragraph (a) shall cease to have effect.

23. In subsection (1) of section 70 of the 1969 Act (interpretation), after the definition of "young person" there shall be inserted the following definition—

""youth offending team" means a team established under section 39 of the Crime and Disorder Act 1998."

Superannuation Act 1972 (c 11)

24. In Schedule 1 to the Superannuation Act 1972 (kinds of employment to which a scheme under section 1 of that Act may apply), at the end of the list of "Other Bodies" there shall be inserted the following entry—

"Youth Justice Board for England and Wales."

Powers of Criminal Courts Act 1973 (c 62)

25. After subsection (1) of section 1A of the 1973 Act (absolute and conditional discharge) there shall be inserted the following subsection—

"(1A) Subsection (1)(b) above has effect subject to section 66(4) of the Crime and Disorder Act 1998 (effect of reprimands and warnings)."

26.—(1) In subsection (1) of section 2 of the 1973 Act (probation orders), the words "by a probation officer" shall cease to have effect and for the words "the supervision of a probation officer" there shall be substituted the word "supervision".

(2)   In subsection (2) of that section, for the words "a probation officer appointed for or assigned to that area" there shall be substituted the following paragraphs—

"(a)   a probation officer appointed for or assigned to that area; or
(b)   where the offender is under the age of 18 years when the order is made, a member of a youth offending team established by a local authority specified in the order."

(3)   After that subsection there shall be inserted the following subsection—

"(2A) The local authority specified as mentioned in subsection (2)(b) above shall be the local authority within whose area it appears to the court that the offender resides or will reside."

(4)   In subsection (4) of that section, for the words "the probation officer" there shall be substituted the words "the person".

(5)   After that subsection there shall be inserted the following subsection—

"(4A) In the case of an offender under the age of 18 years, the reference in subsection (4) above to a probation officer includes a reference to a member of a youth offending team."

(6)   In subsection (6) of that section—
(a)   for the words "the probation officer" there shall be substituted the words "the person"; and
(b)   for the words "that officer" there shall be substituted the words "that person".

27.—(1) In subsection (4) of section 14 of the 1973 Act (community service orders), for the words from "a probation officer" to the end there shall be substituted the following paragraphs—

"(a) a probation officer appointed for or assigned to the area for the time being specified in the order (whether under this subsection or by virtue of Part IV of Schedule 2 to the Criminal Justice Act 1991);

(b) a person appointed for the purposes of those provisions by the probation committee for that area; or

(c) in the case of an offender under the age of 18 years when the order is made, a member of a youth offending team established by a local authority for the time being specified in the order (whether under this subsection or by virtue of that Part)."

(2) After that subsection there shall be inserted the following subsection—

"(4A) The local authority specified as mentioned in subsection (4)(c) above shall be the local authority within whose area it appears to the court that the offender resides or will reside."

(3) After subsection (8) of that section there shall be inserted the following subsection—

"(9) In the case of an offender under the age of 18 years, references in subsections (2), (5)(c) or (6) above to a probation officer include references to a member of a youth offending team."

28. In subsection (2) of section 21 of the 1973 Act (restriction on imposing sentences of imprisonment etc on persons not legally represented)—

(a) after the words "sentence or trial," there shall be inserted the words "or sent to that Court for trial under section 51 of the Crime and Disorder Act 1998,"; and

(b) for the words "which committed him" there shall be substituted the words "which committed or sent him".

29. In subsection (1)(b) of section 32 of the 1973 Act (enforcement etc of fines imposed and recognizances forfeited by Crown Court), after the words "or dealt with" there shall be inserted the words ", or by which he was sent to that Court for trial under section 51 of the Crime and Disorder Act 1998".

30. After subsection (2) of section 23 of the 1973 Act (power of court on conviction of further offence to deal with suspended sentence) there shall be inserted the following subsection—

"(2A) The power to make an order under subsection (2) above has effect subject to section 102 of the Crime and Disorder Act 1998."

31. In section 42 of the 1973 Act (power of Crown Court on committal for sentence), subsection (2) shall cease to have effect.

32. In subsection (1) of section 46 of the 1973 Act (reports of probation officers), after the words "probation officer" there shall be inserted the words "or a member of a youth offending team".

33. In subsection (1) of section 57 of the 1973 Act (interpretation), after the definition of "suspended sentence" there shall be inserted the following definition—

""youth offending team" means a team established under section 39 of the Crime and Disorder Act 1998."

34.—(1) At the beginning of sub-paragraph (1) of paragraph 6 (requirements as to drug or alcohol dependency) of Schedule 1A to the 1973 Act there shall be inserted the words "Subject to sub-paragraph (1A) below,".

(2) After that sub-paragraph there shall be inserted the following sub-paragraph—

"(1A) If the court has been notified by the Secretary of State that arrangements for implementing orders under section 61 of the Crime and Disorder Act 1998 (drug treatment and testing orders) are available in the area proposed to be specified in the probation order, and the notice has not been withdrawn, this paragraph shall have effect as if the words "drugs or", in each place where they occur, were omitted."

(3) After that paragraph there shall be inserted the following paragraph—

"Interpretation

7.   In the case of an offender under the age of 18 years, references in this Schedule to a probation officer include references to a member of a youth offending team."

Rehabilitation of Offenders Act 1974 (c 53)

35. After subsection (6) of section 5 of the Rehabilitation of Offenders Act 1974 (rehabilitation periods for particular sentences) there shall be inserted the following subsection—

"(6A) Where in respect of a conviction a detention and training order was made under section 73 of the Crime and Disorder Act 1998, the rehabilitation period applicable to the sentence shall be—

(a)   in the case of a person aged fifteen years or over at the date of his conviction, five years if the order was, and three and a half years if the order was not, for a term exceeding six months;

(b)   in the case of a person aged under fifteen years at the date of his conviction, a period beginning with that date and ending one year after the date on which the order ceases to have effect."

36. In subsection (2) of section 7 of that Act (limitations on rehabilitation under Act etc), after paragraph (b) there shall be inserted the following paragraph—

"(bb) in any proceedings on an application for a sex offender order under section 2 or, as the case may be, 20 of the Crime and Disorder Act 1998 or in any appeal against the making of such an order;".

Bail Act 1976 (c 63)

37. After subsection (8A) of section 3 of the Bail Act 1976 (general provisions) there shall be inserted the following subsection—

"(8B) Subsection (8) above applies where a court has sent a person on bail to the Crown Court for trial under section 51 of the Crime and Disorder Act 1998 as it applies where a court has committed a person on bail to the Crown Court for trial."

38. In paragraph 8(1) of Schedule 1 to that Act (persons entitled to bail: supplementary provisions), after the words "subsection (6)(d)" there shall be inserted the words "or (e)".

Magistrates' Courts Act 1980 (c 43)

39. In subsection (3) of section 11 of the 1980 Act (certain sentences and orders not to be made in absence of accused), for the words "secure training order" there shall be substituted the words "detention and training order".

40.—(1) In subsection (1)(a) of section 24 of the 1980 Act (summary trial of information against child or young person for indictable offence), for the words "that subsection" there shall be substituted the words "subsection (3) of that section".

(2) In subsection (2) of that section, for the words from "that other offence" to the end there shall be substituted the words "the charges for both offences could be joined in the same indictment".

41. Section 37 of the 1980 Act (committal to Crown Court with a view to greater term of detention in a young offender institution) shall cease to have effect.

42. In subsection (1) of section 65 of the 1980 Act (meaning of "family proceedings"), after paragraph (p) there shall be inserted the following paragraph—

"(q) sections 11 and 12 of the Crime and Disorder Act 1998;".

43. In subsection (2) of section 108 of the 1980 Act (right of appeal to the Crown Court), the words "a probation order or" shall cease to have effect.

44. In subsection (4)(c) of section 125 of the 1980 Act (warrants)—

(a)   the word "and" at the end of sub-paragraph (ii) shall cease to have effect;

(b)   in sub-paragraph (iii), for the words "or 97 above" there shall be substituted the words ", 97 or 97A above; and"; and

(c)   after that sub-paragraph there shall be inserted the following sub-paragraph—

"(iv) paragraph 4 of Schedule 3 to the Crime and Disorder Act 1998."

45. In section 126 of the 1980 Act (execution of certain warrants outside England and Wales)—

    (a)   the word "and" at the end of paragraph (c) shall cease to have effect;

    (b)   after that paragraph there shall be inserted the following paragraph—

"(cc) warrants of arrest issued under section 97A above;"; and

    (c)   after paragraph (d) there shall be inserted the words

"; and

    (e)   warrants of arrest issued under paragraph 4 of Schedule 3 to the Crime and Disorder Act 1998."

46. At the beginning of subsection (1) of section 133 of the 1980 Act (consecutive terms of imprisonment) there shall be inserted the words "Subject to section 102 of the Crime and Disorder Act 1998,".

Supreme Court Act 1981 (c 54)

47. After subsection (1) of section 47 of the Supreme Court Act 1981 (sentences and other orders of Crown Court when dealing with offenders) there shall be inserted the following subsection—

"(1A) The power to give a direction under subsection (1) above has effect subject to section 102 of the Crime and Disorder Act 1998."

48. In subsection (1)(a) of section 81 of the Supreme Court Act 1981 (bail), after the words "Criminal Justice Act 1987" there shall be inserted the words "or who has been sent in custody to the Crown Court for trial under section 51 of the Crime and Disorder Act 1998".

Criminal Justice Act 1982 (c 48)

49. In subsection (2) of section 1 of the 1982 Act (general restriction on custodial sentences), for the words from "remanded in custody" to the end there shall be substituted the following paragraphs—

    "(a)   remanded in custody;

    (b)   committed in custody for trial or sentence; or

    (c)   sent in custody for trial under section 51 of the Crime and Disorder Act 1998."

50,—(1) In subsection (1) of section 1A of the 1982 Act (detention in a young offender institution), for the words "not less than 15 years of age" there shall be substituted the words "not less than 18 years of age".

(2) In subsection (3) of that section, for the words "the minimum period applicable to the offender under subsection (4A) below" there shall be substituted the words "21 days".

(3) In subsection (4) of that section, for the words "the minimum period applicable" there shall be substituted the words "21 days".

(4) Subsection (4A) of that section shall cease to have effect.

(5) At the beginning of subsection (6) of that section there shall be inserted the words "Subject to section 102 of the Crime and Disorder Act 1998,".

51. In subsection (2) of section 1C of the 1982 Act (accommodation of offenders sentenced to detention in a young offender institution), the words "but if he is under 18 at the time of the direction, only for a temporary purpose" shall cease to have effect.

52.—(1) In subsection (1) of section 3 of the 1982 Act (restriction on certain sentences where offender not legally represented), for paragraph (e) there shall be substituted the following paragraph—

"(e) make a detention and training order,".

(2) In subsection (2) of that section—

    (a)   after the words "sentence or trial," there shall be inserted the words "or sent to that Court for trial under section 51 of the Crime and Disorder Act 1998,"; and

(b)   for the words "which committed him" there shall be substituted the words "which committed or sent him".

53.—(1) In subsection (3)(a) of section 19 of the 1982 Act (breaches of attendance centre orders or attendance centre rules), the words "revoke it and" shall cease to have effect.

(2)   In subsection (5) of that section, the words "revoke the attendance centre order and" shall cease to have effect.

(3)   In subsection (5A) of that section, for paragraph (b) there shall be substituted the following paragraph—

> "(b)   in the case of an offender who has wilfully and persistently failed to comply with those requirements, may impose a custodial sentence notwithstanding anything in section 1(2) of the Criminal Justice Act 1991."

(4)   After that subsection there shall be inserted the following subsection—

> "(5B) Where a court deals with an offender under subsection (3)(a) or (5) above, it shall revoke the attendance centre order if it is still in force."

Mental Health Act 1983 (c 20)

54. In subsection (8) of section 37 of the Mental Health Act 1983 (powers of courts to order hospital admission or guardianship), for the words from "pass sentence of imprisonment" to "in respect of the offender" there shall be inserted the following paragraphs—

> "(a)   pass a sentence of imprisonment, impose a fine or make a community order (within the meaning of Part I of the Criminal Justice Act 1991) in respect of the offence; or
>
> (b)   make an order under section 58 of that Act (binding over of parent or guardian) in respect of the offender,".

Mental Health (Scotland) Act 1984 (c 36)

55.—(1)   In subsection (8A) of section 74 of the Mental Health (Scotland) Act 1984 (effect of certain directions), for the words "the Crime and Punishment (Scotland) Act 1997" there shall be substituted the words "Part I of the Prisoners and Criminal Proceedings (Scotland) Act 1993".

(2)   The amendment made by sub-paragraph (1) above shall be deemed to have had effect from 1 January 1998.

Repatriation of Prisoners Act 1984 (c 47)

56. In subsection (4)(b) of section 2 (transfer of prisoners out of United Kingdom) of the Repatriation of Prisoners Act 1984, for sub-paragraph (i) there shall be substituted the following sub-paragraph—

> "(i)   released on licence under section 33(1)(b), (2) or (3), 33A(2), 34A(3) or 35(1) of the Criminal Justice Act 1991 or section 28(5) or 29(1) of the Crime (Sentences) Act 1997;".

57. In subsection (9) of section 3 of that Act (transfer of prisoners into United Kingdom)—

(a)   for the words "section 48 of the Criminal Justice Act 1991 (discretionary life prisoners transferred to England and Wales)" there shall be substituted the words "section 33 of the Crime (Sentences) Act 1997 (life prisoner transferred to England and Wales)"; and

(b)   for the words "section 34 of that Act (duty of Secretary of State to release discretionary life prisoners)" there shall be substituted the words "section 28 of that Act (duty to release certain life prisoners)".

58.—(1) Paragraph 2 of the Schedule to that Act as it has effect, and is deemed always to have had effect, by virtue of paragraph 2 of Schedule 2 to the 1997 Act shall be amended as follows.

(2)   In sub-paragraph (4), for the definition of "the enactments relating to release on licence" there shall be substituted the following definition—

""the enactments relating to release on licence" means sections 33(1)(b), (2) and (3), 33A(2), 34A(3), 35(1) and 37(1) and (2) of the Criminal Justice Act 1991 and section 28(5) and (7) of the Crime (Sentences) Act 1997;".

59.—(1) Paragraph 2 of the Schedule to that Act (operation of certain enactments in relation to the prisoner) as it has effect by virtue of paragraph 3 of Schedule 2 to the 1997 Act—

    (a)   shall have effect in relation to all prisoners repatriated to England and Wales after the commencement of Schedule 2; and

    (b)   as it so has effect, shall be amended as follows.

(2) In sub-paragraph (2), for the words "34(3) and (5) and 35(1) of the Criminal Justice Act 1991" there shall be substituted the words "35(1) of the Criminal Justice Act 1991 and section 28(5) and (7) of the Crime (Sentences) Act 1997".

(3) In sub-paragraph (4), for the definition of "the enactments relating to release on licence" there shall be substituted the following definition—

""the enactments relating to release on licence" means sections 33(1)(b), (2) and (3), 33A(2), 34A(3), 35(1) and 37(1) and (2) of the Criminal Justice Act 1991 and section 28(5) and (7) of the Crime (Sentences) Act 1997;".

60. For paragraph 3 of the Schedule to that Act there shall be substituted the following paragraph—

"Life imprisonment

3.   Where the relevant provisions include provision equivalent to a sentence in relation to which subsection (1) of section 29 of the Crime (Sentences) Act 1997 (power to release certain life prisoners etc) applies, that subsection shall have effect as if the reference to consultation with the trial judge if available were omitted."

Police and Criminal Evidence Act 1984 (c 60)

61. After subsection (4) of section 27 of the 1984 Act (fingerprinting of certain offenders and recording of offences) there shall be inserted the following subsection—

"(4A) In subsection (4) above "conviction" includes—

    (a)   a caution within the meaning of Part V of the Police Act 1997; and

    (b)   a reprimand or warning given under section 65 of the Crime and Disorder Act 1998."

62. After section 47 of the 1984 Act there shall be inserted the following section—

"47A Early administrative hearings conducted by justices' clerks

Where a person has been charged with an offence at a police station, any requirement imposed under this Part for the person to appear or be brought before a magistrates' court shall be taken to be satisfied if the person appears or is brought before the clerk to the justices for a petty sessions area in order for the clerk to conduct a hearing under section 50 of the Crime and Disorder Act 1998 (early administrative hearings)."

Prosecution of Offences Act 1985 (c 23)

63. In subsection (2) of section 23 of the 1985 Act (discontinuance of proceedings), after paragraph (b) there shall be inserted the following paragraph—

"(c)   in the case of any offence, any stage of the proceedings after the accused has been sent for trial under section 51 of the Crime and Disorder Act 1998 (no committal proceedings for indictable-only and related offences)."

64, After that section there shall be inserted the following section—

"23A Discontinuance of proceedings after accused has been sent for trial

    (1)   This section applies where—

    (a)   the Director of Public Prosecutions, or a public authority (within the meaning of section 17 of this Act), has the conduct of proceedings for an offence; and

(b) the accused has been sent for trial under section 51 of the Crime and Disorder Act 1998 for the offence.

(2) Where, at any time before the indictment is preferred, the Director or authority gives notice under this section to the Crown Court sitting at the place specified in the notice under section 51(7) of the Crime and Disorder Act 1998 that he or it does not want the proceedings to continue, they shall be discontinued with effect from the giving of that notice.

(3) The Director or authority shall, in any notice given under subsection (2) above, give reasons for not wanting the proceedings to continue.

(4) On giving any notice under subsection (2) above the Director or authority shall inform the accused of the notice; but the Director or authority shall not be obliged to give the accused any indication of his reasons for not wanting the proceedings to continue.

(5) The discontinuance of any proceedings by virtue of this section shall not prevent the institution of fresh proceedings in respect of the same offence."

Criminal Justice Act 1987 (c 38)

65. After subsection (3) of section 4 of the Criminal Justice Act 1987 (notices of transfer in serious fraud cases) there shall be inserted the following subsection—

"(4) This section and sections 5 and 6 below shall not apply in any case in which section 51 of the Crime and Disorder Act 1998 (no committal proceedings for indictable-only offences) applies."

Criminal Justice Act 1988 (c 33)

66. In subsection (1) of section 40 of the Criminal Justice Act 1988 (power to join in indictment count for common assault etc), at the end there shall be inserted the words "or are disclosed by material which, in pursuance of regulations made under paragraph 1 of Schedule 3 to the Crime and Disorder Act 1998 (procedure where person sent for trial under section 51), has been served on the person charged".

Legal Aid Act 1988 (c 34)

67.—(1) In subsection (4) of section 20 of the Legal Aid Act 1988 (competent authorities to grant representation under Part V), after paragraph (a) there shall be inserted the following paragraph—

"(aa) which sends a person for trial under section 51 of the Crime and Disorder Act 1998 (no committal proceedings for indictable-only offences),".

(2) After subsection (5) of that section there shall be inserted the following subsection—

"(5A) A magistrates' court which has a duty or a power to send a person for trial under section 51 of the Crime and Disorder Act 1998 is also competent, before discharging that duty or (as the case may be) deciding whether to exercise that power, as respects any proceedings before the Crown Court on the person's trial."

(3) In subsection (3)(a) of section 21 of that Act (availability of representation under Part V), after the word "committed" there shall be inserted the words "or sent".

(4) In subsection (4) of that section, after the word "commits" there shall be inserted the words "or sends".

Children Act 1989 (c 41)

68. In subsection (4) of section 8 of the 1989 Act (which defines "family proceedings"), after paragraph (h) there shall be inserted the following paragraph—

"(i) sections 11 and 12 of the Crime and Disorder Act 1998."

69. In subsection (3) of section 47 of the 1989 Act (local authority's duty to investigate), after the words "this Act" there shall be inserted the words "or section 11 of the Crime and Disorder Act 1998 (child safety orders)".

Prisons (Scotland) Act 1989 (c 45)

70.—(1) Section 16 of the Prisons (Scotland) Act 1989 (discharge of prisoners) which, notwithstanding its repeal by the Prisoners and Criminal Proceedings (Scotland) Act 1993, is an "existing provision" for the purposes of Schedule 6 to that Act of 1993, shall for those purposes be amended as follows.

(2) In subsection (1), for the words "or Sunday" there shall be substituted the words "Sunday or public holiday".

(3) At the end there shall be inserted the following subsection—

"(3) For the purposes of this section "public holiday" means any day on which, in the opinion of the Secretary of State, public offices or other facilities likely to be of use to the prisoner in the area in which he is likely to be following his discharge from prison will be closed."

71. In section 39 of that Act (rules for the management of prisons)—
    (a)   in subsection (7)—
          (i)   at the beginning there shall be inserted the words "Subject to subsection (7A) below,";
          (ii)   for the words "a short-term or long-term prisoner within the meaning of" there shall be substituted the words "any person who is, or is treated as, a long-term or short-term prisoner for the purposes of any provision of"; and
          (iii)   the words from "and the foregoing" to the end shall cease to have effect; and
    (b)   after that subsection there shall be inserted the following subsections—

"(7A) Additional days shall not be awarded under rules made under subsection (7) above in respect of a sentence where the prisoner has at any time been released on licence, in relation to that sentence, under Part I of the Prisoners and Criminal Proceedings (Scotland) Act 1993; and any reference to a sentence in such rules shall be construed in accordance with section 27(5) of that Act.

(7B) In the application of subsection (7) above to a prisoner subject to an extended sentence within the meaning of section 210A of the 1995 Act, the reference to his sentence shall be construed as a reference to the custodial term of that extended sentence."

Criminal Justice Act 1991 (c 53)

72. For subsection (3) of section 1 of the 1991 Act (restrictions on imposing custodial sentences) there shall be substituted the following subsection—

"(3) Nothing in subsection (2) above shall prevent the court from passing a custodial sentence on the offender if he fails to express his willingness to comply with—
    (a)   a requirement which is proposed by the court to be included in a probation order or supervision order and which requires an expression of such willingness; or
    (b)   a requirement which is proposed by the court to be included in a drug treatment and testing order or an order under section 61(6) of the Crime and Disorder Act 1998."

73. In subsection (5)(a) of section 3 of the 1991 Act (procedural requirements for custodial sentences), for the words "a probation officer or by a social worker of a local authority social services department" there shall be substituted the following sub-paragraphs—

       "(i) a probation officer;
       (ii) a social worker of a local authority social services department; or
       (iii) where the offender is under the age of 18 years, a member of a youth offending team;".

74. In subsection (4) of section 6 of the 1991 Act (restrictions on imposing community sentences)—
    (a)   after paragraph (a) there shall be inserted the following paragraph—

    "(aa) a drug treatment and testing order;";

(b) the word "and" immediately following paragraph (e) shall cease to have effect; and

(c) after paragraph (f) there shall be inserted the following paragraph—

"(g) an action plan order."

75. In subsection (3) of section 7 of the 1991 Act procedural requirements for community sentences), after paragraph (a) there shall be inserted the following paragraph—

"(aa) a drug treatment and testing order;".

76. In subsection (1) of section 11 of the 1991 Act (combination orders), for the words "the supervision of a probation officer" there shall be substituted the word "supervision".

77. In subsection (3) of section 15 of the 1991 Act (regulation of community orders)—

(a) in paragraph (a), after the words "probation officer" there shall be inserted the words "or member of a youth offending team"; and

(b) after that paragraph there shall be inserted the following paragraph—

"(aa) in relation to an offender who is subject to a drug treatment and testing order, the probation officer responsible for his supervision;".

78. In subsection (1) of section 31 of the 1991 Act (interpretation of Part I)—

(a) immediately before the definition of "attendance centre order" there shall be inserted the following definition—

""action plan order" means an order under section 69 of the Crime and Disorder Act 1998;";

(b) in the definition of "custodial sentence", in paragraph (b), after the word "age," there shall be inserted the words "a detention and training order," and the words "or a secure training order under section 1 of the Criminal Justice and Public Order Act 1994" shall cease to have effect; and

(c) after that definition there shall be inserted the following definitions—

""detention and training order" has the meaning given by section 73(3) of the Crime and Disorder Act 1998;

"drug treatment and testing order" means an order under section 61 of that Act;".

79.—(1) In subsection (1)(b) of section 32 of the 1991 Act (Parole Board), for the words "the functions conferred by Part II of the Crime (Sentences) Act 1997 ("Part II")" there shall be substituted the words "the functions conferred by this Part in respect of long-term and short-term prisoners and by Chapter II of Part II of the Crime (Sentences) Act 1997 ("Chapter II") in respect of life prisoners within the meaning of that Chapter".

(2) In subsections (3), (4) and (6) of that section, for the words "Part II" there shall be substituted the words "this Part or Chapter II".

80.—(1) In subsection (3) of section 33 of the 1991 Act (duty to release short-term and long-term prisoners)—

(a) in paragraph (a), for the words "subsection (1)(b) or (2) above or section 35 or 36(1) below" there shall be substituted the words "this Part"; and

(b) in paragraph (b), for the words "38(2) or 39(1)" there shall be substituted the words "39(1) or (2)".

(2) After that subsection there shall be inserted the following subsection—

"(3A) In the case of a prisoner to whom section 44A below applies, it shall be the duty of the Secretary of State to release him on licence at the end of the extension period (within the meaning of section 58 of the Crime and Disorder Act 1998)."

(3) Subsection (4) of that section shall cease to have effect.

81. After that section there shall be inserted the following section—

"33A Duty to release prisoners: special cases

(1) As soon as a prisoner—

(a) whose sentence is for a term of less than twelve months; and

(b) who has been released on licence under section 34A(3) or 36(1) below and recalled to prison under section 38A(1) or 39(1) or (2) below,
would (but for his release) have served one-half of his sentence, it shall be the duty of the Secretary of State to release him unconditionally.

(2) As soon as a prisoner—
(a) whose sentence is for a term of twelve months or more; and
(b) who has been released on licence under section 34A(3) below and recalled to prison under section 38A(1) below,
would (but for his release) have served one-half of his sentence, it shall be the duty of the Secretary of State to release him on licence.

(3) In the case of a prisoner who—
(a) has been released on licence under this Part and recalled to prison under section 39(1) or (2) below; and
(b) has been subsequently released on licence under section 33(3) or (3A) above and recalled to prison under section 39(1) or (2) below,
section 33(3) above shall have effect as if for the words "three-quarters" there were substituted the words "the whole" and the words "on licence" were omitted."

82, In subsection (1) of section 36 of the 1991 Act (power to release prisoners on compassionate grounds), for word "prisoner" there shall be substituted the words "short-term or long-term prisoner".

83.—(1) In subsection (1) of section 37 of the 1991 Act (duration and conditions of licences)—
(a) for the words "subsection (2)" there shall be substituted the words "subsections (1A), (1B) and (2)"; and
(b) the words "any suspension under section 38(2) below or, as the case may be," shall cease to have effect.

(2) After subsection (1A) of that section there shall be inserted the following subsection—

"(1B) Where a prisoner whose sentence is for a term of twelve months or more is released on licence under section 33A(2) or 34A(3) above, subsection (1) above shall have effect as if for the reference to three-quarters of his sentence there were substituted a reference to the difference between—
(a) that proportion of his sentence; and
(b) the duration of the curfew condition to which he is or was subject."

(3) In subsection (2) of that section, for the words "section 36(1) above" there shall be substituted the words "section 34A(3) or 36(1) above".

(4) In subsection (4) of that section—
(a) after the words "a licence" there shall be inserted the words "under this Part"; and
(b) the words "(which shall include on his release conditions as to his supervision by a probation officer)" shall cease to have effect.

(5) After that subsection there shall be inserted the following subsection—

"(4A) The conditions so specified may in the case of a person released on licence under section 34A above whose sentence is for a term of less than twelve months, and shall in any other case, include on the person's release conditions as to his supervision by—
(a) a probation officer appointed for or assigned to the petty sessions area within which the person resides for the time being; or
(b) where the person is under the age of 18 years, a member of a youth offending team established by the local authority within whose area the person resides for the time being."

(6) For subsection (5) of that section there shall be substituted the following subsection—

"(5) The Secretary of State shall not include on release, or subsequently insert, a condition in the licence of a long-term prisoner, or vary or cancel any such condition, except after consultation with the Board."

84. After subsection (5) of section 39 of the 1991 Act (recall of prisoners while on licence) there shall be inserted the following subsection—

"(5A) In the case of a prisoner to whom section 44A below applies, subsections (4)(b) and (5) of that section apply in place of subsection (5) above."

85. After subsection (4) of section 40 of the 1991 Act (convictions during currency of original sentences) there shall be inserted the following subsections—

"(5)   Where the new offence is found to have been committed over a period of two or more days, or at some time during a period of two or more days, it shall be taken for the purposes of this section to have been committed on the last of those days.

(6)   For the purposes of any enactment conferring rights of appeal in criminal cases, any such order as is mentioned in subsection (2) or (3A) above made with regard to any person shall be treated as a sentence passed on him for the offence for which the sentence referred to in subsection (1) above was passed."

86.—(1) For subsections (1) and (2) of section 41 of the 1991 Act (remand time to count towards time served) there shall be substituted the following subsections—

"(1)   Where a person is sentenced to imprisonment for a term in respect of an offence, this section applies to him if the court directs under section 9 of the Crime (Sentences) Act 1997 that the number of days for which he was remanded in custody in connection with—
   (a)   the offence; or
   (b)   any other offence the charge for which was founded on the same facts or evidence;
shall count as time served by him as part of the sentence.

(2)   For the purpose of determining for the purposes of this Part whether a person to whom this section applies—
   (a)   has served, or would (but for his release) have served, a particular proportion of his sentence; or
   (b)   has served a particular period,
the number of days specified in the direction shall, subject to subsections (3) and (4) below, be treated as having been served by him as part of that sentence or period."

(2)   After subsection (3) of that section there shall be inserted the following subsection—

"(4)   Where the period for which a licence granted under section 33A(2), 34A(3) or 36(1) above to a short-term prisoner remains in force cannot exceed one-quarter of his sentence, nothing in subsection (2) above shall have the effect of reducing that period."

87.—(1) In subsection (3) of section 43 of the 1991 Act (young offenders), for the words "subsections (1)" there shall be substituted the words "subsection (1)".

(2) In subsection (5) of that section, for the words "section 37(4)" there shall be substituted the words "section 37(4A)".

88.—(1) In subsection (1) of section 45 of the 1991 Act (fine defaulters and contemnors), for the words "except sections 35 and 40" there shall be substituted the words "except sections 33A, 34A, 35 and 40".

(2)   In subsection (3) of that section—
   (a)   for the words "subsections (1) to (4)" there shall be substituted the words "subsections (1) to (3)"; and
   (b)   for the words "section 38(2) or 39(1)" there shall be substituted the words "section 39(1) or (2)".

(3)   In subsection (4) of that section—
   (a)   the words "any suspension under section 38(2) below; or" shall cease to have effect; and
   (b)   for the words "section 39(1)" there shall be substituted the words "section 39(1) or (2)".

89. In subsection (2) of section 46 of the 1991 Act (persons liable to removal from the United Kingdom), for the words from "section 37(4)" to the end there shall be substituted the words "section 37 above shall have effect as if subsection (4A) were omitted".

90.—For subsection (2) of section 47 of the 1991 Act (persons extradited to the United Kingdom) there shall be substituted the following subsection—

"(2)   In the case of an extradited prisoner, section 9 of the Crime (Sentences) Act 1997 (crediting of periods of remand in custody) shall have effect as if the days for which he was kept in custody while awaiting extradition were days for which he was remanded in custody in connection with the offence, or any other offence the charge for which was founded on the same facts or evidence."

91.—In section 50 of the 1991 Act (transfer by order of certain functions to Board), for subsection (3) (including that subsection as applied by any order under subsection (1) of that section) there shall be substituted the following subsection—

"(3)   In section 37 above, in subsection (5) for the words "after consultation with the Board" there shall be substituted the words "in accordance with recommendations of the Board", and subsection (6) shall be omitted."

92. In subsection (4) of section 51 of the 1991 Act (interpretation of Part II)—
    (a)   for the words "Subsections (2) and (3)" there shall be substituted the words "Subsection (3)"; and
    (b)   for the words "as they apply" there shall be substituted the words "as it applies".

93. After subsection (7) of section 53 of the 1991 Act (notices of transfer in certain cases involving children) there shall be inserted the following subsection—

"(8)   This section shall not apply in any case in which section 51 of the Crime and Disorder Act 1998 (no committal proceedings for indictable-only offences) applies."

94.—(1) In subsection (1) of section 65 of the 1991 Act (supervision of young offenders after release), for the words from "a probation officer" to the end there shall be substituted the following paragraphs—

    "(a)   a probation officer;
    (b)   a social worker of a local authority social services department; or
    (c)   in the case of a person under the age of 18 years on his release, a member of a youth offending team."

(2)   After that subsection there shall be inserted the following subsections—

"(1A)   Where the supervision is to be provided by a probation officer, the probation officer shall be an officer appointed for or assigned to the petty sessions area within which the offender resides for the time being.

(1B)   Where the supervision is to be provided by—
    (a)   a social worker of a local authority social services department; or
    (b)   a member of a youth offending team,
the social worker or member shall be a social worker of, or a member of a youth offending team established by, the local authority within whose area the offender resides for the time being."

95.—In subsection (1) of section 99 of the 1991 Act (general interpretation), after the definition of "young person" there shall be inserted the following definition—

""youth offending team" means a team established under section 39 of the Crime and Disorder Act 1998."

96.—(1) After sub-paragraph (5) of paragraph 1 of Schedule 2 to the 1991 Act (enforcement etc of community orders) there shall be inserted the following sub-paragraph—

"(6)   Where a drug treatment and testing order has been made on an appeal brought from the Crown Court, or from the criminal division of the Court of Appeal, for the purposes of this Schedule it shall be deemed to have been made by the Crown Court."

(2)   In sub-paragraph (1)(d) of paragraph 3 of that Schedule, the words "revoke the order and" shall cease to have effect.

(3)   After sub-paragraph (2) of that paragraph there shall be inserted the following sub-paragraph—

"(2A) Where a magistrates' court deals with an offender under sub-paragraph (1)(d) above, it shall revoke the relevant order if it is still in force."

(4) In sub-paragraph (1)(d) of paragraph 4 of that Schedule, the words "revoke the order and" shall cease to have effect.

(5) After sub-paragraph (2) of that paragraph there shall be inserted the following sub-paragraph—

"(2A) Where the Crown Court deals with an offender under sub-paragraph (1)(d) above, it shall revoke the relevant order if it is still in force."

(6) After paragraph 12(4) of that Schedule there shall be inserted the following sub-paragraphs—

"(5) Where—
(a) the court amends a probation order or community service order under this paragraph;
(b) a local authority is specified in the order in accordance with section 2(2)(b) or 14(4)(c) of the 1973 Act; and
(c) the change, or proposed change, of residence also is or would be a change of residence from the area of that authority to the area of another such authority,

the court shall further amend the order by substituting the other authority for the authority specified in the order.

(6) In sub-paragraph (5) above "local authority" has the meaning given by section 42 of the Crime and Disorder Act 1998, and references to the area of a local authority shall be construed in accordance with that section."

(7) In paragraph 17(1) of that Schedule, the words from "and the court shall not" to the end shall cease to have effect.

97. In paragraph 1(2) of Schedule 5 to the 1991 Act (Parole Board: supplementary provisions), for the words "its functions under Part II of this Act" there shall be substituted the following paragraphs—

"(a) its functions under this Part in respect of long-term and short-term prisoners; and
(b) its functions under Chapter II of Part II of the Crime (Sentences) Act 1997 in respect of life prisoners within the meaning of that Chapter".

Prisoners and Criminal Proceedings (Scotland) Act 1993 (c 9)

98.—(1) In subsection (1) of section 1 of the 1993 Act (release of short-term, long-term and life prisoners), at the beginning there shall be inserted the words "Subject to section 26A(4) of this Act,".

(2) In subsection (2) of that section, at the end there shall be added the words "unless he has before that time been so released, in relation to that sentence, under any provision of this Act".

(3) After subsection (3) of that section there shall be inserted the following subsection—

"(3A) Subsections (1) to (3) above are subject to section 1A of this Act."

99.—(1) After subsection (1) of section 4 of the 1993 Act (persons detained under the Mental Health (Scotland) Act 1984) there shall be inserted the following subsection—

"(1A) This Part of this Act shall apply to a person conveyed to and detained in a hospital pursuant to a hospital direction under section 59A of the 1995 Act as if, while so detained, he was serving the sentence of imprisonment imposed on him at the time at which that direction was made."

(2) The amendment made by sub-paragraph (1) above shall be deemed to have had effect from 1 January 1998.

100. In section 5 of the 1993 Act (fine defaulters and persons in contempt of court)—
(a) in subsection (1), for the words "and (3)" there shall be substituted the words "to (4)"; and
(b) after subsection (3) there shall be inserted the following subsection—

"(4)   Where a person has had imposed on him two or more terms of imprisonment or detention mentioned in subsection (1)(a) or (b) above, sections 1A and 27(5) of this Act shall apply to those terms as if they were terms of imprisonment."

101. In section 7 of the 1993 Act (children detained in solemn proceedings)—

    (a)   in subsection (1)(b), at the end there shall be added the words "unless he has before that time been so released, in relation to that sentence, under any provision of this Act";

    (b)   after that subsection there shall be inserted the following subsections—

"(2A) This subsection applies where a child detained under section 208 of the 1995 Act is sentenced, while so detained, to a determinate term of detention in a young offenders institution or imprisonment and, by virtue of section 27(5) of this Act, such terms of detention or imprisonment are treated as single term.

(2B) In a case where subsection (2A) applies and the single term mentioned in that subsection is less than four years, the provisions of this section shall apply.

(2C) In a case where subsection (2A) applies and the single term mentioned in that subsection is of four or more years—

    (a)   section 6 of this Act shall apply to him as if the single term were an equivalent sentence of detention in a young offenders institution, if that term is served in such an institution; and

    (b)   the provisions of this Act shall apply to him as if the single term were an equivalent sentence of imprisonment, if that term is served in a remand centre or a prison.";

    (c)   after subsection (4) there shall be inserted the following subsection—

"(4A) Where an order under subsection (3) above is made, the making of the order shall, if there is in force a licence relating to the person in respect of whom the order is made, have the effect of revoking that licence."; and

    (d)   in subsection (5), after the word "construed" there shall be inserted the words "and sections 1A and 27 shall apply".

102. In section 11 of the 1993 Act (duration of licences), subsections (3)(b) and (4) shall cease to have effect.

103. In section 14 of the 1993 Act (supervised release of short-term prisoners), subsections (2) and (3) shall cease to have effect.

104.—(1)In subsection (1) of section 16 of the 1993 Act (orders for return to prison after commission of further offence), after the word "released" there shall be inserted the words "at any time".

(2) In paragraph (a) of subsection (7) of that section, after the word "shall" there shall be inserted the words ", if the licence is in force when the order is made,".

(3) Paragraph (b) of that subsection shall cease to have effect.

105. In section 17 of the 1993 Act (revocation of licence), after subsection (4) there shall be inserted the following subsection—

"(4A) Where the case of a prisoner to whom section 3A of this Act applies is referred to the Parole Board under subsection (3) above, subsection (4) of that section shall apply to that prisoner in place of subsection (4) above."

106. In section 20 of the 1993 Act (Parole Board for Scotland), at the end of subsection (4) there shall be inserted the words—

"and rules under this section may make different provision for different classes of prisoner."

107. After subsection (7) of section 27 of the 1993 Act (interpretation) there shall be inserted the following subsection—

"(8)   For the purposes of this section "public holiday" means any day on which, in the opinion of the Secretary of State, public offices or other facilities likely to be of use to the prisoner in the area in which he is likely to be following his discharge from prison will be closed."

108. In Schedule 6 to the 1993 Act (transitional provisions), after paragraph 6C there shall be inserted the following paragraph—

"6D. Where a prisoner released on licence is treated by virtue of the provisions of this or any other enactment as a prisoner whose licence was granted under section 2(4) of this Act, the validity of his licence shall not be affected by the absence in the licence of such a condition as is specified in section 12(2) of this Act."

Probation Service Act 1993 (c 47)

109. In subsection (1)(dd) of section 4 of the Probation Service Act 1993 (functions of probation committee), for the words "a secure training order (within the meaning of section 1 of the Criminal Justice and Public Order Act 1994)" there shall be substituted the words "a detention and training order (within the meaning of section 73 of the Crime and Disorder Act 1998)".

110.—(1) In subsection (1) of section 17 of that Act (probation committee expenditure), for the words "(5) and (5A)" there shall be substituted the words "and (5)".

(2) Subsection (5A) of that section shall cease to have effect.

Criminal Justice and Public Order Act 1994 (c 33)

111. In subsection (3) of section 12 of the 1994 Act (escort arrangements and officers), after the words "secure training orders" there shall be inserted the words "or detention and training orders".

112. In paragraph 4 of Schedule 1 to the 1994 Act (escort arrangements: England and Wales), in the definition of "the offender", after the words "section 1 of this Act" there shall be inserted the words "or detention and training under section 73 of the Crime and Disorder Act 1998".

113.—(1) In sub-paragraph (1) of paragraph 3 of Schedule 2 to the 1994 Act (certification of custody officers: England and Wales)—
    (a)   in paragraph (b), for the words "person in charge" there shall be substituted the word "monitor"; and
    (b)   in paragraph (c), for the words "person in charge" there shall be substituted the word "governor".

(2) In sub-paragraph (2) of that paragraph, for the words "or person in charge" there shall be substituted the words ", monitor or governor".

Drug Trafficking Act 1994 (c 37)

114. In subsection (7) of section 2 of the Drug Trafficking Act 1994 (confiscation orders), paragraph (a) shall cease to have effect.

Proceeds of Crime (Scotland) Act 1995 (c 43)

115. At the end of section 18 of the Proceeds of Crime (Scotland) Act 1995 (order to make material available) there shall be added the following subsection—

"(12) In this section "constable" includes a person commissioned by the Commissioners of Customs and Excise."

116. In subsection (6) of section 19 of that Act (authority for search)—
    (a)   for the words "subsection (10)" there shall be substituted the words "subsections (10) and (12)"; and
    (b)   for the words "it applies" there shall be substituted the words "they apply".

Criminal Procedure (Scotland) Act 1995 (c 46)

117.—(1) For section 18(3) of the 1995 Act (prints and samples) there shall be substituted the following subsection—

"(3) Subject to subsection (4) below, all record of any relevant physical data taken from or provided by a person under subsection (2) above, all samples taken under subsection (6) below and all information derived from such samples shall be destroyed as soon as possible following a decision not to institute criminal proceedings against the person or on the conclusion of such proceedings otherwise than with a conviction or an order under section 246(3) of this Act."

(2) The amendment made by sub-paragraph (1) above shall be deemed to have had effect from 1 August 1997.

118. In subsection (3) of section 49 of the 1995 Act (references to children's hearings), in paragraph (b), after the words "the sheriff" there shall be inserted the words "or district".

119. In section 106(1)(bb) of the 1995 Act (appeals against automatic sentences), which is prospectively inserted by section 18(1) of the Crime and Punishment (Scotland) Act 1997, for the words "205B(3) or 209(1A)" there shall be substituted the words "or 205B(3)".

120. In section 108A of the 1995 Act (prosecutor's right of appeal against refusal to impose automatic sentence), which is prospectively inserted by section 18(2) of the Crime and Punishment (Scotland) Act 1997, for the words "205B(3) or 209(1A)" there shall be substituted the words "or 205B(3)".

121. In section 118(4A) of the 1995 Act (disposal of appeals), which is prospectively inserted by section 18(5) of the Crime and Punishment (Scotland) Act 1997, in paragraph (c), sub-paragraph (iii) shall cease to have effect.

122. In section 167 of the 1995 Act (findings and sentences in summary proceedings), in subsection (7), at the beginning there shall be inserted the words "Subject to section 204A of this Act,".

123. In subsection (5C) of section 175 of the 1995 Act (right of appeal in summary proceedings), the words "paragraph (a) of" shall be omitted.

124. In subsection (1) of section 307 of the 1995 Act (interpretation), in the definition of "officer of law"—

    (a)   after paragraph (b) there shall be inserted the following paragraph—

        "(ba) any person commissioned by the Commissioners of Customs and Excise;"; and

    (b)   in paragraph (e), for the words "class or persons" there shall be substituted the words "class of persons".

Criminal Procedure and Investigations Act 1996 (c 25)

125. In subsection (2) of section 1 of the Criminal Procedure and Investigations Act 1996 (application of Part I of that Act)—

    (a)   after paragraph (c) there shall be inserted the following paragraph—

        "(cc) a person is charged with an offence for which he is sent for trial under section 51 (no committal proceedings for indictable-only offences) of the Crime and Disorder Act 1998,"; and

    (b)   at the end there shall be inserted the words

        "or

    (f)   a bill of indictment charging a person with an indictable offence is preferred under section 22B(3)(a) of the Prosecution of Offences Act 1985."

126. In section 5 of that Act (compulsory disclosure by accused), after subsection (3) there shall be inserted the following subsection—

        "(3A)   Where this Part applies by virtue of section 1(2)(cc), this section does not apply unless—

    (a)   copies of the documents containing the evidence have been served on the accused under regulations made under paragraph 1 of Schedule 3 to the Crime and Disorder Act 1998; and

    (b)   a copy of the notice under subsection (7) of section 51 of that Act has been served on him under that subsection."

127. In subsection (1) of section 13 of that Act (time limits: transitional)—

    (a)   after the words "section 1(2)(b) or (c)," there shall be inserted the words—

        "(cc) the accused is sent for trial under section 51 of the Crime and Disorder Act 1998 (where this Part applies by virtue of section 1(2)(cc)),"; and

    (b)   after the words "section 1(2)(e)" there shall be inserted the words "or (f)".

128. In subsection (1)(a) of section 28 of that Act (introduction to Part III), after the words "committed for trial" there shall be inserted the words ", or sent for trial under section 51 of the Crime and Disorder Act 1998,".

129. In subsection (1) of section 39 of that Act (meaning of pre-trial hearing), after the words "committed for trial for the offence concerned" there shall be inserted the words ", after the accused has been sent for trial for the offence under section 51 of the Crime and Disorder Act 1998,".

Crime (Sentences) Act 1997 (c 43)

130.—(1) In subsection (3) of section 28 of the 1997 Act (duty to release certain life prisoners), after paragraph (b) there shall be inserted the words

> "and
> (c) the provisions of this section as compared with those of sections 33(2) and 35(1) of the Criminal Justice Act 1991 ("the 1991 Act")".

(2) In subsection (7) of that section, in paragraph (c), for the words from "the time when" to the end there shall be substituted the words "he has served one-half of that sentence".

131.—(1) In subsection (2) of section 31 of the 1997 Act (duration and conditions of licences), the words "(which shall include on his release conditions as to his supervision by a probation officer)" shall cease to have effect.

(2) After that subsection there shall be inserted the following subsection—

> "(2A) The conditions so specified shall include on the prisoner's release conditions as to his supervision by—
> (a) a probation officer appointed for or assigned to the petty sessions area within which the prisoner resides for the time being;
> (b) where the prisoner is under the age of 22, a social worker of the social services department of the local authority within whose area the prisoner resides for the time being; or
> (c) where the prisoner is under the age of 18, a member of a youth offending team established by that local authority under section 39 of the Crime and Disorder Act 1998."

(3) In subsection (6) of that section, for the words "section 24(2) above" there shall be substituted the words "section 46(3) of the 1991 Act", and for the words "the words in parentheses" there shall be substituted the words "subsection (2A) above".

132.—(1) In subsection (1) of section 35 of the 1997 Act (fine defaulters: general), for the words "the 1980 Act" there shall be substituted the words "the Magistrates' Courts Act 1980 ("the 1980 Act")".

(2) In subsection (5)(e) of that section, for the words "paragraph 3(2)(a)" there shall be substituted the words "sub-paragraphs (2)(a) and (2A) of paragraph 3".

(3) In subsection (8) of that section—
(a) in paragraph (a), the words "to revoke the order and deal with an offender for the offence in respect of which the order was made" shall cease to have effect; and
(b) in paragraph (b), for the words "paragraph 3(2)(a)" there shall be substituted the words "sub-paragraphs (2)(a) and (2A) of paragraph 3"

133. In section 54 of the 1997 Act (general interpretation), subsection (2) shall cease to have effect.

134. Subsection (5)(b) of section 57 of the 1997 Act (short title, commencement and extent) shall have effect as if the reference to the Channel Islands included a reference to the Isle of Man.

135.—(1) Schedule 1 to the 1997 Act (transfer of prisoners within the British Islands) shall be amended as follows.

(2) In sub-paragraph (3) of paragraph 6—
(a) after paragraph (a) there shall be inserted the following paragraph—

"(aa) in relation to a person who is supervised in pursuance of a detention and training order, being ordered to be detained for any failure to comply with requirements under section 76(6)(b) of the Crime and Disorder Act 1998;"; and

   (b)   in paragraph (b), for the words "recalled to prison under the licence" there shall be substituted the words "recalled or returned to prison".

(3)   In paragraph 8—
   (a)   in sub-paragraph (2), for the words from "sections 10" to "27 of this Act" there shall be substituted the words "sections 33 to 39, 41 to 46 and 65 of the 1991 Act, paragraphs 8, 10 to 13 and 19 of Schedule 12 to that Act and sections 75 to 77 of the Crime and Disorder Act 1998";
   (b)   in sub-paragraph (4), for the words from "sections 16" to "27 of this Act" there shall be substituted the words "sections 37 to 39, 43 to 46 and 65 of the 1991 Act, paragraphs 8, 10 to 13 and 19 of Schedule 12 to that Act and sections 76 and 77 of the Crime and Disorder Act 1998";
   (c)   in sub-paragraph (5), after the words "Any provision of" there shall be inserted the words "Part II of the 1991 Act or"; and
   (d)   after sub-paragraph (5) there shall be inserted the following sub-paragraphs—

"(6)   Section 41 of the 1991 Act, as applied by sub-paragraph (2) or (4) above, shall have effect as if section 67 of the Criminal Justice Act 1967 (computation of sentences of imprisonment passed in England and Wales) or, as the case may require, section 9 of this Act extended to Scotland.

(7)   Section 65(7)(b) of the 1991 Act, as applied by sub-paragraph (2) or (4) above, shall have effect as if the reference to a young offender institution were a reference to a young offenders institution."

(4)   In paragraph 9—
   (a)   in sub-paragraph (1), paragraph (a) and, in paragraph (b), the words "to that and" shall cease to have effect;
   (b)   in sub-paragraph (2), for the words from "sections 10" to "27 of this Act" there shall be substituted the words "sections 33 to 46 and 65 of the 1991 Act, paragraphs 8, 10 to 13 and 19 of Schedule 12 to that Act and sections 75 to 77 of the Crime and Disorder Act 1998";
   (c)   in sub-paragraph (4), for the words from "section 16" to "27 of this Act" there shall be substituted the words "sections 37 to 40A, 43 to 46 and 65 of the 1991 Act, paragraphs 8, 10 to 13 and 19 of Schedule 12 to that Act and sections 76 and 77 of the Crime and Disorder Act 1998";
   (d)   sub-paragraph (5) shall cease to have effect;
   (e)   in sub-paragraph (6), after the words "Any provision of" there shall be inserted the words "Part II of the 1991 Act or"; and
   (f)   after sub-paragraph (6) there shall be inserted the following sub-paragraphs—

"(7)   Section 41 of the 1991 Act, as applied by sub-paragraph (2) or (4) above, shall have effect as if section 67 of the Criminal Justice Act 1967 or, as the case may require, section 9 of this Act extended to Northern Ireland.

(8)   Section 65(7)(b) of the 1991 Act, as applied by sub-paragraph (1), (2) or (4) above, shall have effect as if the reference to a young offender institution were a reference to a young offenders centre."

(5)   In paragraph 10—
   (a)   in sub-paragraph (2)(a)—
      (i)   for the words from "sections" to "1997 Act")" there shall be substituted the words "sections 1, 1A, 3, 3A, 5, 6(1)(a), 7, 9, 11 to 13, 15 to 21, 26A and 27 of, and Schedules 2 and 6 to, the Prisoners and Criminal Proceedings (Scotland) Act 1993 ("the 1993 Act")"; and
      (ii)   after the word "3," there shall be inserted words "6(1)(b)(i) and (iii)";
   (b)   in sub-paragraph (2)(b), for the words "sub-paragraphs (3) and (4)" there shall be substituted the words "sub-paragraph (3)";
   (c)   sub-paragraph (4) shall cease to have effect;
   (d)   in sub-paragraph (5)(a), for the words from "sections 15" to "37 of the 1997 Act" there shall be substituted the words "sections 1A, 2(4), 3A, 11 to 13, 15 to 21, 26A and 27 of, and Schedules 2 and 6 to, the 1993 Act";

(e)   for sub-paragraph (6)(b) there shall be substituted the following sub-paragraph—

"(b)   in the said sub-paragraph (2) the reference to section 6(1)(b)(i) of the 1993 Act is a reference to that provision so far as it relates to a person sentenced under section 205(3) of the Criminal Procedure (Scotland) Act 1995."; and

(f)   for sub-paragraph (7) there shall be substituted the following sub-paragraph—

"(7)   Any provision of Part I of the 1993 Act which is applied by sub-paragraph (2) or (5) above shall have effect (as so applied) as if any reference to a chief social work officer were a reference to a chief social worker of a local authority social services department."

(6)   In paragraph 11—
    (a)   in sub-paragraph (2)(a)—
        (i)   for the words from "sections" to "1997 Act")" there shall be substituted the words "sections 1, 1A, 3, 3A, 5, 6(1)(a), 7, 9, 11 to 13, 15 to 21, 26A and 27 of, and Schedules 2 and 6 to, the 1993 Act"; and
        (ii)   after the word "3," there shall be inserted the words "6(1)(b)(i) and (iii),";
    (b)   in sub-paragraph (4)(a), for the words from "sections 15" to "37 of the 1997 Act" there shall be substituted the words "sections 1A, 3A, 11 to 13, 15 to 21, 26A and 27 of, and Schedules 2 and 6 to, the 1993 Act";
    (c)   in sub-paragraph (5), for the words "Sub-paragraph (5)" there shall be substituted the words "Sub-paragraph (6)"; and
    (d)   in sub-paragraph (6), the words "or Part III of the 1997 Act" shall cease to have effect and, in the Table, for the entry relating to the expression "young offenders institution" there shall be substituted the following entry—

| "Probation officer appointed for or assigned to such petty sessions area | Probation Officer appointed by the Probation Board for Northern Ireland". |

(7)   In sub-paragraph (5) of paragraph 12, in the Table, the entry relating to the expression "Prison rules" shall cease to have effect.

(8)   In sub-paragraph (5) of paragraph 13, in the Table, the entry relating to the expression "Prison rules" shall cease to have effect.

(9)   In sub-paragraph (1)(a) of paragraph 17 (prisoners unlawfully at large), after the words "section 49(1)" there shall be inserted the words "and (5)".

(10)   In sub-paragraph (1) of paragraph 20, in the definition of "supervision", after the word "purpose" there shall be inserted the words "or a detention and training order".

136.   In Schedule 2 to the 1997 Act (repatriation of prisoners to the British Islands), paragraphs 4 and 8 are hereby repealed.

137.   In Schedule 4 to the 1997 Act (minor and consequential amendments), the following provisions are hereby repealed, namely—
    (a)   in paragraph 6, sub-paragraph (1)(b);
    (b)   paragraphs 9 and 11; and
    (c)   in paragraph 12, sub-paragraph (4).

138.—(1)   In Schedule 5 to the 1997 Act (transitional provisions and savings), paragraphs 1 to 4 and 6 are hereby repealed and the following provisions shall cease to have effect, namely—
    (a)   paragraph 5(2);
    (b)   paragraphs 8, 9(1) and 10(1);
    (c)   in paragraph 11, sub-paragraph (1), in sub-paragraph (2)(c), the words "or Part III of the 1997 Act" and, in sub-paragraph (3), the words from the beginning to "1995; and"; and
    (d)   in paragraph 12, sub-paragraph (1) and, in sub-paragraph (2)(c), the words "or Part III of the 1997 Act".

(2)   In paragraph 11(2) of that Schedule—
    (a)   in paragraph (a)—
        (i)   for the words from "sections 15" to "1997 Act" there shall be substituted the words "sections 1, 1A, 3, 3A, 5, 6(1)(a), 7, 9, 11 to 13, 15 to 21, 26A

and 27 of, and Schedules 2 and 6 to, the Prisoners and Criminal Proceedings (Scotland) Act 1993 ("the 1993 Act")"; and

    (ii)   for the words "the 1989 Act" there shall be substituted the words "the Prisons (Scotland) Act 1989 ("the 1989 Act"); and

  (b) in paragraph (b), for the words from "sections 15" to "1997 Act" there shall be substituted the words "sections 1A, 2(4), 3A, 11 to 13, 15 to 21, 26A and 27 of, and Schedules 2 and 6 to, the 1993 Act".

    (3) In paragraph 12(2) of that Schedule—

      (a) in paragraph (a)—

          (i)   for the words from "sections 15" to "1997 Act" there shall be substituted the words "sections 1, 1A, 3, 3A, 5, 6(1)(a), 7, 9, 11 to 13, 15 to 21, 26A and 27 of, and Schedules 2 and 6 to, the Prisoners and Criminal Proceedings (Scotland) Act ("the 1993 Act")"; and

         (ii)   for the words "the 1989 Act" there shall be substituted the words "the Prisons (Scotland) Act 1989 ("the 1989 Act"); and

      (b) in paragraph (b), for the words from "sections 15" to "1997 Act" there shall be substituted the words "sections 1A, 2(4), 3A, 11 to 13, 15 to 21, 26A and 27 of, and Schedules 2 and 6 to, the 1993 Act".

139. In Schedule 6 to the 1997 Act (repeals), the entries relating to sections 33 to 51 and 65 of the 1991 Act are hereby repealed.

Crime and Punishment (Scotland) Act 1997 (c 48)

140. Section 4 of the Crime and Punishment (Scotland) Act 1997 (supervised release orders) is hereby repealed.

141.—(1) In Schedule 1 to that Act (minor and consequential amendments), the following provisions are hereby repealed, namely—

  (a) paragraphs 1, 9(7), 10(2)(a), 13(3) and 21(3); and

  (b) in paragraph 14, sub-paragraphs (2)(a), (3)(e), (4) to (7), (9), (10)(a), (11)(b), (12), (13) to (15) and (17).

    (2) In paragraph 14 of that Schedule, for sub-paragraph (16) there shall be substituted the following sub-paragraph—

    "(16) In section 27(1) (interpretation), in the definition of "supervised release order" the words "(as inserted by section 14 of this Act)" shall cease to have effect."

142. Schedule 2 to that Act (transitional provisions) is hereby repealed.

143.—(1) Schedule 3 to that Act (repeals) shall be amended in accordance with this paragraph.

    (2) In the entry relating to the Prisons (Scotland) Act 1989, in the third column, the words "In section 39, subsection (7)" are hereby repealed.

    (3) In the entry relating to the Prisoners and Criminal Proceedings (Scotland) Act 1993—

      (a) the words relating to sections 1, 3(2), 5, 6(1), 7, 9, 12(3), 16, 17(1), 20, 24, and Schedule 1;

      (b) in the words relating to section 14, the words "and in subsection (4), the words "short-term"";

      (c) in the words relating to 27(1)—

          (i)   the words "the definitions of "short term prisoner" and "long-term prisoner" and";

         (ii)   in the words relating to the definition of "supervised release order" the words "and the words from "but" to the end"; and

      (d) the words relating to section 27(2), (3), (5) and (6),

are hereby repealed.

    (4) In the entry relating to the Criminal Procedure (Scotland) Act 1995, in the third column, the words relating to section 44 are hereby repealed.

Sex Offenders Act 1997 (c 51)

144. In subsection (1)(a) of section 4 of the Sex Offenders Act 1997 (young sex offenders), after the word "under" there shall be inserted the words "a detention and training order or".

Definitions For "the 1933 Act", "the 1969 Act", "the 1973 Act", "the 1980 Act", "the 1982 Act", "the 1984 Act", "the 1985 Act", "the 1991 Act", "the 1993 Act", "the 1995 Act" and "the 1997 Act", see s 117(1), (2). In the Children and Young Persons Act 1933, for "child" and "young person", see s 107(1) thereof. In the Prison Act 1952, for "remand centre" and "young offender institution", see s 43(1) thereof. In the Children and Young Persons Act 1969, for "supervision order", "supervised person" and "supervisor", see s 11 thereof; for "child", "local authority", "reside", "young person" and "youth offending team" see s 70(1) thereof. In the Criminal Justice Act 1991, for "curfew order" and "supervision order", see s 31(1) thereof. In the Powers of Criminal Courts Act 1973, for "probation order", see s 2(1) thereof; for "court", "local authority" "suspended sentence" and "youth offending team", see s 57(1), as amended; definition "youth offending team" inserted, by para 33 above. In the Bail Act 1976, for "bail" see s 1(2) thereof; for "court", see s 2(2) thereof. In the Magistrates' Court Act 1980, as to offences, see s 150(5) thereof. In the Criminal Justice Act 1982, for "attendance centre order", see s 17(2) thereof. In the Repatriation of Prisoners Act 1984, for "prisoners", see s 1(1)(b) thereof; for "action plan order", "custodial sentence", "drug treatment and testing order" and "supervision order", see the Criminal Justice Act 1991, s 31(1), as amended by s 106 of, Sch 7, para 42 to, this Act, and as amended and repealed in part by para 78 above, s 120(2) of, Sch 10 to, this Act; for "youth offending team", see s 99(1) of the 1991 Act, as amended by para 95 of this Schedule; for "the Board", "long-term prisoner" and "short-term prisoner", see the Criminal Justice Act 1991, s 51(1). In the Prisons (Scotland) Act 1989, for "prison", "prisoner" and "sentence", see s 43(1) thereof; for "long-term prisoner" and "short-term prisoner", see the Prisoners and Criminal Proceedings (Scotland) Act 1993, s 27(1). In the Criminal Procedure and Investigations Act 1996, Pt I, for "the accused", see s 2(1) thereof. In the Crime (Sentences) Act 1997, Sch 1, for "prison", and as to "supervision", see para 20(1) thereof, as amended (definition "supervision") by para 135(10) above; for "Parole Board", see the Prisoners and Criminal Proceedings (Scotland) Act 1993, s 27(1); as to a term of imprisonment, see s 27(5) of the 1993 Act, as substituted by s 111(3).
References See paras 6.32, 6.35.

SCHEDULE 9

Section 120(1)

TRANSITIONAL PROVISIONS AND SAVINGS

Presumption of incapacity

1. Nothing in section 34 of this Act shall apply in relation to anything done before the commencement of that section.

Effect of child's silence at trial

2. Nothing in section 35 of this Act shall apply where the offence was committed before the commencement of that section.

Sexual or violent offenders: extended sentences

3. Section 58 of this Act does not apply where the sexual or violent offence was committed before the commencement of that section.

Drug treatment and testing orders

4. Section 61 of this Act does not apply in relation to an offence committed before the commencement of that section.

Young offenders: cautions

5.—(1) Any caution given to a child or young person before the commencement of section 65 of this Act shall be treated for the purposes of subsections (2) and (4) of that section as a reprimand.

(2) Any second or subsequent caution so given shall be treated for the purposes of paragraphs (a) and (b) of subsection (3) of that section as a warning.

Abolition of secure training orders

6. In relation to any time before the commencement of subsection (7) of section 73 of this Act, section 9A of the 1997 Act shall have effect as if after subsection (1) there were inserted the following subsection—

"(1A) Section 9 above applies to periods of detention which offenders are liable to serve under secure training orders as it applies to sentences of imprisonment."

Sentencing guidelines

7.—(1) Section 80 of this Act does not apply by virtue of subsection (1)(a) of that section in any case where the Court is seised of the appeal before the commencement of that section.

(2) In this paragraph "the Court" and "seised" have the same meanings as in that section.

Confiscation orders on committal for sentence

8. Section 83 of this Act does not apply where the offence was committed before the commencement of that section.

Football spectators: failure to comply with reporting duty

9. Section 84 of this Act does not apply where the offence was committed before the commencement of that section.

Power to release short-term prisoners on licence

10.—(1) Section 99 of this Act does not apply in relation to a prisoner who, immediately before the commencement of that section, has served one or more days more than the requisite period for the term of his sentence.

(2) In this paragraph "the requisite period" has the same meaning as in section 34A of the 1991 Act (which is inserted by section 99 of this Act).

Early release: two or more sentences

11.—(1) Where the terms of two or more sentences passed before the commencement of section 101 of this Act have been treated, by virtue of section 51(2) of the 1991 Act, as a single term for the purposes of Part II of that Act, they shall continue to be so treated after that commencement.

(2) Subject to sub-paragraph (1) above, section 101 of this Act applies where one or more of the sentences concerned were passed after that commencement.

Recall to prison of short-term prisoners

12.—(1) Sub-paragraphs (2) to (7) below have effect in relation to any prisoner whose sentence, or any part of whose sentence, was imposed for an offence committed before the commencement of section 103 of this Act.

(2) The following provisions of this Act do not apply, namely—
- (a) section 103;
- (b) paragraphs 83(1)(b) and 88(3)(a) of Schedule 8 to this Act and section 119 so far as relating to those paragraphs; and
- (c) section 120(2) and Schedule 10 so far as relating to the repeal of section 38 of the 1991 Act and the repeals in sections 37(1) and 45(4) of that Act.

(3) Section 33 of the 1991 Act has effect as if, in subsection (3)(b) (as amended by paragraph 80(1) of Schedule 8 to this Act), for the words "section 39(1) or (2)" there were substituted the words "section 38(2) or 39(1) or (2)".

(4) Section 33A of the 1991 Act (as inserted by paragraph 81 of Schedule 8 to this Act) has effect as if—
- (a) in subsection (1), for the words "section 38A(1) or 39(1) or (2)" there were substituted the words "section 38(2) or 38A(1)"; and
- (b) in subsection (3), for the words "section 39(1) or (2)", in both places where they occur, there were substituted the words "section 38(2)".

(5) Section 34A of the 1991 Act (as inserted by section 99 of this Act) has effect as if, in subsection (2)(g), for the words "section 39(1) or (2)" there were substituted the words "section 38(2)".

(6) Section 40A of the 1991 Act (as inserted by section 105 of this Act) has effect as if, in subsection (1), for the word "39" there were substituted the word "38".

(7) Section 44 of the 1991 Act (as substituted by section 59 of this Act) has effect as if—
- (a) in subsections (3) and (4), after the words "subject to" there were inserted the words "any suspension under section 38(2) above or, as the case may be,"; and

    (b)   in subsection (7), for the words "sections 37(5) and 39(1) and (2)" there were substituted the words "section 37(5), 38(2) and 39(1) and (2)".

(8) Section 45 of the 1991 Act has effect as if, in subsection (3) (as amended by paragraph 88(2) of Schedule 8 to this Act), for the words "section 39(1) or (2)" there were substituted the words "section 38(2) or 39(1) or (2)".

(9) For the purposes of this paragraph and paragraph 13 below, consecutive sentences, or sentences that are wholly or partly concurrent, shall be treated as parts of a single sentence.

Release on licence following recall to prison

13. Section 104 of this Act does not apply in relation to a prisoner whose sentence, or any part of whose sentence, was imposed for an offence committed before the commencement of that section.

Release on licence following return to prison

14.—(1) Section 105 of this Act does not apply where the new offence was committed before the commencement of that section.

(2) In this paragraph "the new offence" has the same meaning as in section 40 of the 1991 Act.

Remand time: two or more sentences

15.—(1) Where the terms of two or more sentences passed before the commencement of paragraph 11 of Schedule 8 to this Act have been treated, by virtue of section 104(2) of the Criminal Justice Act 1967, as a single term for the purposes of section 67 of that Act, they shall continue to be so treated after that commencement.

(2) Subject to sub-paragraph (1) above, paragraph 11 of Schedule 8 to this Act applies where one or more of the sentences concerned were passed after that commencement.

Definitions   By virtue of ss 58(8), 85(5), for the meaning of "sexual offence" and "violent offence", see the Criminal Justice Act 1991, s 31(1), as amended and repealed in part by ss 104, 117, 118(2) of, Sch 7, para 42, Sch 8, para 68, Sch 10 to, this Act; for "the 1991 Act", "caution", "child" and "young person", see s 117(1), (3). In the Crime (Sentences) Act 1997, for "sentence of imprisonment", see s 27(1) thereof. **References**   See paras 6.33, 6.35.

SCHEDULE 10

Section 120(2)

REPEALS

Chapter	Short title	Extent of repeal
30 Geo 3 c 48	Treason Act 1790.	The whole Act.
36 Geo 3 c 7	Treason Act 1795.	The whole Act.
36 Geo 3 c 31	Treason by Women Act (Ireland) 1796.	The whole Act.
57 Geo 3 c 6	Treason Act 1817.	The whole Act.
11 & 12 Vict c 12	Treason Felony Act 1848.	Section 2.
21 & 22 Geo 5 c 24	Sentence of Death (Expectant Mothers) Act 1931.	The whole Act.
23 Geo 5 c 12	Children and Young Persons Act 1933.	In section 47(2), the words from the beginning to "court; and".
		In Schedule 2, in paragraph 15(a), the word "shall", in the second place where it occurs, and, in paragraph 17, the words "or, if a metropolitan stipendiary magistrate, may sit alone".

Chapter	Short title	Extent of repeal
1945 c 15 (NI)	Criminal Justice Act (Northern Ireland) 1945.	Sections 32 and 33.
1967 c 80	Criminal Justice Act 1967.	In section 56, subsections (3), (6) and (13).
		Section 67(5)(c).
1968 c 19	Criminal Appeal Act 1968.	In section 10(2), the words "(other than a supervision order within the meaning of that Part)".
1969 c 54	Children and Young Persons Act 1969.	Section 12D.
		Section 13(2).
		In section 16, subsection (10) and, in subsection (11), the words "seventeen or".
		Section 23(14)(a).
		In section 34, in subsection (1), paragraph (a) and, in paragraph (c), the words "7(7), 7(8),".
		Section 69(5).
		In Schedule 6, the entries relating to sections 55, 56(1) and 59(1) of the Children and Young Persons Act 1933.
1972 c 71	Criminal Justice Act 1972.	Section 49.
1973 c 62	Powers of Criminal Courts Act 1973.	In section 1, in subsections (8)(b) and (8A) the words "37 or".
		Section 1B(10).
		In section 1C(1), paragraph (b) and the word "and" immediately preceding it.
		In section 2(1), the words "by a probation officer" and the words from "For the purposes" to available evidence".
		Section 11.
		Section 14(8).
		In section 31, in subsection (3A), the words "Subject to subsections (3B) and (3C) below," , subsections (3B) and (3C), in subsection (4), the words "4 or" and, in subsection (6), the words "about committal by a magistrates' court to the Crown Court".
		Section 32(5).
		Section 42(2).
		In Schedule 1A, paragraph 6(7).
		In Schedule 5, paragraph 35.
1976 c 63	Bail Act 1976.	In section 3(5), the words "If it appears that he is unlikely to remain in Great Britain until the time appointed for him to surrender to custody".
1980 c 43	Magistrates' Courts Act 1980.	Section 37.

Chapter	Short title	Extent of repeal
1980 c 43 *contd*		In sections 38(2) and 38A(2), the words ", in accordance with section 56 of the Criminal Justice Act 1967,".
		In section 108(2), the words "a probation order or".
		In section 125(4)(c), the word "and" at the end of sub-paragraph (ii).
		In section 126, the word "and" at the end of paragraph (c).
		In Schedule 7, paragraph 120(b).
1982 c 48	Criminal Justice Act 1982.	Section 1A(4A).
		Section 1B.
		In section 1C(2), the words "but if he is under 18 at the time of the direction, only for a temporary purpose".
		In section 3(1)(a), the words "under section 1A above".
		Section 18(7).
		In section 19, in subsection (3)(a), the words "revoke it and" and, in subsection (5), the words "revoke the attendance centre order and".
		Section 66(3).
		In Schedule 14, paragraph 28.
1987 c 42	Family Law Reform Act 1987.	Section 8(1).
		In Schedule 2, paragraph 26.
1988 c 33	Criminal Justice Act 1988.	Section 69(2).
		In Schedule 15, paragraph 40.
1989 c 45	Prisons (Scotland) Act 1989.	In section 39(7), the words from "and the foregoing" to the end.
1991 c 53	Criminal Justice Act 1991.	In section 6(4), the word "and" immediately following paragraph (e).
		In section 31(1), in the definition of "custodial sentence", in paragraph (b), the words "or a secure training order under section 1 of the Criminal Justice and Public Order Act 1994".
		Section 33(4).
		In section 37, in subsection (1), the words "any suspension under section 38(2) below or, as the case may be," and, in subsection (4), the words "(which shall include on his release conditions as to his supervision by a probation officer)".
		Section 38.
		In section 45(4), the words "any suspension under section 38(2) below; or".

Chapter	Short title	Extent of repeal
1991 c 53 *contd*		In section 61(1), paragraph (b) and the word "or" immediately preceding that paragraph.
		Section 62.
		In Schedule 2, in paragraphs 3(1)(d) and 4(1)(d), the words "revoke the order and" and, in paragraph 17(1), the words from "and the court" to the end.
		In Schedule 11, paragraphs 10, 11 and 14.
		In Schedule 12, paragraph 17(3)
1993 c 9	Prisoners and Criminal Proceedings (Scotland) Act 1993.	Section 11(3)(b) and (4).
		Section 14(2) and (3).
		Section 16(7)(b).
		In paragraph 6B(1) of Schedule 6, the word "and" after head (a).
1993 c 47	Probation Service Act 1993.	Section 17(5A).
1994 c 33	Criminal Justice and Public Order Act 1994.	Sections 1 to 4.
		Section 20.
		In section 35, in subsection (1), the words "who has attained the age of fourteen years" and subsection (6).
		Section 130(4).
		In Schedule 10, paragraph 42.
1994 c 37	Drug Trafficking Act 1994.	Section 2(7)(a).
1995 c 46	Criminal Procedure (Scotland) Act 1995.	Section 118(4A)(c)(iii).
		In section 175(5C), the words "paragraph (a) of".
		In section 209(1), the words "not less than twelve months but".
1997 c 43	Crime (Sentences) Act 1997.	Section 1.
		Section 8.
		Sections 10 to 27.
		In section 31(2), the words "(which shall include on his release conditions as to his supervision by a probation officer)".
		In section 35, in subsection (5), paragraph (c) and the word "and" at the end of paragraph (d), and in subsection (8), in paragraph (a), the words "to revoke the order and deal with an offender for the offence in respect of which the order was made" and the word "and" at the end of that paragraph.
		Section 43(4).
		Section 54(2).

Chapter	Short title	Extent of repeal
1997 c 43 *contd*		In Schedule 1, in paragraph 9(1), paragraph (a) and, in paragraph (b), the words "to that and", paragraph 9(5), paragraph 10(4), in paragraph 11(6), the words "or Part III of the 1997 Act", in paragraph 12(5), in the Table, the entry relating to the expression "prison rules" and, in paragraph 13(5), in the Table, the entry relating to the expression "prison rules".
		In Schedule 2, paragraphs 4 and 8.
		In Schedule 4, paragraph 6(1)(b), paragraphs 9 and 11 and paragraph 12(4).
		In Schedule 5, paragraphs 1 to 4, paragraph 5(2), paragraph 6, paragraph 8, paragraph 9(1), paragraph 10(1), in paragraph 11, sub-paragraph (1), in sub-paragraph (2)(c), the words "or Part III of the 1997 Act" and, in sub-paragraph (3), the words from the beginning to "1995; and", and in paragraph 12, sub-paragraph (1) and, in sub-paragraph (2)(c), the words "or Part III of the 1997 Act".
		In Schedule 6, the entries relating to sections 33 to 51 and 65 of the Criminal Justice Act 1991.
1997 c 48	Crime and Punishment (Scotland) Act 1997.	Section 4.
		Chapter I of Part III.
		In Schedule 1, paragraph 1, paragraph 9(7), paragraph 10(2)(a), paragraph 13(3), in paragraph 14, sub-paragraphs (2)(a), (3)(e), (4) to (7), (9), (10)(a), (11)(b), (12), (13) to (15) and (17), and paragraph 21(3).
		Schedule 2.
		In Schedule 3, in the entry relating to the Prisons (Scotland) Act 1989, the words "In section 39, subsection (7)", in the entry relating to the Prisoners and Criminal Proceedings (Scotland) Act 1993, the words relating to sections 1, 3(2), 5, 6(1), 7, 9, 12(3), 16, 17(1), 20, 24, 27(2), (3), (5) and (6) and Schedule 1, in the words relating to section 14, the words "and, in subsection (4), the words "short-term"", in the words relating to section 27(1), the words "the definitions of "short term prisoner" and "long-term prisoner" and" and "and the words from "but" to the end" and, in the entry relating to the Criminal Procedure (Scotland) Act 1995, the words relating to section 44.
1997 c 50	Police Act 1997.	In section 94(4), the word "and" immediately preceding paragraph (c).

References   See paras 6.33, 6.35.

Crime and Disorder Act 1998 (Commencement No 1) Order 1998

(SI 1998/1883)

Made: 31 July 1998.

1 This Order may be cited as the Crime and Disorder Act 1998 (Commencement No 1) Order 1998.

2 The following provisions of the Crime and Disorder Act 1998 shall come into force on the day after the day on which this Order is made—

    (a)   section 41, for the purpose of making appointments under that section and under paragraph 1 of Schedule 2;

    (b)   section 49, for the purpose of making rules which make such provision as is mentioned in subsection (2) of that section;

    (c)   section 114;

    (d)   sections 116 and 117; and

    (e)   paragraphs 1 and 2 of Schedule 2, for the purpose of making appointments under section 41 and paragraph 1 of that Schedule.

3 Section 84 of, and paragraph 9 of Schedule 9 to, the Crime and Disorder Act 1998 shall come into force on the seventh day after the day on which this Order is made.

Crime and Disorder Act 1998 (Commencement No 2 and Transitional Provisions) Order 1998

(SI 1998/2327)

Made: 19 September 1998.

1.—(1) This Order may be cited as the Crime and Disorder Act 1998 (Commencement No 2 and Transitional Provisions) Order 1998.

    (2)   In this Order, "the 1998 Act" means the Crime and Disorder Act 1998.

2.—(1) The following provisions of the 1998 Act shall, subject to articles 5 to 8 below, come into force on 30th September 1998—

    (a)   sections 5 to 9 (crime and disorder strategies; parenting orders);

    (b)   section 10(1) to (5) (appeals against parenting orders);

    (c)   sections 11 and 12 (child safety orders);

    (d)   section 13(1) and (2) (appeals against child safety orders);

    (e)   sections 14 and 15 (local child curfew schemes);

    (f)   sections 17 and 18 (duty to consider crime and disorder implications; interpretation);

    (g)   sections 28 to 37 (racially aggravated offences; abolition of doli incapax; effect of child's evidence at trial; abolition of death penalty for treason and piracy; aim of youth justice system);

    (h)   section 38(4) (definition of youth justice services);

(i)   sections 41 and 42 and Schedule 2 (Youth Justice Board), to the extent that they are not already in force;

(j)   section 43(1) (time limits);

(k)   sections 47 and 48 (powers of youth courts; and of stipendiary magistrates to sit alone);

(l)   section 50 (early administrative hearings);

(m)   section 52(6) (indictable-only offences) and Schedule 3, for the purpose of making both regulations under paragraph 1 of that Schedule and rules which make such provision as is mentioned in paragraph 2(7) of that Schedule;

(n)   sections 53 to 64 and Schedule 4 (criminal justice system: miscellaneous; dealing with sexual or violent offenders; and those dependent on drugs);

(o)   sections 67 to 70 and Schedule 5 (reparation orders; action plan orders);

(p)   section 71(5) (selection of supervisor for supervision order);

(q)   section 72 (breach of requirements in supervision orders);

(r)   sections 82 and 83 (increase in sentences for racial aggravation; power to make confiscation orders on committal for sentence);

(s)   sections 85 to 96 and Schedule 6 (interpretation; extended sentences for sex and violent offenders in Scotland; drug treatment and testing orders in Scotland; offences racially aggravated in Scotland);

(t)   section 97, for the purpose of making an order under section 23 of the 1969 Act (prescribed description of children and young persons who may be remanded or committed to local authority secure accommodation);

(u)   section 100(1), for the purpose of making orders under section 37A of the 1991 Act (responsible officers for offenders released on licence with curfew conditions);

(v)   sections 101 and 102 (early release: two or more sentences; restriction on consecutive sentences for released prisoners);

(w)   sections 104 to 108 and Schedule 7 (release on licence following recall or return to prison; pre-consolidation amendments; amendments to Chapter I of Part II of the 1997 Act; repeal of Chapter I of Part III of the Crime and Punishment (Scotland) Act 1997;

(x)   sections 110 to 113 and 115 (calculation of period of detention at custom office etc where person previously detained; early release in Scotland: two or more sentences; restriction on consecutive sentences for released prisoners: Scotland; deputy authorising officer under Part III of Police Act 1997; disclosure of information);

(y)   sections 118 and 119 and the provisions of Schedule 8 mentioned in paragraph (2) below (provision for Northern Ireland; minor and consequential amendments);

(z)   section 120(1) and paragraphs 1 to 4, 6, 8, 11, 12(1) and (3) to (9), and 13 to 15 of Schedule 9 (transitional provisions and savings); and

(aa)   section 120(2) and Schedule 10 so far as they repeal the provisions mentioned in paragraph (3) below (repeals).

(2)   The provisions of Schedule 8 referred to in paragraph (1)(y) above are—

    (a)   paragraph 2;

    (b)   paragraph 4;

    (c)   paragraph 9(1)(b);

    (d)   paragraph 10(a);

    (e)   paragraph 11;

    (f)   paragraph 13;

    (g)   paragraph 16;

    (h)   paragraph 18;

    (i)   paragraphs 20 and 21;

    (j)   paragraph 24;
    (k)   paragraph 30;
    (l)   paragraph 34(1) and (2);
    (m)   paragraph 38;
    (n)   paragraph 40(1);
    (o)   paragraphs 42 and 43;
    (p)   paragraphs 46 and 47;
    (q)   paragraph 50(5);
    (r)   paragraphs 53 and 54;
    (s)   paragraphs 56 to 60;
    (t)   paragraph 62;
    (u)   paragraphs 68 to 72;
    (v)   paragraphs 74 and 75;
    (w)   paragraph 77(b);
    (x)   paragraph 78(a) and (c);
    (y)   paragraphs 79 to 82;
    (z)   paragraph 83(1)(a) and (4) to (6);
    (aa)   paragraphs 84 and 85;
    (bb)   paragraph 87;
    (cc)   paragraph 88(1), (2) and (3)(b);
    (dd)   paragraph 89;
    (ee)   paragraphs 91 and 92;
    (ff)   paragraphs 96(1) to (5) and (7);
    (gg)   paragraphs 97 and 98;
    (hh)   paragraphs 100 to 108;
    (ii)   paragraph 113;
    (jj)   paragraphs 115 and 116;
    (kk)   paragraphs 118 to 124;
    (ll)   paragraph 130;
    (mm)   paragraph 131(3);
    (nn)   paragraphs 132 to 134;
    (oo)   paragraph 135(1), (2)(b) and (3) to (8); and
    (pp)   paragraphs 136 to 143.

(3)   The provisions which are referred to in paragraph (1)(aa) above are the entries in Schedule 10 to the 1998 Act relating to—

    (a)   the Treason Act 1790;
    (b)   the Treason Act 1795;
    (c)   the Treason by Women Act (Ireland) 1796;
    (d)   the Treason Act 1817;
    (e)   the Treason Felony Act 1848;
    (f)   the Sentence of Death (Expectant Mothers) Act 1931;
    (g)   the 1933 Act;
    (h)   the Criminal Justice Act (Northern Ireland) 1945;
    (i)   section 56(3) and (13) of the Criminal Justice Act 1967;
    (j)   the Criminal Appeal Act 1968;
    (k)   the 1969 Act;
    (l)   the Criminal Justice Act 1972;
    (m)   sections 1B, 1C, 11, 14, 31 and 32 of and Schedules 1A and 5 to, the 1973 Act, and the words from "For the purposes" to "available evidence" in section 2(1) of that Act;
    (n)   the Bail Act 1976;
    (o)   sections 38, 38A and 108 of and Schedule 7 to, the 1980 Act;
    (p)   sections 3, 18, 19 and 66 of and Schedule 14 to, the 1982 Act;
    (q)   the Family Law Reform Act 1987;
    (r)   the Criminal Justice Act 1988;
    (s)   the Prisons (Scotland) Act 1989;

(t)   sections 6, 33 and 37(4) of, and Schedules 2 and 11 to, the 1991 Act;

(u)   the Prisoners and Criminal Proceedings (Scotland) Act 1993;

(v)   sections 35 and 130(4) of the 1994 Act;

(w)   the Criminal Procedure (Scotland) Act 1995;

(x)   sections 1, 8, 10 to 27, 35, 43 and 54 of, and Schedules 1, 2, 4, 5 and 6 to, the 1997 Act;

(y)   the Crime and Punishment (Scotland) Act 1997; and

(z)   the Police Act 1997.

3.—(1) The following provisions of the 1998 Act shall, subject to article 9 below, come into force on 30th September 1998 in the areas specified in Schedule 1 to this Order—

(a)   sections 38(1) to (3) and (5), 39 and 40 (youth justice services; youth offending teams; and youth justice plans);

(b)   paragraphs 17, 19, 23, 26, 27, 32, 33, 34(3), 73, 76, 77(a), 94, 95, 96(6) and 131(1) and (2) of Schedule 8; and

(c)   the entries in Schedule 10 relating to the words "by a probation officer" in section 2(1) of the 1973 Act and to section 31(2) of the 1997 Act.

(2)   Section 46 (date of first court appearance in bail cases) and, to the extent that it is not already in force, section 49 (powers of magistrates' courts exercisable by single justice etc) of the 1998 Act shall come into force on 30th September 1998 in the areas specified in Schedule 2 to this Order.

(3)   Sections 65 and 66 of, and paragraphs 25 and 61 of Schedule 8 and paragraph 5 of Schedule 9 to, the 1998 Act (reprimands and warnings) shall come into force on 30th September 1998 for the purpose of [reprimanding or] warning a person under section 65 in any area specified in Schedule 3 to this Order.

NOTES

Sub-s (3): words in square brackets inserted by the Crime and Disorder Act 1998 (Commencement No 2 and Transitional Provisions) (Amendment) Order 1998, SI 1998/2412, art 2.

4.—(1) The following provisions of the 1998 Act shall come into force on 1st December 1998—

(a)   sections 2 and 3 (sex offender orders);

(b)   section 4 (appeals against orders), so far as relating to a sex offender order;

(c)   section 16 (removal of truants to designated places etc);

(d)   section 20 (sex offender orders);

(e)   section 21 (procedural provisions with respect to orders), but only for the purposes of sex offender orders made under section 20 of the 1998 Act and orders made under section 20(4)(a) of that Act;

(f)   in section 22 (offences in connection with breach of order), subsections (6) and (7) and, for the purposes of their application to an order under section 20(4)(a) of the 1998 Act and to a sex offender order made under section 20 of that Act, subsections (1) to (5);

(g)   section 23 (anti-social behaviour as ground of eviction);

(h)   section 24 (noise-making equipment: police power of seizure);

(i)   sections 25 to 27 (powers to require removal of masks etc; retention and disposal of things seized; power of arrest for failure to comply with requirement);

(j)   Schedule 1 (Schedule 2A to the Civic Government (Scotland) Act 1982); and

(k)   paragraph 36 of Schedule 8.

(2)   The following provisions of the 1998 Act shall come into force on 4th January 1999 for the purpose of sending any person for trial under section 51 of that Act from any area specified in Schedule 2 to this Order—

    (a)   section 51 and, to the extent that it is not already in force, section 52 (no committal proceedings for indictable-only offences etc);

    (b)   Schedule 3, to the extent that it is not already in force;

    (c)   paragraphs 3, 5(1)(a) and (2), 8, 12, 28, 29, 37, 40(2), 44, 45, 48, 49, 52(2), 63 to 67, 93 and 125(a), 126, 127(a), 128 and 129 of Schedule 8; and

    (d)   in Schedule 10, the entries relating to sections 125 and 126 of the 1980 Act.

5.—(1) In relation to any time before the commencement of sections 38 to 40 of the 1998 Act in an area not specified in Schedule 1 to this Order—

    (a)   subsection (4A) of section 37 of the 1991 Act (as inserted by paragraph 83 (5) of Schedule 8 to the 1998 Act) shall have effect as if paragraph (b) of that subsection and the word "or" immediately preceding it were omitted; and

    (b)   section 31(6) of the 1997 Act (as amended by paragraph 131(3) of Schedule 8 to the 1998 Act) shall have effect as if the words "and for the words "the words in parentheses" there shall be substituted the words "subsection (2A) above"" were omitted.

(2)   In relation to any time before the commencement of sections 75 to 77 of the 1998 Act—

    (a)   section 55(1A)(d) of the 1933 Act (as inserted by paragraph 2 of Schedule 8 to the 1998 Act) shall have effect as if the words "section 77(3) of the Crime and Disorder Act 1998 (breach of requirements of supervision under detention and training order) "or" were omitted;

    (b)   section 31(1) of the 1991 Act (as amended by paragraph 78(a) and (c) of Schedule 8 to the 1998 Act) shall have effect as if the definition of a detention and training order were omitted;

    (c)   paragraphs 8(2) and 9(2) of Schedule 1 to the 1997 Act (as amended by paragraph 135(3)(a) and (4)(b) of Schedule 8 to the 1998 Act) shall have effect as if the words "and sections 75 to 77 of the Crime and Disorder Act 1998" were omitted; and

    (d)   paragraphs 8(4) and 9(4) of Schedule 1 to the 1997 Act (as amended by paragraphs 135(3)(b) and (4)(c) of Schedule 8 to the 1998 Act) shall have effect as if the words "and sections 76 and 77 of the Crime and Disorder Act 1998" were omitted.

(3)   In relation to any time before the commencement of sections 99 and 100 of the 1998 Act—

    (a)   section 2(4)(b)(i) of the Repatriation of Prisoners Act 1984 (as substituted by paragraph 56 of Schedule 8 to the 1998 Act) shall have effect as if the words ", 33A(2), 34A(3)" were omitted;

    (b)   paragraph 2(4) of Schedule 2 to the Repatriation of Prisoners Act 1984 (as substituted by paragraphs 58(2) and 59(3) of Schedule 8 to the 1998 Act) shall have effect as if the words "33A(2), 34A(3)," were omitted;

    (c)   section 33A of the 1991 Act (as inserted by paragraph 81 of Schedule 8 to the 1998 Act) shall have effect as if—

      (i)   in subsection (1)(b), the words "34A(3) or" were omitted;

      (ii)   in subsection (1)(b), the words "38A(1) or" or, as that subsection has effect by virtue of paragraph 12(4) of Schedule 9 to the 1998 Act, "or 38A(1)" were omitted; and

      (iii)   subsection (2) were omitted;

    (d)   section 37 of the 1991 Act (as amended by paragraph 83(1)(a) and (4) to (6) of Schedule 8 to the 1998 Act) shall have effect as if—
        (i)   in subsection (1), the words ", (1B)" were omitted; and
        (ii)   in subsection (4A), the words "may in the case of a person released on licence under section 34A above whose sentence is for a term of less than twelve months, and" and "in any other case," were omitted; and
    (e)   section 45 of the 1991 Act (as amended by paragraph 88(1), (2) and (3)(b) of Schedule 8 to the 1998 Act) shall have effect as if, in subsection (1), the words "34A," were omitted.

6.—(1) Paragraphs 2(4) and 30(2) of Schedule 7 to the 1998 Act shall not apply in relation to an offender committed to (but not sentenced by) the Crown Court before 30th September 1998.

(2)   Neither paragraph 17 of Schedule 7, nor the repeal of section 11 of the 1973 Act by Schedule 10, to the 1998 Act shall affect the operation of an order made under that section before 30th September 1998.

(3)   Paragraphs 37(2) and (3) and 38(3) of Schedule 7 to the 1998 Act shall not apply in relation to attendance centre orders made before 30th September 1998.

(4)   In paragraph 46 of Schedule 7 to the 1998 Act—
    (a)   sub-paragraph (1) shall not apply in relation to any proceedings under Schedule 2 to the 1991 Act which have been begun before 30th September 1998; and
    (b)   sub-paragraphs (2) and (8) shall not apply where the breach of the relevant order occurred before 30th September 1998.

7.—(1) The amendment of section 1(2) of the 1993 Act made by paragraph 98(2) of Schedule 8 to the 1998 Act shall not have effect in relation to any person whose licence under Part I of the 1993 Act has been revoked under section 17 of that Act before 30th September 1998.

(2)   The amendment of section 5 of the 1993 Act made by paragraph 100 of Schedule 8 to the 1998 Act shall apply where one or more of the terms of imprisonment or detention was passed on or after 30th September 1998.

(3)   The amendment of section 7 of the 1993 Act made by paragraph 101(a) of Schedule 8 to the 1998 Act shall not have effect in relation to any child whose licence under Part I of the 1993 Act has been revoked under section 17 of that Act before 30th September 1998.

(4)   The repeal of subsections (3)(b) and (4) of section 11 of the 1993 Act made by paragraph 102 of Schedule 8 and Schedule 10 to the 1998 Act and the repeal of paragraph (b) of subsection (7) of section 16 of the 1993 Act made by paragraph 104(3) of Schedule 8 and Schedule 10 to the 1998 Act shall not have effect in relation to any person who is subject to an order under section 16(2) or (4) of the 1993 Act which was made before 30th September 1998.

8.—(1) Where a person is sentenced for a sexual offence within the meaning of Part I of the 1991 Act which was committed before 30th September 1998, the substitution of section 44 of that Act by section 59 of the 1998 Act shall not have effect and, in relation to such a person, neither paragraph 103 of Schedule 8, nor the repeal of section 14(2) and (3) of the 1993 Act by Schedule 10, to the 1998 Act shall have effect.

(2)   The amendments made to section 209 of the Criminal Procedure (Scotland) Act 1995 by paragraphs (b) and (c) of section 86(2) of the 1998 Act shall not apply in relation to a person who is convicted of an offence which was committed before 30th September 1998.

9 Nothing in article 3(1) above shall require the local authority in an area specified in Schedule 1 to this Order, acting under section 38(1) of the 1998 Act, to secure that the youth justice service mentioned in subsection (4)(c) of that section (support for children and young persons remanded or committed on bail while awaiting trial or sentence) is available in their area.

SCHEDULE 1

Article 3(1)

AREAS IN WHICH THE PROVISIONS OF THE 1998 ACT SET OUT IN ARTICLE 3(1) SHALL COME INTO FORCE ON 30TH SEPTEMBER 1998

1. The counties of Bedfordshire, Devon and Hampshire.

2. The Isle of Wight.

3. The cities of Portsmouth, Sheffield, Southampton and Westminster.

4. The Royal borough of Kensington and Chelsea.

5. The London boroughs of Hammersmith and Fulham, and Lewisham.

6. The Metropolitan boroughs of St Helens and Wolverhampton.

7. The boroughs of Blackburn with Darwen, and Luton.

SCHEDULE 2

Articles 3(2) and 4(2)

AREAS IN WHICH THE PROVISIONS OF THE 1998 ACT SET OUT IN ARTICLES 3(2) AND 4(2) SHALL COME INTO FORCE ON 30TH SEPTEMBER 1998 AND 4TH JANUARY 1999, RESPECTIVELY

1. The petty sessions areas of Bromley; Croydon; and Sutton.

2. The petty sessional divisions of Aberconwy; Arfon; Blackburn, Darwen and Ribble Valley; Burnley and Pendle; Colwyn; Corby; Daventry; Dyffryn Clwyd; Eifionydd and Pwllheli; Gateshead; Kettering; Meirionnydd; Neweastle-under-Lyme and Pirehill North; Newcastle-upon-Tyne; Northampton; Rhuddlan; Staffordshire Moorlands; Stoke-on-Trent; Towcester; Wellingborough; and Ynys Mon/Anglesey.

SCHEDULE 3

Article 3(3)

AREAS IN WHICH THE PROVISIONS OF THE 1998 ACT SET OUT IN ARTICLE 3(3) SHALL COME INTO FORCE ON 30TH SEPTEMBER 1998

1. The county of Hampshire.

2. The Isle of Wight.

3. The cities of Portsmouth, Sheffield, Southampton and Westminster.

4. The Royal borough of Kensington and Chelsea.

5. The London borough of Hammersmith and Fulham.

6. The Metropolitan borough of Wolverhampton.

7. The borough of Blackburn with Darwen.

Index